The State and Nuclear Power

The State and Nuclear Power

Conflict and Control in the Western World

Joseph A. Camilleri

Senior Lecturer in Politics
La Trobe University

University of Washington Press
Seattle

Library of Congress Cataloging in Publication Data

Camilleri, Joseph A., 1944–
The state and nuclear power.

Bibliography: p.
Includes index.
1. Atomic power industry—Government policy.
2. Energy policy. 3. Antinuclear movement. 4. Atomic
power industry—Government policy—United States.
5. Energy policy—United States. 6. Antinuclear
movement—United States. I. Title.
HD9698.A2C33 1984 338.4′762148 83–19824
ISBN 0-295-96094-9

Printed and bound in England

To Rita, Kristian and Emil

Contents

Preface

Since the late 1960s, the civil use of nuclear power has provoked intense public debate and prolonged political conflict in most western industrial societies. The intensity of the controversy stems directly from the sharply divergent assessments which the major protagonists have made of the ethical, social and economic implications of the technology. For a time it appeared as if the policies of government, industry and the scientific community rested on widespread expert and public support which sporadic local opposition could do little to undermine. It is doubtful whether the outward façade of unity projected by the nuclear establishment was ever an accurate reflection of political reality. By the early 1970s any semblance of unity was shattered, perhaps irreparably. It was now evident that the commercial development of nuclear energy had become the battleground for sharply competing interests and ideologies. The high stakes involved in the dispute, the political passions they aroused, and the very considerable investment of organisational resources by all interested parties had a pronounced polarising effect on both domestic and international politics.

In recent years a vast body of literature has accumulated, which attempts to assess, from a variety of viewpoints and with varying degrees of insight and objectivity, the relative costs and benefits of nuclear energy. The purpose of this study is not to examine the cases for and against nuclear power. Rather it is to analyse the political, cultural and international dimensions of the conflict to which it has given rise, and more particularly to focus attention on the role of the advanced capitalist state in the establishment and subsequent development of the nuclear industry. The 'socialist' industrial state has no doubt performed an equally significant function in the harnessing of nuclear energy, but when compared to the liberal capitalist state there may well be a qualitative difference in the scope and mode of intervention. On the other hand, the centrally planned economies have had to operate within a framework of economic and military competition whose *modus operandi* is still very much determined by the international capitalist system. Clearly, the linkages tying the socialist economies to the world market economy still await close theoretical scrutiny. In the interests of restricting somewhat an already vast field of inquiry, this study has chosen to exclude from its purview the socialist model of development and to confine its attention to the capitalist state and its relationship to the international division of labour.

Lewis Mumford, Jacques Ellul, Raymond Aron, John Kenneth Galbraith, Jürgen Habermas, James O'Connor and many others, writing from widely different perspectives, have pointed to the increasing integration of the productive process with the political apparatus of society as the dominant characteristic of the industrial age. In *Civilization in Crisis* I have examined the way in which the twin processes of technological change and capital accumulation have been gradually brought under the unifying sphere of state planning. If this is at all an accurate reading of the direction of late capitalism, then it is only to be expected that the state should play an important part in harnessing nuclear energy for both military and civil purposes. What is less clear, however, is the specific role various states have played (in that sense that is a comparative study) in the original development of the technology, and especially in the recent period when the nuclear controversy may be said to have substantially magnified and complicated the related tasks of political and economic management, social legitimation and international regulation.

At this point a word of explanation as to the nature of the state may be appropriate. Here I am indebted to the conceptual framework offered by Ralph Miliband in *The State and Capitalist Society*. Although government is obviously an integral part of the state system, it is by no means synonymous with it. Government may speak on the state's behalf; it may administer and enforce laws, but ultimate authority resides in the state. To use the well-known Weberian phrase, it is the state which exercises 'the monopoly of the legitimate use of physical force within a given territory'. The state's authority is, however, manifested or at least concretised in a number of interacting institutions which constitute the political, legal and coercive arms of the state.

For our purposes the political apparatus may be said to comprise the seat of constitutional and political power (i.e. parliaments or representative assemblies), the political executive to which it is theoretically accountable, and the sprawling bureaucracy attached to ministerial departments, public corporations, central banks and a wide range of other regulatory organisations. It should not be assumed that this bureaucracy is the obedient servant of the executive, let alone of the legislative organs of the state. Yet despite the enormous pressures for centralisation in the modern industrial state, some diffusion of power normally prevails by virtue of the functions and powers assigned to local government, and, in federal systems, to state or provincial governments. These sub-central units of administration can provide a vehicle for the articulation of particular interests at the periphery and may, at times, modify or even thwart the execution of policies formulated by the centre.

Another element of the state system conducive to the dispersion of power is the judiciary which, in many capitalist societies, enjoys at least in principle a constitutional independence designed to defend the rights and liberties of citizens. To the extent that this separation of powers is realised in practice, the state system becomes less monolithic and more susceptible to the clash of competing interests. On the other hand, the degree of control exercised by the executive is normally enhanced by its ready access to the services of a large coercive apparatus that includes not only the armed services but also the forces of internal security. The resources and status enjoyed by these coercive institutions are often such as to enable them to wield enormous influence over the political decision-making process. Clearly, the precise structure of the state may vary considerably from country to country, and such variations may greatly affect the cohesiveness and effectiveness of central authority and its relationship to the periphery.

This study, then, is concerned to elucidate the mode, extent and efficacy of state intervention in nuclear dicision-making. Several questions immediately suggest themselves: What factors account for the commitment of major western governments to the commercial development of nuclear power? How has that commitment evolved since the United States launched its 'Atoms for Peace' programme? What have been the economic and administrative functions performed by the state? To what extent, and in what respect, has the performance of those functions varied from state to state? How may those differences be explained? The very attempt, however, to examine the functions of the state raises the even wider question of the state's relationship to civil society. Here it is necessary to determine the manner in which bureaucratic rationality and technical specialisation, which are central to the modern industrial state, have affected the political process. In relation to the nuclear controversy, it is important to establish whether, and to what extent, the actions of the state have favoured either side of the debate. Has the state acted as a neutral umpire, a representative of sectional interests, a direct protagonist in the conflict, or a political arena for the clash of opposing interests and values?

The political contest which has emerged between pro-nuclear and anti-nuclear elements in society may be said to have confronted the state with a new challenge to its authority in that the division between the proponents and opponents of nuclear power reflect conflicting, and therefore potentially destabilising, attitudes to 'technological progress', centralised modes of economic and social organisation, and personal life-styles characteristic of mass production societies. In this sense, the development of nuclear power programmes brings into question not merely the technical and administrative functions of the state, which are presumably central to the task of capital accumulation, but also its capacity to maintain the legitimacy of the process.

By the very nature of nuclear fission, by virtue of its commercial and military application, the state, operating in a stratified yet fragmented world system, is called upon to perform yet another function. The permanent possibility of economic and military rivalry, inherent in the dissemination of nuclear technology, further taxes the resources of the state as it seeks to balance the pursuit of *national* interests and the preservation of *international* order and security. Here, then, we are concerned to juxtapose the tendency towards disruption and the consequent need for regulation. Several questions would seem to follow from this proposition. To what extent have the nuclear policies of the major western states become intertwined with conflicts of economic interest, and with what implications for the problem of nuclear proliferation? How have national policies responded to the prospect of nuclear proliferation? To what extent have these policies and the institutional arrangements they have created succeeded in devising an effective system of international nuclear regulation?

It should be clear from this long list of complex questions that no single study, however exhaustive, could provide adequate answers specifically valid for all western countries, let alone for all nuclear countries. For this reason, the project has concentrated on an examination of six countries, although consideration has also been given to international negotiations, institutions and commercial transactions in order to make possible conclusions whose applicability might extend beyond the geographical boundaries of the selected countries.

The United States is a choice which hardly needs justification given America's economic and strategic pre-eminence in the post-1945 period. For many years, the United States accounted for more than half of the non-communist world's nuclear business. Within the range of middle powers, France has been chosen because of its commitment to an independent nuclear weapons capability and an ambitious nuclear power programme. Of particular interest is the impact of the highly centralised French political system on the pattern of nuclear development. Although roughly comparable to France, West Germany represents a significant contrast worthy of investigation. Noteworthy features include the absence of a military programme, the more decentralised system of government, and the more powerful and seemingly more effective anti-nuclear movement. The United Kingdom has been included partly because British policies ad initiatives played an important role in the early stages of nuclear expansion, and yet proved singularly ineffective in subsequent years in maintaining the momentum of the industry. Sweden readily suggested itself as a smaller country with no military alignments or nuclear weapons ambitions, but one which had embarked on a very substantial nuclear programme that sharply divided the community and for several years dominated the political landscape. Finally, Brazil was selected as a rapidly industrialising Third World state committed to an ambitious nuclear programme which became the subject of intense conflict between Germany's commercial policy and America's non-proliferation strategy. As far as possible the criteria of selection have been designed to facilitate a comparative and international perspective.

ACKNOWLEDGEMENTS

In establishing the conceptual framework and assembling the empirical evidence for this study I owe a great debt to individuals and institutions too numerous to name. Mention must be made, however, of La Trobe University where I have been teaching for the last ten years. This project would not have been commenced, much less completed, without the general support of the Department of Politics, the wholehearted co-operation of the secretarial staff, the Library, and the very generous financial assistance provided by the Social Sciences Research Committee. But I am most deeply indebted to the Australian Research Grants Committee who have financially sustained this project for three years, enabling me to have the necessary research assistance and to visit several of the countries concerned. Here I want to express my very special gratitude to Gary Smith, Sue Wakefield, Peter Davis and Peter Christoff for their painstaking and methodical work in helping me to locate, classify and process the enormous volume of documentary material and the extensive periodical literature relevant to this study. Finally, I must thank the US Institute of International Education, the Australian Embassy in the Federal Republic of Germany, the French Atomic Energy Commission, the UK Central Office of Information, and the Swedish Institute for arranging for me an extremely valuable programme of discussions and field research in their respective countries. Ultimately, however, responsibility for the judgements and arguments contained in this volume is entirely my own.

Abbreviations

AB Atomenergi	Swedish Atomic Energy Company
AEC	Atomic Energy Commission (US)
AEG	Allgemeine Elektrizitätgesellschaft
AFR	away from reactor storage facility
AGR	advanced gas-cooled reactor
AIS	advanced isotope separation
ANDRA	Agence Nationale pour la Gestion des Déchets Radioactifs
ASEA	Swedish nuclear company
AVM	Marcoule vitrification facility
BBC	Brown Boveri Company
BBU	Bundesverband Bürgerinitiativen Umweltschutz
BEG	Bureau d'Etudes Générales
BFCE	Banque Française de Commerce Extérieur
BNFL	British National Fuels Ltd
BNX	British Nuclear Export Executive
BWR	boiling water reactor
CANDU	Canadian deuterium-uranium reactor
CDFR	demonstration fast reactor
CEA	Commissariat à l'Energie Atomique
CEGB	Central Electricity Generating Board
CERN	Centre Européen de Recherche Nucléaire
CFDT	Confédération Française Démocratique du Travail
CFP	Compagnie Française des Petroles
CGE	Compagnie Générale d'Electricité
CGT	Confédération Générale du Travail
CIA	Central Intelligence Agency
CLAB	central storage facility for spent fuel (Sweden)

CNEN	Comissao National de Energia Nuclear (Brazil)
CNEN	Comitato Nazionale per l'Energia Nucleare (Italy)
CNPRI	Commission Nationale de Protection contre les Rayonnements Ionisants
CRILAN	Comité Regional d'Information et de Lutte Anti-Nucléaire
DM	deutsche mark
DWK	Deutsche Gesellschaft für Wiederaufarbeitung von Kernbrennstoffen mbH
ECCS	emergency core-cooling system
EdF	Electricité de France
ENEL	Ente Nazionale per L'Energia Elettrica
EPA	Environmental Protection Agency
ERDA	Energy Research and Development Administration
Euratom	European Atomic Energy Community
Eurodif	European Gaseous Diffusion Enrichment Plant Study Group
FBI	Federal Bureau of Investigation
FBR	fast breeder reactor
FOE	Friends of the Earth
Fr	French franc
GESMO	Final Generic Environmental Statement on the Use of Recycle Plutonium in Mixed Oxide Fuel in Light Water Cooled Reactors
GHH	Gutehoffnungshütte
GSIEN	Groupement de Scientifiques sur l'Information de l'Energie Nucléaire
GWe	gigawatt (electric) = 1000 MWe
HDR	high temperature reactor (West Germany)
IAEA	International Atomic Energy Agency
IEA	International Energy Agency
INB	Internationale Brutreaktorbau-Gesellschaft mbH
INCFE	International Nuclear Fuel Cycle Evaluation
INFA	International Nuclear Fuel Authority
INSERM	Institut National de la Santé et de la Recherche Médicale
Interatom	Internationale Atomreaktorbau
KBS	Kärnbräslesäherhet (Swedish reactor fuel safety project)

KNK	sodium-cooled, zirconium-hybride-moderated reactor
Kr	Swedish knona
kWe	kilowatt (electric)
kWh	kilowatt-hour
KWU	Kraftwerk Union
LIS	laser isotope separation
LMFBR	liquid metal fast breeder reactor
mtce	million tons of coal equivalent
mtoe	million tons of oil equivalent
mtpe	million tons of petroleum equivalent
MWe	megawatt (electric) = 1000 kWe
NEA	Nuclear Energy Agency
NNC	National Nuclear Corporation
NPC	Nuclear Power Company Limited
NRC	Nuclear Regulatory Commission
NPT	Non-Proliferation Treaty
NUCLEBRAS	Empresas Nuclearas Brasileiras SA
NUCLEN	Nuclebràs Engenharia SA
NUCLEP	Nuclebràs Equipamentos Pesados SA
NYSE & G	New York State Electricity and Gas Company
OECD	Organisation for European Co-operation and Development
OPEC	Organisation of Petroleum Exporting Countries
PEON	Commission Consultative pour la Production d'Electricité Origine Nucléaire
PFR	prototype fast breeder reactor
PUK	Pechiney Ugine Kuhlmann
PWR	pressurised water reactor
R & D	research and development
RWE	Rhenish-Westfalisches-Elektrizitäwerk
RWMAC	Radioactive Waste Management Advisory Committee
SBK	Schnellbrüker-Kernkraftwerks-gessellschaft mbH
SCPRI	Service Central de Protection contre les Rayonnement Ionisants
SERENA	Société Européenne pour la Promotion des Systèmes de Réacteurs Rapides au Sodium
SGHWR	Steam-generated heavy water reactor
SKI	Swedish nuclear inspectorate

SWU	Separative work unit
THORP	Thermal Oxide Reprocessing Plant
TWh	Terawatt-hour = 10^9 kilowatt-hours
UCS	Union of Concerned Scientists
UEA	Uranium Enrichment Associates
UKAEA	United Kingdom Atomic Energy Authority
UN	United Nations
VEW	Vereinigte Elektrizitätswerke Westfalen AG
WVP	Windscale vitrification plan

1 Origins of the Peaceful Atom

As early as 1911 Lord Rutherford had established by theory and experiment that an atom consists of a loose structure of electrons surrounding a heavy central core, the nucleus. Although hundreds of nuclear reactions were subsequently produced and studied, it was not until 1939 that serious consideration was given to the possibility of nuclear fission as a source of energy. The work of Otto Hahn, Lise Meitner, the Curies, Otto Robert Frisch, Rudolf Peierls, Enrico Fermi, Leo Szilard and a handful of other scientists soon confirmed the possibility of a sustainable chain reaction.[1] During the latter half of 1939, Szilard, concerned by the possibility that Germany might be rapidly moving towards the construction of a chain-reacting system, sought through various intermediaries, notably Einstein, to communicate his concern to the President of the United States.[2] In October 1939, the US Administration established a Uranium Committee which held discussions with several scientists, including Szilard and Edward Teller, but no firm action eventuated. It was only in the spring of 1940 that the modest sum of $6000 was made available for continued research in the uranium-graphite project. Following the re-organisation of the Committee several months later, Columbia University was awarded a $40,000 contract in order to develop the Fermi-Szilard system. By that time, however, Frisch and Peierls, now working in England, had already advised the British government of the possibility of making uranium 235 bombs using quantities of material that were industrially available.[3]

THE MILITARY CONNECTION

In January 1942, the American uranium project and the funds which sustained it were moved from the University of Columbia to the University of Chicago. Amid continuous reports of ominous German developments, the British research programme, including many prominent British scientists, was placed at America's disposal. In June 1942 supreme control of atomic research was transferred to a Military Policy Committee. A few months later General Leslie Groves was placed in charge of the whole effort which came to be known as the Manhattan District Project. From this time onwards, all personnel involved in the project, including the most eminent scientists, became captives of the enterprise, obliged to submit to military control and to the most stringent security provisions.

Although many of the scientists themselves had previously argued against the publication of their findings, they could hardly have imagined the veil of secrecy which was soon to descend on almost every facet of research. Perhaps no more than a dozen of the 150,000 people eventually employed in the Manhattan Project had a clear conception of its purpose and scope. From its inception, it was characterised by secrecy, lack of public accountability and the tacit alliance between science and the military establishment, all of which were to become distinguishing features of post-war military and nuclear planning. Indeed, the Atomic Energy Act, 1946, better known as the McMahon Act, granted the newly-established Atomic Energy Commission (AEC) extraordinary powers to call upon the services of intelligence agencies, including the FBI and the CIA, and to conduct the most exhaustive vetting of employees, ostensibly for reasons of national security.

After the war, the United States opted for a policy of atomic secrecy and isolation even in relations with its closest wartime allies, Britain and Canada. Originally, the three Anglo-Saxon powers had agreed at the Quebec summit conference in August 1943 to prevent the spread of nuclear technology by blocking access to the two ingredients essential for nuclear development, that is, uranium and technical know-how. The agreement, however, which was reaffirmed at the Hyde Park discussion in September 1944, at least pending the adoption of a fully effective system of international controls, had precisely the opposite effect. Quite apart from the resentment such a policy was bound to provoke among countries disadvantaged by the agreement, it was predicated on continuing British–American collaboration. But with Roosevelt's death, the conclusion of the second world war and the emerging conflict with the Soviet Union, the

Truman Administration became distinctly less enthusiastic about the Churchill–Roosevelt agreements.[4] In April 1946, after several months of deliberate procrastination, Truman finally turned down British requests for technical assistance in the development of nuclear facilities because of their perceived military potential. This decision, coupled with the provisions of the McMahon Act limiting nuclear collaboration with other countries and the obsessive preoccupation of the American military with the secrets of the atomic project, became a source of deep British resentment and a major factor in Britain's resolve to acquire an independent nuclear weapons capability. Given the fragmented system of sovereign states, and the national rivalries that it encouraged, America's efforts to preserve and strengthen its nuclear monopoly could not but fan the flames of nuclear proliferation.

Following the devastation of Hiroshima and Nagasaki, the United States set about the task of expanding its nuclear armaments. Although two atomic weapons had been used within the space of three days, their appalling destructive power concealed the limitations of the American weapons programme. In August 1945 the United States had no ready-made nuclear arsenal and could not have produced more than one atomic bomb a month. It may well be that the extraordinary secrecy surrounding the Manhattan project was partly designed to obscure the meagreness of its results. This may also to some extent explain the grim determination of the military to retain exclusive control over the elaborate complex of nuclear-related facilities.[5]

The weaknesses of the atomic programme were given frank expression in a report prepared by the five AEC commissioners for President Truman in April 1947. The commissioners stated:

> The present supply of atomic bombs is very small. The actual number for which all necessary parts are available is.... None of these bombs is assembled. The highly technical operation of assembly hitherto has been effected by civilian teams no longer organised as such. Training of military personnel to effect assembly is not yet complete.[6]

The blank space in the report referring to the number of weapons for which components were available, and the President's surprise when informed verbally of the actual number, would indicate that it must have been extremely small. Recently released information about the size of the nuclear stockpile during the period of US monopoly reveals that as of June 1947, nearly two years after the end of the second world war, there were only thirteen nuclear components available, along with twenty-nine Mark III implosion assemblies. This means that in the critical months that ushered in the Cold War; the United States was producing fewer than one atomic bomb every two months.[7]

Within weeks of the briefing he had received in April 1947, Truman authorised the AEC to undertake a rapid expansion of its military activities, including increased production of existing weapons and designing of smaller, more efficient A-bombs. In the ensuing Cold War atmosphere, the call for the development of a thermonuclear fusion bomb rapidly gained momentum. The growing pressure applied by the Joint Congressional Committee on Atomic Energy, certain sections of the Atomic Energy Commission, the Joint Chiefs of Staff, and the Defense and State Departments eventually persuaded Truman in March 1950 to issue the necessary instructions for the stepping-up of the hydrogen bomb programme from research to weapons production, and on to all-out delivery of H-bombs. In that year, the US President also submitted to Congress a request for a $1000 million supplementary appropriation for the AEC and plans for an expanded capability costing $5000 million, which would soon raise the AEC's annual budget to $3000 million and the level of its capital investment to $9000 million.

Military involvement in the atomic energy programme encompassed uranium output, production of fissionable materials, construction of chemical processing facilities and nuclear energy laboratories. In the period 1945–60, two-thirds of atomic research and development (R & D) expenditure and of the construction costs of the AEC's reactor power programme were devoted to military purposes. Military interest, however, was not confined to nuclear explosives. Equally important was the perceived potential of nuclear propulsion. The Navy, in particular, was anxious to develop a method of powering its submarines which would obviate the need to resurface. Accordingly, US designers developed a reactor type using light water as coolant and moderator, and keeping it under sufficient pressure to prevent it from boiling. The first such power reactor was tested in a land-based mock-up of a submarine hull in 1953. The following year saw the launching of the first nuclear-powered submarine, US *Nautilus*, followed in 1955 by US *Seawolf*. The submarine pressurised water reactor system was to serve as the rototype for the Shippingport power station, the first commercial ower reactor built in the United States. By the end of 1961, sixty-our submarines and surface ships were nuclear-powered. As late as 970, the US Navy accounted for more than three-quarters of the ower reactors produced in the United States.

The military thrust of the American nuclear programme, its scale, rganisation and rationale were largely determined by the objectives nd perceptions of a loosely-structured coalition of converging and verlapping interests. The principal actors in this coalition were the rmed services, private industry and finance, the legislative and xecutive organs of government, intelligence organisations and to a esser extent the emerging atomic bureaucracy, sections of the cientific and technological community and even elements of the rade union movement. This is not to say that these constituents of the military–industrial complex[8] were of one mind or always acted in unison. On the contrary, on many issues relating to the scope of the nuclear programme, the level of resource allocation, the degree and form of secrecy to be observed, the organisational arrangements to be enacted, the relationship to be maintained between the military and civil spheres of government, there were deep divisions and prolonged battles. On the other hand, it is also true to say that these groupings recognised one another as legitimate participants in the nuclear project and as sharing a common set of basic assumptions about its value and function. Clearly, in the early stages of development it was the military character of nuclear technology which established its political legitimacy, dovetailing as it did with the overriding ideological and strategic objectives of the American state.

The importance of military considerations, however, was not confined to the American experience. In Britain the decision to continue with the development of nuclear weapons was taken by a handful of people behind a screen of almost complete secrecy. Special precautions were taken to conceal not only the technical and organisational details of the decision, but also the fact that work on weapons production was being done at all. It was not until May 1948 that the Minister of Defence casually informed Parliament that 'research and development continue to receive the highest priority in defence, and all types of weapons, including atomic weapons, are being developed.'[9] Responsibility for the design work, materials research and prototype development of reactors and other nuclear facilities was placed with the Division of Atomic Energy Production in the Ministry of Supply, but the reactors designed at Harwell and Risley were clearly intended for the production of weapons plutonium. Initial military planning involved the construction of a uranium processing plant at Springfields, Lancashire, a uranium enrichment plant at Capenhurst, Cheshire, and plutonium-producing reactors and a plutonium separation plant at Windscale, Cumbria. Although consideration was also given to the civil applications of nuclear technology, these were accorded a much lower priority and were developed largely along lines dictated by military requirements.[10]

In France's case, the intention to develop a weapons capability was less obvious but none the less central to French nuclear plans. Taking advantage of the considerable expertise in atomic research developed before 1940 and of the return after the war of French scientists who had participated in British and Canadian experiments, the French government lost little time in establishing the Commissariat à l'Energie Atomique (CEA) in October 1945 and soon gathered a growing team of enthusiastic scientists and engineers. With the aid of a few tonnes of uranium mined in France and Mexico, some outdated equipment and heavy water supplied by Norway, the CEA was able to set up laboratories and a small chemical plant, and subsequently commissioned the small experimental reactor, ZOE. French nuclear research and development were thus based from the outset on natural uranium and graphite-moderated reactors. The first nuclear five-year plan announced in 1951, which provided for the construction of two reactors at Marcoule, initiated co-operation between the CEA and the nationalised utility, Eléctricité de France (EdF).[11] Despite the trappings of a civil industry and France's formal statement at the United Nations in 1946 that it would not seek military applications of the technology, the Marcoule Centre with its graphite reactors and chemical plant could easily provide the basis for nuclear weapons production.

The military implications of French nuclear policy became clearly visible in 1955 when the CEA undertook, in conjunction with the Ministry of National Defence, the construction of a third reactor at Marcoule specifically designed to provide France with a weapons capability. Indeed, as early as December 1954, the French government under Mendès France had decided to create within the CEA the Bureau D'Etudes Générales (BEG), a cover organisation whose task was to prepare the first atomic explosions and build prototype nuclear weapons. The details of the discussions which took place at the inter-ministerial meeting on 26 December 1954 have not been fully disclosed and are still the subject of conflicting interpretations, but there is little doubt that on that day a critical step was taken towards the development of a French atomic bomb.[12]

Although the precise role played by Mendès France himself remains unclear, one issue is beyond dispute. The decision to accelerate the French nuclear programme was made despite the clear recognition by all the main participants at that meeting that no effective barrier could separate the civil from the military applications of the technology.[13] It has still not been clearly established whether the main responsibility for proceeding with the production of nuclear weapons lies with Mendès France in 1954 or with Guy Mollet in 1956. It may well be that neither prime minister was fully conscious at the time of the magnitude or significance of what was being decided. It may even be that neither prime minister fully authorised the various plans emanating from the Ministry of Defence or the CEA. By the same token, it is evident that neither prime minister had available to him the institutional or technical resources which could effectively challenge the expertise or policy recommendations of France's atomic and military planners. Well before de Gaulle came to power in June 1958, the Fourth Republic had carefully laid the foundations for the Gaullist *force de frappe*.

The desire to develop nuclear, and later thermonuclear, weapons was thus central to the American, British and French nuclear programmes, as indeed it was in the case of the Soviet Union and China, although the scope and timetable of military planning varied widely from country to country depending on the level of technological development, availability of resources, and peculiarities of the political process. The primary role ascribed to the weapons programme was clearly acknowledged by leading spokesmen of the US Atomic Energy Commission. For example, Commissioner Eugene Zuckert stated in 1952:

> The requirement of national defense is the first consideration at the Commission. It is the reason for the extensive development of atomic energy today. Had there been no World War II, no need for advanced weapons, the progress made during the last ten years might have been achieved only in small measure.[14]

The politics of nationalism and the divisions of the Cold War had combined to give nuclear technology the required industrial and financial impetus. Here it is worth noting that the technology was born and developed in the context of international conflict and rivalry within as well as between the major alliance systems.

Only a few small European countries anxious to capitalise on indigenous technology or independent access to uranium and heavy water – notably Norway, Sweden, Belgium and the Netherlands – were able to initiate a modest programme of nuclear research and development unrelated to any military objective. But even here the countries in question were dependent, at least in part, on access to fuels and technology which only one of the existing or aspiring nuclear weapons states could supply. In the case of the United States, Britain, and to a lesser extent France, the fact that reactors were originally built to serve a military purpose meant that they could not provide a reliable basis for forecasting the economics of later, more advanced, reactors built primarily for the generation of electricity.[15]

For the industrial application of atomic energy to become a practical reality, then, it was necessary not only to argue for its economic viability but also to establish, at least theoretically, the distinction between the civil and military uses of the technology. Although nuclear weaponry would always lurk in the background, it was hoped that the public mind would focus on the peaceful uses of the atom and that a system of international controls would soon emerge which would break, or at least weaken, the nexus between nuclear reactors and nuclear weapons. Once sufficient public confidence had been established in the civil application of nuclear power, it might then be possible to initiate a system of international nuclear co-operation. That was precisely the rationale of Eisenhower's 'Atoms for Peace' doctrine. In his address to the UN General Assembly in December 1953, the American President went so far as to describe the peaceful use of atomic energy as a start towards diminishing 'the potential destructive power of the world's atomic stockpiles'.[16]

Given its military origins, civil nuclear power was from the outset faced with a serious problem of legitimacy. Expressions of faith in the inevitability of scientific progress and emotional appeals to the 'national interest' were indeed crucial to the strategy for ideological and cultural legitimation. This carefully orchestrated campaign for greater public acceptance was underpinned by the substantial institutional support lavished on the nuclear industry, which was itself the result of the bureaucratisation of science and the increasingly close partnership between the state and private industry. It is to these two closely-related sets of factors and their international implications that we shall now turn our attention.

IDEOLOGY OF PROGRESS

Demonstration of the enormously destructive power of atomic weapons in 1945 did not dim the basic belief of western civilisation that its material progress was inevitable, perhaps irreversible. If anything, the faith in progress was strengthened partly in order to grapple with, accommodate, and, in a sense obscure, the reality of the nuclear threat. Operating on the assumption that 'the clock cannot be turned back', scientists, politicians, bureaucrats and industrialists gradually developed a conceptual scheme aimed at prohibiting, or at least containing, the harmful uses of nuclear technology while highlighting and encouraging its more positive applications. Central to this strategy was the notion of a system of international controls for the peaceful use of atomic energy.[17] Accordingly, the United Nations established in January 1946 an Atomic Energy Commission and debated for several years various proposals, notably the Baruch plan which argued for an international authority to own and control the 'intrinsically dangerous' aspects of the nuclear fuel cycle, from the processing of ore at a uranium mine to its end uses.

America's international efforts to legitimise the development of atomic energy were also reflected in a domestic campaign to transfer the Manhattan project from military to civilian control, thereby hastening the peaceful application of the technology. After a protracted battle in Congress, the pro-civilian lobby, made up largely of scientists who had grown suspicious of military intentions, won the debate. Two factors, however, were to undermine the victory. In the first place, the expectation that nuclear fission could produce spectacular advances in industry proved to be exaggerated and premature. Secondly, the belief that the United States already possessed a considerable military atomic force proved unfounded. As a result, the Atomic Energy Commission found itself in control of a programme which was years away from even a modest civil application, but which had to concentrate instead on the construction of a military arsenal. As David Lilienthal, the first Chairman of the Commission, explained several years later, 'The AEC as a weaponer has in fact become very much a part of that military establishment as defined by the military.'[18] In spite of these constraints, the general euphoria about the atomic future continued to gain momentum throughout the late 1940s and early 1950s.

The prodigious sums of public money, the enormous scientific, technical and industrial resources, and the broad powers invested in the Atomic Energy Commission reflected the conviction that the energy of the atom represented an overriding national interest deserving special status and the highest policy priority. It was confidently expected that cheaper power derived from nuclear energy might stimulate a wide range of industries, for example, reduction of magnesium and aluminium, refining of copper, production of cement, chlorine and caustic soda, and electric furnace operations like the production of graphite, calcium carbide, phosphoric acid, ferro-alloys and electric steel.[19] More generally, it was argued that nuclear power promised a distinct advantage in abundance, cost and convenience of fuel supply. For some the promise of atomic energy was literally limitless since it offered a source of 'wealth and leisure and spiritual satisfaction in such abundance as to eliminate forever any reason for one nation to covet the wealth of another.'[20] Although not everyone in the pro-nuclear lobby shared these expectations, they were all, in varying degrees, exponents of the same technological optimism.

The introductory words of the McMahon Bill clearly expressed the conviction that the harnessing of atomic energy would unveil unlimited horizons, 'promote world peace, improve the general welfare, increase the standard of living, and strengthen free competition . . .'.[21] Even Lilienthal, who had no great enthusiasm for the military atom and who subsequently became a sharp critic of the Atomic Energy Commission, at first entertained great hopes for the electricity-generating potential of nuclear power. In due course the euphoria spread far beyond American shores, even to countries with limited financial or technical resources, and eventually engulfed Japan itself, although its people had still cause to remember the devastating impact of atomic energy. Carried along by a technological faith of almost religious dimensions, the emerging nuclear establishment in several countries endeavoured to instil a sense of urgency into the debate, stressing the need for risk-taking and much greater allocation of resources. Failure to act quickly and decisively, it was claimed, would amount to negligence for it would deprive the nation, perhaps irreparably, of its legitimate stake in the fruits of technological progress.

But the arguments for an all-embracing financial and ideological commitment to the peaceful atom did not go altogether unchallenged. Many questioned whether the revolutionary source of energy expected from the peaceful atom would ever materialise, and whether it would justify the extraordinary scale of public expenditure advocated by its proponents. The hazards and difficulties surrounding the nuclear enterprise, although often underestimated, were nevertheless understood even by those whose entire career revolved around the development of atomic energy. One of Britain's most eminent nuclear scientists, Sir John Cockcroft, clearly indicated the magnitude of the problem in a major address in June 1950:

> radioactivity taken in excess is undoubtedly harmful, and the nuclear engineer has to take account of health hazards in designing his nuclear boilers, and this slows down development and increases costs. More important still, a world run on nuclear power would increase substantially the amount of radioactive materials in the world, and their safe disposal or storage may prove to be costly and difficult.[22]

Equally significant is the fact that, despite the enormous impetus derived from government expenditure on research and development laboratories, subsidies for the purchase of uranium fuel, and direct financial support for manufacturers of electrical equipment and utilities, nuclear power by the mid-1950s was still not regarded by many of the interested parties as a commercially attractive proposition.

Several early studies warned against over-optimistic forecasts and questioned the assumption that low-cost atomic power would be available in the foreseeable future. In 1947, Dr Walter Zinn, a leading theoretician of nuclear power, called attention to the shortage of nuclear fuel, and concluded that the only hope for nuclear power lay in successful perfection of the breeder, which at the time was considered a distinctly remote prospect.[23] The AEC's General Advisory Committee shared Zinn's pessimism, and in November 1947 more or less rejected the notion that any considerable portion of the world's power supply could be replaced by nuclear power over the next twenty years. According to one informed view expressed in March 1949:

In the short run at least, all available evidence supports the belief that atomic power will cost more – and perhaps considerably more – than will power from existent energy sources. From the economic point of view, then, there is little immediate incentive for the adoption of atomic power.[24]

Later in the same year, Philip Sporn a leading figure in the American power industry, also offered a somewhat discouraging assessment of the prospects of nuclear power, and suggested that commercial development might take another twenty-five years or even longer.[25] Despite the growing mood of optimism in the early 1950s, Sporn, who was also Chairman of the Advisory Committee on Co-operation between the AEC and the Electric Power Industry, retained a healthy scepticism of the economic potential of nuclear power, questioning whether nuclear energy 'could be produced cheaper than conventional power or at least at a comparable cost'.[26]

In addition to the technical difficulties, the development of competitive power-producing reactors, particularly in the United States, was hindered by the economics of conventional electricity generation. Between 1950 and 1955 the installation of new electricity facilities increased America's total supply by nearly 48,000 MWe, that is, more than 50 per cent of the capacity installed at the end of 1949. The ability to generate electricity cheaply and in such relative abundance could hardly encourage efforts to develop radically new methods of production. During this period private industry remained unconvinced of the advantages of atomic power largely because of the enormous capital and maintenance costs involved. Given the magnitude of the required investment and the absence of reliable data on which to base estimates of future gains, the major corporations with a potential interest in nuclear power tended to remain on the sidelines leaving it to the public purse to finance the costly programme of research and development.

In the face of these technical, economic and institutional obstacles, President Eisenhower's UN speech of December 1953, soon to be followed by changes to the US Atomic Energy Act, sought to give renewed impetus to the commercial development of nuclear power. The optimism generated by these initiatives reached its peak at the First International Conference on the Peaceful Uses of Atomic Energy held in Geneva in August 1955. The conference undoubtedly released an unprecedented amount of previously classified scientific and technical information. The exhilarating atmosphere created by the conference was subsequently described by one of the participants in terms of 'the arrival of a new Prometheus' bearing 'a gift richer by far than the gift of Promethean fire'.[27] But for all its success in establishing nuclear power as the symbol of modernity and progress, the conference over-sold nuclear energy, encouraging countries to launch nuclear power programmes which greatly overestimated the promise and underestimated the economic and technical problems associated with the technology.[28] A peculiar blend of technological optimism and institutional opportunism had propelled nuclear power to the forefront of national and international decision-making.

BUREAUCRATISATION OF SCIENCE

At first, the role of the scientist in the development of nuclear weapons posed relatively few problems since he was engaged on a project designed to assist in the defeat of the enemy and hasten the end of the war. But once the technical feat of producing the bomb had been accomplished, scientists were suddenly confronted with the ethics of its use. Such considerations led distinguished members of the scientific community to counsel against the dropping of the bomb on Hiroshima and Nagasaki. Many of the scientists at Los Alamos subsequently formed an organisation to disseminate information about the potential of nuclear power for peace and war. The political and moral awakening that followed the nuclear test explosion in July 1945 has been aptly described by one of the contributing scientists:

> My technical work was done, the race was run and the full, awful magnitude of what we had done came over me.... In this sentiment I was by no means alone.... We wrote manifestos, we gave speeches, we made forays to Washington, we organised the Association of Los Alamos Scientists. *Politics became our new business.*[29] (italics added)

It was precisely this emerging consciousness of the social and ethical implications of their discoveries which prompted scientists to question in the aftermath of peace many of the security measures which, principally out of patriotism, they had readily accepted during war.

The very attempt to remove the conditions of war secrecy brought scientists into sharp conflict with the military. Their campaign was successful in blocking the May–Johnson Bill, thereby closing the door to continued military control of nuclear energy. The Federation of Atomic Scientists and the more broadly based Federation of

American Scientists were also instrumental in persuading the US Administration to consider various forms of international control.[30] But the attraction of political lobbying and moral crusading soon lost its novelty, and a good many of the Los Alamos scientists, widely regarded as the most prestigious element in the new scientific establishment, found their way into the councils of government. Fermi, Oppenheimer, Cyril Smith and others achieved positions of considerable influence and were soon joined by other scientists, including Edward Teller who became a passionate advocate for a crash hydrogen bomb programme. Whatever the motivation of these men, they became part of the bureaucratic apparatus of government, whether it be through absorption into the sprawling empires of the Atomic Energy Commission and the Pentagon, or through membership of numerous committees and advisory groups attached to Congress or the Presidential office.

Despite national variations the same general pattern emerged in other nuclear states, The trend was especially visible in France where government consciously sought to make science an instrument of social, economic and military policy.[31] Whereas scientists were largely responsible for the creation of the CEA and its early development – many of them had participated in the Anglo-Canadian team working on the atomic bomb, were suspicious of private industry and favourably disposed towards the parties of the left – their influence rapidly declined after 1951.[32] Frédéric Joliot Curie, the most prominent of the French atomic scientists, was relieved of his duties as first High Commissioner of the CEA because of his association with the Communist Party. Curie's dismissal from his senior post in the French nuclear establishment was remarkably similar in its political implications to the Oppenheimer case which shook the American scientific community in 1954. Robert Oppenheimer, brilliant wartime director of the Los Alamos laboratory and subsequently Chairman for eight years of the General Advisory Committee established to guide the AEC on scientific and technical matters, became the subject of security hearings in 1954. His strong opposition to the development of the H-bomb was probably the decisive factor which prompted the AEC to withdraw his security clearance, thereby permanently depriving him of access to classified nuclear information. In France, Curie was replaced by Francis Perrin, a man drawn from the bureaucratic tradition of French politics and strongly committed to the military and economic application of atomic energy. The subsequent re-organisation of the CEA provided government officials and industrialists with added leverage within the institution and further circumscribed the role of scientists. The atomic age had thus hastened the trend already apparent for some time whereby science was transformed into a technological activity placed increasingly at the service of national interests and objectives.

The development of the UK Atomic Energy Authority, the US Atomic Energy Commission and the French Commisariat à l'Energie Atomique reflected, in varying degrees and in different guises, the same process at work, namely the bureaucratisation of science. The removal or demotion of independently-minded scientists, the growing supremacy of engineers and administrators, the close institutional and personal connections with the military establishment necessitated and legitimised by the nuclear weapons objective, and the rapidly expanding links with the corporate world of industry and finance became the distinguishing features of the atomic decision-making process. The very scale of the enterprise dictated a change in the traditional relationship between the technological application of science and the political organisation of scientific research. Individual scientists, private research institutes, foundations or universities could no longer be relied upon to provide the necessary financial or organisational resources required by the atomic project. The only institution capable of responding to these demands was the nation-state itself.

During the war the problem had been greatly reduced by placing the whole enterprise under military control. But once the war was over the justification for this procedure could no longer be sustained. It thus became necessary to devise an ideologically more acceptable form of state intervention. The civil atomic energy agency supported by public funds and closely connected with other leading branches of the state apparatus became the standard institutional model. But to the extent that the state assumed primary responsibility for both research and development, the very relationship between science and society was radically changed. Scientific effort could no longer be directed exclusively towards the search for truth as conceived by the founders of modern science and affirmed through the centuries of classical tradition, but had to respond to the specific economic, political and military objectives set by the state with the co-operation of the technological community. In precisely the same way the internationalist aspirations of science had to be subordinated to national perceptions and loyalties as defined by the state. It is not surprising therefore to find the development of atomic energy increasingly implicated in the international rivalries and competition characteristic of the fragmented system of sovereign states.

The national nuclear programme, then, may be characterised in terms of a contract between the state and science, with the former as the senior partner, in which the scientific value of the pursuit and possession of truth is overridden by the practical value of science as a source of power in both the technological and political sense.[33] The state gradually abrogated to itself the role of 'legitimate guardian and rightful exploiter of this national resource' whether for military or civil purposes. Atomic energy was harnessed by the state to assist it in its various functions, including the waging of war. It followed that scientific activity – and the scientist himself – had to be carefully monitored and regulated so as to maximise the efficiency with which these functions were performed. Investigations into the political loyalty of the scientist and political discrimination in access to scientific information were essential tools in the national administration of the nuclear project and an integral part of its inner logic. As a consequence, the expertise which developed within the closely-guarded boundaries of the state assumed an increasingly monolithic character. To this extent, the ensuing consensus among 'experts' may be said to have been bureaucratically programmed to serve institutionalised interests rather than critical inquiry.[34]

In due course, the politician himself, far from shaping policy, became the prisoner of 'expert' advice which he could not independently assess and which effectively pre-empted consideration of alternative options. Where counter-expertise does not exist, the function of the politician is reduced to that of articulating and representing the perceptions of a bureaucratic and technological élite which may not necessarily accord with reality or with the preferred values of society. In other words, the bureaucratisation of science, which the emergence of a nuclear – industrial complex both expresses and reinforces, is part of a larger phenomenon whereby science and technology are wedded to the means of production and the productive process increasingly integrated with the political apparatus of society.

THE NATIONAL INTEREST

Over the last two centuries the modern industrial state has acquired a vast array of agencies and institutions (e.g. armed forces, police force, civil service, statutory authorities, educational system) capable of mobilising an ever-increasing proportion of the community's resources, both physical and intellectual, and of channelling them towards ends which are primarily those of the state itself and only indirectly those of the citizen. This historical movement towards the development of the state as a self-serving, self-contained and self-perpetuating political structure has been greatly assisted by the technological revolution but also by the rise of nationalism as the essential element of statehood. It is precisely the appeal to national identity, national loyalties and to the underlying socio-cultural consensus which has enabled the state to achieve a central position in the minds of most individuals and to project itself as the only political institution capable of arbitrating between competing interests in the name of the *national interest*. But it cannot be automatically assumed that the policies of the state actually express the collective interests of society as opposed to merely sectional interests which, because of their power, may nevertheless succeed in presenting an image of neutrality. What is in question is the very concept of the national interest. It is doubtful, to say the least, whether the interests of the individuals or groups that make up the nation are spontaneously in accord with each other, or whether the addition of these interests constitutes in any meaningful sense *the general interest*.

Yet the development of nuclear power has almost invariably been defended in terms of the national interest and appeals to nationalism have featured prominently in government campaigns to gain public acceptance of the nuclear option. In France's case, the harnessing of atomic energy was depicted in the early 1950s as crucial to the restoration of the country's former greatness. Great play was made of the fact that the economic growth experienced by advanced industrial nations was based on the availability of energy resources, hence the importance of atomic energy for future growth. Unflattering comparisons with the Anglo-Saxon countries, stressing the paucity of funds committed to the French nuclear programme, added spice to the argument and provided further justification for a steady increase in the French atomic energy budget.[35] In 1955, Gaston Palewski, the minister responsible for atomic energy, argued that the meagre financial allocation to atomic research and development was all the more unacceptable given that France had ample scientific and technical resources to undertake a large-scale effort in the industrial application of nuclear energy.[36]

Although historical traditions and national psychology may vary widely from country to country, the advanced industrial state has almost without exception been able to formulate compelling national themes and goals aimed at the legitimation of the state's political and economic priorities. In the case of nuclear policy, several closely interconnected themes, centred on economic growth, modernisation, technological independence, energy security and military preparedness, have dominated the attempts of the state to rationalise and justify its commitment to this ambitious and, in some respects, economically unproven technological project. We have already seen that in the United States, Britain and France, initial nuclear planning had a large military component, and civil programmes were developed either as an afterthought or as a means of obscuring, and perhaps making more palatable, the decision to acquire nuclear weapons.

In the case of West Germany military considerations were not paramount in nuclear decision-making partly because of the severe constraints operating against German rearmament in the post-1945 period. On the other hand, German political leaders made no secret of the fact that they regarded nuclear energy as providing significant muscle in Germany's drive to regain its former industrial power. Despite its essentially civil character, Germany's nuclear programme had nevertheless important domestic political and foreign policy connotations in so far as it challenged the traditional ascendancy of the coal and allied industries, created a need to redefine Germany's interest in European political integration, and raised important questions about the country's technological and commercial relations with both the United States and the rest of Western Europe.[37]

In France, where nuclear policy had a much stronger military orientation, atomic energy was also considered vital to the process of social and economic modernisation. Common to both objectives was the search for technological independence, hence the determination to develop an independent nuclear capability which would demonstrate the achievements of French technology and restore national pride and self-confidence. This consideration led the CEA to support for several years the French graphite-moderated reactor system despite widespread doubts as to its economic competitiveness. While resigned to the fact that nuclear fuel imports might be necessary for some time to come, France was adamant that nuclear equipment and technology would need to be locally produced, since much the greater part of the price of nuclear-generated electricity derived from capital rather than fuel costs. Nuclear nationalism required more than local manufacture of materials and equipment; it implied indigenous designs and techniques which would obviate expensive licensing arrangements and ensure effective independence in the utilisation of nuclear technology. In the words of Francis Perrin, CEA High Commissioner, 'it would be greatly preferable for France to buy from the United States oil and coal than nuclear reactors.'[38]

Another important factor contributing to France's nuclear plans was the relative scarcity of indigenous energy resources. Unlike Britain and Germany which had substantial coal reserves, or the United States which had plentiful supplies of coal, oil and gas as well as access to energy sources in other parts of the world, France, with the exception of its hydroelectric potential, had to rely for its energy requirements almost entirely on foreign sources. Energy security thus became a powerful motive for the development of a nuclear industry based on French technology and uranium reserves to be found either in France itself or in some of its African colonies. The second five-year plan, announced in July 1957, explicitly pinpointed access to energy supplies as crucial to France's future as a major power, to the expansion of the economy and to the improvement of living standards.

By appealing to the national interest, the state found a ready-made cultural–psychological lever for establishing a popular consensus in favour of its nuclear plans. The particular interpretation of the national interest advanced by any state depended on the prevailing national mood and the anticipated degree of public receptivity to the various messages or themes the state might wish to develop. Apart from these socio-cultural variables, the state had also to take account of its own requirements and of the uses to which atomic energy could be put in the performance of economic and political functions. The relative importance of the civil and military programmes, their scale and rate of expansion were to a large extent governed by the internal constellation of power within the state and by its international connections. The power play between sectional interests greatly influenced the nature of the nuclear project, largely determining whether it would proceed under civil or military control, under public or private ownership, on the basis of foreign or indigenous technology. Competing groups and elites used the national interest argument to advance their own preferred version of the project rather than to question its implicit assumptions or desirability.

STATE AND INDUSTRY

As one would expect, interaction between the state and industry during the early stages of nuclear power development was ambiguous and to some extent fluid. Although in most cases the relationship was closely linked to organisational patterns which had emerged during the war, there were nevertheless substantial national differences. As a generalisation, it would be true to say that the nuclear relationship between the state and private capital was gradually strengthened, although the extent of such co-operation and its *modus operandi* varied considerably from country to country. Indeed, the growing interdependence between the public and private spheres became one of the distinguishing characteristics of the nuclear project.

As already indicated, the British nuclear programme was initiated under conditions of strict secrecy and geared to the achievement of military objectives. Civil applications of the technology took place within the weapons laboratories and behind the same wall of secrecy. From 1946 to 1954 all nuclear work was carried out under the auspices of the Ministry of Supply. In 1954 the Atomic Energy Act replaced the existing administrative structure with a new agency, the United Kingdom Atomic Energy Authority (UKAEA), which was given responsibility for all nuclear research and development, both civil and military.[39] The UKAEA was funded by a separate vote of Parliament, which amounted in 1954 to $53,675,000. This direct parliamentary allocation placed nuclear energy in a unique position *vis à vis* other industries, enabling it to disregard normal criteria of efficiency. Notwithstanding the dominant financial and administrative role of the state, the private sector was allowed to participate in various stages of nuclear design and manufacture. The AEI-John Thompson Nuclear Energy Company designed and built the Berkeley nuclear power station in Gloucestershire and the Nuclear Power Plant Company designed and built the Bradwell station in Essex. Several consortia of private companies were initially involved, but by 1963 the number had shrunk to three as a result of the progressive concentration of the industry. Although their contribution to the early stages of nuclear power development was limited, statutory electricity authorities, notably the Central Electricity Generating Board, were to play an increasingly important role as exclusive customers for nuclear services and equipment.

The role of the public sector was even more decisive in France, where the CEA was placed under the direct authority of the prime minister and given a wide-ranging charter for the conduct of 'scientific and technical research with a view to the utilisation of atomic energy in the various fields of science, industry and national defence.'[40] Equally pivotal was the role of EdF which operated as a state monopoly in the electricity sector. Representatives of industry were brought together in a government advisory body, the PEON Commission, but the CEA retained overall financial and administrative control in nuclear reactor construction as well as in the production of nuclear fuels. The CEA was also responsible for providing expert advice on the economics of nuclear power and its likely contribution to energy requirements. In the early phase at least, French industry played a subordinate role as the supplier of reactor materials and components. For its part, EdF had a policy of parcelling out small contracts to a host of firms, thereby maximising competition and reserving for itself the role of industrial architect. Moreover, many of the firms which were established to perform specific operational tasks were jointly run by the CEA and private companies, with the CEA normally retaining overall authority.[41] By the same token, precisely because EdF was the only customer of these firms, it was under some obligation to guarantee their financial viability. To this extent, the profitability of indigenous nuclear-related industries strongly influenced the scale and pace of France's nuclear activities. In theory, EdF had the alternative option of contracting with foreign suppliers, but such a strategy was politically unacceptable since it would have contradicted the principle of national independence and created areas of unemployment, thereby undermining one of the principal economic arguments used to justify the nuclear project.

In sharp contrast to the British and French experience, the German nuclear industry began largely with private and local initiative. Given the political consequences of Germany's defeat in the war, it is not altogether surprising to find in the early stages of nuclear power development only limited public involvement. To the extent that German nationalism had been dealt a severe psychological blow and the political structure of Nazi society seriously undermined, it was virtually impossible for the emerging political system to devise a national nuclear policy based on a coherent nationalist ideology. What occurred instead was piecemeal industrial development.

The gradual relaxation of the allied ban on German nuclear research gave added impetus to industrial participation, but it was not until the Paris Accords of 1954, which lifted all restrictions in return for Germany's pledge not to develop nuclear weapons, that private firms set out in earnest to explore the industrial potential of nuclear energy.[42] Soon after, the German government established a new Ministry for Atomic Questions which assumed overall responsibility for defining the relevant spheres of competence of state, federal and private authorities. In January 1956 the German Atomic Commission (Deutsche Atomkomission) was created, comprised of leading personalities drawn from government, industry and science. Despite its purely advisory function, the commission was able by virtue of its expertise to exert significant influence over the direction of Germany's nuclear programme.

Unlike France, which had sought from the beginning to foster its nuclear independence *vis à vis* the United States, Germany's inclination was to develop close links with the American nuclear industry not only because of its military alliance with the United States but also in order to allay lingering international suspicions of German intentions. Another important constraint on the German programme was the relatively plentiful supply of coal which deprived the nuclear effort of any immediate sense of urgency. The absence of a direct military objective coupled with the lack of sustained government intervention tended therefore to reinforce the role of market forces and to place technical and managerial control of both reactor and fuel activities in the hands of private industry. It was not until foreign policy considerations, notably relations with the United States and attitudes to European integration, assumed greater importance in Germany's nuclear plans that the federal government decided to play a more assertive role.

Clearly, the national pattern of nuclear power development differed substantially from country to country. The role of the state, its relationship with industry, the institutional framework for nuclear planning, depended in each case on such factors as the political traditions of the country in question, its foreign policy objectives, the structure of its energy economy and the disposition of its key industries. Nevertheless, despite important national variations in the initial stages of nuclear policy-making, a marked trend towards convergence soon emerged. The expansion of the nuclear industry sooner or later necessitated an increasing degree of state intervention which, paradoxically enough, also brought in its train the growing participation of industry at various stages of planning, design, investment and production. The latent tension and growing interdependence between the public and private sectors were characteristic of all the European countries we have so far considered but also of the United States.

Although the American nuclear project was, by virtue of its military character, almost entirely dependent on the financial and administrative apparatus provided by the state – it was, in effect, the creation of a public monopoly – powerful pressures soon developed advocating the participation of private enterprise. Thomas Dewey, Republican candidate in the 1948 presidential election, argued that atomic progress could not continue to be left exclusively to the government.[43] In keeping with this objective, the AEC had already appointed in October 1947 an Industrial Advisory Group to study ways in which industry might increasingly participate in atomic energy development. According to AEC Chairman, David Lilienthal, the intention of the commission was to move away from the existing government monopoly provided by law 'as fast as it could be done with due regard for the national security.' His proposal envisaged not only the supply of services and equipment through contractors and sub-contractors, but the creation of new profit-making opportunities for industry. To this end, the Industrial Advisory Group recommended in December 1948 that the government should provide industry with relevant information about atomic energy, increase direct personal contacts between civil servants and industrialists, enhance the effectiveness of industrial advisory committees, and strengthen the contract system.[44] In July 1949, the AEC appointed the Ad Hoc Advisory Committee to explore the possibilities of a closer working relationship with the electric power industry. Once again, particular stress was placed on the need for the private sector to become acquainted with the complexities of atomic energy and for technicians and engineers in the power industry to become more involved in the work of the commision.[45]

Efforts to increase industrial participation in nuclear power development gained further momentum in the ensuing two or three years. By June 1953 Lilienthal's successor, Gordon Dean, was ready to make a series of far-reaching proposals to the Joint Congressional Committee on Atomic Energy. In the interests of making civil power more competitive and encouraging the involvement of private industry it was argued that a variety of incentives would have to be devised. Accordingly, interim legislation was advocated, which would permit ownership and operation of nuclear power facilities by private firms, the lease or sale (under safeguards) of fissionable materials, more liberal patent rights, and the transfer of responsibility to state authorities for the safety aspects of reactor operations.[46] In subsequent hearings conducted by the Joint Committee, support for AEC's statement was expressed by the Departments of State, Commerce and Interior, although no in-depth investigation had yet been carried out into the likely effects of nuclear power on the economy or of commercial involvement on nuclear power development.

The five industry groups which gave evidence before the Committee were all agreed that private enterprise should play a larger role in the nuclear programme, but they readily conceded that 'no company was prepared at this time to undertake alone the entire investment necessary to develop and build a full-scale atomic power plant.'[47] Significantly, the proposals put forward by Monsanto Chemical Company envisaged a dual-purpose reactor producing plutonium for sale to the government for military purposes and electric power as a by-product. The purchase price for the plutonium would be set sufficiently high and guarantees of government purchase of plutonium provided in order to ensure the profitability of the exercise. In other words, private participation was feasible only to the extent that the project remained a government-protected risk.

The state monopoly of nuclear power was, of course, a direct consequence of the military programme. By 1952 a massive, publicly-owned industry had been created, involving the expenditure of some $10,000 million of public funds on plutonium-producing reactors, uranium enrichment plants and a host of other research and ancillary facilities. These could not be turned over to private hands unless the industry assumed a civil character. It thus became necessary to experiment with reactors which could produce both electricity and plutonium. In this sense, the search for peaceful applications of nuclear technology was inextricably intertwined with the attempt to involve private enterprise in the development of nuclear power. The first difficulty related to the fact that until the mid-1950s remarkably little research had been done on the design of reactors specifically suited for economic power production. The second problem arose from the unwillingness of any firm to invest the tens of millions of dollars needed not only for reactor construction but for safety and health measures in heat transfer and chemical processing facilities, and for general research and maintenance.

To overcome these obstacles, corporations such as Monsanto and Union Electric initially proposed that the AEC itself embark upon the design of a pilot plant reactor making use of existing government facilities, technical personnel and public funds. Private industry would nevertheless participate in the design, construction and operation of the plant. In other words, the corporate sector made it clear from the outset that private investment in nuclear power would materialise only when risks had been drastically reduced through government subsidies and purchase agreements with appropriate guarantees. Even then it was expected that private industry would require access to government-owned reactor information and technology.[48] In October 1952, the AEC announced that joint feasibility studies would be undertaken with the Dow–Detroit Edison companies, which would require the government to defray about $750,000 in expenses as against $250,000 for the two firms.

Despite the frenetic activity now under way and the variety of financial and technological incentives being offered by the AEC, the privatisation of the industry was still hampered by the nexus between the military and civil uses of nuclear energy. In the first place, it was hardly possible to split the industry into two parts, assigning one to military purposes and keeping it under government control, while providing the other with a peaceful function and transferring it to private hands.[49] Equally vexing was the problem of the economic competitiveness of nuclear electricity, a problem greatly compounded by the fact that profitability for the private investor could be achieved only through the allocation of public funds. Several voices were now beginning to question the wisdom of turning the 'benefits' of atomic energy into private profits given that the technology itself was 'brought to fruition by public funds'.[50]

These and other impediments were in the end overcome by the combined informational and advertising campaigns of industry and government. By proceeding initially at a relatively slow pace, by encouraging giant public–private projects, and, above all, by exploiting the widespread popular commitment to the market ideology, they effectively undermined the notion that the gradual erosion of government's nuclear monopoly was inimical to the public interest. The important point to note, however, is that both public and private interests were directly involved in the commercialisation of the nuclear industry. Indeed, it can be argued that the state, as the principal custodian of the free enterprise system, had itself played the leading role in this process. For their part, electricity utilities and manufacturing firms tended to be far less enthusiastic about the prospects of the industry and reluctant to participate except under conditions which would remove any substantial risk in capital investment. By contrast, the various arms of the state, notably Congress, more particularly the Joint Committee on Atomic Energy, several of the more influential government departments and the Atomic Energy Commission all helped in varying degrees to create the ideological and institutional environment conducive to nuclear power development. Through a carefully calculated mixture of pressure and inducement they succeeded in integrating industry into nuclear policy-making. The net effect of the strategy was to establish and increasingly institutionalise a *nucleocracy* whose function was to coordinate and fuse ever more closely the interests and objectives of the state, of industry, and of the scientific and technological community.

THE INTERNATIONAL CONTEXT

Although the failure to institute a framework for the international control of nuclear facilities tended to reinforce the American policy of isolationism,[51] pressures soon developed for the relaxation of secrecy in the dissemination of nuclear technology and for the lifting of restrictions on international nuclear commerce. No country had made a greater financial and institutional commitment to the military and industrial application of nuclear power than the United States. The ready availability of relatively low-cost electricity, however, could not but discourage the establishment of an expensive civil nuclear industry. On the other hand, in many European countries and in Japan the shortage of energy fuels and the higher costs of electricity generation could be expected to enhance the competitiveness of nuclear electricity. Here, then, was the prospect of a growing export market in nuclear technology and equipment which the United States – perhaps Britain and even Canada – might be able to exploit given the relatively advanced state of their industry.[52]

By the end of 1952, the US atomic energy establishment, including the powerful Joint Congressional Committee, was convinced of the technical feasibility of the industrial application of atomic fission. The only remaining hurdle was perceived to be that of cost and, therefore, of profitability – a matter which, as we have seen, became inextricably intertwined with the controversy about the participation of private enterprise in the nuclear programme. But even before the resolution of the controversy, the AEC was eagerly exploring overseas outlets for demonstration plants not only as a means of acquiring valuable engineering and operating experience, but in order to tap the export market. AEC Commissioners were now openly proposing a variety of US credits and other financial arrangements with a view to speeding up nuclear power construction in Western Europe.[53] The stage was thus set for the 'Atoms for Peace' statement which President Eisenhower delivered to the UN General Assembly in December 1953.

The presidential announcement signalled the start of US diplomatic efforts to create an international atomic energy agency and opened the way for a network of bilateral agreements between the United States and individual countries wishing to acquire American technical know-how, fuels and equipment. These initiatives, which were to be complemented by a regime of international safeguards, were justified on the grounds that they would reverse the trend towards military escalation and promote instead the peaceful uses of nuclear energy. This self-justifying formulation of American policy could not, however, altogether conceal the more pragmatic considerations underlying US commercial interests. In this context, support for a civil nuclear industry in Europe was considered crucial, hence Washington's active encouragement of European nuclear integration. In keeping with this objective, the US offered in principle to supply other countries with enriched uranium and other scarce materials such as heavy water, provided that agreement was reached on adequate controls for the transfer of these materials. It soon became evident that the 'Atoms for Peace' programme and the subsequent changes to the 1946 Atomic Energy Act were intended, as much as anything else, to preserve American dominance in the nuclear field.

The Panel on the Impact of the Peaceful Uses of Atomic Energy, appointed by the Congressional Joint Committee in 1955, recommended vigorous measures to foster nuclear power development in other countries, including the furnishing of financial assistance through both government and private channels. The explanation offered in defence of this proposal stressed the relevance of the overseas market for the future viability of the US nuclear industry:

> If the equipment manufacturers... are to be expected to carry forward research and development directed towards making atomic power competitive in the United States, the foreign market for power reactors with its high near-term growth potential may offer a solution to bridging this gap. The potential demand may represent a $30 billion market.[54]

The 1954 revision of the Atomic Energy Act was designed in part to exploit this potential market.

The three main levers the US hoped to use in this regard included exchange of scientific and technical information, supply of nuclear fuel materials for research and power reactors, and assistance in the design and construction of these reactors. For this purpose, the AEC created in November 1955 a Division of International Affairs (subsequently renamed the Division of International Programs) and entrusted to it the task of overseeing various types of agreements for international co-operation. The Division was also expected to liaise with the State Department in negotiations for the establishment of the International Atomic Energy Agency. By the end of 1955, the AEC had already completed agreements with twenty-two countries, including Belgium, Brazil, Canada, Japan, Switzerland and the United Kingdom. Agreements with France and Sweden were concluded in 1956, and with West Germany in 1957.[55]

American attempts to foster nuclear power development in other countries involved the training of a growing cadre of scientists and engineers as well as financial and technical assistance in the building of research reactors and demonstration nuclear power plants. As a consequence, the United States was well placed to influence the direction of other national nuclear programmes. By the end of 1957, six research reactors of US manufacture were in operation abroad and nineteen others were under construction or on order.[56] In pursuit of the same objective, the United States had already revised in 1956 its previous policy prohibiting the export of uranium enriched beyond 20 per cent. The decision to permit the supply of up to 90 per cent enriched uranium for use in special testing reactors was made despite the proliferation risk associated with enrichment technology. Two years later, US restrictions were further relaxed with the announcement that highly enriched fuel would be supplied for research as well as test reactors.

Early in 1956, the United States concluded negotiations in relation to power projects reactor with several governments. The agreements, which provided for the transfer of restricted data, were particularly attractive to the co-operating countries as much of nuclear technology was still classified and unavailable in the open literature. They also paved the way for the sale of nuclear fuel to each country, although the United States retained substantial control over the use and movement of the plutonium produced by the power reactors. In February 1956, President Eisenhower announced that he would release 20,000 kg of uranium 235 for use America's partners in bilateral agreements and promised additional supplies as further projects might require, with the added assurance that fuel would be made available for the expected working lifetime of bilateral power reactor projects. In July 1957, an additional allocation of uranium 235 for foreign use brought the total to 50,000 kg. It was made clear that these supplies of nuclear fuel were not a gift and that payment would be required.[57] On the other hand, in addition to security of supply, the United States was able to offer co-operating governments a schedule of charges for uranium 235 which were to be the same as for the domestic nuclear industry.[58]

By way of added incentive, the AEC compiled a list of prices it would pay for plutonium and uranium 235 produced in foreign nuclear power reactors using US fuel. Finally, in October 1956 the US made it known that financial assistance for the construction of nuclear power plants would be provided by the AEC and the Export–Import Bank to nations with which it had concluded bilateral agreements. The Bank announced that it would be willing to consider loans to cover the capital costs of nuclear power plants, provided that utilities were privately- and not publicly-owned, that the country in question could demonstrate its ability to service the dollar debt, and that the funds were used only to buy equipment, materials and technical services from the United States. America's vast technological and financial resources thus provided it with a powerful base with which to promote the commercial interests of its own nuclear industry.

Washington was also able to use its diplomatic and military muscle within the Atlantic Alliance to press for an integrated European atomic agency as a means of binding the six countries (France, West Germany, Italy, Belgium, the Netherlands and Luxembourg) to a US-dominated nuclear market. American pressure on West Germany was particularly effective because German leaders were reluctant to associate themselves too closely with the British and French atomic programmes which had obvious military implications. Links with the American nuclear industry were considered politically more acceptable and economically more advantageous. Certainly, neither Britain nor France could offer a technological or financial package as comprehensive or attractive as that offered under the US 'Atoms for Peace' programme. Moreover, the West German government was peculiarly susceptible to American pressure because of the very deep divisions between different sectors of West German industry, which reflected their widely divergent structural, financial and market positions and were reproduced inside the policy-making apparatus of the West German government.[59] Following the vain attempts of the Ministry for Atomic Affairs, under Franz Josef Strauss, to acquire independent uranium sources and secure a bilateral agreement with the United States, the Bonn government decided to accept US proposals for European atomic integration as the only means of achieving the desired co-operation with the US nuclear industry.

In contrast to the West German situation, conditions in France tended to favour a more independent outlook. The more comprehensive and systematic approach to nuclear policy adopted by the French state combined with the more explicitly nationalist formulation of military, economic and technological objectives to produce a distinctively French attitude to the question of European institutions. France's Euratom proposals, outlined in the autumn of 1955, envisaged the creation of an agency which would monopolise the supply of uranium to member countries and build a joint uranium enrichment plant and a joint reprocessing plant to supply community needs. In addition, the French plan provided for the coordination and financing of national and European reactor research, the exchange of patents and the creation of a common market for the products of the European nuclear industry. The French concept of integration was inspired not only by the vision of European independence *vis à vis* the United States but also by the desire to secure France's own lines of reactor development and to create a western European market for the emerging French atomic programme.

In pressing for its own position the United States was greatly assisted by France's growing isolation within Western Europe. The French role in the collapse of the European Defence Community scheme and persistent French opposition to the creation of a general common market had contributed to mounting friction between France and its neighbours. The American cause was also advanced by the Messina Conference of June 1955, at which the foreign ministers of the six member countries of the European Coal and Steel Community decided to encourage the development of nuclear power. They subsequently commissioned three prominent Europeans, Louis Armand of France, Franz Etzel of West Germany, and Francesco Giordani of Italy, to report on the prospects of nuclear power. This group, often described as 'the three wise men' produced a report, *A Target for Euratom*, which, though not published until May 1957, was nevertheless greatly influential in shaping European thinking on nuclear integration. The authors of the report warned of the dangers of excessive dependence on foreign oil supplies and of the inevitability of vast increases in fuel imports should the six countries fail to develop an alternative source of energy. Accordingly they recommended that the Common Market countries install 15,000 MWe of nuclear power by 1967.[60]

The pro-American bias of this recommendation was evident from the fact that the proposed nuclear capacity was nearly ten times the combined capacity planned by Euratom's two principal members, France and West Germany. One can only conclude that the projection bore much less relationship to estimated European needs and capabilities than to American perceptions of the scale of nuclear power development required to ensure effective integration of European resources on the one hand and a substantial American input into the European nuclear programme on the other.

According to 'the three wise men', Euratom was to assist the six member countries to pool their scientific and industrial resources and to contribute to the construction of a European entity which by virtue of its very size would eventually be able to compete with the two super-powers in a way that was beyond the capacity of any single European nation. In the meantime, it would be necessary for Euratom to co-operate closely with the US nuclear industry. The nature of American participation in the European nuclear power programme was outlined in some detail:

> The United States would make available the necessary fissionable materials and the technical knowledge to set our industries going. Once Euratom is established, a task force composed of some of America's most able men would be at our disposal to continue studying with European experts the many technical problems posed by our programme. America would provide training facilities for our scientists and technicians. Joint projects, for instance to improve and adapt reactors, can be envisaged between American and European industries, as well as between the American and European Atomic Energy Commissions.[61]

The report explicitly envisaged the construction of American-designed reactors, whether through direct imports or under licence, and gave assurances that Europe could rely on the United States to provide the necessary supplies of enriched uranium. This course was favoured on the grounds that enriched uranium produced in Europe would be two or three times more expensive than enriched fuel imported from the United States. In any case, the report argued that the early recycling of plutonium produced as a by-product from other nuclear plants, the use of natural uranium as a fuel, and the rapid development of the breeder rector would lessen the need for enriched uranium.

Predictably, the Eisenhower Administration supported the general thrust of the Armand–Etzel–Giordani report, but was careful to distance itself from any suggestion that Euratom might be a stepping-stone to greater European political independence. On the contrary, US policy was to treat Euratom as a predominantly technical project which would provide American industry with experience as well as a market for its products and technology. Quite apart from strengthening American overall economic influence in Western Europe, Euratom was seen as providing the necessary experience in the operation of large-scale reactors, which would in turn encourage the expansion of the US nuclear programme. This pattern of co-operation was favoured by the United States precisely because it afforded a useful lever with which to shape the character and scope of European programmes in a manner consistent with American economic, diplomatic and even strategic interests.

The strength of America's bargaining position lay partly in its technological superiority which was protected by domestic legislation as well as international aggreements. Moreover, the United

States, together with Great Britain, had a virtual monopoly on known uranium reserves and right to the end of the 1950s exercised control over uranium production in Canada, South Africa, Australia and the Belgian Congo through legal arrangements which precluded the participations of third parties.[62] America's dominant role in Europe was further reinforced by virtue of Euratom's lack of technical staff and independent expertise, without which it was not possible to challenge American projections or policy advice. Finally, the close links that had been forged between the AEC and American private corporations permitted American industry to establish a more intimate relationship with European industrialists than European firms had been able to achieve either amongst themselves or through Euratom.

Because of several factors peculiar to French politics, notably the centralisation of state power and the emotional appeal of nationalism, American plans as reflected in the 'Atoms for Peace' programme met with greater resistance in France than in any other part of Western Europe. No French government was prepared to countenance an agreement which would deny it the option of acquiring a nuclear weapons capability. As a consequence, France agreed to take part in negotiations on the clear understanding that such participation would not restrict its right to manufacture nuclear weapons or interfere with its existing civil programme. The French refusal to accept the American-oriented concept of Euratom was sufficient to obstruct the development of the agency as originally envisaged by American policy-makers and 'the three wise men'. Euratom, for example, was never invested with authority over the energy or financial decisions of the national electricity industries. Research thus became the only effective means by which it could implement its objectives. However, even in this sphere, its competence was severely limited by the requirement of unanimity. Whereas the French consistently argued that Euratom research should focus upon reactors using natural uranium as a fuel, in order to reduce European reliance on imported enriched fuels, others preferred research on the light water reactor.

As a result of competing national interests, Euratom's role became that 'of a broker rather than a prime mover in the commercial use of nuclear energy in Europe'.[63] Member states inevitably acted on the principle that their national programme should have priority over supranational technological co-operation. The emerging dissension within Euratom, which ten years after its establishment culminated in the failure to adopt a third five-year plan, accurately reflected not only the current state of international rivalries but the growing friction that was to dominate intra-alliance politics in the field of atomic energy. Relations regarding the civil applications of nuclear energy would in due course prove as divisive and conflict-ridden as the strategic and diplomatic tensions which had originally governed relations in the military applications of the technology.

2 The Emerging Nuclear State

Initially, the harnessing of nuclear fission was governed largely by American efforts to achieve military supermacy in the second world war. With the conclusion of the war, however, the nuclear weapon remained an important instrument of statecraft and one of the principal levers available to the United States in the management of its adversary relationship with the Soviet Union. But quite apart from its Cold War implications, nuclear fission came increasingly to be seen by America's policy-making élite as an important element in the post-war reconstruction of the international capitalist order and in the continued dominance of American economic and political power. Nuclear technology was thus integrated into an elaborate programme which sought to usher in a new phase of capital accumulation generating growth for the capitalist world as a whole while at the same time buttressing the monopoly position of US capital. The establishment of a technologically-complex, capital-intensive industry likely to yield cheap and abundant energy was deemed essential if the programme of capitalist expansion was to gain added impetus and proceed unhindered by considerations of future energy scarcity. Such an ambitious project would obviously require the extensive and continuous intervention of the state.

THE PLANNING PROCESS

The technical difficulties involved in attaining acceptable levels of nuclear safety, the plentiful supply and relative cheapness of non-nuclear fuels, particularly oil and coal, and the substantial capital costs entailed in nuclear power construction, all tended in the late

1950s to slow down the pace of national nuclear programmes. The enthusiasm with which the nuclear option had been embraced a few years earlier gave way to a more realistic assessment of commercial prospects. Nuclear planning in each of the major western powers thus had to contend with the dual limitations imposed by a relatively small domestic base and an even smaller yet highly competitive export market.

In the United States, the AEC, prodded by the Joint Congressional Committee on Atomic Energy, announced in February 1954 a $240 million five-year programme of atomic power development, which would extend from 1954 to 1958 and encompass five reactor construction projects. The five basic concepts which were chosen for development under this programme were the pressurised water reactor (PWR), the boiling water reactor (BWR), the sodium graphite reactor, the fast breeder reactor (FBR) and the homogeneous reactor.[1] Construction of the pressurised water reactor was to be a joint effort of the Duquesne Light Company of Pittsburgh and the AEC, with the government bearing about 85 per cent of the total cost. The 60,000 KWe plant, located at Shippingport, Pennsylvania, was expected to be in operation during 1957. The boiling water reactor was to be housed at Argonne National Laboratories and to produce about 5000 kilowatts of electricity. Design, fabrication and operation of the sodium–graphite reactor were assigned to North American Aviation, Inc. under a cost-sharing contract, with the AEC bearing about 75 per cent of the cost.

The Atomic Energy Commission devised its Power Demonstration Reactor Program with the expressed intention of involving the private sector in nuclear power business. In response to this invitation, four proposals were received, and contracts negotiated with the Detroit Edison Group. A few months later the AEC announced the second round of the Power Demonstration Reactor Program, but in this instance invitations were specifically aimed at proposals limited to nuclear power plants with capacities of 5–10, 10–20, and 20–40 MWe. But whereas the Commission appeared to have a preference for nuclear power plants of lesser capacities than those proposed in the first round of the programme, the electricity utilities were attracted to much larger units because the ensuing economies of scale offered the greatest hope of nuclear electricity effectively competing with conventional fuels.

The general reluctance of the large utility systems and of the manufacturing companies to enter the nuclear field stemmed principally from their assessment of the high cost of nuclear energy – 2–5 times the cost of conventionally fuelled capacity, and possibly more in the early stages of development. In the first atomic plants, at least, it was widely conceded that the production cost would greatly exceed the 6–9 mills per kilowatt-hour (kWh) of a modern coal-fired plant. The relatively slow pace of nuclear development generated a good deal of stocktaking and additional prodding, notably from the Joint Committee on Atomic Energy which authorised the Hanford convertible reactor, increased allocation of reactor research and development funds, and passed the Price–Anderson Indemnity Law and the Euratom Co-operation Act, 1958. In the same year the Committee issued a staff report which was itself the culmination of a long series of reviews on the current state of the industry, beginning with the McKinney Report in January 1956, the Joint Committee on Atomic Energy Acceleration Report in July 1956, the American Assembly and National Planning Association reports in 1957, the Joint Committee and AEC seminars in the winter of 1957, the Edison Electric Institute Report of March and July 1958, and the Atomic Energy Commission statement of June 1958.[2]

Partly with a view to neutralising increasingly vociferous accusations that it was dragging its feet, the AEC issued in January 1957 a third round of invitations for industrial participation in the atomic energy programme. It stipulated that, unless industry agreed to build the required number and kinds of reactors with a view to having them operational by June 1962, the AEC itself would seek congressional authority to build them. Despite the expressed interest of such companies as the Florida Nuclear Power Group, the Pennsylvania Power and Light Company and Westinghouse Electric Corporation, it became increasingly evident that, as a result of soaring capital costs, the programme would not accelerate unless substantially subsidised by government. The power to be generated by the Shippingport pressurised water reactor was now expected to cost somewhere around 63 mills per kWh (nearly nine times the average cost of conventionally generated power). The capital cost of the plant had risen from an early estimate of \$47.8 million to \$70.0 million. Similarly, the cost of the pressurised water reactor being built by Yankee Atomic Electric Company had increased from \$32.9 million to \$57.0 million, and the boiling water reactor under construction by Commonwealth Edison Co. from \$45.0 million to \$60.0 million.

With electricity utilities unwilling to build costly power stations that would operate at a loss for many years, manufacturers were applying increasing pressure for large-scale federal aid in order to establish the conditions for an expanding nuclear market. For its part, the Commission was now resigned to the fact that atomic power would not be competitive even in high fuel cost areas for another ten years.

The fluctuating fortunes of America's nuclear industry and the transition from euphoric optimism to painful readjustment were also characteristic of the British experience. In 1955, a White Paper was presented to the British Parliament outlining provisional proposals for the building of nuclear power stations to give a capacity of 1500–2000 MWe by 1965,[3] by which time it was projected that the cost of electricity from nuclear power would be competitive with that from conventional sources. This initial target was to be the first step in a much larger nuclear programme designed to provide by 1975 nearly half of Britain's electricity requirements. It should be noted that Calder Hall Station, built by the UKAEA at an estimated cost of $56 million, was designed primarily for the production of plutonium (electricity was a by-product) and was not therefore included in the White Paper programme.

Because of a perceived deterioration in access to fuel supplies, accentuated by the 1956 Suez crisis, and because of errors of judgement as to the future costs of nuclear energy, the British government announced in March 1957 its intention to accelerate this programme and adopt it as the basis for planning a range of 5000–6000 MWe of nuclear capacity by the end of 1965.[4] The target date for the completion of this programme, estimated to cost some £980 million, was subsequently extended by one year. Five nuclear power stations were expected to come into operation by 1961 and two more by 1966. These seven stations were to have a combined output capacity of 3000 MWe, which meant that exceptionally larger orders would still need to be placed in the early 1960s in order to reach the target nuclear capacity of 5000–6000 MWe.[5]

The 1955 White Paper had estimated the cost of nuclear power at 0.6 d per kWh, or 7 mills, after allowing for the value of the plutonium produced. Proponents of the nuclear programme were confidently predicting that, with the increasing cost of coal, nuclear electricity would eventually achieve at least a slight advantage over coal-derived electricity, since 'a new art like that of the nuclear reactor [would] advancc faster than the old-established one of the conventional station.'[6] In fact, even before the first commercial nuclear stations were ordered, the competitiveness of nuclear power had begun to decline, partly because of the fall in the value attributed to plutonium. The general rise in interest rates, from 4 per cent in 1955 to 7 per cent in 1963, also proved damaging to the nuclear industry since capital charges accounted for two-thirds of nuclear generating costs as opposed to one-fifth for conventional energy sources. Moreover, nuclear power had to contend with improvements in coal and oil supplies which brought the generating cost from these sources closer to 0.5 d per kWh than the 0.6 d forecast in 1955. Not surprisingly, by June 1960, when the government issued its second White Paper on the nuclear programme,[7] it was generally recognised that a rapid build-up in nuclear capacity could no longer be justified on fuel supply grounds and that nuclear power would not achieve competitiveness with conventional fuels for some years to come. Seven nuclear stations totalling 2600 MWe were either under construction or approved by 1960. The target of 5000–6000 MWe by 1965 was now abandoned, and instead the White Paper indicated that new orders would consist of about one station a year in each of the four ensuing years. In actual fact, only two more stations were to be ordered prior to 1965.[8]

Instead of the nineteen stations originally envisaged in the 1956–65 programme, by 1971 only nine magnox-type power stations (not including Calder Hall and Chapelcross) had been built with a combined capacity of 4887 MWe. The falling rate of orders, combined with the increasing size of stations being ordered, inevitably meant growing doubt as to the future viability of the major industrial groups competing for nuclear business. In yet another White Paper published in 1964,[9] the government called for 5000 MWe of additional nuclear capacity in England and Wales to be commissioned from 1970 to 1975. Given the current state of the nuclear market, it would seem that the decision to proceed with this programme on the basis of the Advanced Gas-Cooled Reactor (AGR) design developed by the UKAEA, had more to do with the perceived need to ensure the survival of the nuclear industry than with any objective assessment of the comparative costs of nuclear power and other available sources of energy.[10]

It would be true to say that the British nuclear programme as defined by successive White Papers was greatly influenced by the

UKAEA's research and development priorities. Even when the electricity authorities had reservations about the scale or the speed of the commercial application of nuclear energy, or when technical and financial problems confronted the nuclear industry, the UKAEA was nevertheless able to press ahead with its activities. It was greatly assisted in this regard by the very large nuclear establishment it had created as a result of generous government funding over several years and by the disproportionate influence it was able to wield in British energy planning. During the 1950s the Authority experienced a remarkably rapid growth, its total staff increasing from 22,000 in 1956 to 30,000 in 1958 and 40,000 in 1960. As principal adviser to the government in all matters relating to nuclear energy, the UKAEA faced no challenge to the validity of its judgement as to the direction which nuclear research, development and production plans should take. The minister responsible for the Authority had no independent technical staff to provide a check on the advice he was given. According to the 1967 Report of the Select Committee on Science and Technology, the minister's 'control and supervision of the Authority's activities was financial rather than technical.' The Authority's position was further enhanced by virtue of the fact that it acted as sole producer and supplier of nuclear fuels in the United Kingdom. Finally, the Authority, as patentee of all its products, had the right to grant or withhold licences for the commercial exploitations of all reactor types and related equipment of United Kingdom origin.

Although atomic energy development in France had a more humble beginning than in Britain or the United States, the first five-year plan adopted in 1952 represented a major watershed in that it involved a shift from the research to the production stage, that is to the construction of high-power reactors designed to generate electricity. Not surprisingly the plan called for an investment of Fr 37,000 million* as opposed to the Fr 15,000 million allocated over the preceding six years. By the time the second five-year plan was approved in 1957, the first reactor in the Marcoule industrial complex had gone critical, and by 1958 the electricity authorities were associated with this programme in the production of several megawatts of electricity.[11] A second 40 MWe reactor at the Marcoule power station became operational in 1958 and a third in 1959. By

*1952 exchange rate: $1 = Fr 350

1962, the three Marcoule reactors were providing some 70 MWe to the grid, or about 0.67 per cent of the country's total production. These were followed by the three Chinon reactors which came into service in 1963, 1965 and 1967 and had a capacity of 170, 210 and 400 MWe respectively.

To ensure the independence of its nuclear programme, France had developed its own gas–graphite reactor fuelled by natural uranium, thereby avoiding recourse to foreign reactor designs and reliance on American enrichment capacity. In keeping with the same objective, the CEA opened several mining divisions, and four chemical treatment plants were built by industry in different parts of France. In addition, uranium exploration carried out by the CEA in several French colonies resulted in the discovery of a rich deposit in Gabon which was soon followed by the construction of a local treatment plant for the production of uranium concentrates. Despite the methodical expansion of the nuclear industry, the ambitious targets set by the second and third five-year plans – in particular, the projected production of 850 MWe by 1965 – had to be abandoned.

Both the Marcoule and Chinon reactors, which employed gas–graphite techniques, had been specifically designed to serve the dual purpose of plutonium production for military use and power production for industrial use. Whether the objective of a fully-fledged national civil industry, independent of foreign technology and sources of supply, would be attained was still open to question. While maintaining the bias towards the gas–graphite design, a policy of diversification was initiated with EdF's decision in 1960 to collaborate with Belgium in the construction of a 300 MWe pressurised water reactor at Chooz, and was soon followed by the commissioning of a 70 MWe heavy water reactor which came into service in Monts d'Arrée in 1967. Another pressurised water reactor with an 870 MWe capacity, to be built at Tihange as a joint Franco–Belgian project, was placed on order in 1960. Throughout this period, France also maintained its interest in the development of breeder reactor designs.[12]

Indicative of the thinking of the French nuclear establishment and of the perceived function of the state in the development of the industry was the 1964 Report issued by the PEON Commission.[13] Essentially, the Report addressed itself to three questions: the medium-term (1965–70) and long-term (1985 and beyond) role of nuclear power in the French economy; the comparative costs of nuclear power and other sources of energy; and the adequacy of current uranium supplies and industrial infrastructure in relation to the proposed nuclear power programme. The general conclusion of the Report was that the growing demand for electricity, coupled with the declining potential of hydroelectricity, would result in the very rapid development of nuclear power. To ensure the success of such an ambitious programme and to avoid technical or industrial bottlenecks, the PEON Commission, acting on the advice of French industry, recommended the need for long-term planning which would provide companies with advance notice of government intentions as well as with a guaranteed future market. To this end, it was argued that during the life of the fifth five-year plan (1970–5) new orders for nuclear-installed capacity should be placed at the rate of 500 MWe per year, that is, the equivalent of one additional nuclear power station (then averaging at 500 MWe) a year. To this extent at least the scale and rationale of the proposed programme appeared to reflect more closely the financial requirements and productive capacity of French industry than an objective assessment of France's future energy needs.

The single-minded formulation and execution of French nuclear policy was to a large extent made possible by the scientific and administrative authority exercised by the CEA and, ironically enough, enhanced by the political instability of the Fourth Republic. The failure of Parliament to give serious consideration to atomic energy policy contributed to a situation in which initiative and guidance in nuclear matters generally resided with the CEA rather than the political executive. In any case, a regular process of consultation with both the industrial and political hierarchy, formalised in part through the PEON Commission, ensured that the CEA could drastically expand the scale of its operation without incurring the wrath of its political masters.

In striking contrast to the American, British and French experience, German nuclear plans were slow off the mark. Several manufacturing firms, including SSW of Erlanger, AEG of Frankfurt, Babcock & Wilcox of Oberhausen, BBC of Mannheim, and Interatom of Bensberg, set up reactor development groups in the mid-1950s, but little progress was made towards a coordinated nuclear power programme. In order to avoid duplication, the various industrial groups agreed to divide their efforts among the various reactor types: pressurised water, boiling water, heavy water, natural uranium-gas and high temperature.[14] These initiatives, funded largely by private industry but sponsored by the German Atomic Commission, formed the basis of the first unofficial nuclear five-year plan, the so-called 1957 Eltville 500 MWe programme, which initially provided for the construction by 1965 of five prototype nuclear power stations with an output of some 100 MWe each. However, development work under this programme soon bogged down. Germany's late entry into the nuclear field was compounded by the problem of finance,[15] or to be more precise by the refusal of the German power industry to accept a greater investment risk given the comparative advantage enjoyed by conventionally-produced electricity.

During this early period, the federal government was assisted principally by the Atomic Energy Advisory Committee, established by a Cabinet decision in January 1956 and comprising some 220 experts. In the Bundestag, a Committee on Nuclear Energy was established but subsequently merged with the larger Committee on Science, Cultural Policy and Journalism. Another influential but unofficial group, the German Atomic Forum, which included politicians, scientists and individuals interested in promoting nuclear energy, played an important part through lectures, meetings, displays and other public relations work, in allaying public fears about the dangers of the nuclear industry. The initiative for the establishment of research facilities was left largely to German industrialists, although many of these, notably the Karlsruhe Nuclear Research Centre and the Jülich Nuclear Research Establishment, derived most of their financial support from federal and state governments. These initial arrangements were nevertheless insufficient to persuade the private sector of the wisdom of investing substantial resources in nuclear power generation.

In response to this impasse, the German government intervened and urged the Atomic Energy Advisory Committee to establish, in co-operation with the reactor industry, a programme for advanced experimental reactors of an output of 10–30 MWe. Although the scale of these reactors was still too small to be of immediate interest to the power companies, two of the four projects initiated under this programme in 1961 were considered successful. These two projects – AEG's high temperature reactor (HDR) and Interatom's sodium-cooled, zirconium-Hybride-moderated reactor (KNK) – highlighted the importance of central planning and forecasting in the development of advanced technology. Accordingly, the federal government announced at the end of 1962 a second five-year plan which envisaged a total expenditure of $625 million. Following the awarding of a contract in 1963 to General Electric for the construction of a boiling water reactor (BWR), the German power industry decided to build three demonstration power stations: a 237 MWe BWR to be built by AEG and General Electric, a 240 MWe BWR to be built by AEG, and a 282 MWe pressurised water reactor (PWR) to be built by SSW. By this time the principle of government leadership and federal funding was firmly establishment.

It was not until 1967, however, that the German Atomic Commission announced the first official nuclear plan (the two previous plans being unofficial) which called for a federal allocation of more than $1000 million and the establishment of nuclear fuel facilities.[16] The federal government, it is true, was still intent on reducing its participation as soon as reactor programmes reached the commercial stage, preferring to concentrate on the development of long-term projects, including advanced reactor designs. Nevertheless, the federal contribution had assumed considerable importance, particularly in its encouragement of industrial partnerships. The commercial interests of private firms were increasingly equated with the German national interest. A notable outcome of this policy was the establishment in 1967 by Siemens and AEG of the joint nuclear subsidiary, KWU. It would seem that the momentum achieved by the nuclear industry in the late 1960s owed a great deal to direct state intervention in both planning and financing.

In the case of Sweden, the interest in nuclear power was directly linked to the structure of the country's energy economy which lacked the substantial indigenous fuel resources available to the other OECD countries. From 1955 to 1965 energy demand increased by 5.1 per cent per year, and although the rate of increase was expected to decline in the ensuing two decades, it was generally argued that with the production of hydroelectricity likely to remain unchanged, only an ambitious nuclear power programme could moderate Sweden's rapidly growing dependence on foreign oil supplies. In 1947, AB Atomenergi (the Swedish Atomic Energy Company) was formed as a state-controlled company with the government holding 57 per cent of the capital and paying all operating expenses. Other shareholders included private and municipal utilities, industrial and insurance companies. One of the main responsibilities of AB Atomenergi was applied atomic research, hence the construction of several experimental reactors. From the outset, government policy was to develop the Swedish concept of a heavy water, natural uranium reactor. The R3/Adam project, the first in this line, was designed for simultaneous generation of 10 MWe of electrical power and 55 MWe in the form of hot water for domestic heating. Situated at Agesta, about 16 km south of Stockholm, the station came into operation in the summer of 1963.[17]

The next development step in the Swedish heavy water reactor line was the 140 MWe Marviken nuclear power station which was located on the Baltic coast some 150 km south of Stockholm. The Marviken project was a joint venture between AB Atomenergi and the State Power Board, with the Swedish ASEA company as principal contractor. Construction difficulties, however, necessitated costly design changes, leading to doubts about the economic feasibility of the heavy water reactor concept compared to the emerging light water nuclear systems. The project was eventually cancelled in 1970. Swedish utilities were nevertheless confidently predicting that nuclear power would play a dominant role in electric power installations during the 1970s and that by 1985 nuclear reactors would contribute 50 per cent of Sweden's electric power production.[18] The first order for a commercial nuclear power plant, the Oskarshamn boiling water reactor with a 400 MWe capacity, was placed with ASEA in 1965 by a consortium of eight large private and municipal electricity utilities. Construction started in 1966 and commercial operation in early 1982. New nuclear capacity installed thereafter was expected to average about 400–450 MWe per year.

Given the central role played by AB Atomenergi in the Swedish nuclear power programme, close collaboration soon developed with industry and particularly with the power companies, notably with the State Power Board and with AKK, a consortium comprising about 75 per cent of the privately- and municipally-owned power companies formed specifically for the promotion of nuclear energy. To assist further the process of coordination the Atomic Forum was created in 1965 by a group of metal-working industries with special interests in the nuclear field, the largest power companies, and AB Atomenergi. By the mid-1960s the technological and administrative foundation of Sweden's nuclear effort was sufficiently in place to make the country's nuclear planners confident about export prospects, not only in reactor components and fuel elements but in complete nuclear power stations based on Swedish reactor designs.

Yet, by the late 1960s the elaborate arrangements devised by major western governments and the very considerable technological and financial resources allocated to their respective nuclear power programmes had yet to close the gap between promise and performance. The commercial application of nuclear power, particularly in Europe, was proceeding at a far slower rate than anticipated. In many of the leading industrial countries several issues fundamental to the future course of nuclear policy had yet to be satisfactorily resolved. Governments faced the difficult task of assessing not only the relative merits of indigenous and imported technology, but the policy consequence of choosing between alternative reactor designs. Equally important was the need to determine the cost–benefit implications of these alternatives and the degree to which the country was getting, or would in future get, value for money. Closely related to these considerations was the perceived need for national control of, or at least access to, uranium enrichment technology and the fuels and materials required for the development of the various reactor options.

Although Europe, and particularly the United Kingdom, had initially dominated nuclear power developments, by 1970 the relative European share of the world's nuclear business was sharply declining as a result of new countries entering the field and faster growth elsewhere, notably in the United States. At the end of 1968, Europe could boast 7030 MWe of nuclear power capacity, that is, 63 per cent of the world total, with the United Kingdom alone accounting for almost 40 per cent of that total. Two years later, Europe's share of installed nuclear power capacity had fallen to 39 per cent, and by 1975 was substantially below that of the United States. As of 1970 the combined capacity of nuclear power reactors already operating, under construction or planned in the United States was 78,358 MWe compared with 20,261 MWe for the United Kingdom, 12,260 MWe for West Germany, 7560 MWe for Sweden, and 4431 MWe for France.[19] The relative decline of the European nuclear industry was considerably accentuated, and is in some measure explained, by the ascendancy of American-designed light water reactor systems and by their increasing penetration of the European market. By 1968 the greater part of future European nuclear capacity was committed either to BWR or PWR designs of American origin. Here it is worth noting that, whereas the Shippingport light water reactor had a larger electric capacity than the Calder Hall natural uranium reactor, its pressure vessel was by volume only one-eleventh the size of its British equivalent. As a result, the capital cost per kWh was substantially higher for the British Magnox and French gas–graphite than for the light water systems.[20]

As the economic competitiveness of nuclear over conventionally-generated power had yet to be established in Europe for almost any reactor type, it is not surprising that the light water system should have become increasingly attractive. Claims were periodically made by European nuclear authorities suggesting that indigenous reactor types, whether it be the AGR, the heavy water reactor, or the 'high temperature gas reactor' had already achieved, or would soon achieve, an economic breakthrough. But such cost estimates were often subjective and arbitrary in character, particularly in terms of the projected life-span and capacity factor of the reactors in question. Significantly, the British Minister of Power admitted in the House of Commons in July 1966 that the cost of a nuclear-generated kilowatt-hour was about 0.19 d (that is 2.2 mills) greater than for a kilowatt-hour produced in a coal-burning station. While the evaluation of the competitiveness of any new technology is bound to be influenced by the inclusion or exclusion of certain elements of cost as they affect different forms of energy supply, the available evidence indicates that the electricity generated by the Magnox programme had increased the average cost of Britain's electricity production.

The Select Committee on Science and Technology reported in 1967 that the advanced gas-cooled reactor – chosen by the Central Electricity Generating Board (CEGB) in preference to a water reactor at the time of the letting of the Dungeness 'B' contract in 1965 and subsequently accepted as the new standard system for energy generation in Britain – was competitive with American water reactors in respect of running and technical costs and might in due course achieve a cost reduction of some 30 per cent.[21] Yet, Mr Hawkins, Chairman of the CEGB, had to admit five years later when giving evidence before the Select Committee:

> I think we have had a fair share of problems on the A.G.R. and my brief tells me that the A.G.R. is proving to be a high cost system which is difficult to build. It has presented a unusually large number of difficult technical

problems and we cannot yet be confident that these have all been successfully overcome.[22]

One of the reasons given for these difficulties was the decision to proceed with the commercial development of the AGR on the basis of a very small prototype reactor at Calder without first building a demonstration reactor. The problem, however, was more deep-seated and related directly to the enormous research and development costs associated with reactor technology.

In most European countries these costs were considerably magnified by the striving for a wide range of technological innovations on the basis of limited national markets. The failure of Euratom to coordinate the research and development priorities of member countries and to rationalise their commercial policies meant that each of the national markets was unable to absorb all the reactor variants and reap the productivity advantage derived from large-scale production. As a consequence, the export potential of European reactor technology was severaly constrained, usually to the benefit of American designed light water systems. Several European countries attempted to improve the competitiveness of their industry through various forms of structural re-organisation, including, as in the case of Britain, the reduction in the number of nuclear design and construction firms.

The tension between economic and political priorities on the one hand and between domestic and external considerations in the formulation of national nuclear policies on the other became particularly acute in Europe during the late 1960s. Nowhere was dissension within the nuclear establishment more intense or the eventual change of direction more drastic than in France. As already indicated, the CEA had from the outset championed the cause of the gas-graphite reactor and was largely successful in persuading the PEON Commission as late as 1964 to announce a substantially expanded programme based on the construction of gas–graphite plants. But both EdF and French industry were becoming increasingly sceptical of the CEA's commitment of gas–graphite techniques and unconvinced by the arguments of national independence and national prestige on which that commitment was premised.[23] Conscious of the competitive advantage enjoyed by the light water reactor and of the technical difficulties experienced by the gas–graphite system, leading representatives of EdF and French industry took steps to facilitate the development of light water reactors. As a result of mergers the number of industrial groupings involved in reactor design was reduced to three (GAAA, Alsthom and SOCIA), and contracts were initiated with American firms with a view to the licensing of light water technology. However, the CEA remained vehemently opposed to these pressures for it interpreted any move towards alternative reactor models as a threat to its continued hegemony over the French reactor programme.

A top-level review of French policy in 1967, while reaffirming the policy of reliance of gas–graphite technology, signalled a further departure from the *status quo* by approving the construction of a second light water reactor in co-operation with Belgium. The turbulent events of May 1968 accelerated the process by limiting the level of funding available to the nuclear programme, with the result that plans for new gas–graphite plants were abandoned and numerous scientists and technicians released from CEA laboratories. It was left to the PEON Report in April 1968 to set out the principal arguments which would in due course justify the re-orientation of French nuclear policy.[24] It was openly admitted that, irrespective of the reactor type adopted, nuclear power was unlikely to prove competitive during the early years of the sixth plan (1970–75). Breaking with the nationalist perspective of previous years, the Report conceded that the light water system was gaining widespread acceptance, not only in the United States but in Europe and Japan, that its continued development could provide the basis for 'international co-operation', and that its introduction in France might well assist French industry to take greater advantage of the export market. The Report concluded by arguing for the construction of a light water reactor in France on the grounds that the Franco-Belgian plant at Tihange could not provide French scientists with a sufficiently detailed knowledge of the technology.

In the space of a few years, the PEON Commission had radically revised its underlying philosophy by questioning the previously sacrosanct notion of 'national independence' and by substituting the concept of 'economic independence' which it now virtually equated with the capacity to compete on the world market. The stage was thus set for the reformulation of nuclear policy in November 1969 following a high-level inter-ministerial meeting chaired by President Pompidou.[25] While reaffirming the centrality of France's nuclear programme for the twin objectives of energy independence and industrial growth, the presidential statement issued after the meeting announced that EdF would undertake a major programme of diversification based on the light water reactor for the duration of the sixth plan. France's expertise in gas-graphite technology would not be abandoned – the Saint Laurent II and Bugey I plants currently under construction would be completed – but the proposed 650 MWe Fessenheim plant would not proceed on the basis of the gas–graphite system as originally envisaged.

After calling for tenders, EdF awarded in 1970 a contract to Société des Forges et Ateliers du Creusot for the construction of a pressurised water reactor under licence from Westinghouse, while at the same time leaving open the future possibility of commissioning a boiling water reactor under licence from General Electric. Needless to say, the French nuclear industry could not hope to entertain both options without substantially expanding its domestic market and capturing at least a slice of the world market. However this particular issue might be resolved, it was already clear that France, like Japan and other major European countries, would have to give serious consideration to the supply of enriched uranium. If the light water reactor was to make a significant contribution to the nation's future electricity requirements, then total dependence on American enriched uranium would be unacceptable. The question thus arose as to whether France, alone or in partnership with other countries, could develop an enrichment technology which would enhance security of supply yet prove commercially competitive.

It can be readily seen from this brief survey that for all the national differences in the institutional and political arrangements governing the planning process, the state, in each of the countries we have so far considered, was confronted with the same fundamental problem: how to create a viable national nuclear industry given the limitations of the domestic and international market. Stated somewhat differently, each of the European states – and to a lesser extent the American state – had the difficult task of reconciling the twin objectives of economic competitiveness and national independence. The nationalist solution, particularly as applied in Britain and France, had to contend with both technical and economic difficulties reflecting in part the more limited technological and industrial base of European countries *vis à vis* the United States. Increasing state intervention and greater industrial concentration could only partially offset the advantages enjoyed by American capital. The state had thus to determine whether to support indigenous capital and technology with all the economic costs implicit in such a course, or to accept the penetration of foreign capital and technology despite its negative implications for technological independence and assured supply of nuclear fuels. Whichever solution was adopted in the medium or longer term, it was necessary to establish in the intervening period an industry of sufficient size to sustain the momentum for continuing design innovation and provide the future basis for large-scale nuclear power development.

THE POLITICAL ECONOMY OF NUCLEAR ELECTRICITY

In all countries the establishment and expansion of civil nuclear power was closely related to, indeed dependent on, the plans and requirements of the electricity supply industry. Commercial nuclear power reactors would obviously not be built unless electricity utilities were willing to order them. To this extent the prospects of any national nuclear programme were bound to be affected by changes in the level of electricity consumption and in the mix of fuels used to generate electricity. A rapidly expanding electricity supply system was generally considered as creating an environment favourable to the advancement of nuclear power. The case for nuclear electricity was therefore greatly assisted by the substantial growth in installed electric power capacity which occurred in most industrial countries after the Second World War, and which averaged at 6–7 per cent per annum for the best part of two decades. US capacity, which stood at 107,354 MWe in 1953, had increased to 186,534 MWe in 1960 and to 254,519 MWe in 1965. During the same twelve-year period, installed electric power capacity in Britain, West Germany, France and Sweden had at least doubled.[26] According to an IAEA report published in 1970, the total electric generating capacity of the industrial world was estimated at 1,000,000 MWe and was expected to rise to 1,400,000 MWe in 1975 and to 1,950,000 MWe in 1980.[27]

The salient fact, then, about electric power production was its exponential growth curve during the 1950s and 1960s and the widespread belief that such a rate of increase was basic to living standards and to the viability of the economy. For the electricity utilities, such a growth rate was considered vital to profitability and to the financial integrity of the enterprise.[28] Generally speaking the electricity industry was more inclined to overestimate than to underestimate future demand because it was usually possible to promote electricity sales through advertising and the adjustment of tariff rates so as to eliminate idle capacity. Moreover, an excess of supply was welcomed by the utilities because it provided them with greater flexibility in choosing the mix of fuels to be used and reduced their dependence on any one fuel supplier. Underestimating demand, on the other hand, carried several penalties, notably the loss of flexibility and the risk of shortages which might in turn encourage consumers to switch to other fuels, thereby reducing the industry's future share of the energy market.[29]

In the United States the upsurge of population growth at the end of the war, coupled with continued growth of per capita incomes and energy consumption, tended to reinforce the optimistic projections of future electric power requirements. In 1954, the Edison Electric Institute forecast that capability of US interconnected electric power systems would by 1975 be no less than 181,000 MWe and possibly as high as 218,000 MWe. Their lower forecast for 1975 was 301,000 MWe and their upper forecast 423,000 MWe, that is, four times the actual capacity in 1955.[30]

These predictions were in fact exceeded, partly because of the general growth in economic activity, but also because of the ability of the electricity utilities to promote the extensive development and cheap sale of electricity. Whether privately- or publicly-owned, these utilities had become virtual monopolies created by government and regulated by the Federal Power Commission and by state and municipal public utility commissions. The profitability of the industry was legally assured by virtue of the guaranteed rate of return on investment capital. During the period 1948–66, electric and gas utilities recorded an annual average capital growth rate of 5.5 per cent, as opposed to an average growth rate of 3.7 per cent for the economy as a whole. With almost 12 per cent of the power generation and transmission facilities in the United States under its control, the federal government played a leading part, especially through the Tennessee Valley Authority and the Bonneville Power Authority, in the production of cheap electricity and the active encouragement of maximum consumer usage. The concerted promotion of the 'all electric home', in which all heating, air conditioning and appliance operation would be provided by electricity, became one of the major functions of public and private utilities alike.[31] Taking advantage of ineffective government regulation and of the special status conferred on them in the allocation of natural resources, electricity utilities devised a tariff structure which, in practice, provided the cheapest power to the highest users, notably large industrial and commercial firms, and the highest electric rates to the poorest households.

Precisely because of the growth factor electricity utilities were increasingly inclined towards the construction of large generating plants from which they hoped to achieve significant economies of scale. This trend was seen as generally favourable to nuclear power in that nuclear plants were expected to become more economical with increasing size. It was widely claimed that beyond the 400 MWe mark, nuclear power stations would be cheaper to operate than conventional stations, simply because higher construction costs would be more than offset by the relative advantage of nuclear *vis à vis* fossil fuels.[32]

The task of forecasting electricity demand and its likely implications for nuclear power proved somewhat more hazardous in Britain, where the tendency to underestimate electricity requirements in the years prior to 1962 was replaced from then on by consistent overestimation. In England and Wales the three bodies primarily responsible for the forecasting of future electricity demand were the Area Boards which distributed electricity to customers, the CEGB which supplied electricity wholesale to the Area Boards, and the Electricity Council which had responsibility for overall planning and liaison between the electricity industry and government. Whereas the Area Boards and the CEGB based their forecasts largely on the extrapolation of past trends, the Electricity Council premised its projections on the anticipated level of general economic activity as calculated by Treasury and other government departments.

The growth of electricity demand during the 1950s was underestimated mainly because of the industry's failure to anticipate the growth rate of the economy and the rate of acquisition of appliances in the domestic sector. At the end of 1947–8, the installed capacity of the British electricity system (excluding the North of Scotland District) was 11,680 MWe. Ten years later the CEGB, which had been created by the 1957 Act to service England and Wales (Scotland was serviced by the South of Scotland Electricity Board and the North of Scotland Hydro-Electric Board) had an installed capacity of 24,315 MWe. The rapid increase in electricity demand coupled with the extremely severe winter conditions pushed the system to its limits in 1961–3, with the result that the planning margin of 14 per cent additional generating capacity over the above anticipated demand was insufficient to prevent voltage reductions and frequent cuts in bulk supplies of electricity. Thereafter the planning margin was increased to 17 per cent and then to 20 per cent above the estimated peak demand.

The greater provision for excess capacity after 1963 coupled with the consistent overestimation of national growth rates now led to a persistent over-capacity problem. Expectations of high and continuing expansion in electricity consumption failed to materialise partly because of the sluggishness of the economy, the introduction of cheap natural gas which took over the premium growth markets that the electricity industry might have otherwise captured, and the rising price of electricity. These external factors no doubt contributed to, but did not fully explain, the trend away from exponential growth in electricity demand. The trend clearly preceded the advent of North Sea gas (1968), the coal miners dispute (1972–3) and the oil price rises (1973–4). The consistent overestimation of demand, it would seem, had a great deal to do with the internal dynamics of the electricity supply industry, and the tendency of planners and forecasters to view economic growth as a permanent condition and to overlook the significance of saturation effects, particularly in certain sectors of the domestic market. In any event, a conscious policy of overestimation may have been favoured precisely because it offered a form of insurance against underestimates of demand or unforeseen problems which might adversely affect the centralised electricity grid whether at the production, transmission or distribution stage.[33]

The widening excess of capacity resulting from a prolonged period of overestimation could not but seriously affect the prospects of the nuclear industry. Here, it is worth recalling that, though sympathetically disposed to the development of nuclear power, the Central Electricity Authority, the forerunner to the CEGB, had played no significant part in the preparation of the 1955 White Paper announcing the first nuclear programme. In determining the size of that programme, the Government had taken into account not so much the preferences or requirements of the Central Electricity Authority as the need to keep together 'the skilled manpower of the [three] consortia for the time when nuclear power on a large scale would become economic.' When giving evidence to the House of Commons Select Committee on the Nationalized Industries, the then Chairman of the CEGB, Sir Christopher (later Lord) Hinton, made no secret of the differences that had emerged with the UKAEA about the direction and scope of Britain's nuclear programme and of the tendency of the UKAEA to determine its activities without adequate consideration of the CEGB's own requirements.[34] On the other hand, the very fact that Britain's nuclear industry dependend almost entirely on the CEGB for the maintenance of its home market, coupled with the absence of export orders, placed enormous pressure on the CEGB to ensure a sufficient rate of orders to the industrial consortia.

The painful dilemma confronting the CEGB was graphically portrayed by its new Chairman, Mr Hawkins, in evidence he gave to the Select Committee on Science and Technology in August 1972. He made it clear that the recent experience of low growth in the electricity supply system, combined with the effect of rising fuel prices, would further reduce the expectation of higher load growth in the future, thereby extending further the period for which plant already on order would be sufficient to meet future demand. Although conscious of the difficulties of the British nuclear industry, Mr Hawkins was at pains to point out that the CEGB's ability to assist the manufacturers was severely limited by the fact of over-capacity and the sharp reduction in the projected demand of electricity over the next ten years. He went on to explain:

> I would draw your attention to the fact that following ... the pressure on the CEGB, quite rightly ... the CEGB ... adopted the policy of scrapping as much of the old plant as they could possibly justify economically. I am sorry, but we cannot keep on doing it.[35]

Both this and other statements, including comments by senior officers of the Atomic Energy Authority,[36] suggest that the CEGB was under intense pressure to modify its forecasts of future electricity demand or, at the very least, to base its ordering decisions on the most optimistic estimates available in the hope of ensuring the survival of Britain's ailing nuclear industry. But there were limits as to how far the CEGB could yield to such pressure without undermining the economic rationality of its operation.

In France, too, policy differences soon developed between the two principal institutions responsible for the direction of the French nuclear programme, that is, between CEA and EdF. In this case, however, the dispute centred not so much on the scale of the programme as on the choice of reactor designs and the most appropriate industrial organisation of the industry. Despite minor differences in the forecasting of future demand, all parties represented within the PEON Commission tended to accept the general premise of rapid growth in electricity consumption and its corollary, the need for large-scale expansion of installed capacity. In the 1964 Report, the PEON Commission readily accepted the forecast of a 4.8 per cent increase in gross domestic production over the next five years resulting in a 7.2 per cent annual growth rate in electricity consumption. Similarly, when it came to the calculation of nuclear costs, there was a general tendency to defer to EdF's technical expertise, and to accept the view that by 1970 nuclear electricity would become competitive with other forms of electricity generation.

EdF's overriding objective during the early years of France's nuclear programme was to perfect a nuclear power station with a capacity of about 500 MWe, which it could then build in sufficient numbers to achieve the desired economies of scale. Unlike the CEGB in Britain, EdF, acting as its own industrial architect, was able to exercise a measure of influence over costs by parcelling out contracts to outside suppliers on a competitive basis. EdF was normally unwilling to subsidise the manufacture of reactor components simply with a view to improving export prospects. In contracts negotiated in the early 1970s when the nuclear programme rapidly accelerated, EdF succeeded in inserting a special clause which tied the price paid to the supplier to the growth rate achieved in nuclear power construction. By allowing prices to rise if the number of 900 MWe units ordered fell below six, or conversely by allowing them to fall if the target was exceeded, EdF was hoping to provide the industry with a degree of security while at the same time reinforcing the incentive to maintain a vigorous rate of expansion.

The other significant feature of EdF policy was its strong interest in diversification. We have already seen how in early 1960, when the gas–grapite reactor was still considered the keystone of France's nuclear industry, EdF decided to collaborate with Belgium in the construction of a pressurised water reactor at Chooz, and in 1961 commissioned a heavy water reactor at Monts D'Arrée in Brittany with a planned capacity of 70 MWe. In December 1967, a decision was taken to build a second joint Franco-Belgian light water reactor at Tihange. EdF's growing dissatisfaction with the performance of gas–graphite technology was undoubtedly one of the decisive factors responsible for its abandonment in 1969.

In Germany, unlike France, the electricity industry was highly decentralised, comprising over 350 individual companies only 3 per cent of which were predominantly private enterprises. The vast majority were either public enterprises financed by federal, state and local authorities, or mixed-type enterprises in which public authorities held a major interest. In the absence of a central authority, several large supply undertakings were responsible for organising the national electricity grid. The largest company, Rheinisch-Westfalisches Elektrizitätwerk (RWE) was responsible for nearly 30 per cent of the total electricity supply, while the twelve largest producers accounted for 65 per cent of total production.[37] In 1959 gross electricity output was 103 million MWe of which nearly 90 per cent came from coal-fired stations. Both power output and installed capacity had more than doubled since 1950 and were expected to double again in the ensuing ten years. By far the largest electricity consumer was industry which accounted for more than 60 per cent of total national consumption. The other main consumers were private households, commerce and transport, with the electricity industry itself accounting for some 13 per cent of total consumption.

Electricity utilities were initially reluctant to support the commercial application of nuclear power for the simple reason that they were assured of supplies of conventional fuel under relatively advantageous conditions. Knowing that no government funding was yet available for the construction of nuclear power stations, aware that the costs involved would be much higher than for conventional stations and faced with the statutory obligation to provide the maximum amount of power at the lowest possible cost, public utilities were unwilling to make any commitment which would seriously affect their profitability or restrict their capacity to deliver cheap electricity. In the modern thermal plants of the Ruhr and the lignite (brown coal) areas of the Rhine, power costs were estimated to be as low as 2.5 pfennigs per kWh, a figure with which no nuclear power station could compete in the immediate future. In any case, the largest German utilities operated their own coal mines and were to that extent inhibited from establishing facilities in direct competition with coal-fired power plants. Commercial reactors could not be expected to come into operation before the end of the 1960s, and even then primarily in southern Germany and other areas of high conventional power costs.

As a result of these various disincentives, utilities were generally content to adopt a wait-and-see attitude and to limit themselves to contracts for design studies. For example, Gesellschaft fur die Entwicklung der Atomkraft in Bayern mbH, Munich, a limited liability company formed by four electricity undertakings, a chemical firm and the Bavarian state government, placed a contract with Siemens Schukert-Werke AG for the design of a 100 MWe heavy water reactor. Projects such as this, involving the building and operation of research or experimental reactors, had little difficulty in obtaining public funds, including substantial assistance from the federal government.[38] However, the first major advance in German nuclear development did not occur until 1961 when a decision was made to proceed with the construction of the first demonstration-size light water reactor (250 MWe) at Gundremmingen. Conceived within the context of Euratom's participation programme, the project was jointly sponsored by RWE and Bayern Atomkraft and was largely responsible for Siemens' shift in development priorities from natural uranium to enriched uranium systems. The joint Euratom programme and the pressure exerted by RWE were decisive factors in the eventual triumph of American technology in Germany.

Like most other advanced capitalist economies, Sweden's energy requirements during the 1950s increased exponentially at the rate of approximately 5 per cent per annum, with electricity consumption registering an annual growth rate of nearly 7 per cent. Expressed in the equivalent weight of coal, total energy consumption in 1956 amounted to 24 million tons of coal, about half of which was used in the production of electric power. In practice, Sweden's pattern of energy supply was unique to the country, with water power satisfying almost completely the demand for electricity. Hydroelectric power with its high capital costs accounted for the bulk of base load production, whilst power from condensing stations with their high running costs supplied peak load and reserve capacity. Over the next 10–20 years it was estimated that the increase in demand for electrical power would be considerably greater than half the total growth in energy consumption, and that much of this steep increase would be a direct result of rapidly rising domestic usage.

To meet the expected increasing demand for power, especially beyond 1970, new resources were deemed necessary. Given Sweden's lack of exploitable coal or oil deposits, and the fact that it was already importing nearly 85 per cent of its fossil fuel requirements, a consensus gradually emerged within the electricity industry that the gap between power supply and demand could only be bridged by increasing reliance on nuclear energy. If the increasing need for thermal power, it was argued, were met by rising imports of fossil fuels, then the country's balance of payments would be seriously affected. The nuclear option appeared to be the only means of relieving the situation. At the end of 1967 the Central Operating Management, a joint organisation of all Swedish power companies, prepared a study of Sweden's future electricity production which indicated that the contribution of nuclear energy to electric power production would increase from 1.5 per cent in 1970 to 30 per cent in 1980. During the 1970s most new power installations were expected to be nuclear, so that by 1985 nuclear power would contribute nearly 50 per cent of electric power production.

By the late 1960s the Swedish electricity industry was divided almost equally between the public and private sectors, with the former operating through the State Power Board. The remainder of the industry comprised private and municipal utilities, the majority of which had combined to form the AKK group specifically to promote nuclear power development. The State Power Board, enjoying somewhat greater access to hydropower resources than private industry, was not quite in the same hurry to embark on a large nuclear programme, but was nevertheless anxious not to lose any ground to the private groups. It was instrumental in the decision to build the Agesta station and was solely responsible for the construction of the Marviken station. Private companies, for their part, were involved in the commissioning of the Oskarshamn nuclear power station (450 MWe) which became operational in 1972. By the late 1960s they had announced plans for a second unit at Oskarshamn (570 MWe) expected to come on stream before 1975, as well as for a nuclear plant at Barsebäck (570 MWe) near Malmö in southern Sweden. The objective behind these decisions was not merely to raise capacity to a level sufficient to meet demand but also to reduce to a minimum the cost of energy. To this end, electricity utilities were increasingly committed to achieving the economies of scale characteristic of big production units. Optimal economic results and increased energy independence were seen as requiring the greater part of electric capacity to be concentrated in a small number of large nuclear power plants.

It remains to say a word about Brazil, a Third World country whose economic and political conditions were far removed from those prevailing in North American and Western Europe, but whose rapid industrialisation was to produce similar pressures for the introduction of nuclear power.[39] Brazil's electrical generating capacity increased substantially during the 1920s and 1930s from 367 MWe in 1920 to 1244 MWe in 1940. After a hiatus coinciding with the war years, the expansion in generating capacity resumed its momentum and rose from 1342 MWe in 1945 to 2805 MWe in 1954.[40] Throughout this period hydroelectric installations accounted for about 80 per cent of the total installed capacity of the Brazilian power industry.

The principal urban and industrial centres were served by a small number of large power systems, whereas the interior was served by a great number of scattered, small enterprises. The largest power company in Brazil was the Canadian firm, the Brazilian Traction, Light and Power Company whose two subsidiaries served the metropolitan areas of Rio de Janeiro and São Paulo. It had an installed capacity in 1954 of 1462 MWe, or 50 per cent of Brazil's total official capacity. The second largest system, Empresas Electricas Brasileiras, with a total installed capacity of about 330 MWe at the end of 1954, was controlled by the American and Foreign Power Company and had ten subsidiaries serving Brazil's other major coastal cities. These two foreign companies accounted for nearly 65 per cent of total Brazilian electrical capacity. Twenty-seven smaller power systems accounted for another 10 per cent of the power, while the remaining 25 per cent represented the combined capacity of nearly 2000 separate enterprises.

Despite steady increases in output, the electricity industry was intent on accelerated expansion on the grounds that existing power installations were being overloaded and could not keep up with the growth in demand. Severe overload of small utilities, it was claimed, was leading to breakdowns of equipment, sudden shortages of power and wide variations in voltage. Given that hydroelectric power accounted for nearly four-fifths of total installed generating capacity, the power supply, at least in some regions, was particularly vulnerable to prolonged drought conditions. According to advocates of massive electrification, the power shortage was severely affecting the quantity and quality of industrial production. Accordingly, the Brazilian government created in 1954 a Federal Electrification Fund as part of a ten-year electrification plan designed to assist the expansion of both private and public power systems. In the interests of expanding power capacity, private companies were eligible for expansion loans not only from electrification funds, but from the National Development Bank and from international banks under government guarantee.

Enough will have been said to indicate that by the mid-1950s the Brazilian electricity supply industry was ready to embark on a new phase of accelerated expansion. Although hydroelectricity was expected to remain the major source for satisfying energy needs in the foreseeable future, pressures were already emerging for the introduction of nuclear power. According to the findings of one study commissioned especially to investigate the prospects of nuclear power:

> In the period from 1965 to 1975, the prospects for nuclear power plants should improve steadily because of increasing costs for new hydro projects and an assumed reduction in nuclear power costs through technological progress. By 1975, nuclear reactors may become the principal means of expanding power capacity in Brazil, particularly if foreign exchange economies are no longer a predominant consideration in the electric power field.[41]

Nuclear power, it was argued, would greatly assist the more rapid expansion of power capacity and might even ameliorate the country's balance of payments by easing the demand for petroleum imports, by releasing domestic petroleum production for export or through the export of nuclear fuels and materials. Low-cost nuclear power (perhaps as low as 6 mills per kWh) could stimulate expansion in iron and steel production based on Brazil's rich iron ore resources.

Yet, for all these optimistic forecasts, the size of Brazil's nuclear effort was to remain negligible for a considerable time to come. Attention was primarily focused on the exploration and processing of minerals, particularly thorium and uranium. In addition a modest programme was under way for the training of technically-qualified people in the fields of nuclear physics, heat transfer, nuclear engineering and instrumentation. Stimulus was provided to the Brazilian programme with the signing of a nuclear co-operation agreement with the United States in 1955. It was followed a year later by the establishment of the Comissao National de Energia Nuclear (CNEN) which was given the task of coordinating national nuclear policy and placed under the Ministry of Mines and Energy. A series of projects and institutions were established to promote nuclear research and development, including the Instituto de Energia Atomica and the Instituto de Engenharia Nuclear. Consideration was first given to the acquisition of a 150–200 MWe plant using enriched uranium. Subsequently, the Quadros government, in keeping with a policy of greater independence from the United States, explored the possibility of obtaining a natural uranium reactor from France. After the military regime took over in 1964, the project was cancelled and preference was once again given to the enriched uranium method favoured by the United States. However, by the mid-1960s, apart from the general wish to rely more clearly on American friendship and technology, no firm decisions had been taken regarding the scale or timetable of any future commercial nuclear power programme.

ECONOMIC FUNCTIONS OF THE STATE

What emerges from this brief survey of the nuclear planning process and of the particular contribution made by the electricity industry is the very considerable role of the public sector in the establishment and growth of nuclear power. We have already seen how the state intervened directly in support of nuclear power by creating the necessary institutional framework and by defining national energy goals and strategies conducive to the nuclear option. By committing itself to a policy of growth based on an expanding energy sector, and by promoting perceived economies of scale, the state was intent on creating a political and economic environment highly favourable to the consolidation of the nuclear industry. In most cases, however, state intervention was even more extensive, encompassing the direct funding of research and development activities and a wide range of incentives and other forms of financial assistance.

In the United States early reactor research and development was conducted largely in research establishments which, though often operated and staffed by firms or universities, were owned and financed by government. Assistance was also made available to utilities by means of the power reactor demonstration programme under which the government financed research specific to the project, helped with design, provided funds for plant, offered facilities for training operators, and waived some fuel use and fuel fabrication charges. It is estimated that between 1941 and 1955 the American government spent a total of $12,300 million in the atomic energy programme, of which $4,800 million represented the value of the industrial plant. By comparison, the contribution of private capital was rather small and for the period 1951–4 amounted to little more than $8 million, which was channelled principally through the power-study group.[42] It was readily apparent that the private sector would be enticed only when assured of substantial government support not only during the research and experimentation stage but also during the construction phase.[43]

In 1959, Senator Clinton Anderson, Chairman of the Joint Committee on Atomic Energy, made it clear that, in his view, the nuclear industry was unlikely to progress very far unless new impetus was provided by government. More specifically, he called for a programme of government grants to private utilities covering a good part (75–90 per cent) of the differential between the estimated cost of a nuclear plant and a conventional plant. He also envisaged a parallel programme of assistance to public power utilities, whether local, state or federal.[44] The Joint Committee's staff report issued in August 1958 had estimated the capital and operating costs of such an expansion programme at about $875 million over a 5–7-year period. By 1960, the Atomic Energy Commission was openly committed as a short-term objective to making it possible by 1968 'for utility owners in areas where fossil fuel costs were 35 cents per million Btu or higher to select large-sized nuclear plants over large-sized conventional plants on the basis of economics alone.'[45] The longer-range objective was 'to make it possible for essentially all utility owners to make such a choice regardless of location or size of plant.'

Although the Commission generally preferred demonstration facilities to be built and operated by publicly- or privately-owned utilities, it was willing, wherever this was not possible, to assume primary responsibility. In the development, construction and operation of prototype and commercial power reactors, the Commission offered reactor manufacturers and publicly- and privately-owned utilities every possible assistance, including research and development and fuel use charge waivers. From the industry's point of view, direct government grants for construction of nuclear plants were a precondition for the development of a viable industry.[46] Such grants, however, were not seen as providing the utilities with windfall profits or as justifying government ownership or control of segments of the power industry. The Edison Electric Institute argued in 1958 that 'detailed Government controls and Government ownership of nuclear power plants will not serve to create this environment [maximum use of industry's inventiveness and productive capacity] and will be detrimental to the achievement of the program objectives.'[47] In August 1962, the AEC issued a revised third round invitation for construction of nuclear power plants of at least 400 MWe. The importance of the power demonstration reactor programme was its subsidisation of the industry at a time when nuclear power had not achieved economic competitiveness and when many utilities were still reluctant to make available the capital investment necessary for its introduction.[48]

But the refusal to invest in atomic energy was also motivated by fear of the high risks implicit in the new technology. Any company considering entry into the nuclear business had to take account of the legal consequences of a serious accident, including a possible core meltdown, which might well inflict enormous financial losses. Not surprisingly, therefore, representatives of firms with nuclear interests were adamant that they would not proceed with substantial investments 'unless some indemnity legislation was passed to protect the industry.'[49] In response to these pressures, Congress passed in 1957 the Price–Anderson Act, as section 170 of the Atomic Energy Act. The most important provision of the legislation, which was to be effective for ten years, was that 'the nuclear licensee and other persons indemnified' would not, in the event of nuclear accident, be liable to damages in excess of $560 million. Under this arrangement a nuclear company was required to obtain $60 million of insurance – this was all that private insurers would offer – which the US government would complement with an additional indemnity protection of $500 million.

The liability limit was intended as a temporary measure in the expectation that, once demonstrated, the safety of nuclear plants would 'remove the fear of public liability that had previously blocked private investment.'[50] However, in 1965 Congress was forced to extend the Price–Anderson Act for another ten years as a necessary condition for the continued viability of the industry. The limitation placed on the scale of public liability claims was deemed essential by nuclear firms given that in 1957 the government-commissioned Brookhaven Report WASH-740 had concluded that in the event of a nuclear accident 'property damage alone could go as high as $17 billion, quite apart from the anticipated 45,000 immediate deaths and the 100,000 later deaths, injuries and cancers.'[51] To the extent that nuclear plants coming on stream during the 1960s were many times the size of those considered in the original Brookhaven Report, it was evident that the consequences of an accident might be substantially more severe than those calculated in 1957.

Enough will have been said to indicate that the American state apparatus, principally through the agency of the AEC but also through several legislative measures spearheaded by the Joint Congressional Committee, was instrumental in creating the domestic conditions necessary for the establishment of a sizeable nuclear industry. Equally important was the part played by the American state in the development of an export market. Reference has already been made to the various forms of assistance extended to other countries under the 'Atoms for Peace' programme. The United States provided assurances to bilateral partners that it would furnish them with regular supplies of nuclear fuel and undertook to purchase all plutonium and uranium 235 produced from such fuel. In addition, the AEC made available to other countries the training facilities of its laboratories as well as many of the resources of its libraries. Financial assistance to foreign nuclear power projects was often channelled through the Export–Import Bank which provided loans to cover the costs of nuclear power plants for privately-owned (but not state-owned) utilities. Such loans were made available only if supported by a technical report from the US Atomic Energy Commission and by evidence of the ability of the country to service the dollar debt involved. The Bank also insisted that funds so loaned could be used only to buy equipment, materials and technical services from the US nuclear industry.

As an additional inducement, the United States had offered other countries to repurchase plutonium or residual uranium 235 from their nuclear reactors. To this end, foreign reactor operators were given the opportunity to return their spent fuel for reprocessing and storage in the United States. The first return shipment, which came from Sweden, was sent to the AEC's Idaho Chemical Processing Plant. But such fuel reprocessing arrangements lost much of their attractiveness as a result of the unexpectedly slow growth of nuclear power in Europe combined with the high cost of shipping the intensely radioactive spent fuel. By the end of 1960 the American industry had made substantial inroads into the export market, but only a handful of power reactors had yet been sold overseas. Over the next ten years, however, some twenty reactors, ranging in capacity from 150–826 MWe were exported to some nine countries.

The arrangements devised in the United Kingdom in support of the commercial application of nuclear technology were not identical with those in the United States, but equally important for the survival of the industry. The financial responsibility undertaken by the UK Atomic Energy Authority for reactor research and design involved 'the technical performance and economic prospects of a reactor system, including safety R & D and work aimed at the achievement of the performance forecast at the time the first of the series of a system was ordered.'[52] In other words, support for reactor research and development often continued beyond the construction stage and even beyond the point of initial operation. In addition, the Authority carried out specific R & D commissioned either by a reactor company to assist with a detailed design for a particular reactor or by a generating board to assist with the optimal operation of a reactor already in service.

By 1958–9, the net total financial contribution of the UKAEA to nuclear activities – both military and civil – had risen to £100 million. The appropriation for 1961–2 fell to about £78 million, partly because of the completion of major production facilities for the military programme, but some £49 million of this amount was specifically earmarked for civil R & D. In 1970, support for R & D stood at £58.5 million, of which £42 million was directed to reactor design, including £26.3 million for the fast breeder programme. In addition to financial support for R & D, the government had committed itself through the Nuclear Installations (Licensing and Insurance) Act 1959, as amended in 1965 and 1969, to financial backing for third-party liability in the event of a nuclear accident. The 1959 Act limited total liability to £48 million of which a mere £5 million would be covered by companies operating nuclear installations and up to £43 million by Parliament. Various other forms of hidden subsidy were also provided to the nuclear industry, implicit, for example, in the ambiguous financial relationship between the UKAEA and British Nuclear Fuels Ltd (BNFL).[53] When these diverse methods of public funding were insufficient to achieve the competitiveness of nuclear power, the electricity supply industry was required to bear the extra costs of nuclear generation, estimated by the CEGB in 1963 at about £20 million per year. Although the additional cost was eventually borne by the consumer rather than the taxpayer, it was nevertheless directly attributable to the intervention of the state as mediated by the UKAEA, government bureaucracy, Parliament and the electricity generating boards.

It remains to say a word about the attempts of the British government to capture a part of the export market. As we have already observed, these proved largely abortive but not for lack of effort. The financing arrangements for the export of the Latina station to Italy and the Tokai Mura station to Japan were not without government involvement, and provided for the lifetime supply to the importing country of fresh fuel and of reprocessing and waste management services. Within a matter of a few years the cost of these commitments was substantially in excess of that envisaged at the time of sale and presumably incorporated into the contractual arrangements. It soon became apparent, however, that the Magnox-type reactor, despite its advantage in using natural uranium as a fuel, would not be able to compete effectively on the world market with American water reactors. The willingness of the UKAEA to assist other countries in setting up fuel fabrication and reprocessing plants under licensing agreements did little to improve the commercial attractiveness of the Magnox reactor.[54] A concerted effort to re-enter the export field was not made until the CEGB gave a contract for the AGR in August 1965. As a result of collaboration between the three nuclear consortia and the UKAEA, an organisation known as the British Nuclear Export Executive (BNX) was created with the express purpose of promoting the sales of British reactors, acting as a focus for foreign inquiries and arranging for the preparation of tenders for overseas contracts. The UKAEA contributed 40 per cent to the financing of the project and industry the remaining 60 per cent. Despite strong support from government, the effectiveness of BNX was severely limited by the competitive relationship of the three consortia.

The supportive, though not always effective, role of the state in the development of the nuclear industry was equally apparent in France, West Germany and Sweden. As already indicated, in France the CEA was the principal vehicle for public sector participation at every stage of nuclear research and development. Throughout the 1950s and 1960s, the personnel employed by the CEA had increased manifold, reaching 30,000 in 1967. By now, the work of the commission was both extensive and diversified, covering every branch of nuclear science and technology from fundamental research to power generation. It operated four main research centres with elaborate facilities for fundamental and applied studies, several military research and production centres, three metropolitan mining divisions, two uranium-producing mills, a breeder reactor programme, two plutonium extraction plants, one uranium isotope separation plant, and eleven research reactors. In 1967, the CEA's civilian and military budget amounted to Fr 4600 million*. Through its control of large investments, its custody of classified information, its close and continuous co-operation with private enterprise, its supply of uranium and fissile materials, and above all by training and allocating research teams, the CEA became one of the chief instruments for the promotion of nuclear power.

In West Germany, federal financing played a minor role initially, but rapidly accelerated after 1957. Although a good deal of basic research together with technical development and safety work was conducted in private research institutes, much of it was funded by government. Similarly, in the field of reactor development most of the work was carried out by private industry but substantially financed from the public purse. The German government also provided guarantees of bank loans, helped with the excess of capital costs over and above those of an established alternative power station, and met a high proportion of any operating losses after shareholders had contributed by foregoing dividends. Other government aid came in the form of defraying 30–50 per cent of the development cost of work on agreed power reactor design studies and projects and on marine reactor research.

In Sweden, the government's contribution was channelled mainly through AB Atomenergi, which was formed in 1947 as a limited company but operated after 1968 under complete government ownership. In the fiscal year 1962 government grants to the company amounted to 130 million kronor, and the cummulative total since the company's founding to Kr 600 million**. In 1968, AB Atomenergi had a staff of about 1350 employees and an annual turnover of some Kr 150 million. Government spending since the inception of Sweden's nuclear energy programme was now in excess of Kr 1700 million, of which about 90 per cent had been allocated to the company. AB

* 1967 exchange rate: $1 = Fr 4.9
** 1962 exchange rate: $1 = Kr 5.2

Atomenergi undertook research and development in every branch of the nuclear energy field, including advanced reactor systems and the study of fuel cycles of different reactor types. Development work carried out at the Studvisk research station enabled Swedish industry to manufacture uranium fuel and other nuclear components and to deliver complete nuclear power stations without relying on foreign licensing agreements.

REGULATORY FUNCTIONS

Enough will have been said to indicate that the development of nuclear power was in every instance closely tied to, indeed dependent on, the policies and performance of the state. It was the state that helped to establish the ideological momentum, the planning framework, the institutional arrangements, the financial resources, the training and technical facilities, and even the market conditions necessary for the commercial application of nuclear technology. There was, however, one other critically important function for which the state was also expected to assume responsibility, namely that of regulation. We have already seen how nuclear legislation was enacted in various countries establishing agencies which would promote the development of nuclear science and technology, providing outright subsidies and tax incentives for nuclear installations and nuclear insurance, indemnity and public coverage schemes for nuclear liability. But apart from its obviously promotional function, nuclear law was also designed to protect against radiation hazards connected with the civilian application of nuclear energy and radioactive substances, and to prevent the non-peaceful uses of nuclear energy by means of a safeguards system. Nuclear law was thus required to set health and safety standards for radiological protection, to regulate the licensing and supervision of nuclear activities, and to provide for sanctions for offences against nuclear regulations.[55] Its primary function was to inspire public confidence in nuclear energy at a time of mounting public anxiety.

The legal instrument which has perhaps had the most significant influence on the evolution of nuclear, law was the United States Atomic Energy Act, 1946. It established the AEC and conferred upon it powers and duties which exceeded those possessed by any previously established arm of government. The Act created an absolute government monopoly of all fissionable material and all facilities for the production of such material. Pressures for greater industry participation eventually led to passage of the 1954 Atomic Energy Act which paved the way for the private ownership and operation of nuclear reactors but maintained government ownership of nuclear fuels. The Act specified that the private possession of radioactive materials would be conditional on the licensee observing 'such safety standards to protect health as may be established by the Commission' (s. 81). To facilitate administrative control of public health and safety, the AEC established a Reactor Hazards Evaluation Staff whose duties were to develop standards, guides and codes for the design, operation, supervision, containment and location of reactors. The Commission also created a Licensing Division with responsibility for issuing licences to firms and individuals wishing to engage in the application of atomic energy either on a research or industrial basis. Finally, an Inspection Division was set up whose duties included the supervision of staff employed by the Commission and contracting firms with a view to ensuring the maintenance of health and safety standards. Federal regulations were in due course complemented by a complex framework of state legislation and other codes of 'good practice' in order to provide additional safeguards against the potential hazards of the atomic energy programme.

In Britain the Radioactive Substances Act, 1948 established the Radioactive Substances Advisory Committee which, together with the Medical Research Council's Radiological Protection Service, provided a reference point on radiological protection, conducted research and offered advice in the field. As a result of heightened concern about nuclear safety, especially after the Windscale accident in 1957, legislation was passed in 1959 establishing the Nuclear Installations Inspectorate. In 1960 the Nuclear Safety Advisory Committee was created to assist the responsible minister. The Windscale accident also led to the establishment of a UKAEA Health and Safety Branch. The 1970 Radiological Protection Act gave birth to the National Radiological Protection Board which took over the functions of the Radioactive Substances Advisory Committee and the Radiological Protection Service as well as the research responsibilities of the UKAEA's Health and Safety Branch.

In France, responsibility for protection against radiation was placed in 1956 in the Central Service (SCPRI) within the National Institute of Health and Medical Research (INSERM). SCPRI, which was assigned several functions, including research, monitoring and control, particularly in relation to pollution, was assisted by the establishment of a laboratory designed to monitor and control levels of ionising radiation in the workplace.[56] The National Commission for Radiological Protection (CNPRI) was a purely consultative body offering advice only on matters submitted to it by the responsible minister. Decrees setting out standards for radiological protection were issued in June 1966 and March 1967. In the area of nuclear safety, the basic regulation was framed in 1963 in accordance with existing laws dealing with dangerous installations and atmospheric pollution. The main provision of the regulation was to make the construction of any nuclear facility conditional on the authorisation of the Minister of Industry after advice had been received from an Interministerial Commission created specifically for the purpose, and the Minister for Health.

In contrast to the British and French experience, West Germany's federal system and the rather decentralised character of its administration made for a somewhat looser and more complex legal framework.[57] Significantly, the 1959 Atomic Energy Act which provided the legal basis for the development of nuclear power did not establish an atomic energy commission or its equivalent. However, in accordance with the Act, the federal government introduced in September 1960 the first Radiation Protection Ordinance designed to protect persons from the effects of ionising radiation. In 1958 a Reactor Safety Committee was established to advise the Minister of Education and Science who was responsible for the application of the Act. The main function of the Committee was to ensure that safety precautions were observed in the planning, design and operation of nuclear installations. In co-operation with the Union of the Technical Safety Control Services, the Reactor Safety Committee helped to create in January 1965 the Institute of Reactor Safety which was asked to advise the Committee, evaluate new information about safety in nuclear engineering, and develop safety regulations and guidelines for the construction and operation of nuclear installations.

In Sweden's case, the Ministry of Finance, which had overall responsibility for the government's nuclear energy programme, created an advisory committee, the Atomic Energy Board. In addition to its advisory capacity, the Board, through its Reactor Safety Committee, was also the licensing authority for the operation of reactors in Sweden. Matters concerning radiation protection were placed under the authority of the Swedish State Institute for Radiation Protection.

On matters of nuclear safety, France and Germany, as members of the European Economic Community, were also required to adhere to the basic radiation standards determined by Euratom and to take certain measures with regard to instruction, education and professional training for radiological health hazards. By 1970, Euratom had used its authority to establish uniform safety radiation standards throughout the community; to standardise the measurement and control of environmental radioactivity; to review plans for reactor installations and their radioactive waste disposal systems; and to study the movement of radioactive substances in the environment and safety aspects of nuclear marine propulsion.[58]

But the need for regulation could not be confined to the area of domestic nuclear safety. From the outset, it was apparent to most governments, and certainly to successive American Administrations, that special measures would be necessary to ensure that international transactions in nuclear fuels and equipment did not result in their diversion for military purposes. Indeed, the 1946 Atomic Energy Act prohibited US nuclear exports or even exchanges of information until Congress found by joint resolution that 'effective and enforceable safeguards' were in operation. Although no such resolution was ever passed, the 'Atoms for Peace' policy announced in December 1953 eventually paved the way for nuclear trade. To this end, the United States concluded 'co-operation agreements' with several countries on the understanding that nuclear materials and technology supplied under these agreements could be used only for peaceful purposes. To ensure such use the United States reserved the right to verify these uses through periodic inspections arranged on a bilateral basis.[59]

Gradually, with the growth of commercial nuclear power, the United States phased out its bilateral safeguards programme in favour of a new international safeguards regime to be administered by Euratom, but more importantly by the International Atomic Energy Agency (IAEA) which was established by statute in July 1957. This new approach was intended, at least in part, to moderate the political resistance of governments to bilateral intrusion into their territories and to prevent mounting commercial pressures from ending the force of bilateral safeguards.[60] The importance of international regulation was stressed by the State Department, by the

Senate Foreign Relations Committee, and even by the Joint Committee on Atomic Energy. This view was vigorously expressed by AEC Commissioner Thomas Murray:

> In no field does the need for international order exist more imperatively than in the field of nuclear energy. In the concept of order I include a whole set of notions – regulation, control, supervision, commonly accepted standards of health and safety, and above all the institutions of free and orderly procedures of co-operation among nations.[61]

For him, as for many other US policy-makers, the IAEA represented the only chance of avoiding international nuclear anarchy.

The implications of these and other attempts to grapple with the dangers of nuclear proliferation will be considered at some length in a later chapter. Suffice it to say for the moment that the problem of international regulation in the nuclear field was ultimately not amenable to national solutions, hence the IAEA experiment and the related decision of the Common Market countries to invest Euratom with supranational rights of inspection and independent verification. The nation-state was thus confronted with an excruciating dilemma. It could either refuse to surrender any of its sovereignty and thereby encourage a state of atomic anarchy which would eventually undermine the legitimacy and public acceptance of nuclear power; alternatively, it could establish an international regulatory framework which, regardless of its efficacy, might at least create a sufficiently ordered environment to facilitate the worldwide expansion of nuclear technology.

The crucial role played by the state in the commercial development of nuclear power is not open to question. While it would be a gross oversimplification and distortion of the facts to regard the capitalist state as the faithful and obedient servant of corporate interests, there is no denying that in every instance it assumed primary responsibility for establishing the legal conditions for the regulation of the nuclear fuel cycle, for developing the necessary engineering and technical skills, for biasing energy planning towards nuclear power, for supplying credit and subsidies to industry, and for orchestrating the 'information' campaigns needed to persuade the public of the desirability and viability of the nuclear option. The long list of administrative, economic and legitimating functions performed by the capitalist state in the service of the nuclear industry does not imply that every arm of the state automatically or consistently represented the interests of the capitalist producer. As we shall presently see, the state often became the battlefield on which were fought the political and ideological antagonisms generated by the nuclear controversy and in a wider sense by capitalist society as a whole.

3 The State's Authority Under Challenge

The controversy which for more than a decade has dominated nuclear power development in much of the industrial western world arose in the first instance from public anxiety about the immediate effects of nuclear technology. Although economic, legal and political considerations were all to contribute to growing public disenchantment with nuclear energy programme, the initial crystallising factor was the increasingly sharper perception of the environmental and health risks associated with the construction and operation of nuclear power plants.[1] Local apprehensions were fuelled by periodic reports of nuclear accidents, but these do not appear to have had a decisive influence on public attitudes in the early years of nuclear power development. During this period media coverage of the Chalk River accident in 1952, the Enrico Fermi controversy in 1956, and even the serious Windscale fire in October 1957, to name but a few examples, occasioned intermittent local concern but no wide-ranging debate around the complex issues of reactor safety.

Nevertheless, as plans for the commercialisation of nuclear power gained momentum, proposed reactor sites soon became a focal point of opposition amongst communities who viewed with suspicion any project likely to disturb their immediate environment. A more favourable attitude emerged in areas of relatively low employment and income, where workers and tradesmen hoped to derive some benefit, at least during the period of construction activity; on the other hand, in areas where nuclear facilities were expected to threaten existing patterns of land use, the reaction was generally hostile. Local farmers were often fearful that their crops would be adversely affected by the steam from cooling towers; fishermen were concerned by the consequences of thermal and perhaps radioactive pollution, particularly for the value of their catch; and there were often objections to the visual impact of nuclear power stations on the natural landscape, reinforced in many instances by commercial considerations, including the wish to protect property prices and tourist income.

EMERGENCE OF DISSENT

By permitting interested citizens to participate in construction permit hearings, the 1954 US Atomic Energy Act had itself opened up the possibility of public intervention in the nuclear decision-making process. Yet despite the rapid growth of the American nuclear industry during the 1960s, community opposition, apart from a few notable exceptions, remained generally muted. The signing of the partial Test Ban Treaty in 1963 and community preoccupation with other politically sensitive issues, notably civil rights and the Vietnam War, may account for the relatively dormant public involvement in nuclear matters.[2] By 1968, however, the rapidly-growing environmental consciousness that had penetrated deep into middle-class America was beginning to make itself felt in the nuclear arena.

Perhaps the best indication of things to come was provided by the controversy surrounding the proposal for a plant at Lake Cayuga, first announced by New York State Electric & Gas Company (NYSE & G) in June 1967[3]. Groups of scientists and citizens, concerned about the effects of thermal pollution, demanded that design alternatives be considered which would minimise likely damage to the lake. Fearing costly delays, NYSE & G announced in 1969 the indefinite postponement of its application for a construction permit. By 1970 the AEC was openly acknowledging that the increasing opposition of writers, scientists and local communities had slowed down the anticipated growth in nuclear energy.[4]

But the utility companies were determined to proceed with their plans. Accordingly, in March 1973 NYSE & G resurrected their proposal for a boiling water reactor with a once-through cooling system. The local reaction to the utility's decision was swift and effective.[5] The close proximity of Cornell University provided citizen groups with access to a great deal of expert advice and information. The very fact that Cornell scientists were questioning the conclusions and methodology of the technical report issued by the utility and its consultants enabled the local community to point to serious disagreement among technical experts, a fact widely interpreted as sufficient justification for the abandonment of the plan. In response to a succession of letters, polls and petitions, which now formed part of an intensified campaign of outright opposition, the company decided against further participation in public debate, thereby isolating itself from the public and further undermining its credibility. In July 1973, NYSE & G finally abandoned its plans for a nuclear power facility on Cayuga Lake.

Although a little slower in developing, a similar pattern of local dissent emerged in various parts of Europe, particularly in the Upper Rhine valley where the German nuclear industry, in collaboration with its French and Swiss partners, was committed to building one of the densest concentrations of nuclear reactors anywhere in the world. Following a proposal in 1970 for the construction of a reactor at Breisach, south of Wyhl, the local residents, concerned that the steam from cooling towers would damage local vineyards, formed the Karlsruhe Burgeraktion Umweltschutz and organised a petition for which they collected 65,000 signatures.[6] Confronted with such opposition, the electric utility (Kernkraftwerk Sud AG) was compelled to drop the Breisach proposal and applied instead for a construction licence for two large reactors at Wyhl. In spite of a series of demonstrations in 1974, the company received approval for the plant from the Baden-Würtemberg Land government and, after a local referendum necessitated by further legal objections, was granted a construction licence in January 1975. However, as we shall see, this was only the beginning of a bitter and protracted battle between the authorities and anti-nuclear groups whose campaign rapidly assumed national and even international dimensions, and whose objections now encompassed not only the effects of thermal pollution but a wide range of technological problems, including radiation, reactor safety and waste disposal.

As in so many other instances, the Wyhl controversy, which began as a local reaction against a particular siting proposal, soon developed into a far-reaching critique of the entire nuclear programme. The local community, which we may for the purposes of analysis designate as the *periphery*, was naturally resentful of the dictates emanating from the *centre*, increasingly identified with remote and anonymous political, bureaucratic and corporate decision-making structures.[7] What often started as a series of 'peripheral' objections to one or more specific aspects of a proposed nuclear facility thus gradually formed the basis for a generalised response involving a coalition of diverse interest groups – some explicitly anti-nuclear, others espousing a more general environmentalist position.[8]

In most countries the development of significant opposition to nuclear power was a slow and painful process. In Sweden, early nuclear plans encountered little hostility and as late as 1971 and 1972 debates in the Riksdag produced very substantial support for the nuclear programme. A report issued by the electricity industry in 1972 recommended that, in addition to the eleven reactors already in operation or under construction, another thirteen reactors be built by 1990. The critical views of Nobel physicist Professor Alfven and the vigorous debate under way in the United States were nevertheless beginning to have an impact, as may be gauged from the decision of the Riksdag in 1973 to defer any authorisation of new nuclear plants pending a review of reactor safety and waste disposal problems.[9]

A somewhat similar situation obtained in Britain where, despite the 1957 Windscale accident, the nuclear controversy remained extremely low-key. After the early 1970s a network of environmental organisations, notably Friends of the Earth (FOE), became increasingly concerned with nuclear hazards, but few misgivings were voiced in Parliament, where the Conservative and Labour Parties remained staunch supporters of nuclear energy. Yet, by 1975 nuclear opponents had gone a long way towards documenting and publicising the economic and technical grounds of their case.[10] Their arguments were greatly strengthened, and in a sense legitimised, by the publication in September 1976 of *Nuclear Power and the Environment* the sixth report of Britain's standing Royal Commission on Environmental Pollution.[11]

In the early stages of the controversy it was in the United States that concerns about nuclear safety were most widely and sharply aired. Drawing upon the experience gained from earlier skirmishes over specific reactors, scientists, lawyers and economists helped to bring the challenge to nuclear power into public view.[12] A particularly sharp attack came late in the 1960s when, as a logical extension of the concern about atmospheric testing, the question of routine radioactive emmissions was raised by Sternglass, Tamplin, Gofman and others.[13] Sternglass, for example, alleged that there was a correlation between emissions from the AEC's experimental

Brookhaven reactor and a rise in infant morality in Suffolk country. Similar claims were made regarding changes in infant mortality rates in the vicinity of several nuclear power plants in Illinois, Michigan, Pennsylvania, New York and California, but all such correlations were 'routinely rejected by the AEC as unscientific and erratic'.[14] Although the Sternglass estimates were subsequently refuted, the linear relationship between radiation dose, even at low levels, and cancer deaths was accepted by numerous expert committees, including the Advisory Committee on Biological Effects of Ionising Radiation convened by the National Academy of Sciences. In due course, the political pressure generated by the controversy was sufficient to prompt the AEC to impose stricter limits on nuclear power plant emissions.

No sooner was this particular debate dying down than another quickly rose in its place. It involved the adequacy of the AEC's design standards for a key safety system in commercial nuclear power plants, the emergency core-cooling system (ECCS). The question, first raised by the Union of Concerned Scientists (UCS), became in 1971 the subject of a special hearing and a matter of debate in other licensing proceedings across the country.[15] In summarising their case, UCS argued that AEC claims on reactor safety were based on a faulty experimental and analytical structure whose computational predictions were critically weak and unreliable and the subject of serious dispute amongst professional and qualified persons.

The hazards of reactor failure were first examined in 1957 in the WASH-740 study commissioned by the AEC to investigate the consequences of a conceivable catastrophic accident for a 150 MWe reactor. The study was updated in 1965 for the 1000 MWe reactors that were then planned. But neither study had calculated the probabilities of failure, and the fact of 300 reactor-years of catastrophe-free commercial reactor operation did not of itself constitute adequate empirical support for the AEC's low core meltdown probability. This, then, was the background to the new Reactor Safety Study commissioned by the AEC and directed by Professor Rasmussen. Although the probability of major accidents was estimated to be rather low, the study's estimate of the core meltdown probability was nevertheless much higher than previously calculated (5×10^{-5} per reactor-year as opposed to 1×10^{-6}).[16] In any case, the Rasmussen report, far from disposing of the reactor safety debate, merely brought it to a higher level of technical complexity and confirmed that estimates of probabilities and possible effects of accidents would remain the subject of considerable scientific disputation.[17]

Another major source of concern related to the possible entry of highly toxic nuclear waste into the biosphere. The issue of waste disposal was one of the principal considerations in the Sierra Club's 1974 decision to oppose the continued development of nuclear energy.[18] The demand for an acceptable solution to the waste problem featured in several state initiatives and was one of the overriding concerns expressed by an eminent panel of scientists and scholars in a report prepared for the National Council of Churches in 1975 and entitled the *Plutonium Economy*.[19] By the mid-1970s, the dangers posed by the long-term disposal of radioactive waste, whether at sea or underground, had become central to the case against nuclear power which was now gaining currency throughout the western world.

Particularly disturbing for many was the toxicity of plutonium and the adequacy of existing standards and regulations. Not unexpectedly, the decision of the US Administration to proceed with the liquid-metal fast breeder reactor as a matter of priority provoked considerable opposition and gave rise in 1971 to a suit against the AEC. Although dismissed by the district court of the District of Columbia, the case raised many of the issues which were to form the basis of environmental protest against the breeder.[20] The development of reprocessing and breeder technologies tended to fuel fears of the plutonium economy and gave rise to declining public confidence in available safeguards for the handling, storage and transport of plutonium and to a heightened perception of the risks of plutonium diversion into unauthorised hands, whether national or sub-national in character.

Separate from, but closely related to, these criticisms was the argument that nuclear authorities, and particularly the AEC, had been less than frank with the public. A case in point was the failure to divulge the miscalculations that had been made about radioactive fallout from above-ground weapons testing in Nevada. For several years the AEC had done its best to conceal that people had been exposed to low-level radiation throughout the 1950s, that nursing mothers were found to have iodine 131 in their milk, and babies strontium 90 impregnated in their bones and teeth.[21] In subsequent years it was alleged that the AEC had tried 'to suppress discussion of reactor safety issues' even within the nuclear profession, and inhibited top level safety researchers from 'speaking directly with the AEC's own regulatory authorities on matters pertaining to the licensing of nuclear power plants.'[22] The refusal to disclose fully the nature of nuclear power research and the safety implications of a large-scale commercial programme was seen by many writers as part of a deliberate policy by nuclear policy-makers to mislead the public or, at least, to manipulate information so as to minimise opposition to their plans.[23].

Accusations of secretiveness and duplicity against the nuclear establishment were by no means confined to the United States. Such criticism was sharply voiced in France where the public was normally given little or no information about reactor safety, pollution dangers or the economics of nuclear power. Even as late as 1975 the often promised public debate had produced very little except for the perfunctory consultation of regional assemblies on the choice of reactor sites.[24] Although Brazil may be regarded as a special case given the political conditions arising from military rule, it is nevertheless significant that Brazilian scientists should have openly criticised the closed character of nuclear decision-making in their country. They were disturbed, among other things, by the absence of free discussion on the terms of the 1975 German-Brazilian deal and its long-term technical, economic and ecological implications for Brazilian society.[25]

In response to the numerous attacks that were now levelled against it, the nuclear industry insisted on its impressive safety record. Persons living in the vicinity of a nuclear plant, it was argued, were permitted a maximum annual radiation exposure which was considerably below the equivalent exposure from natural and medical sources. Regarding the likelihood of a catastrophic reactor accident, the most detailed studies had placed the probability of a major radioactive release at no more than 1 in 100,000 reactor-years. As for the carcinogenic effects of plutonium, there was no conclusive evidence that they could definitely be attributed to plutonium in the several thousand workers who had handled the material.[26] Yet these confident claims, even when supported by the findings of prominent scientists, did not prove fully reassuring. The opponents of nuclear power may not have swung the whole of public opinion behind them, but they had seriously dented the credibility of the nuclear industry.

WIDENING AGENDA OF DISSENT

By the early 1970s the critique of nuclear power was ready to break new ground as the ecological movement moved beyond purely local and specific environmental concerns to more generic economic and philosophical issues. Several studies challenged the conventional assessment of the so-called energy crisis, stressed the wastefulness of intensive electrification, and cast serious doubts on the future competitiveness of nuclear power.[27] The anti-nuclear movement drew attention to the long-term potential of soft technologies which depended not on depletable energy capital but on energy income derived from renewable sources such as sun, wind, water and vegetation. In the shorter term various bridging strategies were envisaged, combining energy conservation, technical fixes and continued reliance on fossil fuels. As with the issues of low-level radiation, reactor safety, waste management, and diversion of weapons-grade material, so with the analysis of energy alternatives, European opponents of nuclear power were for a long time heavily dependent on the vast technical literature available in the United States. This dependence was itself a reflection of America's technological lead, particularly in the light water reactor field, but also of the greater propensity of American scientists to enter the public arena.

Nevertheless, European anti-nuclear sentiment had an identity of its own, which derived much more from national traditions and institutions than from the American experience. While preoccupied, as were many Americans, with nuclear specific risks, with the potential for long-term biological and genetic effects, and with the perceived connection between nuclear power and nuclear weapons.[28] Europeans were generally more inclined to question the ideological implications of nuclear power, indeed the very structure of the economic and political system which they increasingly associated with the planned nuclearisation of society.[29] But aside from these culturally-derived differences of emphasis, the anti-nuclear movements were at one in challenging not only what they regarded as the dubious economics and deceptive propaganda of the nuclear industry, but the very assumption of continuing exponential growth in energy consumption and especially the equation of growth with technical progress and of such progress with the amelioration of the human condition.[30]

Some writers have interpreted this drastic rejection of prevailing social norms as a cultural revolt nearly Luddite in character, and as an expression of 'a longing for a return to nature or to a more simple life unencumbered by machines'.[31] A profound disenchantment with the fruits of modern technology did certainly surface in most advanced industrial systems – the hippie movement of the 1960s was clear evidence of this phenomenon – but it would be a gross oversimplication to explain the political reaction against the nuclear option purely in these terms. Even less illuminating is the crude notion that unconscious fears were so manipulated by horror stories about meltdowns and radioactivity as to transform atomic energy into a quasi-mythical symbol of evil.

The reality of the situation would seem much less dramatic, but more complex. Once local communities felt threatened by the technological and bureaucratic invasion of their lives, made necessary by the nuclear project, they became increasingly mistrustful of reasssuring official statements aimed at minimising the dangers of the nuclear fuel cycle. References to future energy demand, creation of job opportunities, and maintenance of living standards, were no longer sufficient to allay growing suspicion and resentment. From issues of pollution and toxic thresholds, attention was directed more and more to the kind of society envisaged by the technocratic apparatus of the state and by the large corporation, each striving in its own way to maximise its economic power and organisational ascendancy over various facets of social interaction. To this extent, the nuclear controversy would seem to have provoked an intensive reappraisal of the nature of the modern socio-industrial order.

From the ecological perspective, the development of nuclear energy appeared, despite the 1973 oil crisis, tied to a policy of growth. The continuing exponential increase in energy consumption was seen as leading to the depletion of finite resources and to the pollution of the natural environment. At the same time it risked unleashing social and economic processes of increasing scale, complexity and centralisation and required enormous investments that only *transational* or *state* capital could afford.[32] Growth of this kind was inextricably linked to economic concentration and measured in terms of financial indicators which did not necessarily correspond to any real improvement in living conditions. Rather than reduce inequalities such growth tended to accentuate them, both domestically and internationally.

This analysis was taken even further by writers who argued that the great attraction nuclear power held for its proponents was not merely or even primarily profit but the prospect of economic expansion and greater political control. The economic and bureaucratic interests committed to nuclear power were, according to this view, gambling that the technology would place them in a commanding position over the complex industrial machine on which modern society had come to depend more and more for its existence.[33] Significantly, the far-reaching implications of this ecological critique were well understood by the leading advocates of nuclear power, as the following description by a senior Wesinghouse executive clearly indicates:

> To those who challenge our current social and political institutions, and the economic system upon which they rest, nuclear power has become the foremost symbol and almost obsessional target of their opposition, the visible antithesis of their sociopolitical ideals. For nuclear power represents to them the ultimate symbol of economic power, military power, all that the word technocracy connotes, and it is in the hands of the established institutions – the electric utilities, the large corporations, government agencies.[34]

At issue for ecologists was the very nature of the nuclear state.

Ther was, however, another dimension to the socio-political critique of nuclear power. The concentration of power was seen as stemming not merely from the motives or interests of the nuclear establishment but from the very characteristics of nuclear technology. The tendency towards technocratic management already visible in advanced industrial society was accentuated by the magnitude of nuclear hazards which required high levels of social and political stability over long periods of time. Strict compliance with security regulations at every stage of the fuel cycle – including the physical protection of nuclear installations, the transport of fuels, the reprocessing of spent fuel, and the long-term isolation of radioactive waste – presupposed social and political institutions endowed with a degree of vigilance and permanence for which there was little historical precedent.[35] The very vulnerability of the nuclear edifice pointed to an increasingly centralised and bureaucratised political order wedded to rising levels of secrecy and hostile to any manifestation of dissent.

The expanding power of the nuclear state and its increasing resourse to the techniques of repression represented, then, for the ecological movement a fundamental threat to individual freedom. The domination of the state over civil society, evident not only in the economic realm but in almost every facet of social reality, drastically reduced the scope for human autonomy.[36] Even so-called mass political parties, far from being independent expressions of the popular will, were perceived as little more than appendages of the state. The nuclear project reinforced the technocratic tendencies of the modern industrial state and the resulting erosion of civil liberties by providing additional opportunities and justification for the twin processes of centralisation and stratification.[37]

Hostile to the authoritarian tendencies of the state, suspicious of the ideologies and organisational practice of the established political parties, the ecological movement was obliged to define its alternative conception of society. The intellectual origins of this project are many and diverse but they do have in common a sense of the need to develop a planetary perspective and to restore an existential balance between human activity and the natural order as a prerequisite for a more balanced relationship between man and his cultural milieu. In Germany the cultural and philosophical legacy of the youth movement of the late nineteenth and early twentieth centuries and its rejection of atomisation as experienced in highly urbanised and mechanised society no doubt exerted an important influence. In France, the ecological mood, although less nostalgic in tone, did nevertheless bear the imprint of several earlier conservative and radical traditions, notably Catholic social philosophy with its emphasis on personalism on the one hand, and the Marxist critique of capitalist society with its stress on exploitation and alienation on the other.[38] Despite these cultural and ideological differences, ecologists of all persuasions tended to advocate, in sharp contrast to the proponents of nuclear energy, the establishment of more decentralised communities which would minimise environmental degradation and promote a more labour-intensive mode of production, a more self-sufficient and self-sustaining economy, greater cultural diversity, and a more democratic model of decision-making.[39]

It was the task of the environmental movement to apply this ecological view of the future to a wide range of policy areas, including transport, urban planning, energy conservation and the use of renewable energy sources. The decentralisation of economic and energy systems, the restructuring of cities and the reshaping of the prevailing patterns of production and consumption were seen as part of a larger strategy which would conserve rapidly-diminishing energy resources, encourage grass-roots community action, and generally solidify opposition to nuclear energy.[40] But in pressing for these major policy changes, anti-nuclear activists were eager to retain their political independence and to refrain from identifying too closely with any established political party.[41] Even when deciding to participate in the electoral process by fielding their own candidates, ecological groups were intent on preserving their separate identity and on projecting themselves as a non-aligned third force. Indeed, most anti-nuclear organisations were imbued, by the very nature of their ideology, with a deep mistrust of structure which made them hostile to highly disciplined political organisations and resistant to any move to introduce centralised leadership or hierarchy into their own ranks.[42] The ecological movement was thus characterised by a multiplicity of groups, each jealous of its autonomy, yet lacking in organisational continuity.

Anti-nuclear sentiment in the United States as in Western Europe was to a very large extent inspired by a cultural movement which had married the new ecological insights with the more traditional elements of utopian thinking. Several familiar themes had re-emerged: the advocacy of the steady-state society; the emphasis on self-sufficiency; the bias towards reduced commercial transactions; the need for greater integration of industry and agriculture; the rotational principle in the allocation of social tasks. But certain characteristics were peculiar to the new ecological consciousness, in particular the stress on freedom and individualism. It was not a question of opposing merely the repressive tendencies of technocratic society, but also the growth ethic espoused by some of the most powerful elements of the traditional Left, which, though theoretically committed to social transformation, were in practice tied to outdated notions of technological progress. In this sense, the authoritarianism of the Right and the rigidity of the Left were equally unacceptable. The other distinguisting feature of ecological politics was the internationalism of its outlook equally evident in its analysis of the prevailing social order, its organisational practice, and its prescriptions for the future.

OPPOSITIONAL STRATEGIES

Although the philosophical rationale of the ecological option may not have been fully comprehended, at least in its abstract from, by all opponents of nuclear power, the initially unstructured and largely intuitive resentment to centralised plans did gradually give rise to an informal but widely shared ideology. Ecological concepts were internalised by many who recognised an experienced the current crisis of industrial society. They included not only environmentalists of long standing – the initial core of the movement – but a wide range of other social groupings who, because of their class, ethnic background, education, age or sex, were more likely to resist the blandishments of a consumerist culture. Particularly important in this regard were those counter-cultural currents which were especially sensitive to the dual process of alienation and domination characteristic of contemporary industrial society.

In its organisational practice, however, opposition to the nuclear project, while expressing a common set of general attitudes tended also to reflect several more specific national and even local cultural and political circumstances. In broad outline, the opposition strategy was to prevent further reliance on nuclear power by persuading governments and public opinion that the technology posed a unique health and social risk, and that the issue of nuclear safety was now the subject of acute scientific controversy. The translation of this general approach into practical action, at least in the initial stages, was not so much the product of a national plan as the combined effect of a great many disparate and localised initiatives. The tactics used in each case depended largely on the institutional opportunities available to the local group and on its previous political experience.

In his testimony before the House Energy and Environment subcommittee in April 1975, Senator Mike Gravel argued that the strength of the American anti-nuclear movement derived not only from the well-known environmental organisations calling for a moratorium on nuclear construction (eg. Friends of the Earth, Sierra Club, Wilderness Society) but from the hundreds of smaller but extremely effective community organisations. He went on to explain that many people who might otherwise have been indifferent to the idea of nuclear power were willing to change their minds once confronted with a nuclear facility in their own vicinity. As evidence of the importance of local sentiment Senator Gravel produced a list of about 150 anti-nuclear organisations, most of which were community based.[43]

The localised response to nuclear plans was equally evident in Western Europe. From the late 1960s committees were formed near proposed reactor sites in various parts of France. These included

Fessenheim in Alsace, Bugey near Lyon, Blayais near Bordeaux and Gravelines in Flanders. Apart from petitions, meetings and conferences, sit-ins, rallies and festivals often involving several thousand people were organised in protest against these plants.[44] Despite offers of compensation to disadvantaged communities, the intensity of community feeling was such that that elected local representatives had little option but to lodge formal objections against government plans.[45] The vehemence of regional resistance was in large measure a reflection of the highly centralised character of French nuclear decision-making which denied the opponents of nuclear power virtually any institutional remedy for the expression of their grievances.

Germany, precisely because of its more decentralised political system, proved to be a more fertile ground for effective grass-roots activity. The main organisational entity was the citizen action group (Burgerinitiativen) which quickly captured the imagination of the electorate and provided a vehicle for political participation that neither local government nor national political parties could offer. By the mid-1970s as many as 1000 citizen action groups had emerged, boasting a membership of nearly one million. According to a survey published in 1977, 12 per cent of the West German population was willing in principle to work for a political party, whereas 34 per cent would join a citizen action group.[46] Many of these new groups achieved a limited measure of coordination through a loose affiliation with the Bundesverband Bürgerinitiativen Umweltschutz (BBU).

The Wyhl experience, to which reference has already been made, was to provide a model for action and a good deal of inspiration to anti-nuclear groups in the rest of Germany and beyond.[47] Once permission was given in January 1975 for the construction of the reactor, thousands of people marched to the site and occupied it. The retaliatory tactics of the police immediately made headline news, thereby helping to endow the Wyhl struggle with European-wide significance. In spite of arrests and prosecutions, the local people maintained a permanent occupation of the site for nine months, sustained in their determination by the co-operation of neighbouring villages. The occupation was eventually ended following a partial victory in which the government offered to review the safety of the project.

Even when less successful in achieving their immediate aims, these localised initiatives served two important functions: they enabled the opponents of nuclear power to expose what they perceived to be the coercive power of the state apparatus, while at the same time sustaining the unity and morale of their own movement. The establishment of a network of citizen action groups helped to create new channels of information and communication capable of challenging the legitimacy of established institutions. These groups were all the more effective when, as in the case of Wyhl, they were supported by multidisciplinary research and advice involving environmentalists, lawyers, sociologists, biologists and nuclear physicists. The result was a new form of ecological politics in which citizens were able to participate in the public debate, to raise objections to government planning, and, where possible, to engage in a series of court actions.

The experience derived from these localised conflicts soon suggested to the participants the need for more extensive informational campaigns. Local groups with the assistance of regional and national organisations began to accumulate an impressive collection of audio-visual aids, including tapes, films, displays, posters, periodicals and lists of speakers willing to address a wide range of meetings. In the United States, the efforts of the Sierra Club, Friends of the Earth, the Natural Resources Defense Council and the Consolidated National Intervenors brought the concerns of the anti-nuclear movement to a rapidly growing audience. The formation in 1975 of a new organisation, Critical Mass, under Ralph Nader's leadership, gave added impetus to the dissemination of information and to the publication of a host of new books refining yet summarising for the lay reader the long list of anti-nuclear arguments.[48]

A similar though more limited educational programme was undertaken by the anti-nuclear movement in Britain where the public debate was at a much less advanced stage. To begin with, the foreign opposition experience based largely on the light water reactor was not readily applicable to British gas-cooled reactors. Moreover, public discussion of the issues was restricted by the relative isolation of Britain's nuclear sites which tended to moderate grass-roots dissent and made much more difficult the task of exchanging local experiences. Nevertheless, through its publications and in particular the writings of its two principal consultants, Amory Lovins and Walter Patterson, Friends of the Earth were able to question many of the assumptions on which rested the energy and economic case for Britain's nuclear programme.[49] By 1976 the mass media were beginning to give nuclear matters a higher priority and to cover a little more extensively the views and activities of anti-nuclear groups.

In France, research and the dissemination of information became a priority task for the anti-nuclear movement given its own highly decentralised character and the monolithic control of information exercised by the nuclear authorities.[50] The first opportunity to mount a nationwide educational programme came with the candidacy of ecologist René Dumont in the 1974 presidential election. Although Dumont obtained only 337,000 votes, his campaign exposed for the first time many millions of people to the environmental philosophy and to the critique of the all-electric, all-nuclear society. EdF's electro-nuclear programme also came under fire from the influential Fédération Française des Sociétés de Protection de la Nature, which represented numerous nature conservation organisations. Particularly significant was the 'Appeal of the 400' launched in February 1975, which called for a nuclear moratorium pending a clearer appreciation of nuclear risks, and was eventually signed by some 2200 scientists, many of whom were employed by the Centre National de Recherche Scientifique, Collège de France, CEA and EdF. Statements were also issued by 1300 physicists from the Centre Européen de Recherche Nucléaire (CERN) and by 500 Grenoble scientists against the Super-Phénix breeder programme.

In April 1975, marches and processions were organised in Paris and several other locations as part of an educational campaign to convey to the public at large the hazards of nuclear energy and the potential of alternative energy sources.[51] Further evidence of opposition came with a growing number of scientific publications questioning different economic and technical facets of the French nuclear programme. The Institut Economique et Juridique sur l'Information at Grenoble and the Groupement de Scientifiques sur l'Information de l'Energie Nucléaire (GSIEN) were to play an important role in this regard.[52] By the middle of 1975, the nuclear debate had achieved full prominence in the French press. From being confined to the pages of a few radical newspapers and magazines (e.g. *Le Sauvage, la Gueule Ouverte* and *Charlie Hebdo*), French nuclear plans became the subject of intense scrutiny in *Le Monde, Le Nouvel Observateur, Enterprise*, and other influential journals of opinion.

Informational campaigns could not, however, produce of their own accord the desired shift in policy and were therefore complemented in each country by a variety of more explicitly political strategies designed to extract maximum advantage from existing administrative and electoral processes. This approach was to prove remarkably effective in slowing down the American and German nuclear power programmes.

In the United States, tactics used included participation in power plant hearings, lobbying of state legislatures, instigation of plebiscites, court actions and pressure on government agencies to enforce stricter safety standards. Intervention in licensing hearings compelled anti-nuclear groups to translate their general concerns into allegations of specific deficiencies in plant design, an exercise which normally required very considerable financial and technical resources but which they readily undertook in the hope of forcing the cancellation of the proposed facility or, at the every least, of inflicting long and costly delays.

While continuing to exploit the openings afforded by the legal intricacies of the licensing process, localised opposition gradually assumed a higher political profile. Under the impetus of Nader's Critical Mass, initiative campaigns were launched in several western states. Voters were asked to agree to a nuclear moratorium. The first major test of the strategy occurred in the 1976 California referendum, when voters were invited to approve Proposition 15 which listed a highly complex set of procedures designed to bring the nuclear industry to a virtual standstill. If approved, Proposition 15 would have required the operators of nuclear power plants to satisfy much higher standards of nuclear safety, to provide an acceptable technology for waste storage and disposal, and to ensure unlimited liability in the event of nuclear accident. After a bitterly contested campaign to which the pro-nuclear lobby devoted extensive financial resources, the anti-nuclear proposal was rejected by 67 per cent to 33 per cent. Parallel initiatives in Arizona, Colorado, Montana, Oregon, Ohio and Washington produced a roughly similar result. The failure of these initiatives to achieve their immediate objective was partially offset, however, by the growing grass-roots strength of anti-nuclear organisations and their much enhanced capacity to do battle in the public arena.

By comparison, the British anti-nuclear movement found it much more difficult to operate effectively within the formal political process. While activists attempted to use official channels by presenting, for example, detailed evidence to planning inquiries, such involvement brought few successes and relatively little public visibility. The first significant opening occurred with the British government's decision in December 1976 to hold a public inquiry into BNFL's proposals for the construction of a major new thermal oxide reprocessing plant (THORP). The proposal had caused considerable controversy, in part because it involved the reprocessing of significant quantities of spent fuel of foreign origin. For the first time the British public were treated to an extensive public debate. The press decided to keep a close watch on the inquiry. Innumerable reports and articles appearing in *The Times, The Financial Times, The Economist* and *New Society*, were complemented by a spate of programmes on radio and television, and by several major public seminars and hearings. Mr Justice Parker, who was appointed Inspector on 31 March 1977, eventually forwarded his report to the Environment Secretary in January 1978 after hearing evidence on more than 100 days of sitting from some 146 witnesses and sighting some 1500 documents. The anti-nuclear case was ably put by Friends of the Earth, the Windscale Appeal, the Isle of Man Local Government Board, and the Town and Country Planning Association, all of whom were legally represented.[53] In the end, the Parker Report paid little or no heed to the many objections raised by the opponents of the THORP proposal. Yet, though dismissed with little or no explanation, their arguments had achieved a new level of legitimacy by the very processes of the inquiry and the public interest it had aroused.[54]

In the case of France, opportunities for anti-nuclear activists to influence the political process were even more limited than in Britain. In Parliament the nuclear power programme had been the subject of little debate and remarkably little legislation. Most decisions had taken the form of government decrees with little or no prior consultation and no provision for any legal procedures or public inquiries which would allow new proposals to be subjected to detailed critical scrutiny. In an effort to overcome the seemingly impenetrable barriers to public debate, the ecological movement entered the electoral arena, at first through the candidacy of René Dumont in the 1974 presidential election. In March 1976, the ecologists contested several seats in the departmental elections, and obtained 7 per cent of the vote in the Paris district. They again participated in the 1977 municipal elections, receiving some 400,000 votes, that is, a national average of 10 per cent of the vote. In some areas, the environmentalists' vote was as high as 20 per cent. At the 1978 national elections, the ecological list received a total of some 600,000 votes, and at least 7 per cent of the vote in nineteen electorates.[55] The 1978 performance represented a moderate regression of the ecological vote, and contrasted with the steady progress it had made over the preceding five years. The bulk of support for the ecological parties came from younger voters. Most of them were under thirty five years of age and belonged to relatively affluent middle-class backgrounds. About one-third of these voters identified with the non-Communist Left, but an equally significant proportion appeared to have no clearly defined political sympathies.[56] The anti-nuclear electoral strategy may not have produced a decisive shift in the political balance of power, but it did contribute to a more extensive airing of the issues, to greater media attention to the anti-nuclear case, and to limited but discernible changes in the policies of the established parties of both Left and Right.

An electoral strategy was also adopted by sections of the German anti-nuclear movement. In 1978, the ecological parties, which were presenting candidates in Land elections for the first time, obtained 3.9 per cent and 4.5 per cent of the vote in Lower Saxony and Hamburg respectively. In both cases, they were instrumental in lowering the vote of the Free Democrats below 5 per cent thereby automatically eliminating them from parliamentary representation. A few months later, ecological groups again fielded candidates in elections for the Hesse and Bavarian Parliaments, but this time obtained only 2.0 per cent and 1.8 per cent of the vote respectively. In March 1979, the environmentalist vote for the House of Representatives in West Berlin improved somewhat, but still failed to pass the 5 per cent minimum requirement for representation. The first environmental and anti-nuclear grouping to achieve parliamentary representation was the Bremen Green List which secured 5.1 per cent of the vote and four seats in elections for the Bremen Bürgerschaft in October 1979. In January 1980, the Green Party was formally constituted as a national political party and in March of the same year obtained 5.3 per cent of the vote in the Baden-Württemberg Land elections, thereby securing six of the 124 seats. Following further electoral successes in Lower Saxony and Hesse in March and September 1982 respectively, the Greens achieved their first national breakthrough in the March 1983 elections gaining 5.6 per cent of the vote which entitled them to twenty-seven seats in the new Parliament. It had yet to be demonstrated, however, that electoral success would yield political influence.

The intrusion of the nuclear controversy into Swedish politics will be considered in more detail later. Suffice it to say for the moment that the nuclear issue was a significant factor in the September 1976 elections which saw the defeat of the Social Democrats after an uninterrupted period of office lasting forty-four years. It soon became evident, however, that the Conservative coalition headed by the anti-nuclear Centre Party would not be able to agree on the future direction of Swedish nuclear policy. Following the failure of the Fälldin government to prevent the Barsebäck reactor from coming into operation and the complex political manoeuvres which ensued, the environmental movement concluded that the only viable option still open to it was to press for a referendum. Although the proposal was initially opposed by the Social Democrats and the Liberals, the events at Three Mile Island in the United States in 1979 helped to change their minds, thereby producing a parliamentary consensus in favour of a national referendum to be held in March 1980.[57]

Instead of a clear choice between 'yes' and 'no', the electorate was offered three options.[58] The first advocated the phasing out of nuclear power within the operational lifetime of the twelve approved reactors, but was supported by the Conservative Party which refused to commit itself firmly to the halting of reactor construction. Option two, which was supported by the Social Democrats, advocated the use of all twelve approved nuclear reactors, but emphasised that they would spell the end of the nuclear programme which would have to be replaced with renewable energy sources. By contrast, option three, proposed by the Centre Party and the Communist Party, and supported by the People's Campaign Against Nuclear Power, recommended the complete phasing out of nuclear power within ten years. This last option received 38.7 per cent of the vote as against 39.1 per cent for option two and 18.9 per cent for option one. Inevitably, the referendum result was open to conflicting interpretations. Whereas a majority of voters (58.7 per cent) had decided to proceed with the twelve reactor programme, an even greater majority (77.8 per cent) had agreed to place an absolute ceiling on the number of nuclear power stations and to phase out the entire programme by the year 2010.

It would seem, then, that the diverse electoral strategies employed by the anti-nuclear movement had mixed results. On the whole, the gains were less than conclusive but far from negligible. Although eliciting considerable public support and contributing to the politicisation of the issue, intervention in the electoral arena did not result in a massive vote in favour of ecological candidates or ecologically-inspired propositions. Moreover, electoral politics risked creating sharp divisions within the ecological movement by confronting it with the tactical question of political alignment both during election campaigns and in the parliamentary arena.[59] Anti-nuclear groups, then, could not hope to maintain the morale and enthusiasm of their members, radically modify the public perception of risk, and deflect the nuclear establishment from its course by operating exclusively through conventional electoral processes. For this purpose a more militant grass-roots approach was deemed necessary. This was precisely the function of occupations and demonstrations, a tactic the German anti-nuclear movement was to use with increasing frequency and effect.

Mention has already been made of the vigorous protest which developed in Wyhl. Following several demonstrations and a prolonged occupation of the site involving fierce clashes with the police, the Freiburg administrative court decided, after receiving evidence from numerous experts, to cancel the two-year-old construction permit. Although government and industry did not accept the court's verdict and lodged an appeal in a higher court, the Wyhl phenomenon became a source of inspiration to anti-nuclear activists throughout Germany, France and Switzerland, many of whom now equated the nuclear state with the denial of democratic rights and civil liberties.

A similar public outcry occurred in mid-1976 when residents and citizen action groups around Brockdorf began to suspect that plans were afoot to by-pass the necessary judicial requirements and commence work on a reactor near the village. On 13 November 1976, some 30,000 people attended what was to have been a peaceful demonstration, but when 3000 marches attempted to occupy the newly-commissioned site they were repelled by police who erected steel and concrete barriers around the site and dispersed the crowd with batons, clubs, tear gas, water cannon and chemical repellents. The violent police action and the resulting casualties were widely reported in the German and international press. A few weeks later, in a significant development, the Schleswig administrative court imposed a construction moratorium on the plant on the grounds that the problem of waste disposal had not yet been resolved, an argument used for the first time in a German court ruling. When 60,000 people marched a few days later outside the Brockdorf site, the police authorities were much more restrained and allowed the demonstration to take place without violent incident.

The problem of violence re-emerged when a large rally against the 1360 MWe Grohnde nuclear power station in March 1977 deteriorated into large-scale confrontation in which 237 policemen and at least eighty demonstrators were injured.[60] In September 1977, 60,000 marched in protest against the proposed 300 MWe prototype fast breeder reactor at Kalkar. Even more determined was the resistance to the Gorleben plan, which involved the construction of storage facilities and a reprocessing plant capable of handling 3000 tonnes of spent fuel. Local opposition soon assumed national dimensions and gave rise to several large occupations of the proposed site. Following the Harrisburg accident, an estimated 80,000–100,000 converged on Hanover in opposition to the Gorleben complex. Recognising the intensity of public feeling, the government of Lower Saxony announced in May 1979 that construction of the reprocessing plant was no longer politically feasible and that permission for the project would not be granted.[61]

Militant protest was also a frequent feature of anti-nuclear activity in France, but was generally smaller in scale and politically less effective than in Germany. Although considerably exacerbated by provocative police action, the incidence of violence at several demonstrations helped to mar the image of the anti-nuclear movement, to create divisions within its ranks, and to shift media attention from the issue of nuclear risks to that of law and order.

Situated near the French reprocessing plant at La Hague, Flamanville, which was chosen by EdF for a 5200 MWe nuclear power complex, soon became a focal point of opposition. Following the announcement of the government's decision, some 5000 people protested in April 1975 by marching on the proposed site. A regional committee, the Comité Régional d'Information et de Lutte Anti-Nucléaire (CRILAN), was subsequently established, and close links forged with workers and trade unions, particularly during the three months' strike at the La Hague plant. A series of festivals and marches, each involving from 3000–10,000 people, culminated in February 1977 in an attempted occupation of the site, which was eventually thwarted by the intervention of a paramilitary police force of several hundred men. In March, the second Fessenheim reactor in Alsace, which was set to go on stream within the next few months, attracted 4500 demonstrators in Strasbourg and 3000 in Colmar.

Anti-nuclear protests continued to gather momentum throughout 1977, but the event which more than any other brought home to the French population the trauma of the nuclear debate was the upheaval at Creys-Malville. By this time, over one hundred Malville committees had formed across the country in protest against the project. On 31 July 1977, opposition to the construction of the Super-Phénix crystallised in an attempted occupation of the site by 60,000 people. In a battle which lasted three hours, riot police using batons and tear gas fought with tens of thousands of demonstrators. At least one man died and 200 were injured.[62] The French government promptly reaffirmed its commitment to nuclear power and endeavoured to defuse the political impact of the protest by blaming the violence on foreign participants, notably German anarchists.

In the immediate aftermath of the upheaval, the intensity of anti-nuclear protest generally subsided throughout the country. The opponents of nuclear power had attempted to implement a strategy of non-violent direct action as a means of raising the stakes in the conflict, but in the process had provoked the state into fierce retaliatory action. The reappraisal of tactics which ensued did not, however, put an end to public dissent, particularly in those regions with a long tradition of hostility towards central authority. Nowhere was this phenomenon more evident than in Brittany, where the south side of Cap Sizun had been chosen as the site for four reactors with a total capacity of 5200 MWe. The nearby village of Plogoff became the scene for a series of often violent confrontations with police, culminating in widespread protests in March 1980. In the weeks that followed, opposition to the proposed plant continued to escalate and finally resulted in May 1980 in the largest demonstration ever staged in France.[63] The Plogoff complex was one of the few EdF nuclear projects to be cancelled by the new Socialist government soon after assuming office in May 1981.

Confrontational tactics played a much less important role in the respective strategies of the British and Swedish anti-nuclear movements. This is not to say that demonstrations were entirely absent. In June 1976, some 10,000 people converged on the hills of Billinger near the town of Sköde in protest against the proposed mining of uranium. In September 1977, some 20,000 Danes and Swedes took part in a joint twelve-mile march of the Barsebäck reactor site located near Malmö, Sweden's third largest city, and 19 km from Copenhagen.

Two years later, the Harrisburg accident prompted a 10,000 strong demonstration in Stockholm. As for Britain, several public protests were organised by the local inhabitants of the Orkney Islands in opposition to the mining of uranium. A demonstration against the proposed dumping of nuclear wastes in Galloway attracted 3500 people. In April 1978, some 10,000 attended London's first major anti-nuclear rally called by FOE in protest against the Windscale expansion.[64] A more militant approach was adopted by SCRAM, the anti-nuclear coalition established to oppose the construction of two AGR reactors at Torness. The first large-scale demonstration was mounted in May 1978 and was followed a year later by a three-day protest in which more than 7000 people participated.[65]

The Swedish and British experience was largely replicated in the United States where direct action techniques were relatively little used. It was not until May 1977 that the Clamshell Alliance, a loose coalition of anti-nuclear groups centred on New England, staged what was to be the first large-scale occupation of a nuclear reactor site in the United States. Having lost faith in the legal intervention process, Clamshell, with the aid of the American Friends Service Committee, spent several months training would-be occupiers in the tactics of non-violent resistance.[66] The occupation involved some 2000 people, of whom 1400 were arrested by the National Guard. Many of the demonstrators were imprisoned for a period of two weeks – an event which thrust the nuclear controversy into full public view and generated considerable community support for the anti-nuclear cause. The 1977 Seabrook experience provided considerable impetus for further demonstrations in subsequent years, not only in Seabrook but in many other parts of the United States. In April 1978, for example, 6,000 people protested against the plutonium factory near Rocky Flats, Denver, while at the other end of the country a march by 2000 against the reprocessing plant in Barnwell, South Carolina, resulted in some 280 arrests.[67] Despite the mushrooming of regional coalitions (e.g. the Crabshell, Palmetto, Abalone, Paddleworth, Catfish alliances), few of these protests – with the possible exception of Seabrook – were of the same scale or intensity as those experienced in France and Germany. It was only after the impact of the Three Mile Island accident that the United States witnessed its first national anti-nuclear demonstration. Representing a wide range of interests and organisations, the Washington rally was attended by some 100,000 protestors.[68] Four months later, a newly formed group, Musicians United for Safe Energy, were instrumental in organising a mass gathering of more than 200,000 people at Manhattan Park, New York.[69]

Although varying significantly from country to country in their specific objectives, demands and method of organisation, mass public protest had by the late 1970s become a common feature of anti-nuclear campaigns in all of the countries under review. Even in Brazil, where the system of military rule imposed clear limits on the expression of dissent, resistance to the government's nuclear plans gave rise to public forms of opposition. Several thousand took part in a demonstration against the Angra plant in 1979, and a similar number demonstrated in Rio de Janeiro in April 1980. Protests were also staged in Iguape once it became known that the city had been chosen as the site for the country's fourth and fifth reactors.[70] Whether used as a tactic to obstruct the actual construction of a nuclear facility or as part of a larger strategy aimed at influencing the decisions of governments and electricity utilities, demonstrative action inevitably brought in its wake a wider participation in the controversy and with it a much greater polarisation of public opinion.

Another important but largely unforeseen outcome of public protest was the way in which it helped to invest localised campaigns with a national and even international dimension. In this sense, Wyhl, Brockdorf, Kalkar, La Hague, Malville, Seabrook and Harrisburg, to cite but a few of the better-known examples, provided a sharp focus for an otherwise diverse and fragmented movement. Assisted by geographical proximity, demonstrations in Europe – notably in France, Germany, the Netherlands, Belgium and Switzerland – removed physical barriers and facilitated the rediscovery of a common cultural heritage long obscured by linguistic differences and national rivalries. According to one of its more charismatic leaders, the European anti-nuclear movement gave rise to a new sub-culture, 'a living culture of films, photos, papers, posters and ... songs'.[71] Despite the varying cultural, political and economic circumstances of each country, national campaigns increasingly reflected a common appreciation of the international character of the problem.

The exchange of experiences and information across national boundaries, the regional coordination of events and activities, the development of common or complementary strategies, all contributed to the creation of an informal but potent transational coalition. In April 1977, representatives from organisations in twenty countries met in Salzburg to express and reinforce their commitment to a non-nuclear future.[72] While the conference was totally united on fundamental objectives (i.e. the phasing out of nuclear power programmes, the development of alternative energy technologies, and the need for greater public scrutiny of all levels of energy policy-making), differences emerged between those who were content to operate exclusively or primarily through existing institutional channels and those who favoured more innovative or radical measures, including acts of civil disobedience. This disagreement which reflected vastly different domestic political environments diminished in subsequent years as each organisation gained a more intimate knowledge of the experiences of others and attempted to make use of that knowledge in devising a more flexible and diversified mix of strategies and techniques.

SCOPE AND LIMITATIONS OF ECOLOGICAL DISSENT

The foregoing account has not attempted to give a detailed historical analysis of the evolution of a diverse and fluctuating movement. Rather, the intention has been to analyse the intellectual and organisational origins of anti-nuclear sentiment and to characterise the particular forms of dissent to which it gave rise, and which greatly complicated the task of the nuclear state, obliging it in many instances to plan countervailing actions in order to neutralise the effectiveness of protest. The underlying rationale of the state's response will be examined in the next chapter. Suffice it to say for the moment that the politicisation of the nuclear debate has been a necessary but far from sufficient condition for the achievement of anti-nuclear objectives.

It is true that the extensive use of the legal apparatus of the state has, at least in the case of Germany and the United States, slowed down the momentum of their respective nuclear programmes by imposing delays and increasing the costs of nuclear power. The relatively decentralised character of the German judicial system, with its complex hierarchy of administrative and appeal courts, combined with the multiple administrative procedures for the licensing of nuclear power plants, provided numerous points of appeal, which activists were able to exploit as a means of delaying nuclear power construction. To the extent that German courts were able to consider substantive questions about both safety and technical feasibility, they tended to assume a powerful and independent, though often contradictory, role in nuclear disputes.[73] In this regard, the 1977 court decision ordering the suspension of work at Brockdorf represented a watershed in the nuclear controversy for it interpreted the safe disposal of nuclear waste as a requirement of West Germany's Atomic Law. On the other hand, while courts were used as a political resource in anti-nuclear campaigns, only on rare occasions can it be argued that the legal system was instrumental in the permanent closure or cancellation of a nuclear facility.

The results of intervention in the administrative and regulatory process were no less ambivalent. We have already seen how little impact British environmental groups had on the recommendations of the Parker Report, despite the carefully researched case they submitted to the Windscale inquiry. The presentation of detailed technical evidence before other planning inquiries had proved no more successful. In the United States, the AEC and in subsequent years the NRC were required by statute to hold construction permit hearings and, on a showing of need, licensing permit hearings. These regulatory agencies were also expected to conduct general hearings on key safety issues. Yet, intervening groups often found that they were denied access to all available documents and information, and lacked the power to subpoena witnesses. A detailed study of three major AEC hearings led the authors to conclude

> that despite lip-service paid to citizen participation in governmental decision-making, agency arrogance, expert elitism, stacked deck proceedings and the consigning of citizens to helplessness before the steamroller of big government are more the rule than the exception.[74]

Similar attempts by the AEC to avoid public scrutiny became evident when, from January 1969 to July 1971, it failed to submit for independent assessment the comprehensive environmental impact statements required by the National Environmental Policy Act, 1969. The AEC was forced to alter its procedures only after a judicial ruling determined that it had been violating the Act.

The tendency of the nuclear bureaucracy to circumvent public scrutiny was even more acute in France. It was not until 1978 that EdF was obliged by law to make an impact study of the environmental effects of the construction of nuclear power plants. The primary purpose of these and complementary safety regulations was simply to allay the public's increasing apprehension about actual or potential damage to the environment. Inevitably, the more stringent safety requirements and the more elaborate institutional controls gave rise to additional licensing and construction delays and to rapidly rising capital costs. As we shall see in a later chapter, the problem of cost escalation coupled with the utilities' difficulties in obtaining the necessary finance were important contributing factors to the marked downturn in the rate of nuclear ordering, which became particularly noticeable in the United States in the second half of the 1970s. Notwithstanding these important but indirect effects, the fact remains that the public dispute about the adequacy of the regulatory framework was not of itself a sufficiently powerful lever to bring about a reappraisal of official nuclear policy, much less a significant change of direction.

Attempts to promote anti-nuclear goals through reliance on the electoral process had also limited national impact. The Swedish experience constitutes at best a partial exception to this proposition. Voting trends in several countries suggests that the anti-nuclear case was most successful in eliciting a favourable response in local and even regional elections, but was generally much less able to intrude into the national arena, where the localised concerns arising from the geographical proximity of nuclear installations were often overridden by 'national' issues as defined by mass political parties and by the mass media. In other words, the efficacy of the electoral strategy was most pronounced at municipal and regional elections, that is, at the periphery of the nuclear decision-making process.

At this point it may be useful to say a brief word about the uneasy relationship between nuclear critics and the classical Left. While anxious to secure the support of working-class parties, whether social democratic, socialist or communist in inspiration, the ecological movement was generally suspicious of them. The decision of ecological groups to enter directly the electoral arena or to call for plebiscites stemmed in large measure from this mistrust. Given their past record, there was little reason to expect that the various political groupings of the Lift, and particularly their leadership, would become champions of the anti-nuclear cause. Far from being in the forefront of environmental consciousness, they remained for the most part wedded to Keynesian or Marxist concepts of economic growth and technological progress. At the same time they persisted with hierarchical forms of organisation which shielded them from grass-roots pressure for policy change. The formal endorsement and practical encouragement given to the nuclear option by the parliamentary leadership of these parties in Britain, France, Germany and Sweden merely served to make the break more complete.

As for links with organised labour, attempts by the anti-nuclear movement to develop a constructive dialogue met with relatively little success in Scandinavia, Western Europe or North America. Trade unionism in these countries was generally reluctant to identify with ecological concerns, and had, in some instances, actively campaigned on behalf of the pro-nuclear lobby. This negative attitude reflects to some extent the acceptance by the working class of the values of the consumerist culture which justifies and reinforces the prevailing mode of production and distribution. Moreover, trade unions and social democratic parties in many capitalist countries have themselves developed over the years close financial and organisational links with corporate industry. It is hardly surprising therefore that in Sweden and West Germany nuclear power programmes should have been enthusiastically implemented by social democratic governments and strongly supported by some of the most powerful unions.

Similarly, in Britain the vast majority of trade unions have vigorously supported nuclear power in the belief that no other alternative could effectively underpin prosperity and job security. From the perspective of the unions directly involved in the power engineering and construction industries any move to scale down or phase out the nuclear energy programme constituted a threat to thousands of jobs. The energy policy adopted in 1977 by the Trade Union Congress endorsed not only 'an expanded and socially acceptable nuclear programme' but also 'the construction of a full-scale demonstration fast breeder reactor . . . and the development of reprocessing facilities at Windscale.' TUC policy, it is true, came under fire from certain sections of the trade union movement – for example, from the Yorkshire miners and white-collar unions – who voiced growing concern about potential hazards to health, long-term environmental pollution, and the security of nuclear installations and materials. However, such dissent and the increasing awareness of the economic promise of energy alternatives were as yet insufficient to modify long-standing official trade union support for nuclear technology.[75]

In France, the attitudes of the two main national union organisations, the communist-oriented Confédération Générale du Travail (CGT) and the socialist-oriented Confédération Française Démocratique du Travail (CFDT) were somewhat more ambivalent. For its part, the CGT, despite periodic criticisms of the role of private, and especially foreign, capital in France's nuclear industry, was basically favourable to the development of nuclear energy.[76] The CFDT, on the other hand, advanced a more comprehensive critique of the government's nuclear plans and made this the basis of a major publication covering the technical, economic and environmental aspects of nuclear energy as well as the working conditions prevailing in the industry.[77] This initiative was soon followed by a call for a three-year moratorium on all nuclear power construction to enable a comprehensive reassessment of all facets of French nuclear planning.[78] But while questioning the rationale, scale and speed of the government's nuclear programme, and supporting certain anti-nuclear demonstrations and protests directed against specific installations (e.g. the La Hague reprocessing plant), the CFDT was careful at all times not to hinder the construction or operation of nuclear facilities and not to identify too closely with the demands of the ecological movement.

Whatever the economic, ideological or organisational factors accounting for the attitudes of trade unions, the inability of anti-nuclear groups to forge a close working relationship with them undoubtedly restricted their political clout and denied them any prospect of industrial action as a means of halting or slowing down the process of nuclearisation. Ironically, many of the unions and unionists most directly involved in the nuclear industry were the very ones who supported most vigorously the drive for nuclear power. Clearly, environmentalists were regarded by many workers as a threat to their jobs and families, and anti-nuclear fervour as arrogant, moralistic and even elitist.[79] It is perhaps the absence of effective co-operation between the ecological movement and organised labour which, more than any other factor, explains the result of the Swedish referendum and the defeat of the nuclear initiatives in California and the other American states. In the event, anti-nuclear campaigns gained widespread public support but could not fully neutralise the industry's effective propaganda about threatened jobs, economic stagnation and 'freezing dark winters'.

As a broad generalisation it would be true to say that, whereas public opinion in western industrial societies showed a pronounced bias in favour of the peaceful use of nuclear energy from the early 1950s to the early 1970s, the degree of opposition rose substantially thereafter. During the earlier phase, the proportion of those strongly or moderately in support of nuclear energy in West Germany was estimated at 70 per cent. By contrast, in the period 1975–8, hard-core support for nuclear power had fallen to 30 per cent; opposition was estimated at 25 per cent, with the remaining 45 per cent either indifferent, undecided, or shifting between the two extremes depending on prevailing political circumstances.[80] A similar pattern emerged in France. Whereas in 1974, nearly three-quarters of the adult population supported in varying degrees the development of nuclear power, by 1977 the proportion had fallen to 50 per cent. By contrast those 'strongly' or 'more or less' opposed had risen from 17 per cent to 41 per cent. Whereas in 1974, 35 per cent of the French population was totally unconcerned by the proximity of a nuclear installation, by 1977 the proportion had fallen to 20 per cent.[81]

The shift in public opinion was especially discernible in Sweden. By 1975, the Swedish Institute of Public Opinion Research found that while a large majority of the population accepted the existing nuclear programme, an equally large majority were against any expansion.[82] Several polls published in subsequent years indicated a strong commitment against nuclear power.[83] Even in Britain, where public opinion had always been solidly in favour of the nuclear power programme, a 1977 survey showed that 32 per cent of the population were now opposed to the building of more nuclear power stations for the production of electricity (49 per cent were in favour and 19 per cent did not know). More significantly, when asked about ways of ensuring future energy supplies, 61 per cent of the respondents favoured doing everything possible to save coal, oil and gas and continue looking for sources of energy other than nuclear power, while only 32 per cent supported the construction of more nuclear power stations.[84] Despite substantial regional variations, public attitudes in the United States point to much the same trend. Whereas most Americans continued to favour the development of nuclear power, the size of the majority was steadily eroded, most conspicuously at a regional level but also nationally. A 1976 national Gallop Poll found that more respondents were opposed than not opposed to the building of a nuclear power plant within five miles of their home.[85]

Although a good number of surveys – both localised, in-depth studies and national opinion polls – have now been conducted in much of the industrialised world, the state of the art does not yet permit detailed or definitive conclusions. On the other hand, if taken in conjunction with the results of elections and plebsicites, they suggest that at the very least the opponents of nuclear power have succeeded in provoking a keenly contested, at times acrimonious, debate which in turn compelled the attention of both mass media and the political process generally. Crucial to this success was the ability of the anti-nuclear movement to highlight the area of significant disagreement within the scientific community and to erode public confidence in the regulatory process. However, once opposition to nuclear power became an established fact of political life and the initial level of support for nuclear energy was substantially eroded, public attitudes appeared to stabilise. Thereafter, a continuing flow towards a more widespread perception of nuclear risks became increasingly difficult to achieve and was, in any case, offset by a counter-flow arising from the perceived economic necessity of the nuclear option. Prolonged exposure to information, in the context of sharply competing claims and counter-claims, tended to produce a saturation effect and a corresponding stalemate in the controversy. Following the substantial inroads already made into the pro-nuclear majority, further large-scale attitude conversion, barring some dramatic but unpredictable event, seemed to depend on the continued politicisation of the conflict.

4 The State and the Crisis of Legitimacy

Since the late 1960s the nuclear power controversy has intruded with increasing frequency and intensity into the political process of most western industrialised societies. Even the traumatic events associated with the 1973 oil crisis and the subsequent attempts to reduce dependence on OPEC oil did not significantly moderate the level of public hostility to nuclear technology. By the mid-1970s, the nuclear issue had succeeded in polarising the body politic to a greater extent than almost any other scientific-technological dispute this century. The only other comparable instance of dissension to have arisen during this period related to the development of nuclear weapons, with which nuclear energy was in any case closely connected, both technically and institutionally. The very breadth and persistence of the oppositional movement complicated the tasks facing nuclear authorities and governments generally. Their decision to proceed with nuclear power programmes of varying magnitude was now under serious challenge.

Particularly debilitating for the state were the divisions which had emerged within the scientific community regarding the assessment of a wide range of nuclear-related risks. Whatever the underlying reasons for these divergent assessments, they deprived the state of the aura of scientific objectivity which had initially contributed to the legitimation of nuclear policy. Equally disconcerting was the progressive erosion of public confidence in the competence and impartiality of the regulatory process. The very secrecy often surrounding the administration of the nuclear programme and the perceived institutional connection between the exercise of supervisory and promotional functions inevitably fuelled public suspicions about the adequacy of safety standards and practices.

But even more fundamental to the socio-cultural crisis unleashed by the nuclear controversy was the lack of ethical consensus as to what constitutes an acceptable level of risk. What number of cancers and diseases, for example, ought society to trade for the economic and technological advantages promised by nuclear energy? What degree of political and economic centralisation should it tolerate in the interests of preserving current patterns of energy consumption? How, in other words, could society formulate an appropriate risk–benefit analysis, and on the basis of what moral principles? The inability of the state to provide universally acceptable answers to these questions was at the heart of the incipient crisis of legitimacy which now confronted it.[1]

Taken to its logical conclusion the lack of societal consensus on the ethics of risk-taking, and the growing polarisation which it implied and encouraged, might, if unchecked, jeopardise the state's capacity to perform the administrative and economic functions needed for the continued viability of the nuclear industry. Apart from its adverse effect on the economic competitiveness of nuclear power, public opposition had already raised the social and political costs associated with nuclear development. To begin with, it had greatly reduced the freedom of action previously available to the institutions responsible for nuclear plans and investments. Not only were such decisions now subjected to much greater public scrutiny, but they were vulnerable to long delays arising from more elaborate bureaucratic procedures and from protracted negotiations, hearings and court cases in which electricity utilities were expected to furnish detailed evaluations of the safety and environmental implications of their respective proposals.

In addition, public resistance to nuclear policy had so raised the temperature of political conflict as to dissuade bureaucrats and politicians alike from the enthusiastic support of nuclear technology which had characterised the earlier period of nuclear power development. Given a much less favourable political environment, nuclear policies could no longer be pursued with the same fixity of purpose. Much greater energy and attention now had to be devoted to the public justification of policy. At the same time, individual politicians and political parties generally, conscious of the electoral risks involved in the aggressive advocacy of nuclear electricity, moderated their public utterances and accepted the need for existing plans to be brought under review. In some countries, the controversy had created such severe strains within government and the political system as a whole that a deliberate slowing down of nuclear expansion was seen as the only realistic remedy.[2]

Yet there were limits to which the state could accommodate the demands or grievances of the opponents of nuclear power without at the same time threatening the survival of the industry. As we have already observed, the nuclear project had, since its inception, depended on extensive and continuous intervention by the state. Its technical and financial resources had played a major part in the initiation of this large and risky undertaking which required long-term commitments to be made long before the competitiveness of nuclear power had been fully demonstrated. Similarly, the state's organisational resources had to be placed at the disposal of the nuclear programme since only the state was capable of the high level of coordination needed to marry the requirements of research establishments, manufacturing firms, regulatory authorities, electricity utilities and financial institutions. The state had thus come to fulfil an indispensable planning function which it could not suddenly relinquish without jeopardising the future viability of the industry.

The coordinating role of the state had assumed added strategic importance because of the highly integrated character of the nuclear fuel cycle. It has always been clearly understood that a nuclear programme could not proceed without adequate fuel supplies and access to the necessary enrichment or heavy water production services. But even after the front end of the nuclear fuel cycle had been established, it soon became apparent that a politically and economically stable industry also required mastery of the back end of the fuel cycle, including spent fuel management and eventual waste disposal. The very interconnectedness of the industry was such that problems in any part of it might affect the viability of the whole. In this sense, public disquiet about any aspect of the nuclear fuel cycle, whether it be the environmental hazards of uranium mining, reactor safety, the effects of low-level radiation, or the dangers of reprocessing and waste storage, might, if allowed to fester, threaten the acceptability of the entire industry. It was the function of the state to reassure the public that the cycle could be safely and effectively closed and to ensure that technical failures or political bottlenecks at any point in the cycle did not lead to the paralysis of the entire project.

THE STATE AS CRISIS MANAGER

The intensification of the nuclear controversy during the 1970s posed an agonising dilemma for the state, for what was at issue was not merely the safety of the technology but the very role of the state as the advocate and promoter of that technology. A significant section of the population was now challenging directly the intimate relationship which had developed between the nuclear industry and the political apparatus of society. In other words, the choice facing the state was whether or not to intervene at the ideological level and, if necessary, whether to make use of its repressive powers in order to safeguard the institutional and financial support it had traditionally extended to the industry. The very attempt to intervene in the public arena was itself problematic for much of the dissent was grounded on ethical considerations which called into question the rationale of state activity. Before proceeding with our analysis it may therefore be useful to delineate the contours of the ethical argument.

An important part of that argument relates to the dispute over low-level radiation. Here we are not so much concerned with the disagreement between the results of the various statistical studies of the effects of low-level radiation as with the ethical assumptions on which public policy is based. In most countries the general requirement governing low-level radiation has been that the permissible radiation exposure for any worker or member of the public should not exceed 5 rem per year or 0.5 rem per year respectively. Even if one accepts the assessment that such radiation exposure would produce only 'negligible' increases in cancers and genetic defects, the fact remains that some damage to human life is generally conceded, although justified by reference to the ensuing economic and technological benefits. Quite apart from the morality of such a trade-off is the fact that the enjoyment of benefits and the burden of carcinogenic or mutagenic risk are unlikely to be shared equally by all members of society. In other words, in so far as radiation policy does not afford equal protection to all citizens, it runs counter to concepts of equal justice and due process for all.[3]

The ethical difficulty posed by the radiation standards which are meant to govern the routine operation of nuclear power stations applies with still greater force to the possibility of major or even minor reactor accidents. For even if one is willing to grant that a certain level of risk to human life and health may be legitimately traded for material benefits, there is still the question as to how equitably the liabilities of such a trade-off will be distributed. The moral dilemma becomes even more acute in the case of radioactive wastes, many of which are extremely hazardous and contain elements whose decay times are measured in hundreds of thousands of years. Here the principle of equity is inextricably connected with the question of knowledge. Until recently the social, economic and ecological costs of waste storage and disposal have not been included within cost–benefit analyses of the nuclear generation of electricity, largely on the grounds that additional information was needed before final decisions could be made on the most suitable form of waste management. Yet the failure to consider such costs, which may be substantial, invalidates any attempt at comparative assessments of alternative energy sources and may lead to public policy based on erroneous calculations of the true costs of nuclear energy.

Also at stake is the principle of equity which requires that the costs of disposing of nuclear wastes should be borne equally by all those who benefit from their production. To the extent that radioactive hazards are long-lived and cumulative, it is members of future generations who are most likely to incur a disproportionate share of the health and financial risks involved. So long as the costs of nuclear waste storage and disposal are not fully known, then, it is not possible to provide adequate compensation for those most likely to be disadvantaged, or to determine whether the energy–equity exchange implicit in nuclear power is ethically justified. But the morality or otherwise of allowing society to be subjected to the hazards of nuclear fission is not only a question of how equitably the hazards are distributed, or how well understood they are, but also a question of whether the danger has been voluntarily accepted by the public. Have all those who are likely to be affected by the decision fully participated in its making? The inequity of risk distribution, the inadequacy of available information, and the lack of citizen participation have been central to the ethical case of the opponents of nuclear power.

Faced with the radical challenge to the basis of its action, the state has vacillated in its response between acceptance of the legitimacy of ethical concerns and attempts to reassert the primacy of technical considerations. The first option carries with it considerable dangers, for if the state were to accept the validity of the case based on principles of equity, knowledge and participation, it might be constrained to reconsider its own policies and to impose restrictions and delays which could well prove fatal to the continued development of the nuclear industry. If, on the other hand, the state refused to enter the arena of normative discourse and sought instead to confine discussion to technical questions, the net effect might well be to accentuate public disenchantment and fan the flames of protest.

This latter course was nevertheless attractive to the state for it held out the possibility that the battle-lines would be drawn on its own terms. Indicative of this general approach was the view repeatedly expounded in official circles that the problems of the nuclear industry should not become the subject of confrontation between exponents of alternative world views. In the words of one civil servant, 'acceptable solutions can only be found if decisions are impartial, prudent and based on strictly *scientific* analysis rather than on a trade-off between the views of *extremists*' (italics added).[4] In this context, it is worth noting that the US Atomic Energy Commission, and later the Nuclear Regulatory Commission, attempted to defuse public controversy by removing generic issues of safety from individual licensing hearings and consigning them to a single national hearing. Such a policy was defended on the grounds that it eliminated 'from the public debate over nuclear energy extraneous arguments which cloud and make meaningful dialogue impossible.'[5] Presumably, the object of the exercise was to insulate the decision-making process from the ethical concerns of local communities, and to establish an institutional framework where the controversy would be reduced to a dispute between technical experts.

The same logic appears to have influenced the ruling of the US Supreme Court in June 1978, which validated the existing statutory limitation on liability in the event of a nuclear accident. The attempt to divorce nuclear power from larger ethical considerations was also reflected in official attitudes to the question of nuclear proliferation. For example, Walter Marshall, later to become Chairman of the UK Atomic Energy Authority, argued in 1978 in defence of the fast breeder reactor by suggesting that once these reactors were fully established, recycling would take place so quickly that plutonium would in effect be continuously inaccessible for nuclear weapons. In any case, the problem of proliferation was essentially political and therefore not intrinsic to the debate about nuclear power.[6]

Yet political institutions could not remain impervious to the ethical dimensions of the anti-nuclear case. For what concerned a significant body of citizens was not merely the nature and extent of the risk, but whether or not the risk should be taken in the first place. In order to give at least token recognition to these concerns, the state was driven towards a variety of compromises designed to blur the issues. Here, it is worth noting that the state did not always speak with one voice. Whereas some institutions (e.g. atomic energy commissions, electricity utilities) might remain unquestioning advocates of nuclear energy, others (e.g. public inquiries, political parties) were at times willing to take a more balanced view of the costs and benefits. But whenever the state, or any of its constituent parts, acted or spoke in a way that conceded the relevance of the normative realm, it inevitably enhanced the legitimacy and intensity of dissent. Faced with such a prospect, the natural reaction of the state apparatus as a whole was to retreat from the ethical argument and to reassert the autonomy of technical expertise.

The development of Swedish nuclear policy after the formation of the Fälldin government in September 1976 provides a fascinating illustration of state vacillation.[7] After several months of indecision, the government gained in April 1977 parliamentary approval for the Nuclear Stipulation Act. The main thrust of the legislation was to make any further expansion of the nuclear power programme dependent on a satisfactory method of waste management. An attempt was thus made to put a brake on the operation of any additional nuclear reactor unless the reactor operator could present an *adequate contract* for the reprocessing of spent fuel and an *absolutely safe* method of disposing of the highly radioactive waste resulting from reprocessing. Significantly, recognition of the normative concept of safety, implicit in the Stipulation Act, was from the outset qualified by the ambiguity surrounding the terms 'adequate contract' and 'absolute safety'.

In December 1977 the Swedish State Power Board applied to the government for permission to operate the Ringhals–3 reactor under the Stipulation Act, and submitted in support of its application a reprocessing contract with the French State Company Cogéma and the first report of the reactor fuel safety (Kärnbränslesäherhet or KBS) project. The report recommended storage of spent fuel in a central facility for up to ten years, reprocessing of the fuel followed by vitrification, sealing of the vitrified waste in steel cylinders, intermediate storage under security watch and cooling for about thirty years, followed by final storage at a depth of 500 metres in a dry, stable, rock formation. After extensive reviews of the application, the government concluded that the conditions of the Stipulation Act had not been satisfied, largely on the grounds that the KBS study had not demonstrated the existence of a site with the necessary rock characteristics for the storage of the vitrified waste. At the same time, the government left open the possibility that the KBS scheme might in future be deemed acceptable should an appropriate site be found, and indicated that henceforth in matters relating to the application of the Stipulation Act the recommendations to be followed would be those of the Swedish Nuclear Inspectorate (SKI), an agency noted for its sympathetic attitude to the nuclear industry.

It would appear, then, that by the time the Fälldin government was forced to resign in October 1978, the stage had been set for a retreat from the spirit if not the letter of the Stipulation Act. In February 1979, the new minority Liberal government received a further submission from the State Power Board claiming that drillings carried out at Sternö in south-east Sweden had shown that a suitable site existed for the disposal of vitrified waste. Of the eight Scandinavian geologists appointed by the SKI to review the KBS study, seven found the proposed repository unsatisfactory and reported accordingly. The Inspectorate's Board, for its part, decided to go against the weight of geological opinion and argued instead that, although the Sternö site might not be a suitable repository for Sweden's entire nuclear programme, it might nevertheless provide adequate storage for the wastes generated by the two reactors in question. Taking advantage of this conclusion, the government gave approval under the Stipulation Act for the two new reactors, Ringhals-3 and Forsmark-1, to enter into operation, although implementation of the decision was to be deferred until June 1980.

We have described this sequence of events in some detail because it illustrates rather graphically the way in which the state (not only the political parties, but the nuclear bureaucracy and the State Power Board) had succeeded in redefining what was essentially an ethical choice as a technical issue. The function of the Stipulation Act had thus been to convert the Centre Party's generalised critique of nuclear power into a set of specific technical deficiencies, which were further reduced to the problem of high level waste management. The KBS study was therefore perceived as a technical solution to a technical problem. While the proposed solution was at first found to be deficient and rejected by experts and politicians alike, it was nevertheless expected that the further application of technique would in due course supply the appropriate technical fix. Once the problem had been formulated in these terms, it was only a matter of time before the locus of decision-making reverted from the wider political arena back to the inner confines of the bureaucratic apparatus.

The actual strategies adopted by each state in response to the ethical challenge posed by anti-nuclear activism varied considerably from country to country. A critical factor in all cases was the distribution of power in the political system, that is, the degree of centralisation in the exercise of state authority. As a broad generalisation, it would appear that where the state apparatus operated as a cohesive, well-coordinated, monolithic entity faithfully reflecting the interests of a dominant power group, its actions tended to dismiss the relevance of normative considerations and to reinforce the supremacy of technical rationality. Where, on the other hand, the political system was open to geographical or institutional fragmentation, either because regional or local government had significant decision-making powers or because the judiciary or legislature retained a measure of independence from the executive, groups at the periphery had greater opportunity to make their voices heard and to contest the basic assumptions underlying the exercise of central authority. For example, the fragmentation of responsibility over siting decisions and the corresponding role of regional and local government were much more evident in West Germany, Sweden and the United States than in France, the UK or Brazil. Similarly, the relative autonomy of the courts in West Germany and the United States appears to have provided the opponents of nuclear power with an important lever for intruding the ethical dimension of their case into the political process.

Another important and closely connected factor governing the state's handling of the nuclear controversy was the division between the public and private sectors in the organisation of the nuclear industry. Again as a broad generalisation, it would seem that those countries which came closest to the private-ownership model (e.g. US, West Germany) are those were the state had most difficulty in neutralising public disaffection, whereas countries tending towards a high level of state ownership in the nuclear and electricity supply industries (e.g. France, UK) appear to have been less vulnerable to the criticisms and demands of the anti-nuclear movement. The evidence suggests that, at least in the short and medium terms, the national nuclear programmes which have most effectively withstood the challenge of dissent are those which have benefited from the support of a highly centralised state power structure that is able to allocate resources with minimal regard to the views of the periphery, and from the active involvement of state-owned enterprises in different stages of the nuclear fuel cycle which thus develop a direct stake in the generation of nuclear electricity.

A less easily definable but none the less significant variable in the equation has been the character of the prevailing political culture which has often influenced the modality and efficacy of state intervention. Particularly relevant in this regard is the focus of collective loyalties. At one end of the spectrum are those societies characterised by a highly developed and pervasive sense of national allegiance, and at the other end those in which communalist and regionalist sentiment represent a much stronger pole of attraction. Needless to say, none of the six countries under review fits neatly into either category. On the other hand, it would seem that the ideological defence of nuclear programmes has been most effective where it has successfully linked in the public mind the commercial development of nuclear technology with pre-existing notions of *national* pride or *national* independence. Similarly, it can be argued that the legitimating function of the state has been greatly facilitated by the psychology of the growth cult and the syndrome of rising material expectations to which it gave rise. Public acceptance of nuclear energy was thus directly related to the state's ability to reduce the nuclear debate to one of economic living standards, where the principal question became not which life-styles were most compatible with human or ecological values, but which particular mix of energy fuels was most likely to encourage a specified level of capital investment, credit expansion and consumer purchasing power. This reductionist approach was particularly appealing in countries such as France, where the relative absence of indigenous energy sources could be expected to strengthen the argument based on national economic security.

FORMS OF STATE INTERVENTION

Thus far the discussion of the options available to the state in the performance of its legitimating function has concentrated on the problems posed for it by the normative thrust of the anti-nuclear case

It is worth remembering, however, that the complex and diverse apparatus of the state has at its disposal several instruments for intervention which have, in fact, been used with varying degrees of success to influence the outcome, and even to pre-empt the full maturation, of the nuclear controversy. Four such instruments have been especially important and merit closer consideration. They are the control of information, the manipulation of emotive symbols, the encouragement of civic privatism, and the use of coercive techniques.

Because of its long-standing and intimate connection with the development of nuclear technology in both its military and civilian application, the state has traditionally enjoyed privileged and in some instances monolithic access to nuclear information. It has been able to determine in very large measure what technical knowledge and even what economic and sociological studies would be disclosed. A variety of arguments, usually based on notions of military security, commercial confidentiality and political convention, have been used to justify this practice. Whatever the underlying motive, it is clear that on numerous occasions the agencies of the state have deliberately withheld information or else released information that was either inaccurate or selective.[8]

Nuclear authorities have generally been reluctant to publish all information relevant to the licensing of nuclear reactors. Even in the United States, where a substantial amount of information has been made available for public scrutiny, there are several categories of data that have been routinely denied to the public by the Atomic Energy Commission and its successor, the Nuclear Regulatory Commission. These have included analyses, recommendations and internal memoranda dealing with such matters as evaluations of the safety features of a particular reactor as compared with other reactors, and reports of inspection visits to reactor manufacturers and suppliers. The suppression of information may be aimed at concealing the substantial conflict of opinion that often exists within the regulatory agency, thereby depriving interveners in the licensing process of the technical basis on which to mount their challenge to the reactor proposal.[9] It has also been claimed that research results and safety evaluations have often been suppressed simply because they were deemed potentially embarrassing. Researchers are said to have been dissuaded from incorporating their views in written material or even from disseminating opinions within the agency which might contradict official positions or might reveal negligence and breaches of existing regulations.[10] Even where employees were resentful of this form of internal censorship, they nevertheless refrained from speaking out 'for fear of harassment, reprisals or loss of their jobs'.[11]

The same pressures appear to have operated at German nuclear research establishments and to have severely restricted the flow of information. The appeal of several scientists at the Karlsruhe Nuclear Research Centre and other institutes against the censorship imposed on them suggests that these restrictive regulations may have been designed not merely to safeguard technical secrets but to prevent employees from disseminating critical attitudes on nuclear energy. In the case of Brazil, an official investigation is reported to have found evidence of negligence in connection with a fire which broke out during the construction of the first Brazilian reactor. The Brazilian Atomic Energy Commission apparently tried to conceal the nature of the incident and to extract from a number of engineers a favourable report on the safety precautions applying at the plant prior to the accident.[12]

But the attempt to conceal has not been confined to questions of technical safety. It has been equally evident in relation to threatened or actual acts of nuclear malevolence and, in particular, to instances of illicit diversion of various quantities of strategic nuclear materials.[13] Here again the motive behind the secrecy has probably to do as much with the desire to allay public anxiety as with the need to maintain effective security. In Britain, sensitive information relating to nuclear security is subject to the system of D notices. More importantly, under the Offical Secrets Act, release of even trivial information about a nuclear facility by an employee to an outsider may be treated as a punishable offence.[14] As a result of these legal barriers and the internal regulations of the Atomic Energy Authority nuclear policy has become surrounded by a wall of secrecy which even the most persistent complaints of individual parliamentarians have found it difficult to penetrate.[15]

Of course, the ban on information has never been absolute. Even in France where disclosure of information has been rigidly controlled, nuclear authorities have made available a good number of facts and opinions, although invariably these have been carefully presented under the guise of scientific objectivity to convey an image of an industry that is benign, efficient, and essential to economic well-being. In other words, the object of such information has been to justify, rationalise and pacify rather than to inform or provoke critical inquiry. Traditionally there has been little opportunity, even for scientists, to obtain precise details of proposed nuclear sites or of planned nuclear facilities. This situation was largely the product of the pronounced bias towards secrecy favoured by EdF, government ministers and the administrative authorities.[16] It was not until 1975 that the government finally conceded the legitimacy of public anxiety, and that M. D'Ornano, Minister of Industry and Research, acknowledged the need for a wide-ranging information campaign.[17] But the establishment of information offices and other consultation mechanisms, including the Electronuclear Energy Information Council, was simply an attempt to explain and gain support for decisions already taken.[18] As for the elaborate brochures, slides, films and other resources produced by the CEA and EdF, they amounted to little more than a lavish public relations exercise.

Although couched in the language of dialogue, more or less the same unidirectional approach characterised the West German government's response to increasing public anxiety.[19] In a bid to reassure, an extensive information campaign was launched in 1975 with the aid of free brochures, information kits and saturation newspaper and television advertising. A somewhat more open-ended educational programme had been instituted in Sweden in 1974. It was based largely on the long-standing study circle method and managed by a variety of adult education associations connected with political parties, trade unions, religious groups and other community organisations. By the end of 1974, it was estimated that some 7000 study groups had been formed with the participation of some 100,000 Swedes.[20] In Britain, while no attempt was made to launch educational campaigns of the type conducted on the continent, Anthony Wedgwood Benn, who was Secretary of State for Energy between 1975 and 1979, consistently stressed his wish to adopt 'policies of the greatest possible openness, disclosing and publishing all information that Parliament or the people wish to have, and listening most attentively to the debates that then centre around that disclosure.'[21] In keeping with this policy he initiated a major public debate on the reprocessing question, gave the Commons details of a radioactive leak which had occurred at Windscale, and, subsequent to the Flowers Commission Report, published a list of nineteen questions he had addressed to the Nuclear Installations Inspectorate. The Flowers Report had itself widened the scope of public debate by drawing attention to the risk of nuclear terrorism and more generally to the dangers inherent in the plutonium economy.

Whatever their underlying intention, these government-inspired initiatives, including those that actively cultivated a two-way communicative process, did little to eliminate confusion or reduce concern over risks. More often than not they merely endowed the nuclear controversy with greater public visibility and contributed to the politicisation of the issue. On the other hand, attempts to withhold information or limit the opportunities for public debate were in the long term likely to erode the credibility of nuclear policy-makers. Governments and state instrumentalities had therefore to balance carefully the administrative advantages derived from information control with the ideological disadvantages that might result from the declining legitimacy of the decision-making process.

But the attempt to influence public attitudes was not purely a function of informational strategies. The state was also intent on eliciting a positive response to its nuclear policies by associating them in the public consciousness with established societal objectives, in particular the twin goals of economic growth and national self-reliance. Frequent reference has already been made to the concepts of energy independence, security of electricity supplies and economic living standards which provided the ideological rationale for the official defence of nuclear power programmes. In France, senior CEA officials went so far as to argue that nuclear energy was an essential instrument in the fight against inflation.[22] To the extent that nuclear electricity had a cost advantage over fossil fuels, it could be expected to bring about a reduction in average energy costs. The trend, it was claimed, would be reinforced by the introduction of fast breeders which would ensure the diminishing importance of fuel costs in the energy equation and make the costs of electricity almost entirely dependent on the technical and economic performance of power stations. Moreover, the increasing substitution of oil by nuclear energy would significantly reduce the oil bill, thereby improving the balance of payments, and at the same time moderate inflationary pressures on the economy.

The economic arguments adduced to justify nuclear expansion did not differ greatly from country to country. In virtually every instance, the same stress was placed on the beneficial impact of the nuclear industry on the level of economic activity, availability of jobs and satisfaction of consumer wants. The only slight variations introduced into the argument were those made necessary by the particular economic or energy conditions obtaining in a given country. In Brazil, for example, the development of the industry was portrayed as a sign of the country's growing technological maturity, while opposition to it was likened to protests at the end of the century against a national campaign to innoculate the Brazilian public against yellow fever.

But in time crude appeals to economic and technological progress and to national prestige and security were refined in the light of a more sophisticated analysis of public perceptions. The issue of nuclear power was increasingly treated as 'a problem of public relations – not in the crude sense of merely trying to inform people but in the more important sense of trying to understand why people think as they do and *of trying to help them towards a more rational approach to the problems of the modern world*' (italics added).[23] In order to explain the failure of past publicity campaigns and formulate more effective strategies for blunting the success of anti-nuclear protests, efforts were now made to utilise all the conventional techniques of motivation study as well as the new methods of socio-psychological investigation. Accordingly, the Battelle Institute was commissioned by the West German Ministry of the Interior in July 1975 to investigate popular attitudes to different kinds of energy production.[24] Since then a good deal of research has been conducted in the field of risk-perception, including studies by the IAEA Risk Assessment Group in Vienna.[25] The aim of this research was to determine the factors shaping public attitudes, including sources and content of information, motivational patterns, belief-systems, demographic and social characteristics. It was not unreasonable to assume that buried beneath the academic presentation of many of these studies was a hidden agenda which included the elaboration of new psychological strategies capable of deflecting anxieties about nuclear risks and neutralising the intellectual and emotional appeal of the anti-nuclear case.

Enough will have been said to indicate a third important function performed by the state, namely that of maintaining the ideological and organisational unity of the nuclear industrial complex while at the same time undermining the cohesion of oppositional elements. It was the task of the state – especially those segments of it most closely identified with the industry – to ensure the atomisation of society into individual citizens and to represent itself as the political expression of an all-inclusive common good or 'national interest'. This was to be accomplished by the political and legal institutions of the liberal state which would create the impression of equality, fair play and due process, and through the promise of material rewards – variously expressed in terms of money, leisure, comfort or security – the effect of which would be to transform political conflict into a series of skirmishes between narrow economic interest groups. In order to deny the legitimacy of the anti-nuclear case, it was thus necessary for the state to invoke the democratic basis of its authority and to have recourse to the resources of consultation and co-option.

In the United States, the principle of public participation was enshrined in the 1954 Atomic Energy Act which required that, when 'granting, suspending, revoking or amending... any license or construction permit [for a nuclear power reactor]... the Commission shall grant a hearing upon the request of any person whose interest may be affected by the proceeding, and shall admit any person as a party to such proceeding.' Subsequent amendments to this law changed the circumstances but not the fact of public participation in the licensing process. The requirement for public hearings on reactor licence applications was seen as the most effective method of assuring the public that reactors would indeed be safe. Nevertheless, several obstacles were placed in the path of the intervener. For one thing, he was given rather short notice prior to the beginning of the hearing and therefore relatively little time in which to acquaint himself with the technical complexities of the case. Moreover, he was seldom furnished with the full details of the licence application, and even the Commission's own evaluation was often not made publicly available in its entirety until after the hearing had begun. Finally, the right to intervene was limited to those whose case was related to the radiation and safety hazards of nuclear energy. Larger social and environmental concerns were excluded from consideration until the 1971 Calvert Cliffs court decision which required the AEC, in accordance with the National Environment Policy Act, to make an independent and case-by-case assessment of the total environmental impact of every nuclear facility for which it was asked to issue a permit or licence.[26]

In France, where participatory institutions were much less developed, little attempt was made to establish a process of consultation until 1975. Indeed, it was only after the announcement in 1974 of a major acceleration in the nuclear programme that the decision was made to consult with regional and local authorities. Several ministerial statements now suggested that the government had no intention of imposing its nuclear policies against the wishes of the elected representatives of any region. It was even promised that details of government plans would be widely disseminated and submitted to the Parliament for its approval.[27] The government could afford to adopt this stance since its policies were assured in advance of a solid parliamentary majority. Here the state was apparently contributing to politicisation of the controversy, but on its own terms. Rather than provide a vehicle for the political expression of dissent, it was seeking to confront such dissent with the legitimacy of the democratic process, a task in which it was greatly assisted by the unfamiliarity of most Deputies with the complexities of the issue.

In contrast to the French experience, the British nuclear programme gradually lost much of its earlier momentum, but the relatively closed character of the decision-making process remained virtually intact until the mid-1970s. Increasing unease about the possible dangers of the plutonium economy, coupled with the more sympathetic disposition of certain Labour ministers to the concept of open government, eventually set the stage for the Windscale inquiry, which was to provide the best opportunity yet for public involvement in a major and sensitive nuclear decision. The official report of that inquiry published in March 1978 proved nevertheless a great disappointment to all parties that had objected to the BNFL proposal.[28] Not only did Mr Justice Parker's recommendations accept the BNFL case in its entirety,[29] but they were widely interpreted as a one-sided presentation of the arguments placed before him. The Report failed, it was claimed, to mention the major witnesses and key proposals of the opposition and did not even take cognisance of the exhaustive evidence and cross-examination through which they had sought to demonstrate that reprocessing did not reduce waste management problems and indeed seemed likely to aggravate them.[30]

Particularly unconvincing to objectors and independent observers alike was the Report's treatment of the proliferation question and especially its conclusion that 'a refusal to accept foreign fuel would be in breach of the spirit if not the letter of the NPT.'[31] Yet for all the criticisms of bias levelled against the Report, including the professional standing of the inspector's two assessors, the fact remains that the establishment of the inquiry was essentially a political initiative designed to produce a desired political result. It is not without significance that Mr Justice Parker should have given as one of the principal reasons for his decision the need 'to keep the nuclear industry alive and able to expand should expansion be required'. The development of a reprocessing industry was an important element of the government's nuclear policy, and the inquiry was established with the firm expectation that it would find in favour of BNFL. The appointment of the inspector and his technical advisers was no doubt intended to ensure an orthodox, and to that extent predictable, assessment of the questions before them. Once, Mr Justice Parker had released his conclusions and recommendations, government and parliamentary ratification was little more than a formality.[32]

In Germany, a somewhat different pattern emerged with the courts playing a far more prominent role. The operation of the judiciary, which reflects the more decentralised character of the German political system, was the most useful political lever available to anti-nuclear groups. Certain provisions of the Atomic Law, and particularly amendments made to it in 1976, considerably increased the possibilities for judicial interpretation by making the industrial use of nuclear energy subject to the interpretation of constitutional principles. In this regard, one of the landmark decisions was that made in 1972 by the Supreme Administrative Court which ruled that in the list of objectives specified by the Atomic Law safety must take precedence over economic development and promotion of nuclear technology. Equally significant was the 1976 amendment which made the licensing of a nuclear installation conditional on the introduction of the most stringent safety precautions.

Having been assigned the task of evaluating substantive questions of safety and the limits of technology, German judges took advantage of the wide margin of interpretation open to them to deliver rulings increasingly critical of nuclear policy. Such rulings, however, were far from uniform. Whereas in decisions given at Krümmel and Stade in 1973 and 1974 respectively judges upheld the Immediate Effect Orders requested by the licensing authorities, in 1975 the Freiburg lower court ruling on Wyhl revoked the Order. Within a few years lower courts had ordered the suspension of work on several nuclear power stations for a variety of reasons, including insufficient cooling capacity, insufficiently detailed plans, and above all unsatisfactory proposals for the disposal of nuclear wastes. The 1977 Brockdorf decision was especially significant for it was explicitly based on the long-term problem of waste disposal – an interpretation of the Atomic Law which was subsequently upheld by the administrative appeals court.

The precedent, it is true, set by the Brockdorf and other rulings was not universally followed. For example, the Würzburg administrative court sustained the construction permit for the Grafenrheinfeld nuclear power plant by arguing that considerations based on worst-case risks and the adequacy of waste diposal techniques were not within the scope of the court's discretion.[33] Yet, despite the unpredictability of the German courts, the process of near–endless ligitation greatly increased the costs of nuclear power construction and significantly slowed down the pace of development. In a bid to overcome these legal obstacles, the proponents of nuclear projects explored several avenues, including challenges to the constitutionality of the Atomic Law, attempts to limit or at least rationalise the interpretative powers of the courts, proposals for more direct parliamentary responsibility over nuclear licensing.

The dilemma confronting the liberal state, torn between the implementation of nuclear policies on the one hand and the legitimation of those policies on the other, was nowhere more acutely experienced than in Sweden. It was the inability to reconcile these two conflicting tasks within the confines of the conventional political process that finally precipitated the decision in favour of a referendum. Such a decision necessarily carried with it the risk that the third option listed on the ballot paper, which called for the phasing out of Sweden's nuclear power programme within ten years, might in fact succeed. Several factors, however, could be expected to minimise that risk. Apart from the confusion created by listing three options rather than a straight yes–no choice, the opponents of nuclear power were placed at a considerable disadvantage. Although they conducted a vigorous campaign and even received modest financial assistance from the state, they could not begin to match the resources available to institutions favouring the continued expansion of Sweden's nuclear power programme. These included the vast majority of Sweden's newspapers, almost the entire business sector (which established an energy information service for the exclusive purpose of conducting a multi-million advertising campaign), the two largest trade union federations (the Swedish Trade Union Confederation and the Central Organisation of Salaried Employees), and many of the higher echelons of the scientific and technological community.[34]

The importance attached to technical expertise was well illustrated with the setting up of two investigative committees. The Committee on Nuclear Reactor Safety was to carry out a technical examination of the events leading up to the Three Mile Island accident, make safety comparisons with Swedish reactors, and recommend measures to improve safety. The other committee had the task of evaluating the consequences of rapidly phasing out the nuclear power programme. Both committees submitted their reports in November 1979, in good time to influence the conduct of the referendum campaign. The function of the reactor safety report was to calm public fears by giving Sweden's reactors a clean bill of health, while at the same time recommending a long list of technical improvements. As for the consequences committee, its main finding was that a ten-year phasing out of the present six reactors compared with a programme incorporating twelve reactors running for twenty five years would cost an additional $18,000 million. The study also concluded that an increased use of coal would lead to greater acidification of water and soil, and other kinds of pollution. The report thus provided an authoritative case for those political parties favouring continued nuclear expansion. The argument for or against nuclear power had now become considerably more complex, and was in any case transformed into a debate about alternative energy futures predicated on varying degrees of reliance on nuclear power and operating within varying time-frames.

It remains to say a word about political parties, for in most liberal democratic states they retained a major role in the performance of both administrative and legitimating functions. It is not without significance that in the Swedish referendum, the 'yes' case was supported by the Conservatives, Liberals and Social Democrats, whereas only two parties, the Centre Party and the relatively small Communist Party, identified with the 'no' case. The Swedish experience was not untypical. A clear pro-nuclear bias characterised the attitudes of virtually all Conservative parties, whether in Europe or the United States. Significantly, most large Social Democratic parties were also favourably disposed towards the development of nuclear power. Sharp divisions, it is true, did emerge within Social Democratic ranks, particularly in Austria, Switzerland, Denmark, Norway, Sweden and West Germany, but the parliamentary leadership of those parties was generally successful in steering a pro-nuclear course. As for the powerful Communist parties of Italy, France and Spain, they too were supportive of the nuclear option, although they normally married such support to a demand for complete or partial nationalisation of their country's nuclear programme. It was generally left to minority parties occupying the middle ground or the Left of the political spectrum (e.g. the Centre and Communist parties in Sweden, Free Democrats in West Germany, the Liberals in Britain, and the PSU in France) to adopt more explicitly anti-nuclear policies. This pattern of alignments effectively denied the opponents of nuclear power any prospect of securing a parliamentary majority.

The natural inclination of most political parties – particularly when in government – was to ignore the nuclear controversy, at least initially, and to rely on the expert advice of government departments and nuclear research establishments. Even when significant sympathy developed within its own ranks for the concerns of the anti-nuclear movement, the large party tended to translate ecological and ideological issues into technical problems and to dissociate itself from overt political action. Until compelled by the pressure of events to do otherwise, it was content to pursue a strategy of depoliticisation. A 'centripetal political culture', it has been argued, mediated through overlapping leadership and other structural connections between parties and major interest groups (corporations, farmers' organisations, trade unions, and professional associations) prevented the articulation of policies that ran against the prevailing ideology or the will of the dominant élites.[35] The monopoly of expertise enjoyed by the administrative bureaucracies, the close links between government and the corporate sector, and the electoral risks entailed in deviating from consensus politics all tended to push the major parties towards depoliticisation of the nuclear issue. Such pressures became especially acute as parties moved closer to the exercise of governmental power. The tendency has thus been for the locus of nuclear decision-making to shift from legislatures and political parties to the bureaucratic agencies of the state.

In Brazil, where political parties and the electoral process were virtually paralysed by the 1964 military *coup*, the intervention of the state was mediated principally through public firms and regulatory agencies which expressed the uneasy alliance between the technocracy and the military.[36] The solidity of that alliance and its acceptability to domestic and foreign capital depended largely on its ability to create conditions of social stability and economic growth.

The political dominance of the military, however, and the implementation of their nuclear policies necessitated an authoritarian form of decision-making from which not only the underprivileged stratum of society but all dissenting groups were excluded. Indeed, all scientific, business and environmental organisations opposed to the nuclear accord with West Germany were accused by the state of colluding with foreign interests or at least of acting in a manner contrary to the national interest. These tactics failed to silence the opposition. With the increasing stagnation of the Brazilian economy and mounting pressures for more rapid democratisation, public mistrust of Brazil's ambitious nuclear plans became more widespread and part of a larger challenge to the prevailing model of economic development. In so far as the German–Brazilian deal favoured the penetration of foreign capital, the state, despite the bureaucracy's claim to efficient and modern planning, was increasingly perceived as the agent of dependency and denationalisation.[37]

Once the prevailing system of cultural control was broken or appeared threatened, there was a tendency for the state, whether authoritarian or liberal in character, to employ more openly coercive techniques. Attempts to silence or harass the critics of nuclear power have included massive police and paramilitary mobilisation against demonstrators, surveillance of the leaders of the protest movement, and the illegal installation of listening devices in the homes of nuclear scientists. Recourse to extreme security measures became commonplace in West Germany where several demonstrations occasioned the involvement of military troops, use of helicopters dropping tear gas, and the stationing of tanks, armoured vehicles and water cannons. Even in peaceful rallies, security police were accused of intimidating participants by taking photographs and by conducting extensive stop-and-search operations. This latter tactic is estimated to have prevented some 10,000 demonstrators from reaching a rally organised in September 1977 in protest against the construction of the Kalkar prototype fast breeder reactor.[38]

Even more dramatic was the use of force by the French riot control police (Compagnie Républicaine de Sécurité) who responded to the attempted occupation of the breeder reactor site at Creys–Malville in 1977 by a series of baton charges and the use of rifle-launched tear gas and percussion grenades.[39] The purpose of these harassing tactics was not merely to prevent protesters from achieving their immediate objective but to help discredit the entire protest movement. The very presence of a large police force at a demonstration could, with the willing co-operation of the mass media, help to create the impression that demonstrators were dangerous or guilty of miscounduct. To the extent that violence and arrests ensued that impression was greatly reinforced. But the resulting climate of fear and suspicion served another purpose: it alarmed demonstrators themselves and sowed divisions between moderate and more militant elements of the anti-nuclear movement.

A more subtle form of pressure, particularly in West Germany, was applied by labelling anti-nuclear activists as 'communist subversives' or by associating them in the public mind with terrorist activities. In this way, the authorities hoped to undermine the legitimacy of the opposition and in turn legitimise the increased application of social controls. In January 1979, it became known that the West German Bureau of Criminal Investigation had, since June 1977, been registering all persons who took part in the preparation of 'violent demonstrations'. As a precautionary measure in the fight against terrorism such a method of registration amounted to constant and automatic surveillance, for each time that a registered person was checked by the authorities at a border crossing, an airport, or traffic control point, information about the place, time and any accompanying person would be fed into the computer and added to the data already stored about this person.[40] Apart from directly monitoring the activities of the leadership of the movement, police also carried out general surveillance of citizen action groups by evaluating their publications, registering the names of those disseminating information in public places, registering the licence plate numbers of cars parked in the vicinity of anti-nuclear meetings, photographing demonstrations, infiltrating and observing meetings, tapping telephones, and intercepting mail.

The intimidatory effect of these measures was compounded in West Germany's case with the introduction in 1972 of the *Berufsvertbot* legislation, which allowed for state employees to be placed under surveillance or investigation. If, in the opinion of the Offices for the Protection of the Constitution, an employee was acting against the constitution then, unless he could prove otherwise, he would be liable to the termination of his employment. Civil servants, teachers and academics were particularly vulnerable to this system of surveillance. According to Dr Andreas Dress, a leading campaigner against academic 'Berufsverbot', as at the end of 1978 there were some 4000 cases of investigation carried out under this law. Many of those under investigation were either denied legal assistance or given access to it only after long delays. So intense was the government's commitment to the legislation that it was prepared to spend some DM 70 million in a publicity campaign to justify the existence and enforcement of the law.[41] Activities deemed to warrant investigation included participation in demonstrations, writing for supposedly subversive magazines, and association with anyone considered to be subversive. In confirming the constitutionality of this law, the German courts had firmly established the principle which required the civil servant to act as the absolute servant of the state.[42]

From this brief survey it emerges that state intervention oscillated frequently and often abruptly from reliance on confrontational and coercive tactics to emphasis on democratic procedures and consensual decision-making, as neither of these strategies was entirely successful in resolving the problem of legitimation. At various points in the controversy, the West German state asserted the maintenance of law and order to be its overriding task, and raised the spectre of terrorism perhaps in order to justify its own recourse to violence as it struggled to preserve its authority in the face of mounting dissent. The events at Malville in July 1977 demonstrated that the violence of the nuclear state and the consequent erosion of civil liberties was by no means an exclusively German phenomenon. A coercive strategy, however, if taken to extreme lengths, would in the long run accentuate the crisis of legitimacy. So long as the anti-nuclear movement retained close affinity with significant sections of the community, then the overt use of force to restrict its effectiveness might simply serve to expose the undemocratic structure of the state and bring its activities under greater public scrutiny. It would, in other words, contribute to the politicisation of the nuclear issue by raising far-reaching questions about the legitimacy not merely of nuclear policy but of the entire political process.

A somewhat less risky approach, and one more in keeping with the self-proclaimed ideology of the liberal state, was to explore the possibilities of participation and to move some way towards stricter enforcement of safety and environmental regulations. Such a conciliatory attitude might help to moderate the stridency of oppositional demands, reduce the level of public anxiety and thereby limit the stimulus for mass protest. Despite its obvious appeal, the strategy was nevertheless fraught with difficulties in its conception and xecution. If, on the one hand, the concessions to be offered were to e minimal, then the contradiction implicit in such a gesture would oon become apparent. The pro-nuclear bias of the state would be onfirmed and the vigour of the anti-nuclear campaign intensified. If, n the other hand, the policy of co-option involved more substantive hanges, for example extensive public intervention in the decision-naking process, the net result might be to legitimise the critique of uclear power and erode the capacity of the state to provide the ndustry with effective administrative and financial support. The nore nuclear planners subjected themselves to the pressure of pposing claims and interests the more likely it was that the strain on he planning process would lead to virtual paralysis. Moreover, in ttempting to satisfy the demand for legitimation, the administrative pparatus would become increasingly vulnerable to conservative esistance which would in turn restrict the degree of innovation ossible. As Habermas would argue, for the state to open the door to videspread participation in nuclear decision-making was 'a risky neans of meeting legitimation deficits'.[43]

Alternatively, the state sought on several occasions to overcome he problem of legitimation by offering material rewards compatible vith technocratic requirements. The difficulty with such a solution temmed from the discrepancy between promise and performance. More jobs, increased purchasing power and greater comfort were not easily achievable in conditions of stagflation and, in any case, the contribution of nuclear energy to the achievement of such goals was ikely to be problematic at a time of rapidly rising capital costs and changing patterns of energy supply and demand. Such promises were therefore as likely to aggravate as to relieve the legitimation crisis for they raised expectations which the nuclear technocracy might not be able to satisfy. The problem became doubly acute when expectations were raised – especially in relation to health, physical security and protection of the environment – which simply could not be accommodated within the framework of available rewards.

Lacking a consistent and successful strategy for the performance of its administrative and legitimating functions, the state was transformed into an arena of conflict.[44] It had to provide and organise the elaborate and multi-faceted infrastructure required by the different stages of the nuclear fuel cycle. Simultaneously, it had to respond to a popular movement increasingly capable of articulating its objectives, mobilising in support of them, and asserting its participatory rights.

In order that the new participants in nuclear decision-making should not obstruct the pre-ordained allocation of resources, they were granted only restricted or conditional access. These conditions included disavowal of any use of force or act of civil disobedience, exclusion of critical normative discourse, agreement to abide by the rules of the game, and acceptance of the declining importance of legislatures.

Yet for all these conflicting pressures, and perhaps because of them, the state retained a measure of autonomy and was able to offer anti-nuclear campaigns a wider scope of action than might otherwise have been the case. Court rulings in West Germany and the United States, the Swedish referendum, the decision of the Lower Saxony government not to proceed with the Gorleben reprocessing scheme, and even the Windscale inquiry were so many illustrations of the gains made by the opposition to nuclear power and of the price the state had to pay in the pursuit of legitimation. The very attempt to protect the long-term interests and functional unity of the nuclear industry had placed the liberal democratic state in a contradictory position. The required allocation of resources necessitated the expanded use of the repressive instruments of state power, yet the capacity to do so was severely limited by the need to maintain legitimacy.

In the face of conflicting demands, the state had but one alternative, that is, to manipulate not only the material but ideological resources of society, hence the attempt to fashion a political culture based on economic individualism and political mass conformity.[45] In the nuclear context, the state was obliged to allocate vast resources in order to persuade the public that nuclear technology was the answer to the 'energy crisis', to the 'fear of not having enough', and that only technical expertise rather than ethical preference offered the basis for such a solution. But the ideological manipulation of perceived scarcity was by no means assured of success for, over and above the harsh economic realities, it had to contend with the growth of a mass movement capable of appealing to deep-seated fears and emotions, intent on widening and transforming the cognitive and normative dimensions of social interaction.

5 The Impact of Recession

The political obstacles encountered by national nuclear programmes during the 1970s were greatly accentuated, and in a sense mirrored, by the recession prevailing in most western economies. With a few notable exceptions, the anticipated impetus from the oil crisis either did not materialise or proved short-lived. The ensuing years saw higher levels of inflation, higher interest rates, reductions in public spending and more sustained efforts at energy conservation. All these factors were inimical to nuclear expansion. In most cases assumptions about the future role of nuclear electricity and the economic foundations on which they rested proved unfounded or premature. Rising capital costs, patchy technical performance and growing political opposition severely tarnished the image of the nuclear industry. As for the fast breeder reactor (FBR) its prospects were greatly diminished as a result of the slow growth in the demand for uranium, the high costs of R & D, and increasing apprehension about the dangers of the plutonium economy. This is not to say that all these factors were equally evident or that they produced the same outcome in all countries. Attempts, for example, to reconsider the funding of FBR development were often resisted by powerful lobbies enjoying privileged access to the decision-making process.

Possibly the single most important factor governing nuclear power development in many parts of the western world, especially since 1974, has been the declining rate of electricity growth. Reduced forecasts of electricity demand were themselves a reflection of the slower growth in energy demand which in turn resulted both from improvements in energy efficiency and the general downturn in economic activity. As a consequence many utilities were faced with substantial over-capacity in their grids, which ambitious construction programmes could only exacerbate. The readjustment of construction schedules and more importantly the slump in the nuclear ordering rate were in no small measure a response to these perceived trends. Another contributing factor was the rapid upward movement of capital costs which was itself the product of more elaborate regulatory procedures, lengthening lead times, more stringent safety requirements and higher interest rates. Electricity utilities thus had to operate in an economic environment which threatened both profitability and the capacity to finance investment programmes. The unpredictability of future energy demand coupled with rising capital costs and government restrictions on increases in electricity tariffs could not but undermine the industry's confidence in its own investment plans.

Any decision on the part of electricity utilities to reconsider their commitment to nuclear power was in turn bound to have far-reaching repercussions on the reactor industry which had developed in many countries on the assumption that the relatively buoyant conditions of the 1960s would continue into the 1970s and beyond. Yet in the period 1975–9 the average ordering rate for the leading nuclear countries (i.e. Britain, Canada, France, Japan, Sweden, the United States and West Germany) was approximately 15 GWe (15,000 MWe) per year compared with an actual capacity of 50–60 GWe. The resulting over-capacity in reactor manufacturing posed difficult problems of industrial readjustment. Here, it is worth noting that the manufacture of the nuclear supply steam system investment in sophisticated capital equipment and the assembly and training of highly skilled design and engineering teams. In addition, nuclear production entails the maintenance of a much higher level of quality assurance than is normally needed in other branches of industry. Reactor manufacturers thus faced a difficult dilemma – they could cut their losses and withdraw from the industry but only by abandoning any share in a future revival of nuclear market prospects; alternatively, they could maintain their manufacturing capability during a period of minimal ordering but at the cost of seriously jeopardising the current profitability of their operations.[1] The work created by deficiencies in various reactor designs and the consequent need to redesign and refit parts of reactor systems made it possible to utilise the services of designers and engineers and the productive capacity of the reactor industry generally. There were also possibilities for expanding into other facets of the nuclear fuel cycle and transferring key personnel to R & D projects. Such measures, however, amounted to no more than a holding operation. They could not be indefinitely maintained in the face of a deep and sustained recession in the nuclear market.

The development of the reactor industry was also affected by government attempts to establish and expand an independent technological base. The emerging rivalry between national nuclear scientific and industrial complexes inevitably gave rise to a series of mergers and amalgamations designed to protect the domestic market from the encroachment of foreign firms. On the other hand, considerations of economic and technical efficiency often made it necessary for European countries to enter into foreign licensing arrangements, particularly with the American manufacturers Westinghouse and General Electric. These pressures were particularly acute in a country like Brazil where extensive dependence on foreign technology was perceived as a prerequisite for any programme of rapid nuclearisation.

In the light of the increasing economic and political costs associated with nuclear investments, governments which had set ambitious targets for nuclear power development had to determine whether they would allocate additional public funds and initiate legislative and administrative action in a bid to overcome the technical, structural and financial obstacles which were seriously eroding the relative position of nuclear electricity in the overall energy equation. Private and public organisations, including scientific and military institutions, which had made a large historic investment – both financially and ideologically – in nuclear technology and manufacture were obviously intent on resisting the decline of the nuclear industry. We need, therefore, to consider more closely the changing conditions of the nuclear domestic market in each of the countries under consideration, the economic and political pressures to which they gave rise and the efficacy of government attempts to maintain the momentum of nuclear plans.

FEDERAL REPUBLIC OF GERMANY

In 1976 primary energy consumption in West Germany stood at about 370 million tons of coal equivalent (mtce). In 1973 government forecasts had suggested a primary energy demand in 1985 of

610 mtce. A year later the forecast was lowered to 555 mtce, and in 1977 to 496 mtce.[2] Even this revised projection, however, was regarded as too optimistic by the Institute of Applied Systems Research and Prognosis which estimated West Germany's demand in 1985 at 437 mtce.[3] Equally indicative of the trend was the 5 per cent fall in primary energy consumption registered in 1981 which brought it back to its 1976 level.[4]

Whatever the reasons for declining energy growth – adverse economic conditions and improved energy conservation were no doubt important contributing factors – they were also reflected in reduced expectations of the future role of nuclear power. In the 1970s the government was confidently predicting that by 1980 20 per cent of electricity consumption would be derived from nuclear energy and that the proportion would rise to 50 per cent by the year 2000.[5] According to one scenario based on official estimates, nuclear power was expected to make a contribution of 90 mtce by 1985 and 350 mtce by 2000.[6] The federal government's 1973 energy programme envisaged that Germany's installed nuclear capacity in 1985 would reach 45,000–50,000 MWe, but by 1977 the estimate had been reduced to 30,000 MWe. Independent studies have since indicated that this projection will also be far off the mark and that nuclear capacity in 1985 is unlikely to exceed 18,000 MWe.

The diminishing prospects of nuclear power could not be attributed to government indifference. Public subsidies, which had amounted to DM 1182 million during the first atomic energy programme (1956–62), rose to DM 2959 million during the second programme (1963–7) and to DM 4065 million during the third programme (1968–72).[7] These figures do not include West Germany's financial contribution to Euratom, CERN and other international nuclear agencies or the funding of several nuclear research centres. Even as late as 1980, the federal annual budget for nuclear energy R&D amounted DM 1167 million out of a total budget for energy research of DM 1909 million.[8] Despite such financial support, the nuclear industry proved incapable of sustaining the momentum generated during the 1960s and early 1970s. By 1972, twenty-five reactors with a total capacity of 14,000 MWe were either operating under construction or on order. Yet by 1976, despite a spate of new orders placed in the immediate aftermath of the oil crisis, a good part of the programme was halted or at least postponed because of environmental opposition.[9]

As of 1978, installed nuclear capacity stood at 8765 MWe, in addition to which nuclear power stations with a capacity of 9400 MWe were either under construction or awaiting operating licence. However, even if all these stations were to come into operation by 1985, they would still fall short of the federal government's newly-revised target of 24,000 MWe.[10] KWU, which received no new domestic orders between 1976 and 1980, had little reason to expect a dramatic improvement in the immediately foreseeable future.[11] As of 1980 some ten reactors with a capacity of 12,500 MWe had reached the planning stage but it was by no means certain that a significant porportion of these would be in operation by 1990. Given the prevailing economic and political climate, an installed nuclear capacity in 1990 of 22,000–25,000 MWe appeared a more realistic assessment.

The failure of the nuclear industry to fulfil its expectations of expansion reflected not only depressed market conditions but also long delays in licensing and construction schedules resulting from political intervention, legal disputes and new regulatory procedures. The processing of the licensing application for the Stade plant took a mere four months, whereas the corresponding period for the Phillipsburg-2 plant was two years, and applications filed in 1974 and 1975 were still pending four or five years later. These delays coupled with higher interest rates and modifications in the guidelines and regulations governing specifications for nuclear installations, inevitably meant additional and often unrecoverable capital costs.[12]

Although investment costs were higher for nuclear power plants than for other thermal power plants (perhaps by as much as 50 per cent), electricity utilities were nevertheless attracted to the nuclear option partly because nuclear plants involved lower fuel costs and offered possibilities for exploiting economies of scale.[13] According to the calculations of a representative of the electricity supply industry, nuclear power plants scheduled for commissioning in 1985 would have a cost advantage over their entire service life in the base load range of 6–7 pf/kWh. In the first year after commissioning, the cost advantage was estimated at 4–5 pf/kWh.[14] A study commissioned by the Federal Ministry of Economic Affairs found that on comparing the actual costs for 1977, the cost advantage of nuclear energy over that generated form hard coal was 3.58 pf/kWh at base load operation and about 3.22 pf/kWh at medium load operation. Whatever the accuracy of these calculations, they were seen by the electricity utilities as providing the economic justification for their future investment plans.

A 1974 study by a leading German bank had estimated the capital requirements for nuclear power plants up to 1985 at DM 72,920 million. In addition it was calculated that DM 26,500 million would need to be raised to assure Germany's nuclear fuel supply.[15] By the early 1970s the self-financing ratio of many utilities had fallen from 75 per cent to 50 per cent and reached a low point of 42 per cent for those utilities building nuclear power plants. As a result of the rising unit costs of nuclear construction and longer lead times (and thus later start of depreciation) a growing gap soon emerged between the investment needs of the utilities and the depreciation that could be charged. Such a difference could be filled only with additional income or with credits. To ease the problems arising from a low ratio of self-financing, attempts were made to spread borrowing from different sectors of the capital market. For this purpose investment projects (mainly nuclear power plants) were financed within the framework of affiliates or leasing companies. The financial constraints operating on German utilities were, in any case, less acute than those experienced by their American counterparts. The German industry enjoyed greater flexibility in adjusting its tariffs[16] and benefited from the country's lower rate of inflation as well as from the government's generous subsidy of the coal industry. But the most important factor in averting the expected fall in self-financing ratios was the decline in the ordering of new plants. The resulting slowdown in capital investment meant that the financial requirements of the largest German electricity utilities, including RWE, Vereinigte Elektrizitätswerke Westfalen AG (VEW), Nordwestdeutsche Kraftwerke AG, and Preussenelektra, were raised through self-financing.[17] Ironically, this improved liquidity was a reflection of the much slower pace of nuclear power development and the much reduced forecasts of electricity consumption.

The shrinking domestic market had also far-reaching implications for the reactor industry and especially for KWU which had operated as a 50: 50 per cent shareholding of Siemens and AEG (Allgemeine Elektrizitätgesellschaft) until 1977 when Siemens took over complete ownership of the firm. With about 15,000 employees KWU covered the whole range of nuclear power reactors, including the PWR, BWR and heavy water reactors, and was intent on making major inroads into the turbine generator market which it shared with its major rival, the Swiss–German Brown Boveri Company (BBC). Having broken its connections with the US nuclear industry, except for a technical exchange agreement with Combustion Engineering, KWU achieved a near monopoly in nuclear contracting in Germany and was ready to launch a major offensive into the European and Third World markets. However, the *de facto* moratorium in the domestic market placed considerable strains on KWU and its component suppliers. In order to avoid heavy fixed investments in nuclear reactor manufacture, KWU had made a practice of sub-contracting to local firms, in particular to GHH-Sterkrage, a division of the heavy engineering company Guttehoffnungshütte (GHH) specialising in pressure vessels, steam generators and pressurisers. Components were also supplied by such European firms as Voest–Alpine, Breda and RSV.

The lean years experienced after the mid-1970s thus threatened the long-term profitability of the heavy investments which had been made for the development of production facilities, the installation of quality assurance programmes, and the assembling of teams of highly qualified and often specialised personnel. After losses that reached a peak of DM 81 million in 1972, KWU earned a profit of DM 41 million in 1976 only to see its position deteriorate once again in subsequent years. In 1979–80, KWU was operating at only 52 per cent of its manufacturing capacity – a situation which remained more or less static in the following two years.[18] If KWU remained in surprisingly good health, it was only because of its success in the export market and the capacity of its parent company, Siemens, to subsidise its loss-making activities. Neither of these factors, however, could be expected to provide a satisfactory or permanent solution to the problem of over-capacity.

The federal government's response to the plight of the German nuclear industry was neither coherent nor decisive. In part this was the result of sharply diverging attitudes within Helmut Schmidt's coalition government, which in a sense mirrored the political and ideological divisions within society at large. Increasing pressure from the environmental movement coupled with the impact of the oil crisis had led the government to revise its 1973 energy programme in 1974 and again in 1977. The main thrust of the new policy was to slow down the long-term growth of energy consumption and to diversify Germany's sources of supply. More specifically, government objectives were defined as greater energy conservation, reduced reliance on oil, priority for indigenous hard coal and lignite and expansion of nuclear power at the rate necessary to secure electricity supply.[19] Clearly the intention was to strike a compromise between the demands of the nuclear lobby and those of its opponents. Nuclear expansion would proceed but at a much slower rate than previously planned. The new emphasis on increased efficiency in energy usage and greater reliance on coal, which was endorsed by the Social Democratic Party's Congress in December 1979, was justified in terms of the need to lessen the country's dependence on foreign oil. But the other important consequence of the policy was to reduce the likely contribution of nuclear power to Germany's energy requirements. The implications of that approach became fully apparent with the announcement by the North Rhine–Westphalia government – a coalition of Social Democrats and Free Democrats – in May 1980 that 9000 MWe of coal-fired capacity would be built before any consideration was given to the construction of nuclear power plants.[20]

The German federal government, it is true, remained anxious to secure a favourable climate for nuclear power development and to this end took steps to ensure stability of uranium supplies, to encourage public confidence in the safety and operational reliability of German nuclear power plants, and to initiate studies and proposals for the long-term disposal of nuclear wastes. But none of these actions or the continuing high level of government funding for nuclear research and development had much effect on licensing arrangements, which were the area of most immediate concern to the nuclear industry. Despite the often stated desire to streamline legal and administrative procedures, licensing delays continued to plague the industry throughout the 1970s. In response to representations from the German Atomic Forum,[21] the Cabinet Committee for the Peaceful Uses of Nuclear Power approved in October 1982 a series of measures for speeding up the decision-making process. These included the standardisation of plant designs, timely and complete submission of licensing documents, uniform assessment of plants with respect to the provisions against damages required in accordance with current knowledge, limitation of public participation in the case of modifications to plants which did not entail negative consequences or dangers to third parties.[22] It remained to be seen whether these new procedures could be implemented with sufficient fixity of purpose to achieve the intended result.

Another indication of the political stalemate in the nuclear controversy was provided by the conclusions of the Parliamentary Committee on the Future of Nuclear Energy. The *Enquete Committee*, as it was known, was composed of seven parliamentarians and eight academics representing a wide range of views. Not surprisingly, the Committee was obliged to consider several scenarios, ranging from a complete ban on nuclear plant construction to 60 per cent dependence on nuclear energy for electricity supply by 2025. The failure of the Committee to resolve its internal differences was reflected in the delayed submission of its report and, more particularly, in its eventual recommendation that the nuclear option be left open and that priority be given to a stringent energy conservation programme. The Committee voted 12: 3 to postpone a definitive decision on nuclear power until 1990 and advocated that in the interim modest use be made of nuclear power, including the construction of some new stations 'in line with requirements'.[23] Significantly, the number of stations to be ordered or brought on line over the next decade was left unspecified.

The ambiguity in government policy was to become especially evident in relation to the fast breeder programme. The development of German fast breeder technology was started at Karlsruhe as far back an 1957 and was followed in 1960 with the establishment of a fast breeder project group within the Karlsruhe Nuclear Research Centre. After a period of association with Euratom between 1963 and 1967, co-operation was initiated with Belgium and the Netherlands for the building the 300 MWe prototype fast breeder reactor, SNR–300, at Kalkar on the Lower Rhine. For this purpose the international companies Schnellbrüker-Kernkraftwerks-Gesellschaft mbH (SBK) and Internationale Brutreaktorbau-Gesellschaft mbH (INB) were formed. In SBK the majority share (68.8 per cent) was held by RWE, with smaller shares held by Dutch, Belgian and electricity utilities. As for INB, the majority interest (70 per cent) was held by Interatom (a fully-owned subsidiary of KWU) with minor participation by Dutch and Belgian companies. Notwithstanding the heavy involvement of private firms, the fast breeder project has been the largest government-financed development programme in the Federal Republic. Although the utilities assumed responsibility for construction and future operation, their financial contribution was limited to 8 per cent of the total cost. During the greater part of the 1960s and early 1970s it is the government which remained the dominant actor in policy-making.[24]

The momentum of the programme, however, proved difficult to maintain in the face of licensing delays and rapidly escalating costs. As with light water plants, the SNR–300 had to meet safety criteria prior to each construction step, with time-consuming calculations going into every detail of their design. Moreover, the detailed information supplied to the authorities was subject to review by independent organisations which often requested additional information. Any resulting change to the original design in turn required renewed approval.[25] As the competent authority for issuing construction permits, the North Rhine–Westphalia government exercised its independent judgement, and on occasions delayed the granting of a permit against the express wish of the federal government. By 1976, three years after the start of construction, the project was eighteen months behind schedule. By 1978, the expected date of completion had been put back by four years. By 1981, the SNR–300 had been granted ten partial permits, but the complex licensing procedures meant that as many as another ten such permits would be needed before the reactor could reach full power operation.[26]

These licensing delays had in no small measure compounded the problem of funding the SNR–300. By 1980 the total cost of the project had risen from the 1973 estimate of DM 1700 million* to an official estimate of DM 3700 million – unofficial estimates in 1983 put it as high as DM 7000 million.[27] By 1978 more than DM 3000 million had already been spent on research and development work on the fast breeder. The budget allocation for 1978 was DM 312 million and was expected to amount to DM 1437 million for the 1979–83 period.[28] Although most of these funds were used for the construction of the SNR–300, a significant shortfall emerged by 1980 following the refusal of the Federal Ministry for Research and Technology to raise its financial contribution in line with rising construction costs. The resulting deficit for 1981 amounted to DM 177 million and was expected to rise thereafter to DM 300 million a year.[29]

The attitude of the federal government was that the electricity utilities and industry should assume responsibility for closing the financial gap. The failure of the utilities to respond positively to this suggestion threatened the project with imminent collapse. A partial appropriation for DM 167 million by the BMFT in October 1981

*1973 exchange rate: $1 = DM2.7 (1980: $1 = DM2.5)

temporarily avoided the interruption of construction work. The government decision had followed the offer from RWE and from Preussenelektra and Nordwestdeutsche Kraftwerke AG to contribute a total of DM 557 million, that is, enough to cover half the financial deficit estimated at DM 1100 million. In a bid to find a more lasting solution, the federal government contemplated the possibility of legislation which would compel the utilities to devote a proportion of their income to research purposes. At the same time, it recommended to a number of Länder governments that public utilities be asked to make voluntary contributions to the funding of the breeder. The completion of the SNR–300 now depended on the successful conclusion of these negotiations.

Further doubts, however, on the future of the project were raised by the announcement of the Parliamentary Committee on the Future of Nuclear Energy that the presentation of its study on the risks of breeder technology would be delayed. The Bundestag, for its part, was unlikely to authorise the commissioning of the SNR–300 without first having had the opportunity of examining the study.[30] On the other hand, the electricity utilities, which had undertaken to contribute to the costs of the project, indicated that their financial participation would be conditional on the West German Parliament withdrawing its right of veto. As with the rest of Germany's nuclear power programme, the SNR–300 was caught in a maze of financial and political complications the outcome of which was less than predictable. Equally problematic was the capacity of federal and state governments to provide the coherent policy-making framework and the financial resources needed to ensure the long-term viability of the breeder programme.

FRANCE

In the era of growth which preceded the 1973–4 oil crisis French primary energy consumption more than trebled, increasing from 57.6 million tons of oil equivalent (mtoe) in 1950 to 175.6 mtoe in 1974.[31] The accelerating demand for energy, especially for purposes of heating, transport and industry, had given rise to growing dependence on oil, which rose from 41.6 per cent in 1964 to 63.8 per cent in 1974.[32] During the same period, electricity consumption also experienced a dramatic increase, rising from 93.9 Terawatt-hours (TWh) to 180.7 TWh.[33] This, then, was the context within which governments and energy-planning authorities had conceived of the need for an ambitious nuclear power programme. Economic policy was premised on forecasts of continuing growth in energy consumption, and in electricity consumption in particular. As a consequence of the fourfold increase in the price of oil and the new threat to oil supplies, energy policy placed renewed emphasis on conservation programmes designed to reduce current dependence on Middle East oil. Paradoxically, however, rapid growth in electricity demand was not deemed inconsistent with overall energy objectives since increased electricity production, particularly when derived from nuclear power, was perceived as a substitute for oil and therefore an important part of the strategy for reducing France's oil import bill.

Basing their calculations on the assumption of moderate economic growth (i.e. 3 per cent a year), energy planners were forecasting that electricity consumption would reach 328 TWh in 1985 and 545 TWh in the year 2000. According to 1975 projections the contribution of fossil fuels to primary energy consumption was expected to decline from 90 per cent in 1975 to 68 per cent in 1985 and range between 51 per cent and 67 per cent in 2000. By contrast the contribution of nuclear energy to total energy requirements was expected to climb from 2 per cent in 1975 to 25 per cent in 1985 and range between 26 per cent and 36 per cent in 2000.[36] The fact that four years later these projections remained essentially unchanged was an indication of the dynamism of the French nuclear power programme and of the strong political commitment to it. The CEA's 1979 forecasts suggested that nuclear electricity would account for 20 per cent of primary energy consumption in 1985 and for 32 per cent by the year 2000. The nuclear share of electricity consumption was expected to rise from 9.6 per cent in 1975 to 62 2 per cent in 1985 and 75.2 per cent by 2000.[37]

These forecasts are impressive given that as late as 1970 nuclear power stations were generating only 5.15 TWh of electricity, that is, only 3.7 per cent of total electricity consumption. However by 1978, nuclear electricity accounted for 28.8 TWh or 13.1 per cent of total consumption. This trend was greatly reinforced by the accelerated rate of nuclear ordering which, as Table 5.1 indicates, totalled some 29,982 MWe in the years 1973–8. In 1975 the French government had already set a target of 40,000 MWe of nuclear-installed capacity by 1985.

The steady progress of the French nuclear programme during these years owes a good deal to the success of EdF in limiting licensing and

Table 5.1: *French nuclear orders 1973–8*

Year	*No. of units*	*Capacity (MWe)*
1973	3	2842
1974	13	11840
1975	8	8720
1976	4	3900
1977	1	920
1978	2	1760

Source: Commissariat à l'Energie Atomique, *Rapport Annual 1978*, p. 113.

construction delays. Although initial estimates of the time it would take to build PWR power stations proved somewhat optimistic, the problems did not stem, as in the case of West Germany or the United States, so much from legal or political impediments as from the unpreparedness and inexperience of French industry, the shortage of skilled labour and the introduction of new regulatory requirements. These organisational and technical difficulties did not, however, produce the crippling delays experienced in other countries. The application of highly centralised licensing procedures, offering little or no opportunity for public intervention, greatly reduced the likelihood of delays in the granting of construction and operating permits. The ability to keep lead times for new plants to an average of 6–7 years made it much easier to estimate and therefore to minimise future system costs.

EdF estimated the cost of building the first PWR plant at Fessenheim to have exceeded the budget by only 7 per cent. Nevertheless the capital costs of a 1300 MWe PWR were estimated in 1978 at Fr 2840/kW, which represented a 50 per cent increase on the cost of Fessenheim after allowing for inflation and a 10 per cent margin for economies of scale.[38] These cost increases were attributed by the PEON Commission to technical changes and improvements (34 per cent), higher safety standards (32 per cent), additional siting costs (24 per cent), more accurate cost estimates, and higher quality requirements (10 per cent). The monopoly enjoyed by Framatome in the reactor field and by Alsthom–Atlantique in the production of turbine generators was no doubt a contributing factor. Rising capital costs were not seen, however, as jeopardising the competitiveness of nuclear power stations, in part because of increasing fuel costs in the case of oil-fired plants, and rising construction and operational costs in the case of coal-fired stations. Official estimates released in 1980 indicated that in 1985 the cost of producing 1 kWh of electricity by fuel oil would range between 23 and 30 centimes. The comparable cost for coal was between 19 and 23 centimes, and between 12 and 14 centimes for nuclear power. By 1990, it was argued, the favourable margin currently enjoyed by nuclear power stations would be even wider.[39]

It should be noted in passing that these highly flattering cost comparisons have not been universally accepted. According to one critical assessment, the actual costs recorded in 1978 (as opposed to projected future costs) were much less favourable to nuclear power.[40] The price of nuclear-generated electricity was estimated at 18.82 centimes/kWh as compared with 14.72 centimes/kWh for fossil fuel-fired plants and 7.05 centimes/kWh for hydroelectricity. Apart from the failure to take account of hidden subsidies in the form of R & D carried out by the CEA, it was claimed that EdF estimates had not taken sufficient account of construction delays, of the suspension of interest changes on borrowings for the construction of nuclear installations, or of the rate of inflation (estimated in recent years to have averaged at 13 per cent as opposed to the 10 per cent allowed for by EdF). Another technique used to underestimate the true capital costs of nuclear power was the assumption of a load factor of 75 per cent which compared with an actual load factor of 54.4 per cent for French PWRs in 1979. Whatever the validity of these criticisms, they suggest that the methodology underlying EdF's cost comparisons has yet to be fully verified. They also suggest that these comparisons were designed as much to justify the government's nuclear policies as to demonstrate the economic soundness of EdF's investments.

As a state-owned monopoly, closely integrated into the energy and financial decision-making process, EdF had become a key policy instrument for the implementation of nuclear plans. The replacement of oil by nuclear power in base load electricity generation and the electrification of space heating and other energy end uses were essential to achieving a steady rate of nuclear ordering on which depended the creation of a viable domestic nuclear industry capable of securing a share of the export market. EdF was therefore expected to finance a massive nuclear investment programme which would involve, between 1974 and 1985, the expenditure of some Fr 100,000 million (at 1978 constant prices). Measured in 1978 francs*, EdF's nuclear investments rose from Fr 738 million in 1973 to Fr 8800 million in 1978,[41] to which should be added the capital costs incurred in the construction of transmission and distribution facilities. In 1980, expenditure on nuclear installations amounted to Fr 16,000 million, and during the peak construction period this figure was expected to rise to more than Fr 20,000 million a year.

As a result of its commitment to nuclear power, EdF's self-financing ratio fell from 70 per cent in 1973 to 40 per cent in 1977.[42] The deterioration of its cash flow position was accentuated on the one hand by the increased price of oil and on the other by the government's desire to prevent a sharp rise in the price of electricity. Although higher tariffs might have given EdF the funds needed for its capital investments and kept the utility's debt at a reasonable level, they would also have exacerbated inflationary pressures and discouraged the growth of electricity consumption which had become the foundation stone of France's nuclear programme. EdF was thus obliged to rely on government loans made available on preferential terms through the Fonds de Développement Economique et Social. To supplement the resources of the domestic financial market, EdF also had recourse to foreign borrowing. In 1977, these loans amounted to Fr 4000 million, and by 1979 EdF's accumulated foreign debt had reached Fr 14,000 million. Admittedly, EdF's capital investments as a proportion of total French investments were lower than during the hydroelectric projects of the 1950s. On the other hand, the current level of financial indebtedness had qualitatively different implications given that the prevailing economic environment was no longer one of stable growth but of unpredictable stagflation.

The fact remains that over a period of less than ten years EdF's investment policy had, with the active support of the French government, paved the way for the establishment of a fully-fledged nuclear industry. Soon after the decision had been taken in 1969 to shift from gas-cooled to light water reactors, Framatome, a subsidiary of the heavy engineering company Creusot–Loire (itself a member of the Empain Schneider industrial conglomerate), was awarded the contract for the 900 PWR unit at Fessenheim against competition from Babcock–Atlantique. Between 1970 and 1973

*1978 exchange rate: $1 = Fr 4.2

Framatome received orders for five more 900 MWe units. Following the 1973 oil crisis EdF asked Framatome to consider expanding its productive capacity to six units a year, and, on receiving a positive response, proceeded to the signing of the first multi-annual contract. Another order which had been placed with Compagnie Générale d'Eléctricité (CGE) for two BWR units plus six options was subsequently cancelled as part of a conscious decision to concentrate exclusively on Framatome PWRs.

The underlying strategy was to strengthen and re-organise the reactor industry by taking advantage of Framatome's experience and production facilities. Government intervention was thus instrumental in resolving the long-standing rivalry between the major power engineering groups in France, CGE and Empain Schneider, and in determining their respective roles in the country's nuclear programme. Under an agreement concluded in 1976, CGE, through its subsidiary Alsthom–Atlantique, gained the right to manufacture all steam turbines required for French nuclear plants, while Empain Schneider, through its subsidiary Creusot–Loire, acquired a dominant share of the reactor business with Frametome manufacturing the nuclear steam supply system and Spie Batignolles (also a member of the Empain Schneider group) handling the engineering.[43] It was now confidently expected that Framatome, operating under a licence from Westinghouse, would be able to standardise its designs and thereby minimise capital costs.

The French government was also intent on making CEA a significant shareholder of Framatome in order to facilitate closer technical co-operation between the two organisations and greater government influence over the company's operations. To this end negotiations were held with Westinghouse and a new series of agreements reached at the end of 1975. These provided for a reduced participation by Westinghouse from 45 per cent to 15 per cent, with CEA acquiring 30 per cent of the equity and Empain Schneider retaining 55 per cent of the Framatome capital.[44] This arrangement was to expire in 1982, by which time Westinghouse was to surrender its remaining shareholding to the French parent company. In addition, Westinghouse, Framatome, CEA and EdF agreed to implement a joint research and development programme aimed at improving the safety, reliability and economic performance of the PWR design, and allocated for the purpose an annual budget of Fr 90 million for the next five years.[45] The final step towards the indigenisation of the French industry came in January 1981 with the signing of an agreement formally ending the licensing relationship between France and Westinghouse, thereby removing any legal constraints the United States could apply on the export of French nuclear equipment. A continuing framework of technical co-operation nevertheless provided the American partner with access to French research efforts and to the PWR experience of the most ambitious nuclear programme in the western world.[46]

By the mid-1970s, government policies had gone a long way towards consolidating the position of the highly standardised 900 and 1300 PWR units. By the end of 1979 sixteen units were in operation with a total installed capacity of 8300 MWe. Another thirty-two units (including the Super-Phénix fast breeder) were under construction, representing an additional capacity of 31,500 MWe. Construction on three more 900 MWe units and five 1300 MWe units was expected to start in 1980–1. The steady stream of new orders (averaging 6000 MWe a year) was attributable in large measure to the emphasis on standardisation. The coordination of project capabilities (design, construction, testing) and of engineering capacity (construction, erection of plant components) was facilitated by EdF's monopoly position in the French electricity and supply sector which permitted several diverse functions to be unified under the one authority.[47]

The acceleration of France's nuclear programme, which began under the Pompidou government, reached its peak during the presidency of Giscard d'Estaing who played an active part in the formulation of energy policy generally and nuclear plans in particular. His involvement, no doubt encouraged by his family's substantial commercial interests in various aspects of nuclear production, was influential in committing the resources of the public sector to the financial and industrial organisation of the nuclear project. Following Mitterand's victory in the 1981 presidential elections and the triumph of the Socialist Party in the ensuing general elections considerable attention was focused on possible changes of emphasis or substance in the direction of French nuclear policy.

President Mitterand, it should be remembered, had fought his election campaign on the basis of the Socialist Manifesto which, though not advocating the abandonment of the nuclear option, appeared to place less emphasis on nuclear power in the total energy mix. Whereas the previous government had favoured a strategy which would see nuclear electricity accounting for 30 per cent of national energy needs by 1990 (some 72,000 MWe), the Socialist Manifesto proposed only 48,000 MWe by the same date.[48] To make up for this shortfall, the Socialist Party had proposed a substantial increase in coal production, a more vigorous policy of energy conservation, and renewed efforts to promote alternative energy sources. If implemented the manifesto would have meant a moratorium on nuclear ordering for several years and much less reliance on the development of breeder and reprocessing technologies.

In the first new months of office, the Socialist government's intentions for the nuclear sector appeared ambiguous. The controversial Plogoff project in Brittany was abandoned. Other projects at Belleville, Nogent, Cattenom and Golfech, for which nuclear steam supply systems had yet to be ordered, were temporarily suspended pending a national energy debate.[49] No attempt, however, was made to prevent units already built from being loaded with fuel and connected to the power grid. In 1981, EdF commissioned eight new units with a total capacity of more than 7200 MWe, bringing the total installed nuclear capacity in France to 21,600 MWe.[50] In any case, the vote at the National Assembly, which followed discussion of the government's energy policy, provided for construction to proceed on all nuclear power plants already on order. In addition permission was granted for six new units (5 × 1300 MWe and 1 × 900 MWe) to be ordered in 1982–3, as compared with the nine units previously planned.[51] It was now projected that French installed nuclear capacity in 1990 would reach 56,000 MWe, considerably less than the target set by the former Administration, but more than that indicated by the Socialist Manifesto.

In the short term, at least, the course of the French nuclear programme seemed assured. The socialist government proved less hostile to the demands of the nuclear lobby than many had anticipated, partly out of fear of the increased unemployment that might result from a more drastic contraction of nuclear plans, but also because of financial considerations given the capital already invested in nuclear construction at Cattenom, Belleville and Nogent-sur-Loire. Nuclear planning had gathered such momentum that any attempt to apply a firm brake on it was seen as likely to have seriously disruptive consequences. Indeed, under Mitterand, the nuclear industry was brought even more directly under the unifying power of the state apparatus with the nationalisation of CGE, Péchiney Ugine

Kuhlmann and the Paribas banking group which had a 35 per cent stake in Empain Schneider. While Framatome itself escaped nationalisation and its equity structure remained unchanged, it was placed under the control of a board of directors on which CEA was given equal representation with Creusot–Loire and Framatome and the right to exercise a veto on all important questions.[52] Nevertheless, beyond 1982 the direction of France's nuclear programme seemed less certain. Much would depend on the general climate of opinion, the intensity of regional opposition, attitudes within the Socialist Party, but above all on the state of the French economy and on the evolution of electricity demand. Declining growth in energy consumption might well create powerful pressures for a marked reduction in the rate of nuclear ordering which even the well-organised nuclear lobby might find difficult to resist.[53]

The new mood of uncertainty also had far-reaching implications for the fast breeder programme which previous governments had identified as the key to France's long-term energy independence. Initially, responsibility for the development of the fast breeder was vested with the CEA which in fact commissioned the experimental reactor Rapsodie in 1967. Its power level was low and it was not designed to produce electricity. A year later a decision was made to build the 250 MWe Phénix demonstration plant under the joint supervision of CEA and EdF and with the co-operation of private industry[54] Phénix was put into regular operation in July 1974 and in its first year of operation achieved a capacity factor of 80 per cent.[55] From 1975 to 1978, the plant was periodically out of action as a result of leaks, either in the water pipes or in the heat exchanges,[56] but has since functioned with considerable reliability. This is not to say that Phénix has generated electricity at a commercially-competitive cost. Its doubling time – the time needed for the reactor to recover its original inventory of fuel – was estimated to be 50–60 years, too long for the requirements of a rapidly expanding breeder programme.[57]

Well before the completion of Phénix, arrangements were well under way for the creation of an international company which would build a commercial prototype breeder reactor. In December 1973 an agreement was signed between EdF, RWE and the Italian utility Ente Nazionale per l'Energia Elettrica (ENEL) establishing NERSA, the company which would undertake the construction of the 1200 MWe Super-Phénix plant at Creys–Malville. Some time later, RWE was replaced by SBK, the company it had formed with Belgian and Dutch electricity utilities for the construction of the SNR–300.[58] In May and June 1974, France and Italy signed a series of agreements which aimed at harmonising their research and development programmes and involving Italian companies more closely in fuel fabrication and the manufacture of the nuclear steam supply system. In July 1976 the supply and assembly of the nuclear boiler were entrusted to Novatome and Nira, the two companies which had been specifically created in France and Italy respectively to develop fast breeder reactors. Initially, CEA had a 34 per cent interest in Novatome, the other shareholder being Framatome (36 per cent), Nyerpic (15 per cent) and Alsthom–Atlantique (15 per cent).[59]

The framework of European co-operation was widened still further in July 1977 with the signing of new agreements between France and Germany paving the way for the establishment of a marketing firm SERENA (Société Européenne pour la Promotion des Systèmes de Réacteurs Rapides au Sodium). The company (in which the French- and German-led groups had 65 per cent and 35 per cent of the shares respectively) was given the exclusive rights for granting licences for industrial and commercial uses to all the information and know-how on LMFBRs held by France, Germany, Italy, Belgium and the Netherlands. In line with this function, SERENA granted licences to Novatome and INB in October 1978.[60] The 1977 Franco–German agreements also provided for the exchange of detailed technical information and increased coordination on fast breeder and development between the CEA (representing France and Italy) and Interatom and the Karlsruhe Nuclear Research Centre (representing the Federal Republic, Belgium and the Netherlands).[61]

The obvious interest in international co-operation should not obscure, however, France's determination to assert its leadership in the commercialisation of breeder technology. The single-minded approach of the French nuclear community, which sharply contrasted with the slippage and political hesitation characteristic of the programmes of other countries, was in part inspired by the desire to reduce France's heavy dependence on imported energy, but also by the expectation that the successful operation of Super-Phénix would provide the basis for the international marketing of the technology. Certainly, a high degree of technical and organisational skill had gone into the construction of Super-Phénix which was expected to come on stream, more or less as planned, in 1984. On the other hand, the economic viability of the breeder had yet to be demonstrated.

By the time of its completion, the project was expected to cost in excess of Fr 10,000 million. If one added to this figure the anticipated fuel and generating costs, it became evident that Super-Phénix was unlikely to produce electricity at a cost competitive either with existing PWR plants or even with fossil-fuelled plants.[62] Several hurdles still had to be overcome before the fast breeder could be fully integrated into the French industrial system. Effective commercialisation would in the long run depend on a significant reduction of capital costs, a marked improvement in the economics of reprocessing, technical mastery of the complete nuclear fuel cycle, and greater public acceptance of the technology. The decision of the Mitterand government to permit the completion of Super-Phénix but postpone any commitment to future orders was a clear indication of the continuing uncertainties surrounding the project and of rapidly changing domestic and international market conditions.

THE UNITED KINGDOM

As in other countries, the UK's nuclear programme has been adversely affected by the decline in energy growth and revised forecasts of future energy demand. Over the period 1959–73 the average annual growth in primary energy consumption was 2.0 per cent. However, since the early 1970s, partly as a result of economic recession and higher fuel prices, there has been a marked downturn in the energy sector. Between 1969 and 1974 energy consumption in the UK increased by only 0.7 per cent, and in the period since 1974 has been virtually stagnant. Consumption in 1978 stood at 338.4 mtce as compared with 337.5 mtce in 1974.[63] As a consequence of the steadily deteriorating economic climate, forecasts were now suggesting a net reduction in energy demand during the next decade. According to one scenario, UK primary energy consumption in 1990 was likely to remain below 200 mtoe as compared with 205.6 mtoe in 1979.[64]

Even more instructive have been the changes in the pattern of electricity demand. The average annual growth in electricity consumption, which was estimated at 7.9 per cent in 1959–65, fell to 5.3 per cent in 1966–73. But even before 1973 electrification was levelling off as the market was rapidly approaching saturation point.[65] The failure of the electricity utilities, and the CEGB in particular, to detect this trend led to significant overestimation of future demand, at times by as much as 40 per cent. In 1974, for example, the CEGB forecast a maximum electricity demand of 58,200 MWe for 1979–80. In the event they needed only 44,200 MWe. Towards the end of the 1970s the CEGB finally recognised the need to revise their projections downwards, and in 1980 proposed a reference case in which it was assumed that GDP would grow by 1.3 per cent per annum to the year 2000, with an accompanying growth in electricity demand of 0.9 per cent per annum.[66] Significantly, the CEGB's requirements for 1980–1 were only 214.4 TWh as against the 226 TWh that had been expected. The Electricity Council's *Medium Term Development Plan 1981–88* envisaged only 0.8 per cent annual growth in demand up to 1987–8, with forecasts for the early part of the plan period significantly lower than those of the previous year.[67]

The downturn in energy demand was reflected in the lower estimates of future nuclear expansion. Even as late as 1973, when the reduced growth of electricity usage was already apparent, the UKAEA was still arguing for a dramatic increase in the production of nuclear energy. One unofficial but authoritative estimate predicted that by the year 2000 the nuclear component of the UK power system would lie in the range 120–200 GWe.[68] By contrast, a government Green Paper published in 1978 forecast a steady build-up in nuclear ordering in the second half of the 1980s and 1990s but a maximum total installed nuclear capacity of only around 40 GWe by the end of the century.[69] But even this forecast was unduly optimistic for it assumed an average annual increase in generating capacity of 2.3 per cent up to the year 2000, which was more than twice the average annual increase in maximum demand recorded between 1973 and 1978.

Enough will have been said to indicate that conditions making for ambitious nuclear plans had largely evaporated by the mid-1970s. In May 1974 the Secretary of State for Energy, Eric Varley, conceded that Britain's overall record was disappointing and that since the second nuclear programme was announced in 1964 no decision had been taken for further expansion.[70] Five plants based on the AGR design were ordered between 1965 and 1969. However, the first two commercial AGRs, at Hinkley Point B and Hunterston B, did not begin operating until 1976. By the end of 1980, the other three AGRs, representing a capacity of 3840 MWe, were still under construction and were not expected to come on stream before 1982. All AGRs had experienced costly construction delays owing to managerial and technical difficulties, including corrosion problems with the carbon dioxide coolant. Between 1969 and 1979 the contribution of nuclear power to the country's electricity requirements rose only marginally from 11.6 per cent to 12.4 per cent.[71]

In the mid-1970s, the CEGB floated several proposals for the development of a major light water reactor programme,[72] but these were not sympathetically received by government which was increasingly preoccupied with the limitations of the domestic market and the precarious situation of the British reactor industry. Instead the Labour government announced in 1978 that two more AGRs would be ordered. The first of those to be built at Heysham was expected to be completed in 1986–7; the other station to be sited at Torness would not become operational until the late 1980s. The government also declared their intention to keep open the option of developing the PWR system in the early 1980s, but refrained from any specific commitments.

Normally, the close institutional links between the electricity supply industry and the government – both the CEGB and the SSEB were state-owned utilities – would have been sufficient to ensure the close coordination of nuclear policy. In Britain the national government, acting on the advice of the generating boards, determines the rate of nuclear ordering, authorises changes to electricity tariffs, and oversees the financing of utility investments. While they could not proceed independently of financial constraints and the state of the economy generally, the investment plans of generating boards were nevertheless assured of government support. Yet such protection was not sufficient to guarantee the growth of the nuclear industry.

An important negative factor in this context was the considerable over-capacity accumulated by the electricity generating system as a result of consistent overestimation of future electricity demand. At the end of 1973, the CEGB's over-capacity in relation to net maximum demand was estimated at 46 per cent.[73] After 1976, partly as a result of premature decommissioning of existing plants, the level of excess capacity diminished somewhat but was still estimated at about 33 per cent in 1980 when the net capability of all CEGB power stations was 56,705 MWe as against a maximum system demand of 42,600 MWe. To this the CEGB were expected to add over the next eight years another 13,600 MWe of generating capacity (including 5200 MWe of nuclear plant), or just under one-third of the present maximum system demand.[74] But for the long delays in the commissioning of the AGRs, the CEGB would have been confronted with an even greater excess generating capacity. For its part, the SSEB already had an over-capacity of 86 per cent which meant that the Torness AGR would not be needed for at least six years after the expected completion date. This large surplus capacity, which prompted the Monopolies and Mergers Commission to describe the forecasting record of the electricity supply industry as 'seriously inaccurate',[75] had greatly undermined the case for an ambitious nuclear programme.

In order to buttress their case the CEGB had consistently argued over the years that the cost of producing electricity was significantly lower for nuclear than for fossil-fired stations. For example, the generation costs for nuclear, coal-fired and oil-fired power stations commissioned between 1965 and 1977 were estimated in 1979–80 at 1.30 pence per kilowatt-hour, 1.56 p/kWh and 1.93 p/kWh respectively. Similarly, the generation costs for the first AGR (Hinkley Point B) were calculated as 1.35 p/kWh as against 1.52 p/kWh for the coal-fired station at Drax.[76] But these calculations were sharply criticised for underestimating the true costs of nuclear power and overestimating the costs of competing fuels, in particular coal. According to the Monopolies and Mergers Commission, the apparent economic advantage enjoyed by nuclear power arose from the CEGB's failure to price coal at long-run marginal cost.[77] The Board, it was argued, had not pursued the objective of cost reduction by every means available. First, it had not imported as much coal as it could have done at prices lower than those offered by the National Coal Board. Secondly, it had not entered into long-term contracts for coal imports. Thirdly, it had ordered power stations in advance of need, thereby bringing forward by several years additional capital expenditures.

In a more detailed analysis of the CEGB's calculations, a committee of independent academics concluded that the accounting techniques used by the CEGB for calculating generating costs had seriously prejudiced the results in favour of nuclear power.[78] The 20 per cent generating cost advantage claimed by the CEGB for its Magnox stations, it was argued, would turn into a 50 per cent generating cost disadvantage, if full account were taken of the effects of inflation and therefore of the true capital costs of Magnox plant built up to twenty years ago.[79] Regarding nuclear plants yet to come on stream, the committee questioned the CEGB's assumptions that new plants would be built on schedule, that the performance of new nuclear plants would match expectation, and that nuclear fuel costs would remain low while coal costs escalate. On the basis of what they considered more realistic assumptions, the committee calculated that future nuclear plant would have a generating cost of 3.27 p/kWh compared to 2.34 p/kWh for new coal-fired plant. Accordingly a decision to build one 1500 MWe nuclear power station rather than a coal-fired station of comparable size would entail a loss over the station's lifetime of nearly £2000 million (1980 sterling rate). Although these calculations were themselves open to criticism, they had cast serious doubts on the accuracy of the CEGB's conclusions, and on the soundness of its nuclear investments.[80]

Faced with the realities of over-capacity and doubts as to the true costs of nuclear power, they tended to shift the ground of their defence and to argue that the scale of their nuclear investments plant was necessary to build up a viable British nuclear industry capable of supplying future domestic requirements and of seizing such opportunities as the export market might provide.[81] It was precisely in order to ensure the viability of the reactor industry that a new operating company, the Nuclear Power Company Ltd (NPC) was formed in 1973, which was to act as the executive company of the National Nuclear Corporation (NNC) also established at this time. The NNC's three shareholders were the UKAEA (35 per cent), the GEC (30 per cent) and British Nuclear Associates, a group of seven British companies engaged in reactor manufacturing, which held the remaining 35 per cent. Industrial rivalry, organisational inefficiencies, technical defects in AGR design, and above all the contraction in electricity demand had combined to accentuate the vulnerability of the British reactor industry. Sharply conflicting views about the requirements and potential of British nuclear manufacturing capacity were reflected in the controversy surrounding the question of reactor choice. the claims and counter-claims made for the AGR, SGHWR and PWR (not to mention CANDU) pointed to the weaknesses of British industry but also to the failure of the nuclear decision-making process to reconcile these disparate and often competing interests.[82]

Against this background of political indecision and economic uncertainty, the Secretary of State for Energy, David Howell, announced in December 1979 that Britain's electricity boards could embark on a 15,000 MWe programme in the coming decade.

Although the precise level of future ordering would depend upon the development of electricity demand and the performance of the industry, it was envisaged that orders would be placed at the rate of at least one new nuclear power station a year. The next nuclear order was to be for a PWR, with the aim of starting construction in 1982. With the approval of the government, the CEGB endorsed the NNC's selection of Westinghouse as licensor for the PWR and subsequently issued a letter of intent to the NNC to authorise the design and, subject to the necessary approvals, manufacture of a PWR.[83] If the programme proceeded according to plan, the UK would have by the year 2000 an installed nuclear capacity of 24,000 MWe, comprised of seven AGRs and the 15,000 MWe proposed by David Howell. The Magnox reactors would by then have been decommissioned or be in the process of decommissioning.

In its evidence to the Select Committee on Energy, the UKAEA strongly supported the government's announcement, and went so far as to suggest that with more buoyant economic growth the ordering rate might need to be increased.[84] This was not the view, however, of the Select Committee. In a forthright and wide-ranging critique of the grounds of the government's 1979 statement, the Committee challenged the economic case of the programme, the load factors used to justify it, and the choice of reactors. While expressing support for a modest programme of nuclear plant, it doubted that the eventual figure would be as high as 15,000 MWe. It insisted that the actual rate of installation should depend on realistic cost estimates and take into account any changed circumstances relating to the supply and price of coal and oil, as well as developments in the field of renewable resources. The Committee advocated a review of the standards used by generating boards in setting planning margins, and recommended that the Department of Energy assess the economics of public expenditure to promote energy conservation with the same rigour as that required for the economic appraisal of new generating plant.[85]

The profound scepticism with which the Select Committee treated the CEGB's estimates of construction and unit generating costs and their forecasts of future electricity demand was bound to weaken the credibility and legitimacy of the new nuclear power programme. Ironically, it was these very considerations which had prompted the Thatcher government, despite its unambiguous commitment to nuclear power, to contemplate the deferment of Heysham–2 and Torness. Although the conclusions of the Central Policy Review Staff who were asked to inquire into the matter were not made public, significant differences appeared to emerge between the Energy Secretary who wanted to keep the CEGB within their financial limits and the Board who wanted to keep their AGR programme 'on track'.[86] A decision was eventually made to proceed with the construction of the two AGRs, but by the time the government formulated its response to the Select Committee's report in a White Paper published in July 1981 it was already apparent that the rate of nuclear ordering indicated in the 1979 statement might have to be reviewed.[87]

Further evidence of the government's thinking was provided by the new Energy Secretary, Nigel Lawson, in his statement to Parliament in February 1982. While reiterating his government's belief that there would be a substantial and growing need for generating capacity through the 1990s and into the next century, he was careful not to refer to the 15,000 MWe programme outlined in 1979 and contented himself with a promise to keep the longer-term strategy under regular review. A public enquiry into the CEGB's plans to build a PWR at Sizewell, Suffolk began early in 1983. Its consideration of the economic, environmental, safety and planning aspects of the proposal and its eventual recommendations would no doubt affect the direction of Britain's nuclear programme. But even in the event of the PWR proposal receiving the green light, the necessary planning and consent processes might not be concluded in time for a final decision to be made before 1984. Moreover the possibility of further delays arising from political and economic considerations remained a distinct possibility.

As one might expect, the development of fast reactors was subjected to the same trials and tribulations which had afflicted Britain's thermal reactor programme. While prepared to keep their options open and provide substantial funding to breeder research, both Labour and Conservative governments had been unwilling to commit themselves to the commercialisation of the fast breeder. The UKAEA, for its part, had since its inception been a champion of breeder technology. The first small experimental fast reactor was built at Harwell in 1954 and was followed in 1959 with the opening of the 15 MWe Dounreay Fast Breeder. It was superseded by the 250 MWe Prototype Fast Reactor (PFR) which was completed in 1974 and incorporated some of the features likely to be used in larger commercial reactors. The UKAEA was now pressing for work to proceed on the design and development of a single, full-size fast breeder reactor (CDFR), which would act as a 'lead' or 'demonstration' reactor. According to the Authority, a demand of two fast reactors a year by the year 2000 (2600 MWe) plus a similar number of thermal reactors represented a rate of nuclear ordering which would be well within the industry's capability at that time.[88]

Although the electricity supply industry was itself sympathetically disposed to the breeder as a long-term technological solution to the possible shortfall in uranium supplies, it was much less enthusiastic about early commercialisation. It favoured a start on the CDFR being made some time in the mid-1980s, but argued that further orders should by delayed until the late 1990s to permit sufficient experience to accumulate from the operation of the demonstration reactor. The ambiguous attitude of the electricity authorities indicated that the UKAEA could not expect from them any significant financial contribution towards the cost of the CDFR.[89] These differences in approach, coupled with the uncertainties about future demand and the serious reservations expressed by the Flowers Commission, prompted successive governments to keep their fast reactor plans under review but without making any firm commitment to eventual commercialisation.

Although the UKAEA, which had allocated more funds to breeder research and development than to any other reactor system, remained a vigorous advocate of commercialisation on the basis of the Dounreay prototype, the cost of building the CDFR was becoming increasingly prohibitive. In 1976 the estimated total cost was put at £2000 million. Since then capital costs have risen sharply and are now likely to be double the cost of a comparably sized thermal reactor. In 1980, UKAEA Chairman Sir John Hill pressed for the establishment of a project team comprising the NNC, the CEGB and the Authority which would produce a proposal for a CDFR in time for a final decision to be made in 1984 and construction to begin in 1985.[90] Increasingly, however, the UKAEA was exploring the possibility of combining efforts with the European SERENA consortium. While the experience of the UK prototype reactor would no doubt widen the technological base of the SERENA partners, considerable difficulties stood in the way of collaboration, not the least of which were the financial terms under which Britain would be allowed to join.

By the end of 1980 it appeared as if one of the preconditions for such an arrangement would be a substantial 'entry fee' estimated at

Table 5.2: *Nuclear power reactors in operation and under construction at the end of 1981*

Country	*In operation* Number of units	*In operation* Total MW(e)	*Under construction* Number of units	*Under construction* Total MW(e)	*Nuclear-generated electricity in 1981 (estimated)* TWh(e)	*Nuclear-generated electricity in 1981 (estimated)* %
Brazil	—	—	3	3116	—	—
France	30	29595	26	28585	99.5	37.7
Germany, FR	14	8606	10	10636	50.7	14.6
Sweden	9	6415	3	3025	34.1	15.3
United Kingdom	32	7627	9	5533	33.2	12.7
USA	75	57008	79	87217	272.4	11.9

Source: IAEA, reproduced in *Nuclear Engineering International*, August Supplement 1982, p. 3.

between $50 million and $120 million. The notion of a large cash payment represented a major financial and political hurdle for it could not be easily reconciled with the often repeated claims of successive governments that Britain remained in the vanguard of breeder technology.[91] As late as February 1982, the Energy Secretary, Nigel Lawson, was willing to do no more than promise to keep open the option to introduce fast reactors as and when they became economic. Indeed, he freely admitted that the time-scale for fast reactor introduction as a competitive source of power now looked much longer than a few years earlier.

SWEDEN

The impact of increasing oil prices and economic recession on Swedish energy consumption reflects the same trend as that observed in most other OECD countries. Whereas during the period 1965–73 energy consumption increased by an average of 3.4 per cent per annum, the corresponding increase during 1973–9 was only 0.6 per cent. If the figures for 1979 are corrected for temperature variation, the rate of increase is only about 0.2 per cent.[92] During the 1960s electricity consumption rose by more than 7 per cent a year, but at a much slower rate during the 1970s. Electricity production amounted to 77.3 TWh in 1973 and 89.1 TWh in 1978, representing an average annual increase of less than 3 per cent.[93] Forecasts made in 1975 had suggested a total energy consumption of about 540 TWh in 1985, but five years later revised projections were pointing to a consumption level of between 424 TWh and 455 TWh. No increase was envisaged for the period 1985–90. Electricity production was expected to rise from 93.8 TWh in 1979 to 120 TWh in 1985, but this was a modest increase when compared with the 159 TWh forecast in 1975. On the other hand, the contribution of nuclear power to electricity production was expected to rise dramatically from 20.1 TWh (21.4 per cent) in 1979 to 47.3 TWh (39.4 per cent) in 1985, to 54.5 TWh (40.7 per cent) in 1990.[94]

As already noted, Sweden's first commercial nuclear power plant, Oskarshamn-1 was based on the boiling water design. It was ordered by OKG in 1965 and started commercial operation in 1972. The adoption of LWR technology was reinforced by the decision of the State Power Board in 1968 to order Ringhals-1 (a boiling water reactor form ASEA) and Ringhals-2 (a pressurised water reactor from Westinghouse). OKG followed in 1969 with an order for a second BWR unit (Oskarshamn-2), and was followed in turn by Sydkraft which ordered an identical unit (Barsebäck-1) in the same year.

By 1973 Sweden's nuclear programme proposed the commissioning of eleven nuclear power plants, representing an installed capacity of some 10,000 MWe. The first six of these units (Oskarshamn-1 and 2, Ringhals-1 and 2, Barsebäck-1 and 2) were in operation by 1977. In 1981 nine units were installed and operable, and another three were under construction.[95] Political factors had been largely responsible for delays ranging between one and four years in the initial operation of several reactors. Compared to the original timetable, Ringhals-3 was delayed by four years, Ringhals-4 by three years, Forsmark-1 by two years and Forsmark-2 by one year. Oskarshamn-3 and Forsmark-3, both under construction, had experienced delays of up to three years and were not expected to come on stream before 1985–6. According to nuclear industry spokesmen, these delays represented a cumulative cost of $1160 million.[96]

Sweden's nuclear programme was initially the product of a consensus involving the main political parties, industry and the electricity utilities. Over the years, R & D priorities, the financial requirements of the nuclear industry, the organisation of the electricity supply system, and the whole philosophy of energy and economic policy had created a powerful momentum in favour of nuclear expansion. Ironically, the over-capacity achieved in the electricity supply sector during the 1960s was used to discourage co-generation by industries and local authorities and to justify increased electricity consumption. More specifically, there developed among utilities a marked tendency to promote inefficient end use patterns, such as electric space-heating, thereby establishing a market for nuclear generated electricity. The very nature of large-scale, utility-operated electricity production and the setting of tariff rates reflecting the cost structure of utilities, each competing for large customers and distributors, were themselves significant factors leading to the adoption of nuclear power as part of a centralised, high energy consumption economy.[97]

Government was an integral part of this process since the largest utility, the State Power Board, which accounted for some 45 per cent of Sweden's electricity output, was wholly owned by the Swedish state and under the authority of the Ministry of Industry. In any case, the government as the final licensor of new power plants was intimately connected with all decisions related to investment in nuclear generating capacity. An equally close link existed between government and the reactor industry. The major nuclear manufacturer in Sweden, ASEA–ATOM, was established in 1969 from the nuclear department of ASEA with the state holding 50 per cent ownership. ASEA–ATOM became the only company outside the United States able to offer complete BWR plants independently of foreign licences. ASEA–ATOM also carried out all activities from the conversion of uranium hexafluoride to the fabrication of fuel assemblies, and was thus able to supply its own reactors. Another company, UDDCOMB, was also formed in 1969 for the manufacture of heavy components, in particular reactor pressure vessels. As with ASEA–ATOM, government participation amounted to 50 per cent. In 1973, the Swedish Parliament gave its stamp of approval to the nuclear programme which then envisaged eleven units. In the interests of minimising dependence on imported oil a new Energy Bill was presented by the Social Democratic government in 1975, which made provision for two more units, giving a total of thirteen units and a projected nuclear electricity output of 63 TWh in 1985.

Despite this intricate web of institutional support for the nuclear programme, the upsurge of public opposition made a deep impact on the political process. Anti-nuclear sentiment was an influential factor in the outcome of the 1976 general election which produced a new parliamentary majority, and eventually a new government. A more restrictive attitude to nuclear power resulted in two initiatives: new legislation concerning final disposal of high level waste and spent fuel, and a review of the energy programme by a government commission.

As indicated in the previous chapter, the Stipulation Law became the linchpin of the Fälldin government's nuclear policy and the lever which it hoped would prevent or at least postpone the commissioning of four new plants then under construction: Ringhals-3 and 4, and Forsmark-1 and 2. The utilities responded by concluding hastily arranged reprocessing contracts with Cogéma and proposed the KBS study as the basis for the handling and storage of high level waste. They were thus able to claim that they had satisfactorily complied with the requirements of the Stipulation Law. The focus of attention shifted back to the coalition parties which now had to assess the validity of that claim.[98]

The Centre Party's task was made all the more difficult in the wake of the Energy Commission's report in 1978 which recommended that the nuclear power stations under construction should be completed. A majority of the commissioners were of the view that fossil fuels posed an even more serious threat to the environment than nuclear power, and that the central storage facility proposed by the KBS study offered a promising approach to the problem of radioactive waste disposal. The Commission's pro-nuclear report made it even more difficult for the coalition partners to reconcile their widely divergent attitudes to nuclear policy. Following the disintegration of the coalition a new minority government was formed under the leadership of the Liberal Party. In line with the main recommendation of the Energy Commission a Bill was introduced in Parliament which stressed the high priority attached to energy conservation and proposed the completion and operation of all nuclear power plants currently under construction but with the proviso that the programme should be limited to twelve reactors.[99]

While approving the government's proposals on conservation, fossil fuels and renewable energy sources, the Parliament chose, in the wake of the events at Three Mile Island, to defer any decision on the future role of nuclear power pending a consultative referendum and the recommendations of the Commission on Nuclear Reactor Safety established to re-evaluate the risks associated with nuclear power in Sweden. The Respite Law of May 1979 prevented the start-up of any new reactor until after the referendum. The implications and results of the plebiscite which was held in April 1980 have already been examined. Suffice it to say that it confirmed and legitimised the proposals previously put forward by the Liberal government. A new Bill presented to Parliament in April 1980, and approved in June, provided for the phasing out of the nuclear power programme over the next thirty years. Measures to improve reactor safety which had been recommended by the Reactor Safety Commission, such as venting filter systems, were to be carried out by 1985. The safety analysis of each reactor would be intensified; and the Nuclear Power Inspectorate re-organised and allocated increased personnel and economic resources.[100] A few days after the referendum the loading of fuel was approved for both Ringhals-3 and Formsark-1. Two weeks later approval was also given for the loading of Ringhals-4 and Forsmark-2, but the permission to operate these reactors was limited up to and including 1986. This permission would be extended if the utilities concerned could present to the government an extended reprocessing agreement or an acceptable plan for ultimate disposal of unreprocessed fuel.

Issues of safety and public acceptability aside, the 1980 referendum had obliged Sweden's energy planners to reconcile the long-term policy of developing new energy sources to replace nuclear stations (and to meet any increases in energy demand after 1990 when the contribution of nuclear power to electricity production was expected to reach a peak of 54.5 TWh) with the immediate need to find substitutes for oil. To this end an oil substitution fund was created under the 1981 Energy Act. For the first three-year period the fund, to be financed by a fee on oil products, was allocated Kr 1700 million. Its main purpose was to support oil-saving technologies based on durable, preferably indigenous and renewable energy resources, in particular solar energy, peat, wood chips, biomass and coal. Provision was also made for an extensive conservation programme involving the industrial, residential, commercial and transport sectors.[101]

The Swedish state apparatus had enabled the opponents of nuclear power, in part through the agency of certain political parties and more specifically by recourse to a plebiscite, to impose a ceiling on future nuclear expansion. This limit, however, was placed sufficiently high to permit the completion of all nuclear plants then under construction or on order. The actual phasing out of nuclear power would occur only after a decade of rapidly increasing production of nuclear generated electricity. The precise timetable to be followed had yet to be clarified by the Social Democratic minority government elected in September 1982. On the other hand, the decision to restrict the programme to twelve reactors meant that no new orders would be possible and that by the mid-1980s the reactor manufacturing industry, in particular ASEA–ATOM, would be deprived of a domestic market.

Faced with the prospect of having to wind down its operations, industry, in concert with other elements of the nuclear establishment, could be expected to pressure policy-makers to abandon or at least review the decision taken in the aftermath of the referendum. The effectiveness of such pressure would in large measure depend on the evolution of Sweden's energy policy. If the use of the price mechanism and the proposed institutional and financial incentives succeeded in achieving the desired equilibrium between energy supply and demand, then the long-term prospect of the Swedish nuclear industry appeared extremely bleak. If, on the other hand, it proved difficult to effect the transition to a sustainable energy economy, then the case for continued nuclear expansion might be re-opened. Overall energy policy had thus become the new battlefield which would shape Sweden's nuclear future.

THE UNITED STATES

America's nuclear power programme was very much a product of the era of economic growth which saw energy consumption rise by nearly one-third between 1950 and 1960 and by more than one-half between 1960 and 1970.[102] The annual growth rate during the 1960s averaged about 4.3 per cent. In 1973 energy consumption was still increasing at the rate of 4.2 per cent, but recorded negative growth in 1974 (– 3.0 per cent) and 1975 (– 2.3 per cent), and after a short-lived recovery in 1976–7 reverted to a much slower rate of increase than that experienced during the previous two decades. The same pattern emerged with respect to electricity production. Whereas it increased by 6.0 per cent in 1960, by 7.2 per cent in 1970 and by 6.3 per cent in 1973, the growth rate fell to 0.1 per cent in 1974, recovered to 6.1 per cent in 1976, only to fall back to 3.3 per cent in 1978.[103] The decline in installed generating capacity was, it is true, much less acute given that construction programmes with long lead times are less susceptible to abrupt changes in demand, but the same trend was nevertheless evident.

The rapidly changing economic climate and increasing energy prices were bound to have considerable impact not only on energy consumption but also on the prospects of the nuclear industry. The commitment of electricity utilities to nuclear power had been largely premised on the expectation that the exponential growth rates achieved during the 1960s would continue indefinitely into the future. Once it became apparent that this trend would not eventuate, forecasts of nuclear capacity for 1985 and beyond were drastically revised. In 1972 the Atomic Energy Commission reduced its projection for 1985 from 300 GWe to 280 GWe. Despite this more conservative outlook, it was still confidently predicted as late as 1974 that by 1985 uranium would be the fuel for nearly 30 per cent of all electric power generation, and that by the end of the century it would supply nearly half of the country's electricity requirements.[104] By

1976, however, the Energy Research and Development Administration was forecasting a much lower nuclear capacity for 1985 – 127–66 GWe.[105] These revised forecasts were subjected to further change in the wake of unfavourable conditions. In 1978, for example, the US Energy Information Administration forecast a nuclear capacity of 127 GWe for 1985 and 162 GWe for 1990. Even these forecasts, however, proved unrealistic, and in 1981 independent and well-informed studies suggested a nuclear capacity of 96.6 GWe in 1985 rising to 132.3 GWe in 1995.[106] In less than ten years the forecasts of nuclear installed capacity for 1985 had been reduced by more than 300 per cent.

How, then, did America's nuclear programme actually fare during the 1970s and early 1980s? An upsurge of orders for nuclear reactors, it will be remembered, had occurred after 1965 – 105 units were ordered in the period 1966–71. Uncertainty concerning the future availability of fossil fuels sustained the momentum in 1972–3, when contracts were signed for the construction of sventy-four large nuclear power plants, representing a total capacity of almost 80,000 MWe. By the end of 1973, forty nuclear generating stations with a capacity of over 24,000 MWe were operable, fifty-six units with a total planned capacity of approximately 53,000 MWe were in various stages of construction, and an additional 101 units, representing almost 110,000 MWe, were on order. In 1974 the trend towards nuclear expansion continued. Despite uncertainties related to future load growth rates and financial constraints over rising construction costs and high interest rates, utilities placed orders for twenty-nine new nuclear units in the first nine months of the year, with the result that, by September 1974, 221 power plants totalling nearly 215,000 MWe were operational, under construction or on order in the United States.[107] The production of nuclear-generated electricity rose from 114,000 MWe/h to 276,400 MWe/h in 1978, which meant that the nuclear contribution to total electricity generation had increased from 6.1 per cent to 12.5 per cent.

Notwithstanding this dramatic expansion, several contrary trends began to emerge in the mid-1970s. After 1975 the rate of new orders fell drastically. Less than twelve units were ordered during the period 1975–8. The average annual ordering rate fell from 21,600 MWe in 1970–4 to 2400 MWe in 1975–9, a trend compounded by a growing spate of deferments and cancellations. In 1977–8 alone orders for twenty-one units were cancelled.[108] As of 1980, sixty-nine reactors

Figure 5.1: *Nuclear reactor orders 1967–81*

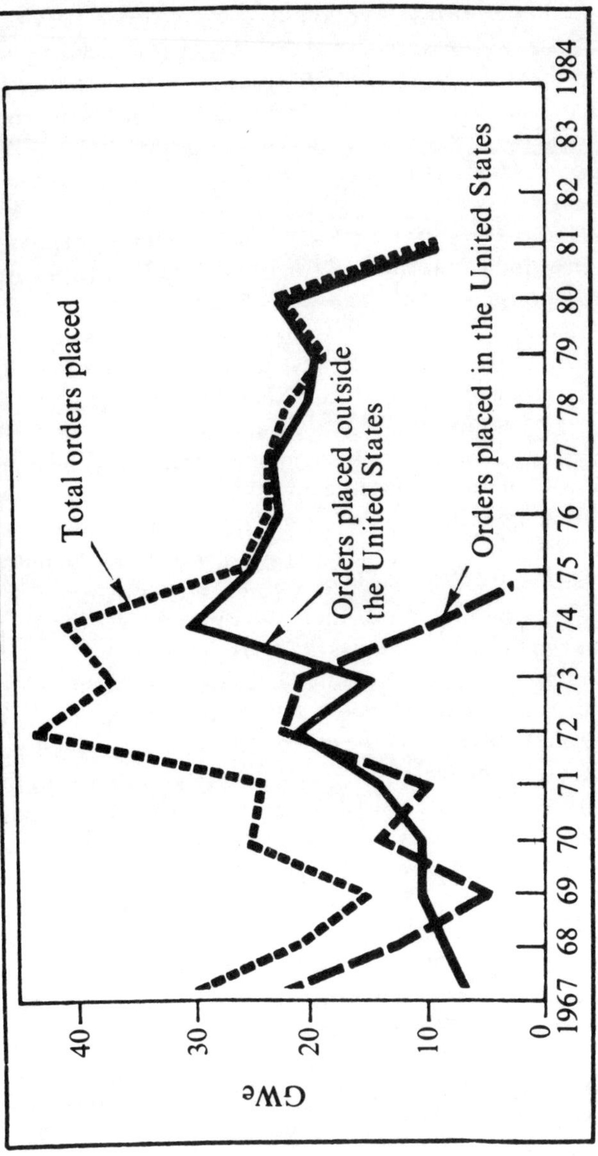

Source: Kidder, Peabody & Co., reproduced in *Nuclear Engineering International*, August 1982 Supplement, p.2.

were licensed for commercial operation, three reactors were ready to come on stream, and another three were shut down indefinitely. However, no new orders were received in that year, previous orders involving sixteen units (18,085) MWe) were cancelled, and construction of another sixty-nine units were delayed for periods ranging from six months to four years.[109] Exactly the same trend emerged in 1981: no new orders were received; six units (5811 MWe) were cancelled; and forty-four were delayed for periods ranging from one month to six years.[110]

From the utilities' point of view, the declining attractiveness of nuclear investments was directly attributable to the rapid escalation in construction costs. Although all electric power plants were subject to the same economic pressures, nuclear plants appeared to be the hardest hit. Apart from late delivery of equipment, scarcity of skilled labour, declining productivity of field labour and continuing inflation in the cost of equipment, materials and wages, cost factors with a peculiarly severe impact on the economics of nuclear power included changes in regulatory procedures, delays in the licensing process, and modifications in reactor design arising from newly-established safety and environmental standards. According to Charles Komanoff, the capital costs of US nuclear power plants during the 1970s had increased annually at more than three times the rate of general inflation, and nearly $1\frac{1}{2}$ times as fast as the cost of building coal-fired plants equipped with anti-pollution devices. Whereas in 1972 nuclear costs were estimated at $ 146/kW, the corresponding costs by the end of 1978 were $718/kW. On the other hand, nuclear power's principal competitor, coal-fired electricity, saw its capital costs during the same period rise from $145/kW to $377/kW ($483/kW with pollution control devices). On the basis of these estimates and taking into account fuel cost differences, it appears that a nuclear plant's overall generating costs in 1978 were roughly equivalent to that of a scrubber-equipped coal plant. Assuming an inflation rate of 7 per cent and the continuation of recent trends, Komanoff calculated that the capital costs of nuclear plants expected to come on stream in the late 1980s would average at about $2500/kW, as compared with $1250/kW for small, efficient coal plants equipped with anti-pollution devices. Total generating costs were estimated at 11.0 cents/kWh for a nuclear plant and 7.0 cents/kWh for a coal plant.[111]

Although the details of these estimates and the method of

accounting were vigorously disputed by spokesmen of the nuclear industry, the general trend and the underlying explanation for it were widely understood and accepted. The sharp increases in nuclear capital costs were a direct result of the efforts of government and regulatory agencies to reduce the societal costs associated with accident risks, pollution of the environment, and radioactive emissions. However, in contrast to coal pollution controls, the remedial measures proposed for nuclear reactors required frequent mid-course design modification which not only lengthened significantly the construction process but required pervasive engineering changes to many plant systems and structures. According to one independent study, stricter design criteria imposed since 1969 by the NRC and its predecessor the AEC had accounted for two-thirds of the capital costs of a nuclear plant completed in 1978 ($591 out of a total of $913 per kilowatt of capacity), whereas for a coal-fired plant cost increases from regulatory and statutory changes accounted for $397 out of a total of $639 per kilowatt of capacity.[112]

Further evidence of the cost implications of regulatory change was provided by the industry's response to the NRC's action plan formulated in the wake of the Three Mile Island accident. The plan was estimated to cost the industry $3500 million in capital costs, $32,000 million in construction delays and shut-downs, and 13,000 technical man-years.[113] Lengthening lead times had already proved the most intractable problem for electricity utilities. Whereas it took 4½–6 years to complete a nuclear power plant in the 1960s, the period required for subsequent plants steadily increased, and by the late 1970s total planning lead times from site selection to operation were estimated to average 12–15 years. A paper published by the International Consultative Group on Nuclear Energy calculated that delays due to siting and regulatory problems had added 'from 3.5 to 7 years to the time from project definition to commercial operation in the U.S.'[114] Lead times of this magnitude required planning horizons which greatly exceeded the industry's forecasting capabilities.

More importantly, in periods of inflation lengthening lead times were likely to result in spiralling capital costs, particularly if the delays came late in the construction process. In 1975 it was estimated that a 1200 MWe plant which might cost $1075 million if built in six years would cost $1600 million in ten years, that is, an additional $525 million. Of this amount, $265 million represented extra interest during construction assuming a rate of 12 per cent, while the remaining $260 million represented cost escalation with inflation at 12 per cent. In addition, it was estimated that the repayment of the additional cost of $525 million would involve a further $661 million in interest changes over thirty-five years. The full cost of the extra four years was therefore estimated to be as high as $1186 million.[115] In other words, electricity utilities had to take into account not only the initial investment cost of a nuclear plant but also the costs arising from inflation and interest during construction. In periods of high inflation and high interest rates these latter costs, assuming a construction period of seven years, were likely to exceed the initial investment cost. Increasing the investment cost even by one year might raise the investment cost by as much as 20 per cent. Increasing the construction time by 5–8 years, as was now the practice in the United States, meant that interest repayments might actually exceed the initial investment cost.[116]

There was, then, nothing very surprising in the fact that electricity utilities were increasingly shying away from nuclear investments, and in some instances cutting their losses by abandoning projects to which they had already committed significant sums of money. They were driven to this course of action by their own deteriorating financial position. Historically, the electricity supply industry had generated two-thirds of its capital requirements from internal sources such as depreciation charges and retained earnings. With the acceleration in capital costs, this ratio had by the mid-1970s dropped alarmingly to less than 25 per cent and for some utilities below 10 per cent. Steeply rising electricity tariffs might have enabled the utilities to absorb the costs and risks of expansion. However, the Public Utilities Commissions, which were responsible for rate regulation in the United States, were intent on restraining the rise of electricity prices. The utilities thus found it increasingly difficult to finance expansion through internal cash flow and were obliged to consider unorthodox financing techniques, including various leasing arrangements and the formation of generation subsidiaries able to sidestep restrictions on the borrowing of new capital. But these measures provided at best a partial solution and could not indefinitely avert the deferment or cancellation of investment decisions.

Nuclear power had become the victim of a complex and increasingly adverse financial and organisational environment. The extremely decentralised character of the American electricity industry, made up predominantly of privately-owned utilities but including also a good number of municipal, state and federal utilities, mirrored the fragmented structure of the American federal system and contrasted sharply with the monolithic position enjoyed by EdF in France and to a lesser extent by the CEGB in the UK. The apparatus of the American state had not only contributed directly, through regulatory intervention, to the financial plight of the electricity supply sector, but had proven singularly incapable of providing the financial relief and instituting the political framework capable of reviving confidence in the security and profitability of nuclear investments.

Electricity utilities were not of course the only parties disadvantaged by the recession in the nuclear market. Even more seriously affected were the reactor manufacturers who, after 1975, had to contend with rapidly diminishing orders and numerous deferments and cancellations. After a period of steady expansion culminating in a productive capacity of 30 GWe of nuclear power plant annually, the US reactor industry was now confronted with a negative ordering rate and with little or no respite in sight. The American government, unlike its counterparts in France, the UK or Sweden, had little direct involvement in the planning or ownership of nuclear production. Reactor manufacture was almost exclusively the preserve of four private corporations, with the two electrotechnical giants, General Electric and Westinghouse, dominating the domestic market with their respective BWR and PWR technologies. As of 1980 General Electric had received orders for eighty-five nuclear reactors, and Wastinghouse for 107. Both firms had a comprehensive manufacturing capability, although General Electric tended to rely more extensively on joint ventures or sub-contracting for the production of various components. The two other major participants in the industry were the heavy engineering firms Babcock and Wilcox (twenty-seven orders) and Combustion Engineering (thirty-one orders) which were the chief suppliers of heavy nuclear components to the US market as well as contractors for complete nuclear systems.

The collapse of the US nuclear market affected different reactor vendors in different ways. General Electric, which had received no new orders since 1975, was also disadvantaged by the relatively poor performance of its BWRs. While anxious to remain in touch with new developments in BWR technology, it appeared likely that General Electric would continue to diversify away from its traditional involvement in the power plant industry and gradually retreat from

Table 5.3: *Nuclear reactor equipment orders at the end of 1981*

Manufacturer	*Cumulative Total*		
	Number	*Capacity (MWe)*	*% of world total*
Asea-Atom	11	8 182	2
Babcock & Wilcox	19	17 705	4
Babcock–Brown Boveri	2	2 507	1
Framatome	54	52 876	12
General Electric (US)	81	69 049	16
Kraftwerk Union	34	32 481	8
NNC (UK)	43	12 271	3
Westinghouse	98	85 227	20

Source: Kidder, Peabody & Co., reproduced in *Nuclear Enginnering International*, August Supplement 1982, p. 3.

the nuclear market which constituted a small proportion of its total sales. As for Babcock and Wilcox, its prospects as a nuclear systems contractor had suffered irreparable damage from the Three Mile Island accident. It might nevertheless seek to retain its manufacturing capability by supplying nuclear components and continuing its involvement in the nuclear submarine programme. Combustion Engineering was in a somewhat stronger position partly because of its success in the American domestic market in the late 1960s and early 1970s, and was probably intent on weathering the current storm.[117]

The firm most heavily committed to the nuclear industry was undoubtedly Westinghouse. Despite lucrative military contracts and other attempts at diversification, Westinghouse's dependence on reactor sales was too great for it to abandon the nuclear market. While waiting for the US moratorium on nuclear ordering to be broken, Westinghouse and other reactor vendors were deriving revenues from their backlog of orders. They were also doing profitable business in such areas as nuclear fuel fabrication, replacement parts and operating plant maintenance and support services.[118] But only additional orders could assure the long-term viability of their manufacturing capacity. Contractors and sub-contractors alike were therefore looking to government and Congress to initiate measures which might once again create the economic and political conditions conducive to expanded investment in reactor development and production.

The sympathetic attitude of successive American administrations to nuclear expansion was not in question. The efficacy of their policies was an altogether different matter. Even before the 1973 oil crisis, President Nixon had repeatedly referred to nuclear energy as the major alternative to current dependence on fossil fuels. In a bid to reduce licensing and construction delays he had proposed to Congress in 1971 that utilities prepare and publish long-range plans for the siting of nuclear power stations and transmission lines. Having failed to secure congressional co-operation, the President resubmitted the legislation in 1973 with several new provisions, including the requirement that government act on all completed licence applications within eighteen months of their reception.[119] As if to underscore the Administration's resolve, William Simon, Administrator of the Federal Energy Office in the White House, stressed in his evidence to the Joint Committee in February 1974 the need to increase installed nuclear capacity in the US to 200,000 MWe by 1980, an eightfold increase over existing capacity.[120] To accomplish this objective it was essential to streamline the licensing process.

Under President Ford the commitment to nuclear power was given renewed impetus with the launching of 'Project Independence' which, among other things, envisaged the construction of 200 large nuclear power plants over the next decade. In addition the establishment of the Energy Research and Development Administration and the Nuclear Regulatory Commission to succeed the AEC were seen as providing the organisational stimulus and the funding needed for an expanding nuclear programme.[121] In 1975, Ford submitted new legislation designed to expedite nuclear licensing and the rapid selection of sites. To ease the financial problems of the industry he recommended that the one year investment credit of 12 per cent be extended for another two years. In 1976, he proposed once again the streamlining of licensing procedures for the construction of new power plants and requested greatly increased funding to accelerate research and development efforts aimed at improving nuclear safety and encouraging industry to enhance the reliability and reduce the construction time of commercial nuclear power plants.

Despite his decision to defer the reprocessing and recycling of plutonium, Ford's successor, President Carter, was no less sensitive to the demands of the nuclear industry for a less obstructionist regulatory framework. During his term of office, the NRC made strenuous efforts to promote a standardisation programme and to reduce the number of hearings required by the licensing process.[122] These initiatives were no more successful than previous attempts to overcome the intractability of a complex and disparate system of state laws and administrative procedures, and the competing and often contradictory influences on congressional decision-making. Whatever hopes may have been entertained for reducing licensing delays, they were dealt a severe blow by the Three Mile Island accident and the series of official inquiries established to investigate its causes and implications. These investigations cast doubts on the adequacy of the plant's design; claimed that the plant's operations had violated plant specifications and federal safety regulations; and described the NRC's handling of the early stages of the accident as 'seriously deficient'.

In its final report, the Kemeny Commission appointed by the President confirmed many of these criticisms, and as part of its forty-four recommendations advocated the drastic re-organisation of the NRC, the periodic renewal of operating licences for nuclear power plants, and the tightening of regulations concerning the location and equipment of such plants. In accepting many though not all of these recommendations, Carter was careful to reaffirm the need for nuclear power. As for Congress, it considered several proposals but decided against a recommendation for the immediate suspension of all licensing. The refusal of either the President or Congress to support draconian anti-nuclear legislation did not, however, imply that the difficulties of the industry had been overcome or that a more favourable regulatory or economic climate was around the corner. Even the advent of the Reagan Administration, which had made no secret of its pro-nuclear stance, did little to restore financial confidence in nuclear investments. In the prevailing economic conditions even the dismantling of part of the regulatory apparatus offered no guarantee of recovery in the nuclear market. Indeed, Reagan's attempts to limit federal influence in the formulation of energy policy and his willingness to rely on 'free and fully informed' market decisions to achieve the required energy balance might simply aggravate the plight of the nuclear industry.[123]

Nor was there any certainty that the Reagan Administration would successfully reverse recent trends in the development of breeder technology. A brief survey of the evolution of policy may be instructive in this respect. In 1971 President Nixon had designated the fast breeder programme as the highest priority item in his nuclear policy. At the Congress hearing on the 1972 Budget, the AEC estimated total government expenditure on the programme at over $2000 million and precast the rapid commercialisation of the technology. The combined influence of the reactor industry, the utilities, the Joint Committee and the Atomic Energy Commission had paved the way for the construction of a demonstration liquid metal fast breeder reactor (LMFBR) at Clinch River in Oak Ridge, Tennessee. The AEC had selected the LMFBR for priority development because of 'its predicted performance, existing industrial support, established base of technological experience, and proven basic feasibility'.[124]

The first major setback came with the Calvert Cliffs decision of the US Circuit Court of Appeals for the District of Columbia which obliged the AEC to produce a detailed environmental impact statement on the whole of their fast breeder programme.[125] Moreover, despite solid congressional support and a Budget allocation which rose from $236 million in the fiscal year 1972 to $320 million in the fiscal year 1973 – the cumulative cost by 1982 was expected to climb above $6000 million – several political clouds were forming on the horizon.[126] In addition to objections based on safety and environmental grounds, the economic viability of the project was increasingly under challenge. (It is perhaps worth noting in parentheses that ERDA's philosophy, in sharp contrast to the approach followed in several European breeder programmes, was to develop a broad technological base and component testing programmes rather than to establish the capability for a competitive industry.[127]) Even with the early resolution of the uncertainties surrounding safety, safeguards and environmental effects, a start on the commercialisation of the LMFBR was not considered feasible before the mid-1990s.[128]

Together with the growing appreciation of proliferation risks the economic case against early commercialisation[129] began to influence congressional thinking and eventually formed the basis for President Carter's decision to restructure the US breeder reactor programme. In April 1977 it was announced that greater priority would be given to alternative breeder designs and the date for the commercial introduction of fast breeders indefinitely deferred.[130] In the President's view, the Clinch River project was likely to contribute to nuclear weapons proliferation; it was prohibitively expensive; its design already obsolete. In any case, given the current availability of uranium supplies, the United States had as yet no need of the fast breeder. The aim of the Carter Administration was to evaluate alternative breeder concepts and fuel cycles and to establish the technical basis for selection of an advanced nuclear system consistent with US nonproliferation objectives and anticipated energy requirements.[131]

The response of industry, Congress and important sections of the bureaucracy was predictably hostile.[132] The deadlock between Congress and the White House and the resulting search for compromises inevitably delayed further work on the Clinch River project. Although large sums of money continued to be allocated to LMFBR research and development, the United States had now fallen considerably behind its main European rivals in the race to build the first commercial-scale demonstration breeder reactor. On coming to office the Reagan Administration sought to revise the Clinch River project by requesting Congress to allocate $254 million for the fiscal year 1982. Government funding was finally fixed at $195 million. Less successful was the Energy Department's formal application to the NRC to permit work on the Clinch River reactor site to begin before hearings on the project's environmental impact were completed. The refusal of the NRC to grant the exemption was thought likely to increase the cost of the plant, perhaps by as much as $150 million, a factor bound to weaken future congressional support for the project.

BRAZIL

The Brazilian 'economic miracle' of the late 1960s and early 1970s was associated in the minds of the country's economic planners with rapidly increasing energy consumption. Indeed, primary energy demand more than doubled during 1967–77, rising from 51.5 million tons of petroleum equivalent (mtpe) to 103.2 mtpe. Despite a high rate of population growth, per capita demand had increased from 0.6 tpe in 1967 to 0.9 tpe in 1977. The trend was, if anything, more pronounced in the area of electricity demand which rose from 34,238 GWh in 1967 to 99,869 GWh in 1977, representing an annual increase of between 9 per cent and 13 per cent.[133] During the same period per capita electricity consumption climbed from 394 kWh to 870 kWh.[134] There was a natural tendency, then, reinforced by the ideological bias of Brazilian economic policy, for official forecasts of future energy demand to extrapolate from this recent history of exponential growth. Indeed, whereas primary energy consumption had increased by an average annual rate of 6.4 per cent during 1965–75, projections made in 1976 for the following decade indicated an average rate of growth of 7.4 per cent per annum.[135] Forecasts in later years were moderated, but only slightly to take account of the downturn in economic activity. In 1978, primary energy consumption was still expected to grow at a rate of 6.2 per cent and to reach 167.0 mtpe in 1985. Two years later the estimate was lowered to 154.7 mtpe.[136]

From the standpoint of nuclear policy, the more relevant forecasts related not so much to total energy consumption as to electricity demand. Again, on the basis of extrapolation from past trends, official projections envisaged that electricity demand would rise at an average annual rate of 11 per cent from 110,018 GWh in 1978 to 263,199 GWh in 1987.[137] To satisfy this dramatic growth in demand installed electric capacity was expected to increase from 22,280 MWe in 1976 to 51,470 MWe in 1985 and reach 185,000 MWe in the year 2000. Given that these load forecasts greatly exceeded Brazil's hydroelectric potential, officially estimated at about 100,000 MWe, a powerful case seemed to exist for the large-scale introduction of nuclear power. Accordingly, the Brazilian Atomic Energy Commission (CNEN) predicted that nuclear-installed capacity would grow from 626 MWe in 1978 to 10,000 MWe in 1990 (13 per cent of total installed capacity), and to 75,000 MWe in 2000 (40 per cent of total installed capacity).[138]

Within the space of a few years, however, two of the major assumptions underpinning this ambitious nuclear programme appeared to be under serious challenge. In the first place, a reassessment of Brazil's hydroelectric resources now indicated a potential of 200,000 MWe, less than one-quarter of which was presently or about to be harnessed.[139] Secondly, government predictions of future electricity demand were proving grossly over-optimistic. Contrary to forecasts and recent trends, declining economic activity and industrial production meant that electricity demand grew by only 3.3 per cent in 1981. In São Paolo, one of Brazil's major industrial centres, demand for electricity actually fell by 0.3 per cent, leaving a generating over-capacity of 15 per cent, which was expected to rise to 25 per cent in the following year.[140]

After the decision was made in the mid-1960s to proceed with

American light water technology, Brazil agreed to buy its first commercial reactor from Westinghouse. The plant, to be built at Angra dos Reis on the coast near Rio de Janeiro, was to have a capacity of 626 MWe and was to come into operation in 1977. A second plant, Angra-2, was to be completed by 1980. Both reactors were to be fuelled by uranium mined in Brazil and enriched in the United States. Brazilian policy-makers, however, increasingly dissatisfied with the conditions attached by the United States to nuclear exports, were striving for greater nuclear independence.[141] It was this consideration, more than any other, which accounts for Brazil's intermittent contacts with European sellers of nuclear technology, for the decision not to proceed with the purchase of the second Westinghouse reactor, and for the eventual announcement in June 1975 that a contract had been signed with West Germany for the acquisition of a self-contained nuclear industry. Initial plans entailed the construction of eight KWU-type 1300 MWe PWRs by 1990. Construction of the first two, Angra-2 and 3, began in 1976 and 1978 respectively. It was expected that they would go into operation in 1982 and 1983 and that the other six stations would be commissioned thereafter at the rate of one a year.[142]

Several difficulties soon emerged making it necessary to reassess the original timetable. The first of these related to the location of the Angra site which had been selected without a detailed geological survey. To secure Angra-2 and Angra-3, concrete piles had to be driven more than 45 metres into the ground.[143] Doubts as to the adequacy of the cooling system also contributed to delays and escalating costs, with the result that in 1978 the dates for the commercial operation of Angra-1, Angra-2 and Angra-3 were rescheduled to 1979, 1984 and 1985 respectively.

In the ensuing years continuing technical problems, coupled with declining growth in electricity demand and the rising cost of nuclear construction, forced further changes to Brazil's nuclear programme. Fuel loading for Angra-1 did not start until the beginning of 1981,[144] and even as late as April 1982 the station was operating only on test at low power, some six years behind the original schedule. In the revised nuclear programme, Angra-2 was expected to start production in 1988; construction of Angra-3 was unlikely to start before 1984. Construction of two more reactors in the south of São Paolo state, on the coast of Iguape, was now planned for 1986 and 1987 respectively, and completion envisaged for 1991 and 1992. With the next two reactors, which were to be built on a site yet to be determined in São Paolo state, work was expected to begin in 1990 and 1993 respectively and to be completed in 1995 and 1998. The location of the remaining two reactors was yet to be finalised but the states of Cearà, Espirito Santo and Rio de Janeiro were the most likely candidates. Work was planned to start in 1994 and 1995 and to be completed in 1999 and 2000.[145] Although the Brazilian Ministry of Mines and Energy conceded that the eight PWR programme would not be realised before the end of the century, even this revised forecast was now widely regarded as unrealistic for it was premised on a five-year construction period which contrasted sharply with the fourteen years taken by Angra-1 and the eleven years currently projected for Angra-2.

Of the various factors which had contributed to the rapid loss of momentum in Brazil's nuclear planning, none was more important than rising capital costs. In 1974, the Furnas Power Authority, one of Brazil's major electricity supply companies, elaborated a *Plan 1990* which formed the basis for the country's nuclear policy. It assumed an annual growth rate of 11.4 per cent in the demand for electrical energy; estimated the cost per installed kilowatt from nuclear power to be slightly in excess of $500; and allowed for a load factor of 80 per cent for nuclear power plants compared with a load factor of 50 per cent for hydroelectricity. Five years later Furnas presented a revised *Plan 1992*, which estimated an annual demand growth rate of only 7.5 per cent; a nuclear load factor of 65.5 per cent; and an investment cost of up to $1700/kW.[146] Adding generating and transmission costs, the Furnas estimates (in 1979 dollars) for Angra-1 and Angra-2 were $1850/kW compared with $1100–50/kW for comparable hydroelectric plants.[147] The disparity between nuclear and hydroelectric costs was even greater according to John Cotrium, former head of Furnas and now technical director of the Itaipù Binacional Authority responsible for the construction of the Itaipù dam with Paraguay on the Parana river, who claimed that nuclear power would eventually cost $3000/kW, thereby raising the total cost of the nuclear programme to $20,000–25,000 million.[148]

What made these unfavourable cost comparisons even less palatable was the added strain they placed on Brazil's already considerable balance of payments difficulties. With a foreign debt well in excess of $50,000 million, Brazil was committed to heavy purchases of foreign nuclear components and technology which would easily outweigh any gain derived from the sale of heavy nuclear parts to neighbouring countries. To give but one example, the design modifications and delays caused by the anchoring of foundation columns for Angra-3 had resulted by 1980 in additional financial charges, mainly in the form of interest payments, amounting to $320 million. Significantly, the contract with German firms provided that the costs of technical difficulties would be passed on to the Brazilian user-company, and that imports of German nuclear know-how and equipment would be paid for in deutsch marks, thus obliging Brazil to borrow on the international money market. To finance the first two nuclear plants, export credits amounting to $1700 million were guaranteed by the West German government and raised largely by loans from kreditanstalt fur Wiederaufbau (DM 1850 million)*, Dresdner Bank (DM 1850 million) and Compagnie Luxembourgeoise de Banque Sa (DM 570 million.[149] The contractual requirements of the German deal tended therefore to reinforce the preference of electricity utilities for hydroelectric plants which were not only cheaper but costed almost entirely in Brazilian currency.

The marked deceleration of the Brazilian nuclear programme at such an early stage of its execution had obvious ramifications for the manufacturing and fuel cycle capacity originally envisaged. In anticipation of a large-scale nuclear industry, the Brazilian government had established as far back as 1971 the Brazilian Nuclear Technology Company to facilitate the formation of a technical and industrial infrastructure. The company, which was at first conceived as the executive branch of CNEN, was transformed in 1974 into the state-owned Empresas Nucleares Brasileiras Sa (NUCLEBRAS), a company with much greater operational flexibility, independent of CNEN, and reporting directly to the Ministry of Mines and Energy. The primary function of NUCLEBRAS was to create in Brazil a capability in the area of nuclear power plant design engineering, construction execution, heavy component fabrication, and production in the different phases of the fuel cycle, mainly production of uranium concentrates, conversion, enrichment, fuel element manufacture and reprocessing.

In line with this general objective, which was enshrined in the German-Brazilian agreement, several 'joint ventures' were estab-

*1976 exchange rate: $1 = DM 2.4

lished between NUCLEBRAS and a number of German companies. The role of NUCLAM in uranium exploration mining and processing, and NUSTEP and NUCLEI in uranium enrichment will be discussed more fully in the next chapter. In the area of nuclear power engineering, a joint venture company, Nuclebràs Engenharia SA (NUCLEN) was formed in which NUCLEBRAS had 75 per cent control and KWU the remaining 25 per cent of the shares. Another joint venture company, Nuclebràs Equipmentos Pesados SA (NUCLEP) was funded with NUCLEBRAS holding 75 per cent of the shares and a consortium comprising KWU, GHH and Voëst-Alpine the remaining 25 per cent. Initial plans called for a capacity to make one complete set of large components (e.g. pressure vessels, steam generators, pressurisers, heat exchangers) a year, expanding to two sets a year, with the possibility of further expansion to cope with the increase in demand anticipated around 1986.[150] Here it is worth noting that these industrial arrangements obscured an intense conflict of interests. For, whereas current plans envisaged 10 per cent Brazilian participation in the manufacture of turbogenerator sets for Angra-2 and 3, gradually increasing to 30 per cent, Brazilian industry could have made a substantially greater contribution to the programme. Clearly KWU's commercial interest was to keep Brazilian participation as small as possible.

What emerges from this brief survey is the critical importance of the state in shaping the pattern of nuclear development. The government's decision to create a large nuclear industry constituted a direct form of state economic intervention, but was seen by the policy-making bureaucracy as an effective means of complementing, supporting and reinforcing the role and activities of private corporations. In other words, state resources were used to cement the alliance with both national and transnational capital. On the one hand, the establishment of the nuclear fuel cycle represented another step in the internationalisation of the country's production through increasing reliance on foreign capital and technology. On the other hand, it promised the progressive indigenisation of the industry by fostering local accumulation and a more extensive national industrial infrastructure.

But the military and bureaucratic elements controlling the core of state power were also motivated by geopolitical considerations, in particular by the notion that Brazil should play a dominant role in the South American continent. By most conventional measures of national power, Brazil in the 1970s was without peer in the region. Its most serious rival, Argentina, was experiencing prolonged economic and political instability. In the nuclear field, however, the Argentine programme based on natural uranium technology appeared to be considerably more advanced.[151] With a nuclear power station and a pilot reprocessing plant already in place, Argentina not only enjoyed a more comprehensive nuclear capability, but a tempting option to fabricate a nuclear device. Reasons of prestige and security thus combined to produce in Brazil a powerful military lobby for the development of a comparable capacity. This factor, more than any other, explains Brazil's decision to terminate its previous dependence on the United States, a country increasingly perceived as an unreliable source of enriched fuel. The Germans, on the other hand, offered the full transfer of the technologies involved in each stage of the nuclear fuel cycle and, therefore, the long-term prospect of nuclear self-sufficiency.[152] The Brazilian state was ready to form an alliance with foreign capital, but in so doing was prepared to choose between competing metropolitan centres in order to maximise its own leverage and freedom of action. Some writers have even gone so far as to suggest that the military and civilian élites were not satisfied with Brazil's recent promotion to the capitalist semi-periphery, but were intent on forcing their way into the core.[153]

As we have already observed, however, the coincidence of political, economic and security objectives which had underpinned Brazil's nuclear programme was severely undermined by the economic recession of the late 1970s. After 1973, industrial growth declined, inflation resumed its upward curve, a serious trade imbalance emerged, and with it a large deficit in the balance of payments. Brazil's foreign debt rose from $600 million in 1973 to $50,000 million in 1980 and $95,000 million in 1983. The economic conditions which had justified and set the stage for Brazil's ambitious nuclear programme no longer existed. Partly as a consequence of the deteriorating economic climate, the military-imposed unity of the state apparatus rapidly gave way to attacks on the authoritarian regime and to calls for democratisation.

In the area of nuclear policy, criticisms were now voiced with mounting vehemence. In keeping with the gradual relaxation of political controls, the National Congress instituted a Commission of Inquiry to investigate the nuclear programme. Evidence presented to the Commission by independent experts, and even by former advisers to the nuclear establishment, pointed to the spiralling costs of nuclear power and to the economic and technical disadvantages arising from the agreement with Germany.[154] In a bid to play down these difficulties, the government maintained an outward appearance of determination and used the occasion of Chancellor Helmut Schmidt's visit to Brazil in April 1979 to reaffirm its commitment to the agreement. In 1980, the President of NUCLEBRAS claimed that the decision of the government was not open to divergence or dissention and confirmed that expenditures of $15,000 million for the eight reactors and $2500 million for the fuel cycle would proceed as planned. It remained to be seen whether this official demonstration of confidence could indefinitely obscure, let alone overcome, the vastly different political and economic realities now confronting the Brazilian nuclear programme.

6 The Politics of the Fuel Cycle

A careful examination of the strategies and options underlying nuclear policy cannot be limited to the fluctuating fortunes of the reactor industry. It also requires us to consider the highly integrated character of the nuclear fuel cycle and the relative importance of such factors as security of fuel supplies, access to enrichment services and mastery of the back and of the nuclear fuel cycle. The very interconnectedness of the industry tends to create new areas of economic and political uncertainty, which in turn impose additional demands on the state's coordinating function.

URANIUM SUPPLY AND DEMAND

Even though uranium availability is not directly or exclusively determined by the decisions of any one state or group of states, there is little doubt that considerations of uranium supply and demand form an integral part of nuclear policy. A viable nuclear programme requires adequate uranium supplies to fuel all existing and projected reactors over their entire life-span. Fuel availability, security of supply and price are important factors governing the scale and timetable of nuclear expansion. They are also bound to influence the debate surrounding the proposed introduction of fast breeder reactors and the economics of reprocessing. In this sense, fluctuations in the uranium market may have profound implications for government decisions relating to the development of sophisticated capital-intensive technologies.

Viewed from a global perspective, estimates published by the OECD Nuclear Energy Agency (NEA) and the International Atomic

Energy Agency consistently indicated throughout the 1970s that existing uranium reserves could support sufficient production to meet any likely levels of demand at least to the year 2000. Indeed, reasonably assured low cost resources (i.e. proven deposits recoverable at costs of less than \$15/lb U_3O_8 in 1975 dollars) increased from 494,000 tonnes in 1965 to 645,000 tonnes in 1970, and were in excess of one million tonnes in 1975.[1] A further one million tonnes of low cost uranium were now estimated to exist which could be categorised as 'less assured'. In the \$15–30/lb range there were another 700,000 tonnes of reasonably assured resources and about the same amount of less assured resources. Two years later, reasonably assured resources, exploitable at a cost below \$30/lb, totalled 1,560,000 tonnes, that is, an increase of 482,000 tonnes over the 1975 estimate where a cost of \$15/lb U_3O_8 was used to define reserves.[2] In other words, reserves grew rather than diminished as consumption increased, in part because of increased exploration. In the case of US domestic supply, ERDA estimates published in 1977 showed that uranium reserves and probable resources available at \$30/lb or less would be sufficient to fuel approximately 315 reactors of the 1000 MWe size range over their thirty-year life-span assuming no recycling of plutonium or uranium.[3]

The first decline for many years in the overall level of the non-communist world's uranium resources was recorded in 1981. Compared to 1979, the 1981 estimates represented a decrease of 297,000 tonnes in the level of reasonably assured reserves recoverable at less than \$130/kg, but this was virtually offset by a corresponding increase of 270,000 tonnes in the level of estimated additional resources. In any case, the main reasons for the decrease were inflation and rising production costs which pushed resources into higher cost categories.[4] However, because of the sluggish growth of nuclear power and the consequent over-capacity in the uranium industry, producers had stopped the exploitation of some deposits and reduced the level of investment in the industry, thereby curtailing the level of exploration in many countries. Here it should be noted that, while representing an accurate measure of the physical limits to supply capacity, at least over the medium term, estimated reserves need to be placed in a larger political and economic context so as to take account of trade and financial policies, safeguards and other institutional arrangements, health, safety and environmental regulations, public perceptions and attitudes, all of which may impose significant constraints on existing and planned supply capacities.[5]

Having reached a peak production of 33,000 tonnes in 1959, much of it earmarked for military purposes, world uranium production declined throughout the 1960s and remained fairly constant in the range of 19,000–20,00 tonnes annually between 1972 and 1975. It then increased sharply in subsequent years, largely as a result of new mines opening in Canada, the United States and South Africa, reaching some 30,000 tonnes in 1977. Of this the United States accounted for 40 per cent, South Africa and Namibia together 23 per cent, Canada 17 per cent, Niger 8 per cent, metropolitan France 6 per cent, and Gabon 2 per cent.Australia, where only the Mary Kathleen mine was in operation, was only just beginning to exploit its large production potential. By 1981 world uranium production capability was approaching 50,000 tonnes, and was expected to reach a maximum of a little under 78,000 tonnes in 1986.[6] Estimates for 1990 ranged from 64,000 tonnes to 82,000 tonnes a year depending on the outcome of projects currently under evaluation.[7]

Of the six countries under review, the United States has by far the largest uranium reserves. Reasonably assured and estimated additional resources exploitable at a cost of $30/lb U_3O_8 were calculated to be 1,361,000 tonnes in January 1977.[8] Indeed, since the early 1960s the uranium industry has suffered from over-capacity. Actual production during the early and mid-1970s averaged at about 10,000 tonnes a year, but by 1977 production capability stood at about 14,700 tonnes and was expected to reach 36,000 tonnes in 1985 and 47,000 tonnes in 1990,[9] a level greatly in excess of likely domestic requirements.[10] Although less generously endowed, France was the only Western European country producing uranium within its own borders. In 1977 its low cost, reasonably assured and estimated additional resources amounted to 61,800 tonnes.[11] In addition some 35,000 tonnes were available in the upper price range, of which about 20,000 tonnes were reasonably assured resources. Annual production during the 1970s ranged between 1500 tonnes and 2500 tonnes, and a production capability of 4000 tonnes a year was forecast for 1990.

The growth of a French uranium industry owed a good deal to the formation in 1972 of the Péchiney Ugine Kuhlmann (PUK) group which brought together a number of fragmented holdings in nuclear subsidiary companies.[12] PUK was nationalised in 1981 following the election of the Socialist government. Equally important, however, was the early involvement of the CEA in the development of French domestic resources which provided a launching-pad for exploration and processing by private enterprise and subsequent expansion of these activities in various French speaking countries in western and central Africa. After 1973 French companies became involved in geological work in Gabon, Niger, Indonesia, Canada, South America and Australia. Several of these are currently exploiting reserves totalling more than 200,000 tonnes (e.g. Somair and Cominak in Niger, Comuf in Gabon and Amok in Canada), in which the main participants are the CEA, Imetal and Minatome, the latter representing an amalgamation of the uranium mining interests of PUK and Compagnie Française des Pétroles (CFP).[13]

Of the other European countries, only Sweden could boast any substantial uranium deposits. Although reasonably assured resources were estimated in 1977 at 300,000 tonnes, they were comprised of low grade ore recoverable only at prices in excess of \$30/lb U_3O_8. Uranium prospecting conducted with government support identified the Pleutajokk deposit as economically the most favourable, but despite test drillings and continuing environmental studies, determined local opposition to uranium mining had thus far prevented the exploitation of any deposit. Sweden, therefore, like Britain and West Germany, has been almost entirely dependent on imports for its uranium requirements. Given the absence of commercial indigenous supplies of suitable uranium ores, Britain has attempted to maximise security of supply through geographical and political diversification, overlapping contracts and direct involvement in mining equity. The CEGB's recent policy has been to provide 75 per cent of its needs through long-term contracts with suppliers and 25 per cent through direct involvement in mining.[14] During the 1970s the bulk of British supplies came from Canada and Namibia. Germany's principal suppliers were South Africa, Canada, Gabon, Niger and the United States.[15] In the case of Brazil, estimates of future dependence on foreign supplies were radically revised as a result of the much slower rate of nuclear power development and the very considerable additions to Brazil's low cost reasonably assured resources. In 1978 these reserves were considered adequate to meet the total cumulative needs of the Brazilian nuclear programme up to 1997, that is, sufficient to supply ten reactors of a size comparable to Angra-1 during their entire lifetime. Apart from the first core of Angra-1, the uranium for which had been contracted in 1973, no further imports were anticipated.[16] By January 1981, Brazil's low cost, reasonably assured resources had increased to 119,000 tonnes, thereby ensuring that available production would be greatly in excess of domestic requirements.

By the early 1980s security of supply was no longer the dominant consideration governing uranium policy. Contrary to the conditions which had prevailed in the early 1970s, an over-supply had emerged resulting from the increased supply capabilities and production of the major producing countries on the one hand, and the sluggish growth of nuclear power on the other. Worldwide uranium demand had risen from 18,000 tonnes in 1973 to 23,000 tonnes in 1977, but the projections which had been made for 1985 and beyond were drastically scaled down. In 1975 estimates published by the IAEA and the Nuclear Energy Agency of OECD had forecast that uranium demand would rise to 80,000–100,000 tonnes by 1985, and by a further 50 per cent by 1990. By 1981, the forecast for 1990 was lowered to 53,000–65,000 tonnes. In the medium term (1991–2000) there was increasing uncertainty as to how many reactors would be built, although the light water reactor was expected to be the main type in operation. Accordingly, projected uranium requirements for 1995 ranged from 64,000 tonnes to 85,000 tonnes and for the year 2000 from 80,000 tonnes to 130,000 tonnes. In 1981, the Uranium Institute's most probable growth scenario envisaged a demand of 64,000 tonnes in 1990 and 74,000 tonnes in 1995.[17] This was a far cry from the optimistic predictions of a few years earlier made by industry, governments and international agencies alike.[18] There was, moreover, every likelihood that the downward trend in the estimates of future demand would continue for some time to come. World production in 1981 was more than double the level of consumption, thereby adding to mounting uranium stockpiles now estimated to be in excess of 200,000 tonnes. Given the reduced growth estimates for nuclear power, world uranium supply was expected to exceed demand to the year 2000 and possibly well beyond.[19]

Nowhere was the recession in the uranium industry more acutely felt than in the United States where the maximum supply capacity from existing mines or those committed to future production was likely to be of the order of 47,000 tonnes in 1990 – enough to supply 230 GWe of installed nuclear generating capacity. By contrast, the firm base of reactors in existence and those well under construction was identified by the Department of Energy to represent some 118 GWe by 1990, which would require approximately 23,600 tonnes of uranium production per year. In these circumstances production capability was likely to be vastly in excess of domestic requirements. The only hope, therefore, that new US uranium projects had of avoiding financial collapse was the export market. But uranium production capacity outside the United States was itself increasing faster than the number of reactors in operation, under construction or on order. It is hardly surprising therefore that Congress should have sought to assist the ailing US uranium industry by imposing import quotas as well as other discriminatory measures against the use of foreign uranium.

With most utilities already carrying substantial stocks of uranium, the effect of the fall in demand on the uranium market was to cause mining projects to be delayed or cancelled and mills to close or operate at partial capacity. But the most immediate result was the decline in uranium spot prices, reversing the trend which had operated during the greater part of the 1970s. In February 1973, the price of U_3O_8 for immediately delivery, as measured by Nuexco's Exchange Value, was \$6/lb. It rose continuously thereafter, reaching \$15/lb in December 1974, \$35/lb in December 1975, \$41/lb in September 1976, and averaging \$43.95 in 1978.[20] Several factors had contributed to the price escalation, notably the Arab oil embargo in late 1973, the election of a Labor government in Australia in December 1972, rising uranium production costs, new environmental, health and safety regulations which changed the economics and delayed the opening of new mines, continuing delays in the anticipated introduction of reprocessing and recycling of uranium and plutonium.

Perhaps the most decisive factor was the change in American contractual policy with respect to enrichment services. The AEC's decision in 1973 to opt for 'fixed-commitment contracts', which required customers to purchase specified amount of enriched uranium at specified dates, greatly exaggerated requirements for production of enriched fuel. The revised contracting process thus accentuated the perceived need for uranium supplies. By June 1974, requests had been received to cover enrichment services needed to fuel the equivalent of 257,000 MWe of nuclear-installed capacity. In addition to these contracts, which specified deliveries of initial cores prior to July 1982, the demand for uranium supplies was further augmented by the US announcement in January 1975 that the tails assay, which determines the uranium feed requirements of enrichment plants, would be raised from 0.20 per cent U_{235} to 0.275 per cent in 1976 and to 0.30 per cent in 1981. The net effect of this change alone was to raise the demand for uranium by 28 per cent.[21] In other words, the policies of the US Atomic Energy Commission were a major cause of over-contracting in enrichment services, which in turn stimulated an artificially high demand for natural uranium and a corresponding over-expansion of uranium productive capacity.

It remains to say a word about the impact of the international uranium cartel which was established in 1972 and operated through to 1974 under the title 'Uranium Marketing Research Organisation'. The group, which comprised Canada, France, South Africa, Australia and the British-based mining giant, Rio Tinto Zinc Corporation, succeeded in formulating major rules that would govern the cartel. Besides the basic pricing policy, market quotas, and discrimination against certain customers and middlemen, agreement was also reached on contract conditions, notably the currency to be used, payment schedules, and flexibility in delivery dates.[22]. Once a few contracts had been negotiated at cartel-desired prices, it was confidently expected that a world market price clause would ensure that all other transactions would automatically take place at satisfactory price levels. There is reason to believe, however, that the cartel did not so much create as take advantage of the new market conditions to which a great many other factors had contributed.

This brief examination of the uranium market as it evolved between 1973 and 1978 would suggest that the complex interaction between government policies and corporate decisions which helped to shape the price of uranium did not accurately reflect the long-term trends in the nuclear industry. Indeed, from 1973 onwards plans for nuclear expansion were being scaled down almost as steeply as uranium prices were rising. It was therefore only a matter of time before the conditions of apparent uranium scarcity would give way to the situation of over-supply characteristic of the late 1970s and early 1980s. Accordingly, the uranium spot price fell dramatically after 1979, sinking to $20.75 in April 1982.[23] Although the spot market was not faithfully reflected in pricing arrangements under long-term contracts, it did nevertheless indicate the recessionist conditions now prevailing in the uranium industry. The net result of this trend was to reduce the economic incentives for closing the nuclear fuel cycle, at least for the foreseeable future, and to lessen the vulnerability of consumers to the financial or political demands of supplying countries. In a buyer's market, the efficacy of state intervention was bound to diminish and the threat of interrupted supplies likely to appear much less credible.

ENRICHMENT

The foregoing analysis of recent trends in the uranium market has not considered in any detail the relationship between uranium supply and nuclear policy for each of the six countries under review. Rather its aim has been to highlight in more general fashion certain recurring themes in the role of the state, namely the uneasy but extensive partnership between the private and public sectors, the emphasis on national independence, and the propensity for international competition and conflict. All of these domestic and foreign policy issues are even more starkly evident with respect to the supply of enrichment services, which is in any case not unconnected with the question of uranium supply. Here it is important to remember that for a great many years the United States enjoyed a monopoly of commercial enrichment capacity within the western world. Under the authority of the 1954 Atomic Energy Act, the AEC was able to provide enrichment services needed to fuel domestic and foreign power reactors, using for the purpose the three enrichment plants at Oak Ridge, Tennessee, Paducah, Kentucky, and Portsmouth Ohio, all of which were originally built to meet national defence needs. During the 1970s more than 90 per cent of the world's nuclear power stations were fuelled with enriched uranium, most of which was supplied by the United States. During the fiscal years 1973 and 1974, AEC revenues from the supply of enrichment services to domestic customers amounted to $116.7 million and $160.7 million respectively. Revenues from foreign customers totalled $140.3 million in 1973 and $381.4 million in 1974.[24] Although abnormally high in these years because of special advance sales to Japan, these figures nevertheless point to the commercial incentives associated with the export of enriched fuel.

A significant change in US enrichment policy ensued with the amendment in 1964 of the Atomic Energy Act, which opened the way for the private ownership of special nuclear materials. The movement towards complete privatisation of the nuclear fuel cycle and, therefore, towards private ownership of enrichment plants was given further impetus by the Nixon Administration. No firm commitment, however, was forthcoming from the private sector to build and operate a uranium enrichment plant, primarily because of the large capital investment involved. Uranium Enrichment Associates (UEA), a consortium headed by Bechtel, had proposed the construction of a 9 million SWU gaseous diffusion plant. In addition, Garret, Exxon, and CENTAR, a joint venture involving Atlantic Ritchfield and Electro-Nucleonics, had each expressed interest in building a 3 million SWU centrifuge plant. It soon became evident that these private projects would not proceed without government guarantees. To this end the Ford Administration proposed in June 1975 the Nuclear Fuel Assurance Act, under which ERDA would have been authorised to negotiate and enter into contracts with private firms interested in building, owning and operating enrichment plants. Provision was made for various forms of assistance and assurances under such arrangements, including a maximum government liability of $8000 million in the event that the private ventures failed and had to be taken over by government. The proposed legislation also provided for foreign participation in these plants, although it was envisaged that they would remain firmly under US control.[25]

In the course of negotiations between ERDA and UEA, it emerged that more specific concessions were being sought, including the supply of essential components, technical assistance and know-how; an assurance that government would assume all liabilities and obligations if the plant could not be successfully completed; and the purchase by ERDA of up to 6 million separative work units (SWUs) during the first five years. The proposed legislation, which was designed to let the public sector shoulder the risks while allowing the private sector to realise profits in the event of commercial success, narrowly failed to secure the necessary majority in Congress. Opponents of privatisation were concerned not only by the public costs of private ownership but also by the prospect of diminished government control over a sensitive technology with far-reaching implications for non-proliferation objectives and foreign policy generally.[26]

During the Nixon years encouragement of privatisation had gone hand in hand with support for the concept of multilateral joint ventures. To the extent that enrichment had become a more conventional industrial undertaking, it was now deemed feasible to consider the participation of foreign governments as well as of

American private industry. By this time, several European organisations were contemplating the construction of European enrichment plants. The multilateralisation proposal was in part justified as a mechanism for enhancing control of the military use of the technology. But it was also designed to serve American economic interests in that joint ventures were likely to provide American firms with a ready market for equipment and know-how. Moreover, by limiting the development of national plants, it might be possible to prevent over-capacity which would adversely affect the profitability of the American enrichment industry.[27] Far from achieving their objective, American initiatives may well have encouraged more widespread enrichment efforts. The major nuclear powers in Europe and Japan and major uranium producers began enrichment project studies, resulting in some instances in actual project planning. Current dependence on the United States stimulated the drive towards enrichment autonomy or at least the desire to diversify sources of supply.

It is against this background that one has to assess the impact of the AEC's revised contract policy which came into effect in September 1973. Whereas previously customers could obtain through 'requirement contracts' as much enriched fuel as they needed with less than one year's advance notice, they were now expected to sign 'fixed-commitment' contracts at least eight years in advance of delivery of the first core. In addition, they had to agree to purchase specified amounts of enriched uranium over a moving ten-year period and to deliver the required uranium supplies regardless of their actual need for enriched fuel.[28] The principal objective, it was claimed, of this revision was to firm up the demand for enrichment services to achieve more realistic and reliable planning. The net effect of the new contract system was to shift the risks to the user. The long lead times and down payments required meant that electricity utilities had to finalise their plans at a very early stage. In the case of the European and Japanese electricity supply industries, requests for enrichment contracts would have to be placed before work on a reactor project had actually started.

As a consequence customers for US enrichment services signed contracts far in excess of likely needs in order to ensure security of supply. By June 1974, the demand on AEC's enrichment services for both executed and pending contracts totalled 364,000 megawatts,[29] representing a rate of nuclear expansion more rapid than the most optimistic AEC projection. Having over-committed itself by a significant margin, the AEC temporarily suspended signing long-term contracts. It soon became apparent that many domestic and foreign electricity utilities were eager, as a result of the slowing down of nuclear power development, to terminate or delay deliveries scheduled under long-term contracts. ERDA, for its part, perceived a need to increase its inventory of enriched uranium and so offered a one-time opportunity for customers to adjust their requests for enrichment services.

The potential of this offer for producing a more realistic estimate of enrichment requirements was nevertheless limited by the fact that the opportunity for revision was not to be repeated and was in any case limited to two months. Moreover, initial core deliveries could not be deferred beyond fiscal year 1985. Rising stockpile levels were thus used to offset the reduced requirements of domestic and foreign customers. In fiscal year 1975, for example, ERDA produced about 3 million kg of enriched uranium, but sold only a little over 60 per cent of this amount. The remainder was added to its stockpile, which at the end of that year amounted to 5 million kg – the equivalent of almost four years' supply for the US domestic programme.[30] The stockpiling policy, strongly supported by ERDA and the Joint Congressional Committee, was in part inspired by the need to justify the expansion of government enrichment capacity to meet the anticipated surge in demand during the 1980s, particularly in the event that private enrichment ventures did not materialise. Equally important was the beneficial impact which the sustained demand for enriched fuel, coupled with the low uranium 235 utilisation rate, was expected to have on the uranium market, notably on the price of uranium, and the consequent flow of investment capital into new mining and milling facilities.[31]

Underpinning all these policies was the projected expansion of US enrichment capacity. This was to be achieved through the Cascade Improvement Program (which would increase efficiency by introducing the most recent technological advances) and the Cascade Uprating Program (which would enlarge the plants' electrical systems and cooling capability). Upon the completion of these programmes in 1983, ERDA expected to obtain an additional annual increase of about 8.7 million SWU. Authorisation had also been given for the construction of another enrichment facility. In April 1977, President Carter expressed his preference for a gas centrifuge plant, and subsequently indicated that it should be located at Portsmouth, Ohio.[32] Upon completion of the plant US enrichment capacity was expected to increase to about 36.1 million SWU per year.[33] Additional US enrichment capacity was defended in terms of America's traditional efforts to limit the proliferation of nuclear and weapons capability and improve the nation's balance of payments.[34] Yet the prospect of so much additional US enrichment capacity, taken in conjunction with the plans of other countries to enter the enrichment supply market, raised the possibility that what was once expected to be an acute shortage might soon become a glut.

By the late 1970s, the proliferation of enrichment techniques was already well advanced. As of May 1979, Brazil was committed to the development of a small facility (0.22 million SWU per year) based on the as yet unproven nozzle technology supplied by West Germany, and expected to come on stream in 1985.[35] South Africa was constructing a plant of comparable size also scheduled to commence operation in 1985, and based on the helikon process. Japan was planning the construction of a gas centrifuge plant with a projected capacity of 5.5 million SWU per year by 1995. The Soviet Union was already operating a gas diffusion plant with an estimated capacity of 3.9 million SWU per year.[36] But the two projects which were expected to have the most far-reaching effect on the worldwide supply of enriched fuel were the Urenco and Eurodif European multinational ventures.[37]

The signing of the Treaty of Almelo in March 1970 represented a watershed in the international transfer of enrichment technology. Through the treaty the governments of the United Kingdom, the Federal Republic of Germany and the Netherlands agreed to pool all their technical resources and to establish a centrifuge-based commercial enrichment enterprise. Initially, it had been intended that the collaboration would function through a centralised structure with a prime contractor, Centec, responsible for research and development, component supply and plant construction, and with Urenco as the owner-operator of the enrichment plants. A more decentralised arrangement was subsequently adopted, with Urenco (UK), Urenco Nederland and Urenco Deutschland set up as legally constituted partnerships to construct, own and operate the enrichment plants at Campenhurst, Almelo and Gronau respectively.[38] The Capenhurst and Almelo plants began producing enriched uranium in 1976, and by the end of 1979 had in operation an enrichment capacity of 0.22

and 0.24 million SWU per year respectively. The Gronau plant with an initial capacity of 0.4 million SWU per year was not expected to become operational before 1985. The flexibility inherent in the gas centrifuge method of enrichment enabled Urenco to establish additional capacity only as required to meet contractually secured commitments. On the other hand, the total planned capacity for the three plants in 1985 was now only 2 million SWU per year compared with the 10 million SWU anticipated in the early 1970s. This dramatic scaling-down of capacity expectations meant that Urenco would not achieve the economies of scale envisaged, a fact that was bound to influence the cost structure of the organisation.

Apart from the utilities of member countries, the only other significant customer of Urenco's enrichment services was Nuclebras of Brazil. However, both the Dutch Parliament and the US Administration were hostile to the supply of enriched uranium for use in the reactors being constructed by West Germany under the June 1975 agreement. They objected on the grounds that the uranium could be treated in the reprocessing plant also being supplied under the agreement to make plutonium suitable for use in nuclear weapons. A formal agreement for the delivery of enriched uranium to Brazil was not reached until September 1978. Public and parliamentary opposition in the Netherlands had hitherto prevented the extensive expansion of the Almelo plant which West Germany needed to provide Urenco fuel for Brazil's reactors.[39] Following the resignation of Mr den Uyl's Centre-Left coalition, the new Dutch government decided to give its approval to the project because of Brazil's agreement to accept tighter safeguards, and place the storage of plutonium under international controls. The Dutch Parliament, however, made the expansion of the Almelo plant and the supply of uranium to Brazil conditional upon the negotiation of strict safeguards against its misuse before the first Urenco shipments were due to be delivered. The proliferation implications of enrichment exports to Brazil coupled with the rapid loss of momentum in the Brazilian nuclear programme – not to speak of the slow rate of nuclear growth in the three member countries – had thus created new uncertainties about the market potential for the Urenco venture.

By comparison, the French-based Eurodif gaseous diffusion venture appeared at first sight to have a sounder commercial base. Gaseous diffusion was indeed chosen to minimise technical risks. Construction of the Eurodif project started in 1974; in 1978, the first cascades were taken into commercial production; in 1979 production reached 2.2 million SWU; and by 1982 the full capacity of 10.8 million SWU per year was achieved as originally planned.[40] The shareholders of Eurodif were: Cogéma, the French, state-owned subsidiary of CEA (36.53 per cent); Sodidif, jointly owned by Cogéma and the Organisation for Economic and Technical Aid and Investment of Iran (25.0 per cent); Agip Nucleare, the Italian, state-owned fuel company, and CNEN, the Italian Nuclear Research Agency (16.25 per cent); Enusa from Spain (11.11 per cent); and SOBEN from Belgium (11.11 per cent). To ensure the commercial viability of the project, all shareholders were committed to buying Eurodif's production – apart from that sold to foreign customers – in proportion to their shareholding. By 1980, enrichment services equivalent to 10 million SWU were sold to Japanese utilities for delivery over a ten-year period beginning in 1981. Similar quantities were contracted by one Swiss and one German utility.

But even as the Eurodif management was claiming to have its order books almost filled until 1990, problems were beginning to loom on the horizon.[41] In the first place, the Iranian revolution had put an end to the country's ambitious nuclear plans and placed in jeopardy its 10 per cent participation in Eurodif. Secondly, the Italian nuclear programme had made remarkably little progress, with the result that only 3400 MWe of nuclear capacity was in operation or under construction by 1980. Yet Italy's original 25 per cent shareholding obliged it to take up enrichment services equivalent to the needs of about 20 × 1000 MWe nuclear power plants. To compound the problem, Italy had already negotiated enrichment contracts with both the United States and the Soviet Union. To reduce its take-off obligations, Italy negotiated in 1980 the sale to Cogéma of 9 per cent of its 25 per cent shareholding in Eurodif. In a bid to reduce the ever-growing stockpile of enriched fuel, the Italians also purchased from the United States some 20,000 tonnes of uranium in the form of 0.3 per cent U 235 tails assay (the percentage of uranium 235 remaining after the production of enriched uranium) with a view to having it enriched by Eurodif up to the equivalent of natural uranium, that is 0.711 per cent U 235. But these were no more than short-term expedients which could not resolve the growing imbalance in Eurodif's long-term supply and demand position.

Belgium and Spain, which had also signed contracts with the United States and the Soviet Union, faced similar difficulties. Spain had entered into its separative work obligations on the assumption that it would have a nuclear installed capacity of more than 20,000 MWe by 1985. It was now thought unlikely that 12,575 MWe would be exceeded by 1990 even according to the most confident official projections. To reduce the expected enrichment surplus, Spain converted its long-term fixed commitment contract with the United States to an adjustable fixed commitment contract and took advantage of the one-time delivery rescheduling opportunity. Nevertheless, Spain could not fulfil all of its commitments without adding the equivalent of 10 million SWU to existing stockpiles during the 1980s. Belgium, for its part, was expected on the basis of all its enrichment commitments to add during the decade about 6 million SWU to its inventory. Only France among the Eurodif shareholders could be said to have anything approaching a balanced supply and demand position, and this before taking into account its acquisition of 9 per cent of the Italian shareholding and the possible consequences of the Iranian dispute. Any delays or reductions in France's projected nuclear programme would obviously accentuate the problem of excess capacity. Nor was there much likelihood, given the current condition of the world enrichment market, that member countries would have much success in selling off their surplus separative work or their surplus Eurodif shareholdings. Should the Eurodif partners fail to absorb the quantities involved, their only way out of the dilemma would be either to operate Tricastin at something less than full capacity, or attempt to use as many SWUs as possible by adopting a much lower tails assay (a policy inconsistent with the current situation of falling uranium prices); or alternatively consider the cancellation of enrichment contracts with the United States.

Competing national interests as defined by the major nuclear powers had thus contributed to the present glut in enrichment supply. The US Department of Energy was still the major supplier of enrichment services which it offered at $100–10 per SWU (compared with Eurodif's price of $140–50 per SWU). Its European competitors claimed that the Department of Energy was not a commercial enterprise, that its prices were fixed by considerations of national policy, and that its plant was paid for from the military budget.[42] Nevertheless, the price of US enrichment services was steadily increasing, with a rise of 27 per cent in 1981 and further rises expected in subsequent years.[43] Whereas the United States was intent on maintaining its share of the western world's enrichment market for economic and security reasons, the Europeans were seeking to curtail American dominance in the interests of 'energy security and independence'. State intervention, which had proved necessary for the achievement of these national goals, was thus instrumental in creating a worldwide enrichment supply vastly in excess of current and foreseeable demand. Supply capability for 1983 was expected to be in the vicinity of 42 million SWU per year compared with a demand projection of 22 million SWU rising to a maximum of 38 million SWU in 1990. The existing inventory of about 38 million SWU of enriched uranium was expected to double by 1990.

In these rapidly changing circumstances it became necessary for the major enrichment suppliers to abandon their grandiose schemes. The progress of the US centrifuge programme now depended on the complex and volatile budgetary process. Its justification no longer rested on demand grounds but on the displacement of the energy intensive diffusion process. In any case, the plant, which was expected to cost $5700 million in constant 1980 dollars, would be built step by step, with the first building unlikely to be completed before 1989. The Coredif enrichment plant was likely to suffer a similar fate. A parallel project to Eurodif, with the same countries participating but with a different share-ownership structure, Coredif was to have an installed capacity of 10 million SWU per year by 1990. By 1980 the time-scale was widely recognised as unrealistic, and the future of the project placed in considerable doubt. As for the Urenco venture, it was originally expected to have a total annual capacity of 10 million SWU but only one-fifth of that capacity was likely to be realised by 1985.

The very substantial over-capacity in enrichment services had developed partly as a result of decisions based on optimistic assumptions about future nuclear growth. Once European countries had acquired an independent but costly enrichment capability, they were obviously intent on maintaining that technological independence and commercial leverage despite the depressed state of the world enrichment market. To preserve their newly-acquired position, they were prepared to cancel, revise, or at least not renew, existing enrichment contracts with the United States. They were also seeking new foreign customers for their services and hoping to be assisted in this task by what they perceived to be growing international dissatisfaction with US non-proliferation policy.

The United States, for its part, was out to reassure all traditional customers of its reliability as the leading international supplier of enrichment services and, as we shall see in a later chapter, was willing for this purpose to moderate, through a process of administrative reinterpretation, many of the requirements of the 1978 Non-Proliferation Act. In the longer term, the US Department of Energy was investing considerable resources into the next generation of enrichment technology – called advanced isotope separation (AIS).[44] Three processes were under investigation: atomic vapour laser isotope separation; molecular laser isotope separation; and plasma separation. The existing gaseous diffusion method, because of its excessive reliance on electric power, was thought unlikely to survive any successful alternative. On the other hand, gas centrifuge plants, though they needed much less power and hence had relatively low operating costs, required very high capital outlay. By contrast, the AIS processes, once perfected, were likely to enjoy low construction and production costs. They were considered feasible for large-scale operation in the 1990s with a possible delivery cost ($20–40/SWU) vastly inferior to that currently offered by the US Department of Energy or by Eurodif. By achieving a decisive lead in this area of research and development, the US was no doubt hoping to re-establish its dominance in enrichment technology and recapture a major share of the world market.

REPROCESSING

In our necessarily brief and selective analysis of the front end of the nuclear fuel cycle we have alluded to the close interconnection between the uranium mining, enrichment and reactor industries on the one hand and between them and other stages of the nuclear fuel cycle on the other. It has long become apparent that the long-term success of any large nuclear programme would depend on mastery of the back end of the nuclear fuel cycle. As we shall see, the reprocessing of spent fuel and the management of radioactive wastes were to prove particularly sensitive policy areas of critical importance to the technological competence, profitability and political acceptability of the nuclear industry.

Until the mid-1970s, the major nuclear states had operated on the assumption that commercial reprocessing, or more specifically the extraction of uranium and plutonium from irradiated fuel and the recycling of these materials for use in thermal or breeder reactors, would enhance the economic competitiveness of nuclear power.

Reprocessing was also viewed as part of a comprehensive waste management strategy. In the case of France and Britain at least, immediate reprocessing of spent fuel from gas-cooled reactors was seen as preferable to prolonged storage.

The reprocessing technique was first developed in the United States at Hanford, Washington with a view to producing plutonium for the weapons programme.[45] The first important step in the establishment of a light water reactor reprocessing industry was taken in 1966 with the opening of the Nuclear Fuel Services facility at West Valley, New York. Although designed to recover 300 tonnes per year, technical and other difficulties meant that only 630 tonnes had been processed by 1972 when the plant was shut down for rebuilding and enlargement. It was not expected to re-open until the early 1980s. Plans by General Electric to establish a 300 tonnes per year pilot plant at Morris, Illinois were eventually abandoned after persistent design deficiencies and an outlay of $64 million. Allied General Nuclear Services was seeking to build a much larger plant (1500 tonnes per year) at Barnwell, South Carolina, but due to regulatory delays and rapidly escalating costs the project was thought unlikely to become operational before 1978, and then only with significant assistance from the federal government. Another commercial reprocessing facility with a 1500 tonnes per year capacity had been proposed by Exxon Nuclear and was under active consideration but was not expected to be completed before the mid-1980s.

In the UK, BNFL had long operated uranium metal reprocessing plants at Windscale.[46] A 1500 tonnes/year facility, which became operational in 1964, handled spent uranium metal fuel from the domestic Magnox stations and the reactors sold to Italy and Japan – the latter with provision for the return of plutonium but not for return of waste. In 1969 a 400 tonnes/year plant was added to treat oxide fuel. However, following an accidental release of radioactivity within the head-end plant, the facility was closed down for subsequent modification but was not expected to re-open until the late 1970s, and even then with only limited reprocessing capacity. By 1975, BNFL was attaching much greater priority to the construction of a completely new oxide plant with a capacity of about 1000 tonnes/year, designed to serve the domestic as well as the overseas market.

In France, the first reprocessing plant (UP–1) with a 1000 tonnes/year capacity was built in 1957 at Marcoule to handle material from the adjacent military reactors, and was followed in 1967 by a second plant with an 800 tonnes/year capacity, known as UP–2, and designed to treat the fuel from EdF's natural uranium/gas graphite power stations.[47] This plant, located at the new site of La Hague on the tip of Cherbourg Peninsula, was extended with the addition in 1969 of a pilot-scale facility for handling highly irradiated fuels from the new light water reactor programme as well as from the Rapsodie and Phénix fast reactors. The CEA was responsible for the construction and operation of both UP–1 and UP–2 until early in 1976 when Cogéma was formed as a wholly-owned CEA subsidiary inheriting all of the CEA's fuel cycle activities.

In Germany, commercial reprocessing was slower in getting off the ground. Four German companies had formed Kernbrennstoff-Wiederaufarbeitungs-Gesellschaft mbH (KEWA) to operate the pilot reprocessing plant at Karlsruhe. By the mid-1970s, KEWA were considering the construction of a large industrial reprocessing plant in collaboration with German utilities, but there was little prospect of such a plant becoming operational before the mid-1980s. By 1976, then, several major European reprocessing facilities were already in operation, under construction or under active consideration. It was partly in order to forestall the possibility of over-supply in reprocessing capacity in Europe that BNFL (United Kingdom), CEA (France) and KEWA (West Germany) had merged their reprocessing interests in October 1971 through the formation of United Reprocessors. The aim of the company was to rationalise new investments in reprocessing plants and to co-ordinate the marketing of reprocessing services.

Enough will have been said to indicate the powerful institutional momentum which had developed in Europe and to a lesser extent in the United States for the commercialisation of reprocessing technology. The scientific and bureaucratic communities which had combined in each country to create the framework for the establishment of the first generation of nuclear engineering were now pressing for the development of more complex and sophisticated technologies. The direct support and participation of national institutions (e.g. CEA and its subsidiary Cogéma in France, the UKAEA and BNFL in Britain) were cemented by the coordinating role of regional organisations, notably Uniting Reprocessors, and by the research and promotional activities of the OECD's Nuclear Energy Agency (NEA).[48] According to NEA estimates published in 1977, even 'under the best of circumstances' nuclear fuel reprocessing capacity would lag behind demand to the point that the cumulative amount of unreprocessed material in OECD countries would increase from 4000 tonnes in 1977 to 16,000 tonnes in 1986 and remain more or less at that level through to 1990. Under the worst circumstances (high reprocessing demand/low reprocessing capacity), the backlog could be as high as 33,000 tonnes in 1986 and 58,000 tonnes in 1990.[49] By the mid-1970s the technical and economic case for commercial reprocessing already enjoyed the support of some of the most influential domestic and international institutions associated with the nuclear industry.

The case for reprocessing rested in part on the argument that it would ease the problem of radioactive waste disposal by converting wastes to a safer and more manageable form, thereby hastening permanent storage in underground repositories. Such a strategy, it was claimed, would greatly reduce the need for interim fuel storage facilities.[50] Moreover, uranium recovered through reprocessing could be recycled for use in thermal reactors, thus reducing the rate at which low cost resources were exhausted. The efficiency of energy usage would be enhanced and the costs of nuclear power correspondingly reduced. According to its proponents, reprocessing was a technical device essential to the mastery of the fuel cycle and to the long-term competitiveness of the present generation of nuclear power stations. As uranium prices rose and supply became tighter, the economics of reprocessing and recycling would become increasingly attractive.[51]

Another factor contributing to the interest in reprocessing was the anticipation of rapid development in breeder technology. The recovery of fuel-grade plutonium from spent fuel was seen in Britain, France and Germany as a necessary step in the introduction of fast breeder reactors. Governments which had made a large commitment to nuclear power in a context of limited indigenous uranium resources were therefore strongly attracted to the reprocessing option. For these states the reprocessing of spent fuel from thermal reactors offered the opportunity of gaining experience with mixed oxide fuels and accumulating plutonium in sufficient quantities for future use in commercial fast reactors. In the case of the United States, these considerations, though they exerted a strong influence over US nuclear policy, were nevertheless partly offset by the country's more privileged access to uranium supplies.

Governments committed to large-scale reprocessing were also impressed by the commercial opportunities entailed in such an option. They tended to regard large facilities as likely to be more efficient, less expensive, and therefore capable of attracting overseas customers. The export of reprocessing services was seen as having a beneficial effect on the national balance of payments and as helping to create employment opportunities, hence the determined efforts of some nuclear states to gain an early competitive advantage. Here, France and Britain were particularly well placed, partly because of their long-standing investment in the technology – itself a consequence of their military programme – but also because of the consistent administrative and financial support extended by French and British governments either directly or through the involvement of publicly owned companies. The official endorsement of commercial reprocessing was undoubtedly one of the factors which assisted Cogéma and BNFL in negotiating substantial overseas contracts. By the end of 1978, Cogéma's foreign customers included Japan, Sweden, West Germany, Switzerland, Austria, the Netherlands and Belgium, representing some 5660 tonnes of reprocessing capacity.[52] In May 1978, BNFL signed contracts worth nearly £500 million for the transport and reprocessing of 1600 tonnes of spent nuclear fuel with representatives of ten Japanese utilities. Together with the European business and Britain's domestic requirements, these contracts were expected to provide the loading for the planned Windscale expansion (6000 tonnes capacity over ten years) aimed for by BNFL.[53]

These signs of apparent progress could not, however, conceal the very serious obstacles that stood in the way. Foremost amongst these was the possible diversion of plutonium for military purposes. To prevent the theft of plutonium, formidable security measures would be necessary, including the use of locks, vaults, fence detectors, guards, body searches, security clearances, polygraph tests and television.[54] Whether this extensive form of surveillance likely to be exacerbated by nuclear threats and hoaxes, would be compatible with democratic traditions remained open to question. But aside from the risk of theft or sabotage on the part of criminal groups was the possibility that access to a reprocessing facility might considerably hasten a country's capacity to produce nuclear weapons. The construction of a reprocessing plant in West Germany, for example, would almost certainly raise the suspicion that one purpose of the plant was to endow the country with a nuclear weapons option, thereby encouraging other states to follow suit. Serious proliferation consequences were also attendant on the export of reprocessing services which necessarily entailed the return of separated plutonium to non-nuclear weapon states. Between 1971 and 1981, BNFL had returned 1930kg of plutonium to its overseas customers, which included Belgium, Canada, West Germany, Italy and Japan.[55] Other countries were likely to be added to the list with the signing of new contracts.

The issue of security was not the only limiting factor in the development of the reprocessing industry. More decisive, at least in the short run, were considerations of technical and economic performance. According to a study published in 1982, which examined the operating records of La Hague, Windscale, Karlsruhe, Mol (Belgium), West Valley (US) and Tokai Mura (Japan), the average life of commercial reprocessing plants throughout the world was six years, during which time plants operated at only 10–35 per cent of their capacity.[56] This assessment, though regarded by the proponents of reprocessing technology as unduly negative, was nevertheless reflected in the early American experience, to which reference has already been made. By the time Jimmy Carter assumed the presidency, the NRC had yet to grant the $250 million Barnwell plant a licence to operate. Rising federal safety standards had made it unlikely that the plant would ever be allowed to operate without substantial additional investment.[57]

Although the British and French reprocessing industries were less hampered by licensing or regulatory requirements, they were nevertheless affected by repeated technical failures. At Windscale, a brief criticality occurred in 1972 in a facility used for the recovery of small amounts of residual plutonium from process chemicals, thus drawing attention to the fact that fissile material can build up to critical levels at unexpected points in a plant. In November 1973, a second incident at Windscale did not involve criticality but had greater repercussions as it occurred in the oxide head end facility.[58] It revealed the build-up of long-lived residual fission products and highlighted the risks involved even in the handling of non-active solutions. The French reprocessing plant at La Hague has also been the subject of controversy. Between May and October 1976, the workers at the plant, backed by the CFDT, went on strike to protest against inadequate safety conditions and the proposed expansion of the plant under Cogéma.[59] In April 1980, an interruption in the electricity supply from the French national grid to the La Hague plant was followed by the breakdown of the emergency generator. According to one account, once the plant's electrically-operated mechanisms were out of action, the possibility existed for the plutonium to reach criticality. The cooling of the reservoirs containing radioactive wastes may also have been in jeopardy. In January 1981, a fire broke out in a trench used for dumping cladding removed from around the used fuel rods of graphite-gas reactors. It was subsequently alleged that the level of beta and alpha radiation had risen several times above the permitted level.[60] Whatever the true facts about the plant's safety, it is clear that La Hague had fallen considerably behind schedule in the reprocessing of oxide fuel. Whereas its planned capacity was 800 tonnes/year, the total amount processed by 1980 was only 340 tonnes.

These technical difficulties inevitably called into question the commercial viability of the technology. In 1970 a Foratom study had estimated that the price for reprocessing services at a 1500 tonnes/year plant, including the cost of transport and waste treatment and allowing 30 per cent for interest charges and commercial profits, would be $33/kg. Six years later, the NRC in a comprehensive analysis of the comparative economics of reprocessing and recycling (referred to as GESMO) assumed a cost of $150/kg.[61] More realistic estimates based on the European and American experience indicated that the cost was more likely to be in the range of $200–400kg.[62] In France, reprocessing costs had increased more than tenfold in the space of four years, rising from Fr 290/kg in 1973 to Fr 3000/kg in 1977*. If the GESMO study had assumed a cost of $250/kg instead of the $150/kg estimate, then the net discounted benefit in favour of uranium and plutonium recycle (as compared with the disposal of unreprocessed spent fuel) for the period 1976–2000 would not have been $3200 million as calculated by the study, but only $400 million. With a cost assumption of $300kg the economic benefit would have been altogether eliminated. After the mid-1970s the continuing escalation in reprocessing costs and the steep decline in uranium prices further undermined the economic case for reprocessing. The financing of large and expensive reprocessing plants has therefore proved a serious disincentive, particularly in the eyes of electricity

*1973 exchange rate: $1 = Fr 4.7.

utilities which have often been asked to provide advance funding for plant construction in accordance with the 'user pays' principle.

The other factor militating against the rapid expansion of reprocessing facilities has been the growth of public opposition. We have already noted how the Flowers Commission in Britain placed considerable emphasis on the proliferation implications of reprocessing. In the view of the environmentalist lobby and of many independent observers the contribution of reprocessing to waste management was marginal, and perhaps counter-productive.[63] On the other hand, the health and safety risks associated with the wider use and transport of large amounts of plutonium were far from negligible. These considerations prompted to prestigious panel of science policy advisers in the United States to recommend in the Ford–Mitre Report the shelving of reprocessing plans and the indefinite postponement of the programme to build a commercial fast reactor. The conclusion of this study was all the more significant in that many of the participants had impeccable establishment credentials and years of experience in the US policy-making process.[64]

In France, serious questions were raised about the safe functioning of commercial reprocessing and about the waste disposal strategy on which it was premised. These misgivings were repeatedly voiced by the CFDT and became the focus of anti-nuclear agitation both locally and nationally. In West Germany, the proposed Gorleben complex attracted sustained opposition which in turn compelled the government of Lower Saxony to institute a major public hearing to which technical and scientific evidence was submitted by the proponents and critics of the proposal. The airing of sharply conflicting views and the intense public response which it aroused made it politically impracticable for the government to proceed with construction of the facility.[65]

Despite the institutional momentum and the powerful blend of economic and technological nationalism favouring the development of national reprocessing industries, governments had, then, to content with technical, financial and political impediments of varying magnitude. In the case of Britain, the political obstacles were largely overcome through the procedure of a public inquiry which, though it provided an important public forum for the objectors, nevertheless found in favour of BNFL.[66] Once Justice Parker forwarded his report to the Environment Secretary in January 1978, the government moved rapidly to accept the Inspector's recommendations, and in May the Commons approved the special development order by a majority of 224 to 80. In March 1981, Parliament increased the support available to BNFL by authorising a government guarantee for the repayment of loans up to £500 million as well as payment of the loan interest.

By far the largest slice of BNFL's programme was allocated to reprocessing – approximately £2000 million. The first irradiated fuel started reaching Sellafield (formerly Windscale works) in 1980 from Hunterston B and Hinkley Point B. When the current programme of AGR stations was fully on stream the amount was expected to rise to 300 tonnes/year. Should Britain also proceed with the proposed 15GWe programme over the next ten years, the total quantity of spent oxide fuel arising by the year 2000 would reach some 7000 tonnes. In addition BNFL was committed to reprocessing 3000 tonnes of LWR fuel from overseas. To meet this anticipated demand, BNFL was constructing THORP at a cost of £800–1000 million. Another £350 million would be spent on research and development over the next ten years, mainly in connection with the project. THORP, which was to have a design reprocessing capacity of 1200 tonnes/year, was scheduled to be in operation by the late 1980s.[67] It remained to be seen, however, whether the project would achieve the desired technical performance, whether the demand for reprocessing, especially from the domestic programme, would reach the anticipated volume, and whether Britain would be able to handle to the satisfaction of all parties the delicate issue of the return of recovered plutonium and radioactive waste to customer countries.

If anything French plans were even more ambitious. Reprocessing requirements from the domestic PWR programme were likely to reach 800 tonnes/year by the mid-1980s, thus making it necessary for additional reprocessing capacity to be available on this time-scale. In 1976, Cogéma's intention was to construct by 1984 one plant (UP3A) with a capacity of 800 tonnes/year, which would be assigned largely to foreign business. A second plant of equal capacity (UP3B) to deal with the rapidly accumulating domestic spent fuel would be ready by 1986. The combined oxide reprocessing capacity of UP2 and UP3 would therefore amount to 2400 tonnes/year. However, the UP2 plant was far from achieving its full capacity in 1980, and as for UP3 the construction schedule was likely to be delayed by at least a few years.

In sharp contrast to the British and French experience, West

Germany's reprocessing plans made much less headway, in large measure because of the inability of the federal system of resolve the sharp political conflict to which these plans had given rise. The proposal to build an integrated spent fuel element disposal centre (Nucleares Entsorgungs Zentrum) was first submitted to the Lower Saxony government in March 1977 by DWK. The centre, which was to include all processes involving the back end of the fuel cycle, was to be located in Gorleben. The reprocessing facility was directly coupled to the storage pond and was to have a nominal capacity of 1400 tonnes/year. However, as a result of the pressure exerted by the local landowners' association, the fierce reaction of the Gorleben community and of neighbouring towns and villages, the adverse findings of the twenty foreign experts who had been officially invited to make an independent assessment of the project, and the sustained campaign of anti-nuclear organisations throughout the country, the Lower Saxony government concluded that the project was not politically feasible.[68] Following the abandonment of the Entsorgzentrum concept, DWK revised their plans and instead proposed in 1980 the construction of a much smaller reprocessing plant (350 tonnes/year) in the state of Hesse. Long-term intermediate storage was now considered an acceptable means of dealing with waste so that reprocessing capacity was no longer required to correspond exactly with the demand created by the operation of existing and planned nuclear power plants.

Despite the modest scale of the proposal, the Hessian initiative was nevertheless confronted with the difficult task of finding a geographically and politically suitable site.[69] The Wethen site was introduced into the licensing process in 1981[70] only to be withdrawn later in the same year for geological reasons in favour of two other possible sites. These proposals were themselves the subject of considerable debate and placed under a political cloud by the results of the Hesse elections in October 1982 which saw the Green Party list gain 9 per cent of the vote and the balance of power in the new Parliament. The DWK was also investigating the possibility of building a reprocessing facility in Bavaria, Rhineland-Palatinate and Lower Saxony.[71] But even in Bavaria, where the political environment was likely to be most favourable, the inspection of possible sites and the licensing procedure alone were expected to take another five years. Even in the most optimistic scenarios, construction was unlikely to start before 1986. For the foreseeable future, DWK was likely to rely on contracts it had signed on behalf of its shareholders with Cogéma. Under these contracts Cogéma would store and reprocess 1705 tonnes of spent fuel, beginning in 1985.[72] Additional spent fuel produced in German plants would have to be stored in intermediate storage pools.

For reasons to which we have already alluded, American reprocessing plans were experiencing serious economic and licensing difficulties even before President Carter's policy announcement in April 1977. The decision to abandon commercial reprocessing and develop instead a comprehensive and long-range spent fuel storage capability simply crystallised previous trends. President Reagan, it is true, subsequently revised Carter's anti-reprocessing policy and in his speech of April 1981 supported the resumption of commercial reprocessing, but significantly designated the private sector as responsible for providing these services. One option was to complete the Barnwell facility. However, given the need for modifications to improve plant reliability and comply with current regulatory requirements, even with an expeditious licensing process the plant was unlikely to come on stream before the late 1980s. In any case, the owners of Barnwell, Allied Corporation and General Atomic, were reluctant to invest additional funds, while other major nuclear companies were equally unenthusiastic about the economic prospects of such a private venture. The capital investment to complete the plant (excluding plant acquisition cost, inflation, and interest during construction) was expected to be of the order of $800–900 million. In these circumstances foreign participation appeared the only other available option. Such an approach, on the other hand, involved the resolution of controversial regulatory and public policy issues, including the receipt and transport of spent fuel, the return and use of recovered plutonium, the return of radioactive wastes, and, possibly the transfer of sensitive technologies. Several more years might have to elapse before commercial reprocessing in the United States could successfully overcome these technical, financial and administrative hurdles.

In Sweden, a study commissioned by the government and published prior to the 1976 general election had strongly recommended the establishment of a Swedish reprocessing capacity.[73] The study proposed an immediate start with a view to having a national reprocessing plant in operation in the early 1990s with a capacity of 800 tonnes/year, enough to reprocess the spent fuel expected to accumulate from the thirteen reactors then in operation or committed. These recommendations were largely pre-empted by the election of a new government later that year. Following enactment of the Stipulation Law in April 1977, the Swedish nuclear industry initiated the KBS project which proposed a method of waste management based on optional ten-year storage of spent fuel and the use of French reprocessing services followed by vitrification of the aqueous solvent extraction waste.[74] By 1981, the Swedish Government had agreed to reprocessing contracts with Cogéma and BNFL, accounting for about one-third of the spent fuel due to be discharged before the end of the 1980s, or 12 per cent of the total amount of spent fuel produced during the operational lifetime of Sweden's twelve reactor programme.[75] The decision to pursue the reprocessing option, by relying on foreign rather than domestic services, was not so much the result of a carefully considered or comprehensive policy on the back end of the fuel cycle as a partial, and perhaps temporary, compromise designed to allow Sweden's nuclear power programme to proceed in conditions of growing public polarisation and political instability.

This brief review of the status of commercial reprocessing in Europe and the United States has served to highlight significant national differences reflecting in part the different economic and political conditions of each country. In France's case, the commitment to reprocessing was reinforced by the rapidly expanding thermal nuclear power programme. In Britain, where nuclear power development had proceeded much more slowly, the momentum was nevertheless maintained partly by building on the experience and infrastructure accumulated in connection with the military programme and subsequently through the reprocessing of uranium metal gas-cooled reactor fuel – a path more or less similar to that followed by French industry. The consolidating factor in each instance was the centralised government advocacy of nuclear energy in general and reprocessing technology in particular. Both governments devised co-operative arrangements with their respective industries, reached specific understandings designed to expedite the necessary initiatives, and offered extensive assistance through government-sponsored research and development, construction and operation of pilot-scale facilities, and guarantees of construction loans.

In the case of both Sweden and the Federal Republic, government support was much less direct, consistent or effective, partly because plans to develop different stages of the fuel cycle gave rise to sustained opposition which succeeded in penetrating, and to some extent shaping, the decision-making process. As for the United States, several factors, including local anti-nuclear sentiment, the reluctance of the private sector to invest the necessary levels of high-risk capital, internal divisions within the bureaucratic establishment, and considerations of international security, combined to inhibit the growth of commercial reprocessing. To the extent that other countries lacked the technological base, economic capacity or political will to proceed with reprocessing, the two states that had established a lead in this area were determined not only to preserve that lead but to extend it by supplying reprocessing services for the international market. In the process they were able to secure advance payments which alleviated the financial difficulties inevitably encountered in the construction of high-cost, capital-intensive, technologically-immature industrial facilities.

THE POLITICS OF WASTE

The controversy over reprocessing was inextricably intertwined with the larger question of waste disposal, regarded by many observers as the single most intractable technical and political problem facing the nuclear industry. The management of high level waste had become so sensitive an issue and contributed to such widespread scepticism about the future of nuclear power that several American state legislatures were considering, and often passing, laws preventing further nuclear power plant construction until adequate means for long-term storage were available. The task was made even more difficult by environmentalist demands for a nuclear waste policy that was both ecologically acceptable and consistent with local participation in decision-making.

In the United States existing fuel storage facilities were thought likely to reach the limits of their capacity by the mid-1980s if not sooner. The expansion of these storage facilities would at best provide a temporary solution. If waste management were based on the reprocessing of spent fuel, the radioactive elements would be separated into new physical categories (high level, transuranic elements, gaseous effluents, etc.), each of which would have to be treated and stored or disposed of in some suitable form. If, on the other hand, the spent fuel were not reprocessed, storage facilities providing security against accident and sabotage for several decades would have to be built until technologies had been developed and demonstrated for the permanent disposal of spent fuel wastes. The problem was further complicated by the accumulation of waste arising from the decommissioning of plant. In the UK alone, for example, most of the Magnox reactors now in operation would probably have to be withdrawn from service and shut by the end of the century. To dismantle and remove them would pose a major waste disposal task.[76]

Against this background of unresolved technical and institutional difficulties, it is not surprising that the UK Royal Commission on Environmental Pollution should have recommended against any commitment to a large programme of nuclear fission power 'until it [had] been demonstrated beyond reasonable doubt that a method [existed] to ensure the safe containment of long-lived, highly radioactive waste for the indefinite future.'[77] These sentiments were echoed soon after by the Australian Ranger Uranium Environmental Inquiry which concluded: 'there is at present no generally accepted means by which high level waste can be permanently isolated from the environment and remain safe for very long periods.'[78] By way of an organisational solution to the problem the UK Royal Commission had recommended that responsibility for waste management strategy should rest with the Secretary of State for the Environment. In addition it advocated the establishment of a Nuclear Waste Disposal Corporation to be charged with the task of managing all nuclear wastes. In similar vein, an OECD report published in 1977 recommended that the respective functions of industry and government should be clearly defined in each country, but stressed that final decisions on waste disposal were the responsibility of national governments.[79] More and more the function of the state was seen as injecting public resources into research, development and demonstration of promising waste storage techniques and disposal alternatives, as a first step towards formulating a comprehensive waste management strategy. The other equally important function was to invest the strategy eventually adopted with the mantle of state authority, and, where possible, to portray it as a rational solution consistent with national interests. By the late 1970s it was widely accepted that countries with large nuclear power programmes would establish their own national facilities and institutions for spent fuel management, thus limiting their dependence on foreign nuclear industries and services.[80]

The performance of government did not always match these expectations. Governments and political parties generally, when confronted with awkward institutional and technical choices, tended to avoid making firm decisions, preferring politically less damaging compromises. This was the principal factor accounting for the fluctuating time-scale proposed for various waste disposal strategies. The INFCE study, for example, concluded that spent fuel storage should be considered as a step in the fuel cycle preceding either the reprocessing or permanent disposal of spent fuel. The storage period would range from one to three years in cases where reprocessing was chosen, to a minimum of ten years if spent fuel disposal were selected. Significantly, it conceded that these optimum times would not be achieved given insufficient reprocessing or disposal capacity. As a consequence, longer interim storage times were envisaged with obvious implications for fuel integrity, proliferation, costs, generation of additional low and medium wastes and increased number of storage sites.[81] Although the pressures operating on the nuclear waste policy-making process were remarkably similar in many countries, national political institutions and traditions were often important in determining the way these pressures were handled, and in helping to explain some of the emerging policy differences.

In France, the official commitment to reprocessing was parallelled at an early stage by an equally determined effort to proceed with the vitrification of high level waste. The French system, developed by CEA on behalf of Cogéma, is comprised of a rotary kiln calciner heated by a resistance furnace, fed with the slurry waste, coupled to a continuous metallic melter which deposits the glass periodically into the waste canister.[82] The Marcoule Vitrification facility (AVM) came on active stream in June 1978. By the end of 1980, the AVM plant was capable of handling up to 36 litre/h of high level waste solution, equal to about 20kg/h of glass. It was claimed that plant capacity would eventually reach 80–100 tonnes/year of glass, corresponding to the reprocessing of some 4000 tonnes of spent fuel a year from gas-cooled reactors. A second plant was being installed at the La Hague reprocessing plant.[83]

The French AVM process was adopted by other European countries as it was the only one to have been demonstrated on an industrial scale. The reprocessing–vitrification strategy was neverheless dependent for its eventual success on the adequacy of vailable sites for long-term disposal. In November 1979, the adioactive waste control agency, Agence Nationale pour la Gestion des Déchets Radioactifs (ANDRA), was formed jointly by the Ministries of Industry, Economy and the Budget.[84] The new agency, tself part of the CEA, was to be responsible for low and medium level and eventually high level waste management. It was financed by fees paid by waste producers, which were complemented, where necessary, by state subsidies. No decision, however, had yet been taken about repositories for long-term waste disposal.

Unlike France, Sweden did not develop its own reprocessing and vitrification facilities, which is not to say that the issue of waste management did not receive extensive attention by both government and public. The 1976 report of the Government Committee on Radioactive Waste had proposed the establishment of a special government agency to be responsible for all long-term management of radioactive waste, in particular the conduct of connected research and development. The report also recommended that the electric power utilities should meet all expenses related to the management and storage of spent nuclear fuel and radioactive waste. As already indicated, these recommendations were overtaken by the change of government and the subsequent proposals contained in the first KBS report. Based on the assumption of reprocessing, the KBS method of management consisted of the following steps:

Optional ten-year storage of spent fuel in a facility to be built in Sweden, the *Centrallagher*;

reprocessing in France followed by vitrification of the aqueous solvent extraction waste;

intermediate storage of air cooled waste canisters for at least thirty years in Mellanlager, a Swedish facility; and

emplacement of encapsulated waste in a final repository in a suitable bedrock formation in Sweden, but not before the year 2020.[85]

The central storage facility (CLAB) was designed to provide an element of flexibility to the planning of the back end of the fuel cycle. It was to be built in stages up to a total capacity of 3000 tonnes of spent fuel, corresponding to some 100 reactor-years of operation. Following government approval in August 1979 in accordance with the Nuclear Energy Act, construction of the facility was started in May 1980, and was expected to be ready for operation in 1985. The total cost of CLAB, not including interest or inflation costs, was estimated at Kr 1000 million (in January 1980 prices).[86] As for the intermediate storage facility, which would receive the vitrified waste from France, it was to be placed underground and to have a capacity sufficient to take care of reactor wastes over the operating lifetime of the twelve reactors. Providing that the necessary permits were quickly obtained, site construction would commence in 1983.[87]

The institutional and financial arrangements for the back end of the fuel cycle were crystallised in legislation passed by the Swedish Parliament in May 1981. The four utilities currently holding licences for nuclear power operation were required to pay annual charges to cover future costs related to spent fuel management and decommissioning. Responsibility for technical activities would rest with the utilities or their subsidiary, SKBF. A government body, the National Board for Spent Nuclear Fuel, would scrutinise technical planning on an annual basis, advise the government annually on the appropriate level of charges, and administer the fund built up by these charges. The government had thus attempted to maintain a supervisory role, while leaving the technical and financial organisation of the programme to the utilities concerned. In the longer term, however, it was recognised that terminal waste storage would become a state responsibility.[88]

In Britain, where some 32,000 m^3 of radioactive waste were thought to be in store at power stations and at Windscale by the end of the 1970s, the formulation of a national waste strategy followed a more tortuous path. Public opposition, although lacking the national visibility to be found in Sweden, had at times impeded or at least delayed waste disposal plans. With respect to low level waste, Britain had shown a marked preference for sea disposal. Between 1976 and 1980 alone some 11,200 tonnes of radioactive waste were dumped at sea.[89] An Expert Group appointed to review the government's 1959 White Paper on the control of radioactive waste, recommended in 1979 that the practice of sea disposal be maintained, and where possible expanded, and that research be carried out to demonstrate the soundness of this approach.[90] Indeed, the review went so far as to suggest that, in spite of reservations expressed in the Flowers Report, there was insufficient information to rule out the sea disposal option even for highly active waste.[91]

The Radioactive Waste Management Advisory Committee (RWMAC), a group set up by the Department of the Environment to advise on nuclear waste disposal, concluded in their second annual report that arrangements for disposing of low level wastes at sea were based on sound radiological principles, and argued that deep-sea disposal for low and intermediate level wastes could be increased. These official endorsements of the practice did not, however, reassure everyone as evidenced by the increasingly vehement protests of environmental groups who insisted that this method of waste disposal could pollute the sea and return radioactivity to man.[92]

With regard to high level waste, it was announced in November 1980 that BNFL wanted to build the first Windscale vitrification plant (WVP) on the basis of the AVM process operated by Cogéma at Marcoule. Although research into vitrification techniques was started by the UKAEA at Harwell in the late 1950s, it was felt that the French process had been substantially proven whereas the Harvest process developed at Harwell would require a considerable amount of further work before it would be possible to proceed to the construction of a full-scale plant with the same degree of confidence.[93] But the vitrified and encapsulated waste, quite apart from the need for cool storage in the early stages, did not of itself resolve the question of ultimate disposal. Several options were under consideration: emplacement in deep and stable geological formations underground, emplacement in sediments or rocks under the sea-bed, or deposition on the ocean-bed. Other possibilities included burial in the polar caps or extraterrestrial disposal by rocket.[94]

Although several waste management systems appeared feasible, in practice choices were likely to be limited. The Department of the Environment was carrying out a Systems Engineering Study with a view to developing a strategic framework.[95] Geological disposal being one of the main options under investigation, much effort was devoted to geological research extending over a range of types of rock formation distributed throughout the UK. Inevitably test drilling aroused public concern and in some instances vociferous opposition by those living in the vicinity of sites, thereby demonstrating once again the political constraints on waste management policy. It was in part recognition of the political pitfalls which inclined the British government to support research while postponing final decisions. Indeed, RWMAC went so far as to suggest that instead of a permanent repository, 'containment in an engineered storage system might be the best way to deal with solidified high-level wastes for decades or even centuries.' In any case the transition from storage to disposal, it was now claimed, was unlikely to take place until at least fifty years after vitrification. In the words of Dr Marshall: 'the simplest, most straight-forward way of proceeding is simply to wait, simply wait!'[96] which was perhaps an elegant way of sidestepping, at least for the present, the difficult political decisions lying ahead.

In West Germany, nuclear waste policy proved even more vulnerable to the vagaries of the political process. Some of the confusion surrounding the allocation of responsibilities for the final storage of radioactive wastes was clarified in 1976 with the addition of a fourth amendment to the Atomic Law. The amendment required the federal government to provide facilities for long-term storage and final disposal of radioactive waste. The PTB, a national scientific and engineering laboratory under the authority of the Federal Ministry for Commercial Affairs, would be responsible for the building and running of facilities, although provision was also made for the federal government to call on the services of a private organisation. The relevant company in this context was DWK which was formed in 1977 by reconstituting the Project Company for Reprocessing of Nuclear Fuel (PKW). All twelve nuclear power plant operating utilities were involved in its operation, although RWE, Preussenelektra and NWK were by far the largest shareholders.

Reference has already been made to the integrated spent fuel disposal centre favoured by the federal government. The centre, to be located on top of a salt dome, was to include a plant for the conditioning of radioactive wastes and a final storage facility. The advantage claimed for the integrated concept was the avoidance of all external transporting of radioactive materials except for the spent fuel elements from the power plants. Different solidification processes were under development, but following a decision in 1977 the Pamela process became the focus of West Germany's vitrification work. In addition to a Pamela demonstration plant which was planned to start hot operation in 1985–6, DWK had also chosen the French process. An AVM plant was planned for the Karlsruhe reprocessing facility and was also due to start hot operation in 1986.[97]

Despite pressure from the federal government, Germany's ambitious plans to build an integrated waste disposal centre at Gorleben were eventually abandoned. Instead, Chancellor Helmut Schmidt and the Minister-Presidents of the German Länder agreed that the back end of the fuel cycle would be based on small units at different sites. No reprocessing plant would be built at Gorleben, but testing of Gorleben salt domes for final storage would continue. Lower Saxony and North Rhine-Westphalia agreed to build two or three intermediate storage facilities which would be needed for about twenty years in anticipation of a final solution to the storage problem. Support was also expressed for research into alternatives to reprocessing, in particular final storage of unreprocessed spent fuel.[98]

The new political compromise still left many questions unanswered. In the first place, the siting of intermediate storage facilities was likely to prove almost as controversial as had the siting of reprocessing plants and final storage facilities, with potentially the same local and regional electoral consequences for the party in power. Equally problematic was the attitude of the courts which might not find intermediate storage an accepable solution to the waste management problem. In the meantime, the Gorleben test drillings were unlikely to be received with equanimity by the local population or by the anti-nuclear movement. In view of these difficulties, it is understandable that the agreement reached between the federal and Länder governments should have postponed any final decision on the handling of spent nuclear fuel until 1985. By the same token, the proposed expansion of the West German nuclear programme was unlikely to eventuate so long as detailed and publicly acceptable arrangements had not been made for managing the back end of the fuel cycle.

The magnitude of the nuclear waste problem and its political ramifications were perhaps nowhere more acute than in the United States where over 2500 tonnes of spent fuel had accumulated by 1980 as a result of commercial nuclear power plant operation. Some $2200 m^3$ of liquid high level radioactive waste had been produced by commercial and military reprocessing at the West Valley facility. In addition, approximately $380{,}000 m^3$ of high level radioactive waste had been generated by government-operated reactors as part of the military programme, principally for nuclear weapons production. President Carter's decision to foreclose the reprocessing option, at least for the foreseeable future, thus focused attention even more firmly on the back end of the fuel cycle.

To restore a measure of order to what had become an increasingly confused situation, the Carter Administration announced in October 1977 a new fuel storage policy outlining the general terms under which a utility company could arrange for the government to store and dispose of its spent fuel.[99] The policy was to be extended to foreign countries 'on a limited basis' as part of US non-proliferation policy to induce selected nations to store their spent fuel at secure sites in the United States. It was calculated that a federal storage unit would cost $50–100 million, but no indication was given of the number of units that might be required. Even before details of the plan had been elaborated, the policy became the subject of vigorous political debate. Fears were expressed about the long distances over which highly radioactive materials would have to be transported. Another complicating factor was the decision of several state legislatures and New York City to ban the transport and/or storage of nuclear wastes within their boundaries. Questions were also raised as to the safety standards for such facilities in the light of the Department of Energy's contention that NRC licensing would not be needed if the facility were government owned.

A series of studies on radioactive waste by the Department of Energy and the Interagency Review Group on Nuclear Waste Management failed to produce an acceptable long-term solution.[100] Nevertheless, in the absence of clear congressional or executive guidance, a *de facto* policy gradually emerged with the Department of Energy and the NRC encouraging the expansion of spent fuel storage capacity at existing reactor sites and exploring the possible establishment of away from reactor (AFR) storage facilities. Although this approach was defended as consistent with continuing efforts to develop a long-term strategy, critics within and outside the Congress argued that such temporary measures might merely serve to relieve the urgency of the problem and delay a permanent solution. In his message to Congress in February 1980 President Carter outlined his long-awaited plan for the final disposal of nuclear wastes.[101] He called for high-level wastes ultimately to be disposed of underground in geological repositories, the first of which would be chosen after several years of geological research. The site for the first full-scale repository was to be selected by 1985 and ready for operation by the mid-1990s. The President's proposals were not well received by the nuclear industry or its supporters in Congress. Other critics expressed concern over the vague provisions for state consultation and concurrence in the site selection process. It was certainly not made clear whether states would exercise a veto over the siting of waste facilities within their boundaries. Although the President established a nineteen member State Planning Council to advise the

Administration on nuclear waste questions, the actual role of the Council remained ambiguous, no doubt because of the unresolved issue of federal–state rights in waste facility siting.

Other provisions in the Carter plan included the construction of one or more AFR facilities to accommodate the spent fuel from overcrowded reactor storage pools. In the Department of Energy budget for the current fiscal year, $300 million was allocated to the development of AFR capacity at Barnwell, South Carolina, Morris, Illinois, and West Valley, New York. Despite this form of federal assistance, it was envisaged that utilities would retain primary responsibility for the wastes they generated, that is, the bulk of spent fuel would continue to be stored in pools at reactor sites. The President also indicated that he favoured the extension of NRC's licensing authority to cover all future civilian and military waste sites (including sites for transuranic and low level waste).

Despite prolonged bargaining Carter's nuclear waste plan did not receive congressional approval, partly because several other nuclear waste Bills were already circulating in no less than five different committees in the House of Representatives and Senate. Some Bills emphasised AFR and long-term storage of spent fuel and high level wastes, other sought to restrict the development of AFR storage capacity and to increase the degree of state involvement in federal waste planning, while others still wanted to link new nuclear plant licensing to demonstrated waste disposal capability.[102] Following extensive negotiations between several committees, the House reached a compromise under which the Department of Energy would choose two possible burial sites by 1982 and two more by 1985; and by 1987, after an elaborate series of public hearings, the President would recommend to Congress the site or sites he considered safe for the storage of waste. The compromise, however, proved unacceptable to the Senate which was strongly biased towards short-term AFR storage capacity. By the end of Carter's term of office (1980), then, the US was still without a national plan for nuclear waste management. Congress had objected to several aspects of the Carter plan but had failed to reach agreement on an alternative plan of its own. No legislation had been finalised, although Congress seemed to be moving towards retrievable spent fuel storage rather than geological disposal, no doubt to pave the way for resurrection of the reprocessing option. At the same time, Congress was unenthusiastic about active state participation in nuclear waste policy-making, partly for fear of allowing additional road-blocks to retard visible progress in waste storage and disposal. Conclusive evidence of such progress was now deemed psychologically necessary to inspire greater public confidence in the industry's capacity to resolve the problem of waste management.

Following Carter's exit from the White House, the Reagan Administration's strong commitment to nuclear power and to the expeditious resolution of outstanding issues was widely expected to have far-reaching consequences for waste management policy. On the other hand, a viable long-term solution had to overcome difficult problems of financing as well as the continuing conflict of views and interests evident within both Congress and the nuclear bureaucracy. In the Senate, three committees, Energy and Natural Resources, Environment and Public Works, and Armed Services were involved in waste legislation. Similarly, in the House the Science, Interior, Energy and Commerce, and Armed Services committees all had a stake in the outcome. The uncertainty and indecision arising from the often divergent approaches favoured by these committees were in any case compounded by two sets of extraneous considerations weighing heavily on the minds of the nation's legislators: the budgetary debate in conditions of deepening economic recession on the one hand, and the 1982 congressional elections on the other.[103]

The compromise Bill finally passed by both Houses of Congress in December 1982 required the Department of Energy to conduct environmental assessments of five potential sites and to recommend three of them for more detailed study by January 1985.[104] The President would then select the first site to be built by March 1987, and the second by March 1990. Following the preparation of an environmental impact statement by the Energy Department, the construction and licensing of a repository would be required to comply with NRC procedures. Significantly, the Bill conferred on states the right to veto the selection of any site on their territory unless both Houses voted to override the veto. The legislation also allowed for the temporary AFR storage of up to 1900 tonnes of spent fuel. The site for this storage would be owned by the federal government, but here again states were given a veto over storage in excess of 300 tonnes of spent fuel.

The intention of the legislation was to demonstrate that high level waste could be disposed of in a safe and environmentally acceptable manner. How realistic the proposed timetable would prove depended on the degree to which the relevant federal agencies, notably the Department of Energy, the Environment Protection Agency (EPA) and the NRC would effectively coordinate their respective responsibilities. Inconsistencies in safety standards prescribed by the NRC and the EPA had already injected an element of uncertainty.[105] Equally unpredictable was the stringency with which the NRC would formulate and enforce its regulations. The timing and process of site selection, the amount and quality of information available to the affected states and to the public, and the closely-related issues of spent fuel transportation and storage were all likely to be a source of public controversy and intense political conflict.

The fragmented character of the American political system, as reflected not only in the separation of powers but in the divisions within the legislative and executive arms of government, clearly militated against the formulation and implementation of a coherent waste management policy. Nor was the severe erosion of public confidence in the federal government likely to be overcome by congressional legislation.[106] In the first place, there was no guarantee that future Administrations would act consistently with current policies. Secondly, it was by no means self-evident that government had the institutional capacity to pursue a technologically complex and politically sensitive programme over several decades. Finally, government had yet to establish a policy framework which effectively internalised the diverse concerns of states and numerous interest groups all seeking to influence the politics of waste management.

This cursory review of the political economy of the nuclear fuel cycle has attempted to demonstrate the extraordinarily complex and at times contradictory functions the nuclear state was called upon to perform. National governments were expected to ensure the security of uranium supplies for their respective industries, ready access to enrichment technologies, the development of reprocessing facilities designed to improve the competitiveness of nuclear power, and politically acceptable methods of handling radioactive waste. While required to provide the technical and institutional framework necessary for the growth of the nuclear industry, the state was also expected to maintain the legitimacy of the process.

The very attempt to satisfy these multifaceted, cumulative and often conflicting demands was constrained by the limits of the state's resources, and by sharp divisions in the body politic that emerged with the growth of the nuclear industry. Decisive action by the state tended to accentuate these divisions and undermine the fragile social and political consensus on which the efficacy of its action ultimately depended. Procrastination or indecision, on the other hand, could only deepen the predicament of the nuclear industry and help to polarise further the shifting domestic and international alignments to which it gave rise. Clearly, the state was both agent and victim of the nuclear controversy. But before we are able to offer a more definitive evaluation of its role, we shall need to consider more fully the global dimensions of the controversy and the interplay of commercial and security interests.

7 International Nuclear Politics

Although much of our study has so far focused on the development of nuclear power in its domestic context, frequent reference has been made to the international dissemination of the technology, to the role of international agencies, and above all to the patterns of international conflict and co-operation arising from nuclear transactions. In initiating or facilitating international nuclear trade, the state has had to grapple with conditions of economic rivalry but also with the reality of military insecurity characteristic of a hierarchical yet fragmented world system. Because of the close link between the civil and military uses of nuclear power no state could indefinitely ignore the disruption of international order that might ensue from the uncontrolled spread of nuclear fuels, equipment and technology. The state has therefore had the task of reconciling economic, diplomatic and strategic objectives. It has had to formulate a nuclear policy consistent not only with narrowly defined national interests but also with the need for international regulation. It is to the difficult dilemma posed by this dual and at times contradictory function that we shall now turn our attention.

THE EXPORT MARKET

Countries that have initiated large nuclear investment programmes, established capital-intensive reactor industries and mastered the technical and organisational difficulties of the nuclear fuel cycle have invariably sought to reduce the unit costs and maximise the commercial benefits of such an enterprise by launching an offensive on the world nuclear market. For the best part of two decades the

American nuclear scientific and industrial complex enjoyed unchallenged dominance in nuclear commerce. Quite apart from its overwhelming control of the reactor export market and the very substantial advantage it had earned from the adoption of LWR technology by other countries, the United States exercised a virtual monopoly on the uranium enrichment business. By the early 1970s, however, several factors, most notably the drive for national independence, had paved the way for a more competitive trading relationship.

As we have already observed, in June 1974, the US stopped accepting new long-term contracts for the supply of enriched uranium as its existing enrichment plants were fully committed through the early 1980s. As a consequence, Western European countries, which had previously purchased uranium almost exclusively from the US, turned increasingly to the Soviet Union with a view to diversifying their sources of supply while developing their own production capacity.[1] By the early 1980s the Eurodif and Urenco projects were capable of meeting a rapidly growing share of the domestic requirements of member countries and were beginning to erode the American presence in other countries. As a result of European initiative other important fuel cycle elements also entered the commercial realm. France, the UK and the Federal Republic of Germany were all endeavouring to expand their domestic reprocessing capabilities and, unlike the United States, were offering either reprocessing technology or reprocessing services.

While not underestimating the strategic importance or financial value of commercial transactions involving the front or back end of the fuel cycle, it is clear that reactors remained the principal item on the international nuclear market. Against a background of rising energy consumption and perceived oil scarcity it was widely expected in the early 1970s that the volume and value of nuclear sales would rapidly expand. One projection in 1975 estimated a worldwide investment in reactors of $250,000 million for the period 1971–85 with an additional $45,000 million to be invested in uranium mining, milling, enrichment, fuel fabrication and reprocessing.[2] The major international agencies were confidently predicting a marked increase in the nuclear power capacity of developing countries over the next decade. According to OECD projections, by 1985 these countries would have a capacity of 25,000 MWe[3] – even higher estimates were suggested by the IAEA.[4] The scale of nuclear plant ordering by such countries as Brazil, Iran and Taiwan and the emergence of new potential markets in the Middle East, south-east Asia and Latin America tended at first to confirm these optimistic predictions. The number of countries committed to the use of nuclear power had risen from thirty-two in 1974 to forty-one by mid-1976.[5]

Stimulated by the perception of a large and increasingly diversified market, the world's major nuclear suppliers were now locked into a highly competitive structure. Whereas up until 1972 the United States had filled 85–90 per cent of export orders for nuclear power plants, the American share declined to 70 per cent over the following three years and to less than 50 per cent by 1977.[6] In other words, the international nuclear market had become increasingly multipolar with the entry on the supply side of West German, French and Canadian firms. Ironically, commercial rivalries in the ensuing years greatly intensified precisely because of steadily declining projections

Table 7.1: *Plants under construction in some Third World countries*

Plant	*Type*	*Output MWe*	*Reactor manufacturer*	*Service date*
Republic of Korea				
KN-5 (Kori)	PWR	900	Westinghouse	1984
KN-6 (Kori)	PWR	900	Westinghouse	1985
KN-7 (Yeonggwang)	PWR	950	Westinghouse	1986
KN-8 (Yeonggwang)	PWR	950	Westinghouse	1987
KN-9 (Ul Jin Kun)	PWR	950	Framatome	1988
KN-10 (Ul Jin Kun)	PWR	950	Framatome	1989
Philippines				
PNPP-1 (Morong)	PWR	620	Westinghouse	1985
Taiwan				
Maanshan 1	PWR	910	Westinghouse	1984
Maanshan 2	PWR	910	Westinghouse	1985
South Africa				
Koeberg 1	PWR	922	Framatome	1983
Koeberg 2	PWR	922	Framatome	1984
Argentina				
Rio Tercero	Candu	600	AECL	1983
Atucha 2	PHWR	692	KWU	1988
Brazil				
Angra 2	PWR	1245	KWU	1987
Angra 3	PWR	1245	KWU	1988
Mexico				
Laguna Verde 1	BWR	645	GE	1984
Laguna Verde 2	BWR	645	GE	1985

Source: *Nuclear Enginnering International*, May 1983, pp. 34–5.

of future nuclear power generation capacity.[7] The lack of new orders in West Germany, Sweden and the United States meant that reactor manufacturers were under mounting pressure to find alternative markets in order to maintain their cost effectiveness and industrial viability. Even in France, where the rate of ordering was appreciably greater than in other countries, Framatome's capacity to produce nuclear steam supply systems was in excess of French requirements. To make matters worse, the export market itself was not expanding as anticipated. Dwindling load growth, high cost inflation, and scarcity of technical skills and financial resources had greatly undermined the plans for nuclear expansion in several Third World countries.

Of the six countries under review neither the UK nor Brazil can be regarded as important competitors in the world reactor market. Except for small experimental and research reactors, the British have been unable to break into the commercial export arena, although they have been quite successful in the field of nuclear fuel services, including uranium enrichment and reprocessing carried out by British Nuclear Fuels Limited. The value of these exports increased from £11.1 million in 1977 to £40.8 million in 1981.[8] As for Brazil, it has been an importer of nuclear technology and equipment, relying first on the United States and more recently on West Germany. The Brazilian government, it is true, often expressed the hope that an indigenous industry would eventually be established capable of exporting not only enriched uranium but reactor pressure vessels, steam generators and perhaps even complete nuclear steam supply systems.[9] But even with the expertise gained from the construction of nuclear power units at the Angra dos Reis complex, there was little likelihood that Brazil would, in the foreseeable future, become a significant nuclear exporter.

By the mid-1970s Westinghouse and General Electric, the two American firms which had until then dominated the world market, were facing severe competition from reactor manufacturers in France and West Germany, and to a lesser extent Canada and Sweden. As of December 1978, Westinghouse and General Electric had received the lion's share of export orders from Belgium, Italy, Spain, Switzerland, India, Japan, South Korea, Taiwan and Mexico. However, Framatome and KWU had made inroads into the Belgian, Spanish and Swiss markets and were also establishing a foothold in several Third World countries.[10] The Canadians had successfully marketed ıeir CANDU reactor in India, Pakistan, Argentina, South Korea nd Romania. The CANDU system, which does not require enichment services for fuel, was especially attractive to countries intent n achieving independence from foreign enrichment technology and ossessing their own supplies of natural uranium. The Japanese had ot yet completed any major foreign reactor sale, but three companes, Mitsubishi (Westinghouse licence), Hitashi (General Electric icence) and Toshiba (General Electric licence) were selling reactors n Japan. Given their strong industrial base, there was every ikelihood that one or more of these companies would soon enter the vorld market.[11]

Although US manufacturers had clearly lost the monopoly they once enjoyed, they remained nevertheless major suppliers of nuclear plants, reactor components and the associated technology. In addition to turnkey contracts for reactor systems, both Westinghouse and General Electric had pursued a strategy of co-operation with foreign firms, including licensing and technical exchange agreements with companies in Belgium, France, West Germany, Sweden, Switzerland, Spain, Italy and Japan. Even where they allowed for the transfer of technology and production capability to domestic companies, these arrangements enabled American firms to take advantage of nuclear expansion in Europe and Japan, thereby extending their own industrial base, technical competence and financial leverage, and giving added impetus to their export drive in Third World countries. Of the two largest American suppliers, Westinghouse was the more successful, partly because of its heavy investment in the design, development and manufacturing of nuclear facilities.[12] Nuclear sales represented in any case a much larger proportion of total business for Westinghouse than for General Electric. By 1975, pressurised water reactors in service or on order clearly outnumbered any other single reactor type, and Westinghouse and its licensees accounted for two-thirds of them, or 147 units.

Though smaller than its main American rivals and with a relatively late start, KWU quickly achieved the technical and engineering capacity needed to offer independently of US company licenses turnkey contracts for a variety of light water reactors, the primary one being a PWR design. Apart from becoming the major supplier for the German nuclear power programme, KWU spearheaded Germany's entry into the world reactor market.[13] Export sales began with an order in 1968 from Argentina for the Atucha natural uranium heavy water reactor. In the ensuing ten years nine other nuclear sales (eight PWR, one BWR) were concluded with seven countries (Netherlands, Austria, Switzerland, Iran, Brazil, Spain and Luxembourg). Some of these plants would not be commissioned until 1985, but they represented highly lucrative business – seven of these nine orders totalled some DM 8000 million.[14] Given KWU's capacity to deliver at least four and perhaps as many as seven reactor units, and the marked contraction of the German market after 1975, it is not difficult to understand the increasing vigour with which KWU and the nuclear bureaucracy should have sought to maximise the export potential of the German reactor industry.

In France's case, Framatome, which originally operated under licence from Westinghouse, soon became a fully integrated company capable of producing all major PWR components. In spite of the very substantial domestic contracts secured during the 1970s, the French company perceived the export market as crucial to its commercial future. France's first reactor export went to Belgium in 1969, and was followed in 1974 by an order for two additional reactors. In 1976 South Africa ordered two units and Iran submitted a letter of intent also for the purchase of two units. Framatome, which had achieved its technological and production capabilities through its relationship with Westinghouse, was now anxious to shed the connection which it regarded as restrictive, particularly as exports to certain countries required prior US government approval. While learning a great deal from the Westinghouse PWR design, Framatome now argued that it had made sufficient modifications to it to be able to approach foreign customers as an independent PWR vendor.[15] This objective, which was consummated with the expiry of the licensing arrangement in 1982, reflected Framatome's intention to pursue a global marketing strategy and to intrude in geographic areas previously regarded as Westinghouse's exclusive domain.

On a more modest scale, the Swedish company ASEA–ATOM, which also acquired a good deal of its know-how from the United States, in particular from General Electric, was able to make its own contribution to light water technology in reactor and fuel design as well as in station layout and construction. Although a relatively small company, ASEA–ATOM was nevertheless committed to competing for overseas orders in countries such as Turkey, Iran and Taiwan,[16] but its ability to do so was constrained by the size of its domestic market, uncertainty regarding the future structure of the company, and the result of the 1980 referendum. ASEA–ATOM's only success on the export front was the sale of two nuclear power stations, each with a net output of 660 MWe, to the Finnish TVO Power Company. The two orders were placed in 1974 and 1975 respectively.[17] Conscious of the limited export opportunities available to it, ASEA–ATOM established a US subsidiary, Aros Corporation, capable of supplying LWR products, design, engineering and operational know-how, in the hope of capturing at least a fraction of the growing US market for these services.

The picture that emerges from this brief survey of the major firms active in the export market is of intense commercial rivalry, made all the more acute by conditions of industrial over-capacity which they all experienced in varying degrees. Moreover, large nuclear component manufacturing facilities were at various stages of construction in several importing countries, notably in Italy (Breda) and Spain (ENSA), followed by Brazil (NUCLEP) and South Korea (KHIC), with Taiwan, Yugoslavia, Argentina and Finland also aiming to acquire their own facilities. The more advanced importers were already beginning to flex their muscles with a view to securing a share of nuclear trade either independently or in collaboration with large nuclear contractors. The net effect of this trend was to reduce the scope and heighten the competitiveness of international nuclear commerce.

To understand more clearly the stakes involved in international competition, it may be helpful to outline the geographical contours of the demand side of world nuclear trade. Leaving aside the centrally planned economies closely aligned with the Soviet Union, Western Europe and Third World countries have constituted the core of the export market. In both areas the United States was able to make use of the leverage afforded by its alliances to establish a commercial presence, although the Europeans and to a lesser extent the Canadians gradually eroded that advantage, particularly in South Asia, the Middle East and Latin America.

In Europe itself the diminishing prospect for nuclear investments in the smaller importing countries (e.g. Austria, Denmark, Netherlands, Norway, Switzerland, Finland) left only Spain and Italy as potentially lucrative markets. As a result of mounting opposition to nuclear power, falling demand for electricity, and the combined impact of declining economic activity and high or rising inflation, the outlook for nuclear exports to Northern and Central

Europe became distinctly bleak. Even in Spain, where nuclear plants with an estimated capacity of 16,000 MWe were ordered during the 1970s, principally from Westinghouse but also from General Electric and KWU, every indication was that the rate of nuclear ordering in the 1980s would fall far below that recorded in the preceding decade. It remained to be seen whether the leftward shift in Spanish politics and the proposed entry into the European Economic Community would be sufficient to undermine the dominant position of American nuclear corporations, which was itself a reflection of Spain's long-standing economic and military dependence on the United States. As for Italy, long delays in the construction of plants ordered during the late 1960s and early 1970s – arising in part from regional and municipal obstruction – meant that, despite ambitious projects, Italian governments were unable to bring their plans to fruition. Italy eventually decided to standardise its programme on the basis of the Westinghouse PWR design, but the resulting American advantage was partly offset by Italy's increasing capacity to supply its own nuclear hardware and its growing links with France in uranium enrichment and breeder development.

Much more intense and diplomatically significant was the competition for markets in Third World countries, for it is here that commercial penetration was thought likely to yield the richest rewards and cut across traditional spheres of influence with far-reaching implications for both regional and international security. The possibility of gaining access to Third World energy resources (whether uranium from South Africa and Brazil, or oil from Iran) in exchange for nuclear technology provided another strong incentive, especially for resource-poor European countries. The major suppliers, for their part, had constantly sought, through co-operation agreements, technical and scientific exchanges and demonstrations of the latest technological advances, to propagate the notion that nuclear power was the energy source of the future. The message found a receptive audience amongst western-trained Third World scientific, bureaucratic and military élites. Although the reactor market in these countries, which averaged less than 3000 MWe a year during the 1970s, could not solve the overall problem of potentially unused production capacity in the West, it was nevertheless perceived as helping the leading US and European manufacturers to stay in the nuclear business.

In Asia, by far the most promising countries for the marketing of nuclear power appeared to be South Korea and Taiwan, where a programme of rapid industrialisation was taking place within the framework of market economy principles and the increasing penetration of foreign capital. South Korea's nuclear industry was from the outset dominated by US capital and technology. Of the seven orders placed between 1969 and 1979, six were supplied by Westinghouse and one by AECL of Canada. All Westinghouse reactors were financed in whole or in part with US funding, often through the agency of the Export–Import Bank. In 1978, the South Korean government announced a grandiose plan to build forty-four nuclear power plants by the year 2000, thereby making South Korea the focus of a concentrated lobbying campaign involving American, West German and French companies.[19]

Intense diplomatic activity, visits by high-level trading missions, a variety of political and financial inducements became an integral part of the scramble for contracts. Westinghouse's victory in securing orders for the seventh and eighth units at Gyamari, near Kwongju, was followed by even greater pressure by the French who finally succeeded in 1980 in breaking the North American monopoly with a contract for two 950 MWe reactors to be built on the east coast.[20] South Korea's desire to acquire advanced fuel cycle technology and reduce its current dependence on US know-how and enriched uranium was an important factor in the success of the French bid. France's pledge to support South Korean intevests in Western Europe and North Africa may also have played a part. It remained to be seen, however, whether Framatome would be able to consolidate its penetration of the South Korean market, particularly in view of the scaling-down of South Korea's nuclear programme necessitated by slower economic growth and balance of payments difficulties. Nor could one underestimate the continuing role of US military and economic influence in South Korea and the very considerable advantage it conferred on US reactor manufacturers. It is worth noting here that several US nuclear energy companies had entered into technology-sharing agreements and joint ventures with South Korean firms. The licensing agreement between Hyundai Yangheng and General Electric for the production of turbine generators for nuclear and conventional power plants, the establishment of Daehan Bechtel (a joint venture supplying engineering services for nuclear power stations), and Hyundai–Westinghouse (providing for the manufacture and sale of nuclear reactors) were a good indication of the entrenched US position in the South Korea market.[21]

The United States exercised even tighter control over the Taiwanese market where all six units operating or under construction were purchased either from General Electric or from Westinghouse. Taiwanese interest in diversification might in future provide an opening for French and West German companies, but they were likely to remain at a considerable disadvantage given Taiwan's increasing political and strategic dependence on the United States. In any case, lower than expected growth in electricity demand coupled with a deteriorating economic climate had compelled the Taiwanese authorities to reassess their ambitious plans for nuclear investments in the 1980s. Nor was the Chinese market any more promising, although the new leadership in China had intermittently expressed interest a launching a civil nuclear programme as part of its economic modernisation strategy. Detailed contract negotiations with France in 1978–9 for the supply of two 900PWRs proved abortive. Given ample fossil and hydroelectric resources, the urgency for nuclear power was far from self-evident to China's economic planners.[22] The announcement that a 300 MWe PWR would be built in the Shanghai region and the two tentative agreements concluded with Britain and France in March and May 1983 respectively for the construction of two 900 MWe PWRs in Guangdong province, represented more a wish to keep the nuclear option open than a firm decision to develop a fully-fledged nuclear industry.[23]

The Indian sub-continent, often regarded as a potentially significant market, had not by the early 1980s provided much encouragement to the major exporters. In India's case autarkic policies had militated against the establishment of a large nuclear programme. After the Tarapur and Rajasthan reactors were ordered during the 1960s from General Electric and AECL respectively, India chose to develop a small indigenous industry partly with a view to minimising dependence on foreign technology and avoiding additional strains on its scarce foreign exchange resources. As for Pakistan, political instability and chronic economic difficulties had limited the nuclear programme to a single reactor supplied by Canada and commissioned in 1973.

Turning to the Middle East, French, German and American attention, particularly after the mid-1970s, focused mainly on Egypt and Iran. Negotiations between Egypt and the United States gained momentum in 1976, but no firm orders materialised despite the

Egyptian government's avowed intention to instal some 6600 MWe of nuclear plant by 2000.[24] In 1982 France appeared well placed, particularly because of the close ties between EdF and Egyptian electricity authorities, to supply two turnkey nuclear power stations to Egypt, although any final agreement was likely to depend on the attractiveness of the financial arrangements offered by the various bidders. Other Middle Eastern countries to attract the interest of reactor suppliers included Israel and oil-rich Iraq and Libya. But, in each case, limited electricity requirements, financial difficulties or security considerations curtailed the prospects for nuclear power. The Israeli bombing raid which destroyed Iraq's Osirak research reactor supplied by France was ample evidence of the strategic sensitivity of nuclear capability in the Middle East region.[26]

Under the Shah's modernisation programme Iran was rapidly transformed into one of the most enticing markets for the international nuclear suppliers. Despite its vast oil resources, Iran had the most ambitious nuclear energy plans of any Third World country. If projections had been realised, the nuclear share of total generating capacity would have reached 50 per cent (23,000 MWe) by 1992.[27] The first nuclear station comprising two 1200 PWRs from KWU was under construction in Bushehr on the Persian Gulf. Construction of these plants commenced in 1976 and was to have been completed within a six-year period. The first plant was 70 per cent complete when the revolution terminated the programme. Contracts had also been placed with France in 1977 for the second twin 990 MWe PWRs at an estimated cost of $3000 million. In addition an agreement had been reached with KWU for the supply of another four 1200 PWRs at a cost of $8500 million which Iran intended to pay for by oil. Negotiations were in progress for another four plants from France and two from Germany, while an in principle agreement with the US for the purchase of 6–8 large units was awaiting ratification by the US Congress in 1978.[28] Following the Islamic revolution all nuclear plans were abandoned and after protracted negotiations a settlement reached between KWU and the Iranian Atomic Energy Commission aimed at minimising losses on the Bushehr project on which some $2100 million had already been invested. The change of regime in Iran had produced almost overnight the collapse of nuclear business with a potential value in excess of $30,000 million.

On the Africa continent, with the possible exception of a few Islamic countries, the only prospect for nuclear expansion appeared to be in South Africa. In 1976, France secured a contract, against strong opposition from an American – Dutch – Swiss consortium, for the design manufacture and commissioning of two 920 PWR units and associated ancillary plant. The commercial operation date for Koeberg-1 was December 1983 with Koeberg-2 following one year later.[29] France's readiness to offer favourable credit terms and adopt a more relaxed attitude towards safeguards' requirements had been sufficient to clinch the deal, which is not to say that other major suppliers including the United States and West Germany were not eager to establish themselves in the South African market or willing to contribute, perhaps somewhat more discreetly than France, to the development of a South African nuclear capability.[30]

It remains to say a word about Latin America, and more specifically about the three important nuclear markets: Brazil, Argentina and Mexico. Brazilian nuclear plans have already been described in some detail as has KWU's success in capturing the reactor market from Westinghouse. The perceived unreliability of the United States as a reliable supplier of enrichment services coupled with its unwillingness to provide access to enrichment technology greatly strengthened West Germany's hand. Having secured the 1975 contract, the West Germans subsequently attempted to erect a protective wall around their nuclear trade with Brazil, but the technical and economic difficulties surrounding the Brazilian programme and growing Brazilian disenchantment with dependence on foreign capital and technology greatly reduced the advantage West Germany was hoping to derive from its monopolistic position.

The Argentinian nuclear market had even more limited export potential partly because of Argentina's smaller economic base but also because of a more conscious policy of self-reliance.[31] Here again, Germany was able to establish an early lead. Following a feasibility study on the installation of Argentina's first commercial nuclear power plant, a turnkey contract for a natural uranium heavy water 340 MWe reactor was awarded to Siemens. A second contract for a 600 MWe unit was awarded to a Canadian–Italian consortium in 1973, although in this case Argentina's National Atomic Energy Commission took responsibility for the erection of critical components and systems. Following a period of intensified nuclear activity during the late 1970s aimed at closing the fuel cycle and acquiring a domestic manufacturing capability, an order was placed with KWU for the import of supplies and services for a 745 MWe natural uranium heavy water reactor scheduled to begin commercial operation in 1988. KWU's success in the face of stiff Canadian competition may well have been influenced by economic considerations, but West Germany's less stringent safeguards' requirements are more likely to have tilted the balance in KWU's favour.[32] The circumstances surrounding the Atucha II contract suggest that West Germany was now well placed to take advantage of any additional orders which might be forthcoming in line with Argentina's stated intention to have a 4000 MWe installed nuclear capacity by the year 2000. In the early 1980s, however, most international interest was focused on Mexico for most of the important decisions concerning the future direction of the country's nuclear programme had not yet been taken. Mexico's decision in 1969 to purchase two 645 MWe BWRs from General Electric had not foreclosed the country's nuclear options in terms of the size and pace of the programme or of the reactor strategy to be pursued.[33] Canada, France, West Germany, the United States and even Sweden were now fiercely competing for at least a slice of the Mexican market, each trying to use their respective strengths to put together a nuclear package likely to appeal to Mexican economic, diplomatic and strategic interests.

What emerges from this necessarily brief survey of Third World markets is the very limited scope for major nuclear investments and the fierceness of the competition where market opportunities had yet to be fully exhausted. Commercial rivalry in the Third World arena had thus become an integral part of the nuclear industry's short-term strategy for survival. It was a strategy in which the state played an increasingly important role since the use of its resources could considerably influence the outcome of international competition. Nuclear suppliers had traditionally operated within statutory frameworks created by various laws, decrees, ordinances, and in particular through bilateral agreements setting out the terms of international nuclear co-operation. These agreements normally provided for the transfer of resources and the training of scientific and industrial teams, on which underdeveloped countries depended for the establishment of the necessary institutional and technological infrastructure. In this sense both peripheral and core states played a key role in the promotion of nuclear exports. The web of bilateral transactions was supplemented and reinforced by a wide range of international agreements and institutions also funded by national governments.[34].

In addition to providing the technical and organisational basis for nuclear planning in Third World countries, core states also attempted to endow domestic manufacturers with a comparative advantage in the reactor market by offering the recipient country various forms of financial assistance. Under the 'Atoms for Peace' programme from 1953 to 1962 the United States made available to twenty-six countries some $9 million in grants for research reactors. In addition, nineteen countries received $2.7 million in research equipment grants. The Agency for International Development provided at least $83.3 million in financial assistance to twenty-seven countries, including $27 million in loans to India for the construction of the Tarapur nuclear power station.

It is the Export–Import Bank, however, which has provided the largest source of US assistance to foreign nuclear energy projects, both through direct financing and commercial and political risk insurance and guarantees. From 1958 to 1974, the Bank authorised $2100 million for the construction and/or fuelling of forty-two nuclear power projects. In addition, the Bank extended approximately $736 million in in financial guarantees to private sources that participated in financing several of the projects. Between 1974 and 1980 another $5000 million was made available in direct loans and financial guarantees, much of this to assist nuclear sales in South Korea, Taiwan and the Philippines.[36] The interest rates offered by the Bank have normally been well below market rates, and its repayment terms far more favourable than in the case of commercial loans. Significantly, the Bank's financing practices have shown a consistent bias towards nuclear as opposed to conventional power projects. As well as the unintentional subsidy resulting from the greater capital intensiveness of nuclear technology nuclear plants have benefited from a deliberate subsidy associated with the financing of the initial fuel inventory, an advantage not enjoyed by fossil-fuelled plants.[37]

Use of public funds to facilitate the export of nuclear goods and services was by no means unique to the United States. Although government policy in West Germany has been to leave the financing of exports to commercial sources, nuclear sales to Brazil, Argentina and Spain are known to have received official financial assistance, mainly in the form of highly subsidised loans.[38] French financial support for exports was provided through long-term credits of the Banque Française du Commerce Exterieur (BFCE) and the Bank of France. In Framatome's sale of two reactors to South Korea in 1980, for example, BFCE agreed to finance 85 per cent of their cost at an interest rate of only 7.6 per cent. France also had an insurance and guarantee programme administered by the Compagnie Française d'Assurance pour le Commerce Extérieur.[39] In addition, French reactor sales often benefited from active government intervention resulting in barter arrangements with the recipient country or in other attractive trade packages including the option of military sales.

We have also seen how, in a bid to offset their limited political and economic leverage and improve their competitive position *vis à vis* the United States, European governments sanctioned the sale of sensitive fuel cycle facilities. The greater range of fuel cycle services they could offer coupled, at least in France's case, with the apparent success of its domestic nuclear programme, might go some way towards neutralising the advantages enjoyed by leading US firms, in particular their technological strength, organisational flexibility and geographical mobility. The West German deal with Brazil and the French decision in March 1976 to supply Pakistan with a reprocessing plant were obviously intended to capitalise on America's more restrictive safeguards policies.

The complex relationship between commercial and security considerations will require fuller examination. Suffice it to say for the moment that governments were not reluctant to make use of military or diplomatic influence to enhance their commercial prospects, which is not to say that the exercise was always successful as the United States found to its cost when opposing the West German–Brazilian contract. There was in any case another aspect to state conduct. Commercial sales were often encouraged not only for their own snake but as part of a larger strategic design. Nowhere was this phenomenon more evident than in the Middle East. In 1974 President Nixon sought to promote US regional objectives by offering the sale of nuclear reactors to both Egypt and Israel. Similarly, France attempted to achieve privileged status with Iraq by agreeing to the sale of a large research reactor. The United States, France and West Germany were all eager to become principal partners in the Shah's ambitious nuclear programme not only for economic reasons but as a means of cementing a close and more durable relationship with a country that was rapidly asserting its dominance in the Persian Gulf region. International nuclear trade thus became inextricably intertwined with geopolitical rivalries and with the realignment of power occurring in regional and global politics. Commercial rivalry and military insecurity were at the heart of international nuclear relations.

PROLIFERATION IMPLICATIONS

Ever since 1945 governments concerned about the risks of nuclear proliferation have advanced a variety of proposals, beginning with the Baruch Plan, with a view to establishing a system of international controls which would facilitate the peaceful development of atomic energy while at the same time restricting its military applications.[40] The horizontal proliferation of nuclear weapons has been widely regarded as inherently dangerous in that it would fuel regional nuclear arms races, increase the risk of the inadvertent use of nuclear weapons, encourage the spread of nuclear terrorism, heighten the international repercussions of domestic instability, in short create conditions tending towards global anarchy. Quite apart, however, from the problem posed by a fragmented system of sovereign states, the non-proliferation objective has had to contend with the technical and institutional difficulty of disentangling the civil and military facets of nuclear power. Could the worldwide dissemination of nuclear technology proceed without unleashing the destructive potential of nuclear fission?

It was precisely in the hope of providing an affirmative answer to this question that the IAEA was formed in 1957. One of its main functions was to replace or at least reinforce the bilateral agreements which had hitherto governed transfers of nuclear materials and equipment. Initially, IAEA safeguards, which consisted of voluntary agreements by member states, were conceived only for research facilities and prototype plants. They were subsequently extended to reactors of greater power and later still to reprocessing plants and nuclear material in conversion and fuel fabrication plants. These various guidelines, which were eventually consolidated in document INFCIRC/66, were legally binding only to the extent that they were incorporated in a safeguards agreement, the precise contents of which could vary from signatory to signatory. It was not until the adoption of the Treaty for the Non-Proliferation of Nuclear Weapons (NPT), which came into force in March 1970, that the entire civil nuclear power programmes of all non-nuclear weapon signatories were placed under IAEA safeguards. The other main innovation of the NPT regime was the requirement that non-nuclear weapon states refrain from acquiring a nuclear weapons capability, including peaceful explosives.

The extension of these institutional arrangements was a direct response to the vastly enhanced role envisaged for nuclear energy. By the end of 1975, nineteen countries – Argentina, Belgium, Bulgaria, Canada, Czechoslovakia, France, the German Democratic Republic, the Federal Republic of Germany, India, Italy, Japan, the Netherlands, Pakistan, Spain, Sweden, Switzerland, the UK, the US and the USSR – had installed 157 reactors, each with an output greater than 30 MWe producing a total output of 71,900 MWe.[41] Another thirteen countries – Austria, Brazil, Finland, Hungary, Iran, Luxembourg, Mexico, the Phillippines, Poland, Romania, South Korea, Taiwan and Yugoslavia – had nuclear power plants under construction or on order. Several other countries, including South Africa, Egypt, Israel, Iraq, Libya Indonesia, Thailand and Turkey, had announced their intention to harness nuclear energy.

The military implications of this vast programme could not be ignored since the plutonium produced in nuclear power reactors, while not ideally suited to the manufacture of the most efficient atomic weapons, could nevertheless be used to build effective nuclear devices. In 1977, Dr Frank Barnaby estimated that within a few years the world's nuclear reactors would be capable of producing about 45,000 kg of plutonium annually, 40 per cent of which was likely to be located in the non-nuclear weapon states, sufficient for them to develop some 2000 weapons.[42]

The NPT–IAEA arrangements were designed to interfere as little as possible with the free flow of nuclear know-how and materials. They were intended to safeguard against nuclear weapons proliferation through the timely detection of diversion of significant quantities of nuclear material for military purposes, and deterrence of such diversion by the risk of early detection. Such strategy did not, however, preclude a country from acquiring an unsafeguarded national fuel cycle, or taking advantage of a safeguarded facility to construct an unsafeguarded duplication. In such circumstances, any help given to a peaceful nuclear programme might well serve the military objectives of the recipient country by enabling it to release materials or equipment which would otherwise be needed for civil purposes. As of December 1977 several nuclear facilities operating in Egypt, India, Israel, South Africa and Spain were not subject to IAEA or bilateral safeguards.[43]

Equally troublesome was the possibility of covert or officially unacknowledged assistance contributing to a nuclear weapons capability either by helping to develop the necessary infrastructure (e.g. supply of enrichment or reprocessing technology and equipment) or by transferring sensitive know-how in weapons design and fabrication. Notwithstanding official denials, evidence of this process was provided by documented reports of West German collaboration with South Africa's uranium enrichment project, and by Pakistan's use of several front organisations around the world for the purchase of centrifuge plant components. The international dissemination of nuclear fuels and equipment thus provided a convenient cloak behind which a growing number of countries could engage in covert transactions, thereby enabling them to reduce the time-lag between the initial decision to acquire a nuclear capability and the actual deployment of nuclear weapons. As for exporting countries, commercial incentives were a potent factor encouraging clandestine assistance or the transfer of equipment and technology under minimal safeguards arrangements.[44]

But even where IAEA safeguards were fully applicable, they were subject to several important limitations or constraints. International safeguards were designed to detect and, it was hoped, deter the diversion of nuclear material but not to protect the material against theft or sabotage. IAEA safeguards did not include safe international transport of nuclear material and equipment. Even under NPT agreements, the safeguarded country could exempt some nuclear material from IAEA safeguards. In the case of non-NPT countries, although IAEA safeguards specifically precluded 'furthering any military purpose', this clause was not universally interpreted as precluding development of peaceful nuclear explosives. IAEA inspectors did not enjoy unlimited access to safeguarded facilities, and had no authority to seek out possible undeclared or clandestine facilities or stockpiles of nuclear material.[45] Finally, there was considerable doubt as to what precise international sanctions would apply in the event that diversion had been established, and the extent to which such sanctions constituted effective deterrence. Critics of the IAEA safeguards system even questioned whether timely detection could be assured given the inadequacies of the monitoring and inspection process.[46]

As for the NPT system, although it represented the most effective barrier to nuclear proliferation yet devised, it remained a weak and ultimately self-contradictory instrument of control. Non-nuclear weapon signatories had agreed to renounce nuclear weapons and nuclear explosives and accepted the application of nuclear safeguards across their entire national nuclear industry, but in return they were promised the right to participate in 'the fullest possible exchange of equipment, materials and scientific and technical information on the peaceful uses of nuclear energy'. In other words, the underlying rationale of the NPT system was premised on the thin dividing line between the civil and military uses of nuclear energy. Yet, given the information available from the open technical literature, much of it stemming from nuclear reactor technology, every country with a significant industrial base now had the capacity to build a military useful fission bomb provided it had access to the necessary material. The task would be made even simpler if the intent was merely to demonstrate nuclear capability rather than technological sophistication.

Notwithstanding the claims of the nuclear industry, it was increasingly understood that use of reactor-grade plutonium of high irradiation levels for weapons purposes did not present formidable technical challenges.[47] As NRC Commissioner, Victor Gilinsky, put it in 1976:

> Countries much less advanced than the major industrial powers but possessing nuclear power programmes can make very respectable weapons... of course when reactor-grade plutonium is used there may be a penalty in performance that is considerable or insignificant, depending on the weapon design. But whatever we might once have thought, we now know that even simple designs, albeit with some uncertainties in yield, can serve as effective, highly powerful weapons – reliably in the kiloton range.[48]

The distinction between the peaceful and military atom was now under serious challenge.

As a consequence of the new technological realities and the wider appreciation of their implications, the increased pace of civil nuclear power deployment gave rise to a growing sense of insecurity. Stocks of plutonium in excess of immediate needs for specific civil power and research purposes were beginning to accumulate in an increasing number of countries in which reprocessing plants were already operating or under construction. A suitable small-scale reprocessing plant, not designed to be commercially viable, clean or safe, could be built in a year or two at an estimated cost of $1–3 million and on a scale sufficient to yield several bombs a year. By the mid-1970s, in addition to the United States, France, West Germany, the UK and Japan, which had already built or were contemplating large commercial reprocessing plants, India, Italy, Spain, Yugoslavia, Argentina and Taiwan were operating or building experimental or pilot scale reprocessing plants. Brazil was expecting to acquire such a facility from West Germany, and both Pakistan and South Korea had made overtures to France with the same end in view.

By accepting the notion that these separation facilities could be safeguarded even though many of the countries in which they were located were not parties to the NPT, exporting nations had helped to create a situation in which a government could come close to developing a nuclear weapons capability without violating any international agreements. Intensified competition for foreign nuclear sales had sharply exacerbated the conflict between non-proliferation goals and the pursuit of national commercial advantage. French and German suppliers, eager to break the American monopoly over the international nuclear market, were willing to offer sensitive elements of the nuclear fuel cycle despite the possibility of their misuse. To make matters worse most of the potential customers for these facilities were precisely those Third World states most likely to harbour military ambitions.

The emerging trend in European export policies was perhaps most graphically illustrated by the West German contract with Brazil, which involved the transfer of all requisites for the production of nuclear explosives. Although the Brazilians undertook not to use the know-how derived from these facilities to make explosives and not to duplicate the German technology except under agreed conditions, the distinction between foreign and indigenous processes remained somewhat imprecise as did the extent to which Brazilian nuclear facilities would be covered by international controls.[49] Nor was it clear why West Germany had agreed to supply Brazil with uranium enrichment technology rather than give it access to Urenco's enrichment services. As for the reprocessing plant, the economic case for it had yet to be demonstrated. Brazil's steadfast refusal to sign the NPT and the uncertainties of domestic and regional politics cast further shadows on the country's nuclear future.[50] American reactions were predictably hostile. Senator Pastore, Chairman of the Congressional Joint Committee on Atomic Energy, described the contract as a 'likely peril in our backyard'. The *New York Times* warned, 'Should Bonn perpetrate this nightmare upon the world, it will put at risk three decades of effort in gaining the high regard of its neighbours and allies.'[51]

The proposed sale of French reprocessing technology to South Korea and Pakistan provoked similar disquiet precisely because of the continuing ambiguity about the military intentions of both countries. The Indians, it will be remembered, had used a small-scale separation plant at Trombay to extract from the spent fuel discharged by a Canadian-supplied heavy water reactor the few kilograms of plutonium needed to assemble the nuclear device that was exploded in May 1974.[52] Statements such as that by President Bhutto after the Indian nuclear explosion – that his country would, if necessary, 'eat grass but produce the bomb' – did little to enhance the credibility of the Pakistani government's assurances that it did not wish to build nuclear weapons.[53] Other indications included Pakistan's refusal to become a party either to the Test Ban Treaty or to the Non-Proliferation Treaty. As for Pakistan's interest in reprocessing, it did not appear to have a sound economic basis given the small scale of its nuclear programme and the fact that the spent fuel derived from its heavy water reactor – the only one in operation – had a high plutonium concentration.[54] The rivalry and instability characteristic of Indo-Pakistani relations since Independence, coupled with India's progress in developing a nuclear explosives capability, made it difficult to avoid the conclusion that Pakistan's nuclear policies were guided at least as much by strategic as by economic or energy considerations.

Although the South Korean and Taiwanese nuclear programmes appeared to be more closely related to the industrial requirements of their respective economies, it was also true that both states had to contend with a precarious regional balance of power, and that their elites might well be attracted to a nuclear weapons option either for purposes of deterrence or as an instrument of diplomatic bargaining. The military potential of nuclear power no doubt held a similar fascination for the South African and Israeli governments whose policies were largely determined by the perception of a hostile external environment. Equally, in the case of Iran, any explanation of the Shah's interest in acquiring enrichment and reprocessing technologies could not be altogether divorced from his geopolitical ambitions.[55] Common, then, to all these regional balances was the perceived predisposition of one or more actors to consider the bomb as a possible weapon of last resort in a future military conflict.

The security implications of nuclear proliferation thus became a matter of growing international concern not only in a regional context but also in relation to the global strategic balance. The development of a nuclear weapons capability in an area of international tension risked unleashing a regional confrontation which might in turn provoke the military intervention of one or both superpowers. It is hardly surprising therefore that serious misgivings should have arisen in the United States and the Soviet Union about the indiscriminate transfer of sensitive elements of the nuclear fuel cycle. To this extent, at least, the American reaction to French and West German nuclear sales should be interpreted not only in the light of commercial interests, which were no doubt important, but also in the context of strategic and diplomatic considerations. By the mid-1970s the steadily deteriorating climate of expectation with regard to the NPT system,[56] amply confirmed by the meagre results of the NPT Review Conference of May 1975,[57] acted as a powerful catalyst for official reassessment of the adequacy of existing arrangements and the formulation of new proposals.

US PERCEPTIONS AND POLICIES

That much of this rethinking was to occur in the United States and eventually influence the policy-making process there should not be taken to mean that the American state had not itself contributed to the problem. Apart from the general promotional activities carried out internationally by the Atomic Energy Commission in tandem with the main nuclear corporations, the United States had agreed to sell substantial amounts of plutonium and weapons-grade enriched uranium to several countries, including South Africa. The fact that the material sold was intended for research and development purposes did not necessarily eliminate the proliferation potential of such transfers. Moreover, despite its consistent championing of the NPT system, the US was not averse to conducting nuclear transactions with countries which had refused to ratify the NPT. As of 1975, no less than thirteen of the US agreements for nuclear co-operation were with non-NPT countries. Even where certain limitations were imposed in respect of sales to non-NPT nations, no concerted effort was made to have the same guidelines applied by other countries though many of them were dependent on the import of US nuclear equipment and technology. The failure to devise stringent safeguards and book-keeping methods, even within the

United States, provided further evidence of the ambiguity of American intentions.[58]

The deficiencies of the international safeguards regime were perhaps not fully appreciated until some time after the 1974 Indian nuclear explosion when it became clear that US heavy water sold to India strictly for peaceful purposes had been used in the Indian reactor which had produced the necessary plutonium. It soon emerged that the US government had not investigated the matter at the time of the sale and not even lodged a protest following the detonation of the device.[59] The alleged contrast between the American commitment to non-proliferation and the more cynical European interest in capturing a share of a potentially lucrative market was more apparent than real. It is equally true, however, that the concern for security, which was never altogether absent, gained currency particularly after 1975, although it remained closely intertwined with the wider economic and strategic interests of the American state.

As congressional committees continued throughout 1975–6 their investigations of nuclear proliferations issues, they became increasingly sceptical of the adequancy of international controls and safeguards. In October 1975 Senator Symington stated:

> Present international safeguards against diversion of nuclear material from peaceful power programs to military purposes would appear virtually useless. The Non-Proliferation Treaty itself may be of more value to a determined violator than to a nation which wishes to be responsible in its nuclear program.[60]

In similar vein, when Secretary of State Kissinger appeared before the Senate Committee on Government Operations, several senators drew attention to the inherent dangers of plutonium stockpiling and to the ambiguities in existing safeguards agreements.[61] In a succession of speeches, Bills and amendments to Bills, members of Congress made it abundantly clear that the *status quo* was no longer acceptable.

Expressions of concern were by no means confined to Congress. In its annual report to Congress in February 1976 the Arms Control and Disarmament Agency stressed the proliferation potential of the civil nuclear industry, particularly in regions of intense rivalry.[62] By this time even the nuclear bureaucracy was beginning to sound the alarm. NRC Commissioner, Victor Gilinsky, was the most outspoken but certainly not the only voice affirming that reactor-grade plutonium could be used for nuclear warheads at all levels of technical sophistication. More importantly, he highlighted the fact that no plutonium controls were in force under IAEA or Euratom safeguards agreements. Given that separation facilities currently could not be safeguarded, he argued that the only effective form of control available to the US was to veto the moves by America's overseas customers towards domestic reprocessing of spent fuel and national stockpiling of plutonium extracted from it.[63]

While cautious in their reassessment of existing policy, the Nixon and Ford Administrations could hardly remain impervious to congressional scrutiny and mounting public pressure. Before the end of the Nixon presidency some tentative first steps in mutilateral diplomacy and national export policy were taken to strengthen the international non-proliferation regime. Following consultations with other nuclear suppliers, the United States was able to gain in 1975 informal agreement for the application of certain guidelines in the conduct of international nuclear trade. The seven countries which participated in these discussions, the US, the Soviet Union, Britain, Canada, West Germany, France and Japan, came to be known as the Nuclear Suppliers' Group. The initial membership of seven nations was later increased to fifteen including some states from Eastern Europe. Possibly the most contentious and ill-defined guideline agreed to was the undertaking to exercise self-restraint in the transfer of nuclear technology and know-how, particularly in the sensitive areas of fuel enrichment, reprocessing and heavy water production. Other principles enshrined in the guidelines included: prohibition against providing assistance for any explosions including those for 'peaceful purposes'; application of IAEA safeguards on exported material, equipment and technology; and requirements for physical security measures on nuclear equipment and materials. In addition, know-how derived through use of supplied technology and equipment was to be subjected to controls, as was the subsequent generation of fissile materials and any plant or equipment 'contaminated' by supplied material. Finally, no material or equipment could be transferred to a third country without the prior approval of the supplier-nation, and supplied technology could not be used to duplicate facilities without these too being subjected to IAEA safeguards.[64]

The establishment of the Nuclear Suppliers' Group was significant in that it went beyond the confines of the NPT system and made the major suppliers primarily responsible for limiting the risks inherent in unfettered commercial nuclear competition. On the other hand, the agreement was limited in substance allowing only for partial restrictions on national export policy.[65] There was no obligation on suppliers to require NPT adherence as a precondition to the supply of nuclear materials and equipment. Nor were the recipient nations expected to submit their entire civil industry to IAEA inspection. In any case, the guidelines were so phrased as to allow a good deal of flexibility in interpretation. Supplier countries had done no more than agree to pursue roughly parallel policies.

The guidelines agreed to by the nuclear suppliers represented a compromise between two opposing perspectives. On the one hand, the United States, Canada and the Soviet Union, sceptical of the efficacy of the NPT–IAEA regime, appeared to favour some kind of selective embargo to prevent the national acquisition of sensitive nuclear technologies. The Europeans and Japanese, on the other hand, expressed greater confidence in existing legal arrangements and argued that the sale of material or equipment on the sensitive list was acceptable so long as the importing state agreed to submit its fuel cycle facilities to IAEA safeguards. On the proliferation issue at least, a closer coincidence of perceptions and policies appeared to exist between the two super-powers than between the United States and its allies.[66]

For all its moderation the Kissinger approach could not conceal, let alone eliminate, the very serious differences in nuclear trade policy that had emerged between the United States and the two leading European suppliers, France and West Germany. The 1975 German–Brazilian deal and French readiness to provide South Korea and Pakistan with reprocessing plants were to prove major bones of contention. Despite IAEA approval of the German–Brazilian and Franco–Pakistani agreements in February 1976, the US remained unconvinced as to the safeguardability of these proposed transfers. Accordingly, pressure was applied on both suppliers and recipients not to proceed with the implementation of these agreements. In 1976 the United States threatened to cut off economic and military aid to Pakistan in a bid to persuade the Bhutto government to abandon its reprocessing plans.[67] Similar pressure was successfully exerted on South Korea to cancel its agreement with France for the construction of a pilot scale reprocessing plant.

American intervention was also a contributing factor in France's decision to modify its export policy.[68] With regard to the Pakistani contract, the French government at first refused to cancel it, arguing that a policy of denial would not prevent Pakistan from assembling a nuclear device. By withholding assistance it would merely be encouraging Pakistan to go it alone, with the added disadvantage that the Pakistanis might then no longer wish to operate their facility under IAEA safeguards. Following the creation in September 1976 of the Conseil Supérieur de Politique Nucléaire Extérieure under the chairmanship of the President of the Republic, it was announced that France would strengthen the conditions and safeguards attached to nuclear sales, continue consultations with other suppliers and with importing countries, but retain unilateral control of its export policy.[69] In December 1976 it was announced that no further bilateral contracts would be concluded involving the export of reprocessing technologies. France subsequently initiated bilateral discussions with Pakistan and proposed the supply of a co-processing instead of reprocessing plant. The offer proved unacceptable to Pakistan and the deal eventually fell through.

By the time the 1976 presidential election campaign got under way, nuclear proliferation had already become a significant issue in American politics. Anxious to refute criticisms of his non-proliferation policies and project an image of firmness, President Ford took the further step in October 1976 of announcing that the US government no longer viewed reprocessing 'as a necessary and inevitable step in the nuclear fuel cycle'. Indeed, he foreshadowed a moratorium on the commercial reprocessing of spent fuel and plutonium recycling in the United States unless it could be demonstrated that they were consistent with America's international objectives. President Ford had thus prepared the ground for his successor, Jimmy Carter, who made non-proliferation one of the major themes of his campaign, openly criticising not only the timidity of the Ford Administration but also what he perceived to be the ambivalence and inadequacy of Western European policies.

Almost immediately on assuming office Carter launched an intensive public media and diplomatic drive in opposition to the German transfer of enrichment and reprocessing technology to Brazil. In a bid to convey the full extent of American displeasure Vice-President Mondale and Deputy Secretary of State Warren Christopher were dispatched to Bonn and Brasilia respectively. In both capitals the US negotiators attempted in rather crude fashion to secure a cancellation of the objectionable elements of the German–Brazilian contract. American leverage, however, proved insufficient for the task and, if anything, American tactics appeared to generate considerable animosity against the United States, particularly in Brazil where nationalist fervour helped to create a newly-found unity between opposing factions of the domestic nuclear establishment in support of the German deal.[70]

The Carter Administration's frenetic but ill-prepared efforts to reverse an agreement that two of its main allies had concluded some two years earlier were perhaps doomed to failure. Yet, precisely because the deal was largely a *fait accompli*, Carter's last minute attempt at obstruction cannot be considered a valid test of his non-proliferation strategy. As we shall see, the Carter approach involved an elaborate mixture of unilateral and multilateral initiatives, designed to enhance the efficacy of international safeguards, promote self-restraint in the transfer of proliferation-prone technologies, and provide countries with incentives for renouncing the acquisition of such technologies.[71]

Perhaps the most dramatic but ultimately least effective unilateral measure was the deferment of commercial reprocessing and plutonium recycle in the United States. Allied to it was the decision to restructure the US breeder programme by giving greater priority to alternative designs of the breeder and deferring the date when breeder reactors would be put into commercial use. It was also proposed to redirect funds for nuclear research and development so as to accelerate research into alternative nuclear fuel cycles which did not involve direct access to materials usable in nuclear weapons.[72] Moreover, the US would continue the existing embargo on the transfer of reprocessing and enrichment technology; avoid new contracts for the supply of separated plutonium except for gram quantities needed for research purposes; and agree to provide significant quantities of highly enriched uranium only in exceptional circumstances.

Although the Carter moves could be construed as a rejection of the philosophy underlying the nuclear programmes of other advanced industrial nations, they were largely symbolic in nature since they entailed few penalties and foreclosed no options for the United States. The economic argument for commercial reprocessing, at least in the American context, was open to serious challenge. Equally questionable was the argument that reprocessing was an essential step in the final disposal of nuclear waste. In any case, the technology and facilities developed for the nuclear weapons programme would be maintained. Furthermore, the President's objectives could not be fully implemented without the co-operation of Congress which, it seemed, was intent on frustrating or at least modifying his termination of the federal subsidy for the Barnwell reprocessing plant and the restructuring of the Clinch River breeder project. Congressional refusal to abandon these two important elements of the plutonium economy reflected once again the fragmented character of the US policy-making process, a factor that was bound to weaken America's international advocacy of its non-proliferation strategy.

As for the decision to re-organise US nuclear research and development and minimise direct accessibility of fissionable materials, it was premised on the dubious proposition that technical fixes could overcome the proliferation hazards implicit in nuclear fission. Even if a proliferation-proof system could be devised, its efficacy would depend largely on the willingness of other governments to apply the technical solution to their respective nuclear power programmes.[73] Unilateral initiatives might help to set a useful example for the rest of the world, but they were unlikely to succeed unless they were supported by other actions capable of changing the political conditions governing international nuclear trade.

In a bid to gain at least limited international compliance with its non-proliferation objectives, the Carter Administration submitted in 1977 to Congress a Nuclear Non-Proliferation Bill which was intended to establish the new criteria to be used by the NRC for nuclear exports. It defined additional conditions which would be required in new agreements for civil nuclear co-operation. In particular, it stipulated that, as a condition of continuing US supply, recipients would have to place all their nuclear activities under IAEA safeguards. In the case of existing agreements a process of renegotiation was proposed with a view to achieving the same standards as those required for new agreements. This approach was justified on the grounds that the automatic imposition of new export licensing conditions would be counter-productive in that it would undermine America's credibility as a reliable supplier of nuclear fuel and equipment, create international resentment likely to speed up the indigenous development route, and preclude the possibility of granting exemptions where this was deemed necessary for reasons of security and consistent with non-proliferation objectives.[74] The Carter Administration had appreciated the limits to

American power and the need to reconcile conflicting US interests, each of them competing for a share of the state's limited resources.

In order to reinforce yet soften the coercive element of its strategy the Carter Administration adopted the notion of incentives based on bilateral and multilateral arrangements. To this end, the US was willing to offer 'assured supply of non-sensitive nuclear fuels on a timely, adequate, reliable, and economic basis at the front end of the fuel cycle', and 'sufficient spent fuel and nuclear waste storage capacity at the back end of the fuel cycle'.[75] On the question of assured fuel supply, a three-tiered approach was contemplated involving bilateral fuel supply commitments based on parallel policies by major fuel exporters; multilateral guarantees to consumers to ensure access to fuel supply; international mechanisms such as an 'international fuel bank' to act as a contingency reserve in case of breakdown of other supply arrangements. Central to the concept of assured fuel supply was Carter's intention to increase US production capacity for uranium enrichment. To the extent that the assurance of adequate fuel supplies implied continued dependence by foreign governments on the United States, it was unlikely to arrest the increasing diversification of national sources of uranium enrichment services.

In respect of spent nuclear fuels, the policy announced in October 1977 envisaged that, in addition to the possible establishment of regional and international storage sites, the US government would accept and take title to spent fuel from other countries on payment of a one-time storage fee.[76] As with fuel assurances, this initiative was seen as alleviating the pressure for the acquisition of reprocessing facilities. But the entire incentive package remained little more than a series of interesting but inconclusive proposals lacking firm financial and organisational foundations. US concepts of spent fuel management were unlikely to halt the spread and use of plutonium unless they satisfied the economic and political requirements of states committed to the reprocessing option. The failure of the Carter Administration to formulate a concrete and detailed policy in this area further weakened Washington's leverage and credibility in pressing for an indefinite moratorium on the reprocessing and recycling of plutonium.

Given the difficulties and inconsistencies surrounding many facets of President Carter's multilateral strategy, nuclear export policy remained the only tangible instrument which could be used to stem the dispersion of fuel cycle technology. After a lengthy process of negotiation, compromise and amendment in the Congress, the Nuclear Non-Proliferation Bill was signed into law in March 1978. The resulting Act, which enshrined many of President Carter's proposals, codified an elaborate set of criteria with which all agreements for co-operation and export licences would need to comply.[77] The most important among these were: application of full-scope safeguards to all peaceful nuclear activities in non-nuclear weapon–state recipients; prohibition of reprocessing without US approval; and prohibition of third-party retransfer without US approval. The full-scope safeguards requirement was expected to prove particularly delicate in nuclear relations with South Africa and several Third World countries, notably India, Pakistan, Israel, Egypt and Argentina. The reprocessing and retransfer requirements were likely to be most troublesome in relations with Japan and the Euratom countries.

So long as the United States continued to supply at least a fraction of Euratom fuel, the renegotiations of nuclear co-operation agreements and export licences in line with the provisions of the Act carried with it the possibility of the Americans achieving virtual control over French and British reprocessing plans. Contracts with countries such as Japan, Switzerland and Spain would also be affected since some of the fuel would again be of US origin. In practice, however, the difficulties promised to be less intractable in that, under the Act, the necessary approval of reprocessing could be granted if, in the view of the Secretary of Energy and the Secretary of State, such reprocessing did not constitute a serious proliferation risk. Existing Western European and Japanese facilities were presumably covered by this clause. Even in the case of new reprocessing plants, Euratom countries were expected to be given the green light for the application of Euratom safeguards was deemed adequate for ensuring timely warning of diversion.

While the 1978 Act did not proscribe the reprocessing and nuclear trading policies of America's major allies, it did impose a highly visible form of extra-territorial control over their economic and foreign policies. If nothing else it called into question the independence of their national programmes. This form of external intervention was likely to be particularly unwelcome since it rested on a highly intricate procedural framework involving not only the President and Secretary of State but several other agencies of the Executive Branch and Congress itself.[78] The issuing of an export licence was to be the responsibility of the NRC, but only after notification from the Secretary of State that the proposed export was not 'inimical to the common defense and security'. The NRC would base its decision on information obtained from the Secretary of State and other government departments, and through public hearings where these were deemed appropriate. A licence approved by the NRC would remain subject to normal court review procedures. Where the NRC declined to approve the licence application, the export could nevertheless be authorised by Executive Order of the President provided that, on being submitted Congress for a period of sixty continuous session days, such an order was not disapproved by majorities of both Houses of Congress. The very attempt to endow the legislation with a measure of flexibility and presidential oversight had created a complex and unpredictable decision-making process likely to accentuate the scepticism of foreign governments.

INTERNATIONAL FALL-OUT

The international response to President Carter's non-proliferation strategy, if judged by the reactions of governments, nuclear corporations and international organisations, was generally hostile. The nuclear industry in the United States as in most other countries tended to argue that nuclear weapons proliferation was principally a function of the political motivation of governments rather than the technological capabilities at their disposal. The danger that reprocessing of civil fuel would be used by non-weapons countries to obtain plutonium for military purposes was discounted as negligible. Other routes for the production of weapons-grade fissionable material was already available, and several others might soon be within the reach of any nation bent on acquiring a nuclear arsenal. In the words of one leading advocate of the US nuclear industry, 'if the dike is leaking in at least eight places, maybe more, why are some so anxious to plug only one of the leaks?'[79] Representatives of the nuclear industry perceived Carter's policies as a threat to breeder and recycling technologies which they considered essential to the longevity of nuclear fission as a worldwide energy source.

Somewhat paradoxically, the pro-nuclear lobbies in Europe and Japan tended to regard the new American approach as motivated more by economic self-interest than by concern for proliferation. The US nuclear industry, it was feared, might benefit from the continued dependence of other countries on the purchase of American nuclear fuels and technology. It is precisely in order to break from such dependence that Britain, France, Germany and Japan had made such a strong commitment to reprocessing and breeder technologies. This capability was seen as valuable insurance against rising world uranium prices or interruption of supply by one or more uranium producing nations. Moreover, reprocessing represented a major nuclear export prospect which, if abandoned, might endanger the future of the nuclear industry in many of these countries.

These varied, often conflicting, but consistently negative assessments of President Carter's policies were given full expression at international conferences attended by government and industry representatives. In April 1977 the Persepolis Conference, sponsored by the Atomic Energy Organisation of Iran, the IEA and the European, American and Japanese Nuclear Societies, vigorously attacked Carter's attempts to legitimise the principle of discrimination in the transfer of nuclear technology for peaceful purposes.[80] This principle it was argued, violated the spirit and the letter of the Non-Proliferation Treaty. Some even went so far as to characterise the Carter approach as a unilateral abrogation of international agreements. Another fear widely expressed was that it would encourage and strengthen the band of groups opposed to nuclear power not only in the US but in other countries where they had also succeeded in obstructing nuclear power programmes. Although more tactfully expressed, many of the same themes surfaced in the public comments of senior IAEA officials. Dr Sigvard Eklund, the Agency's Director General, stressed on more than one occasion that proliferation could not be prevented by technological constraints or policies of denial.[81]

The new direction in US non-proliferation policy met with an equally unfavourable response in many parts of the Third World. The Carter package of incentives and disincentives was widely seen as denying less developed nations 'access to essential nuclear technology needed for self-reliant power generation'.[82] The excessive concentration on the problem of horizontal proliferation and the consequent attempt to prevent Third World countries from developing fuel cycle technology and even a nuclear explosives capability was said to contrast sharply with the scant attention paid to the much more pressing danger of vertical proliferation.[83] To the extent that nuclear technology and nuclear weapons were considered avenues to international prestige and power, Third World élites, particularly in countries which had developed a powerful nuclear lobby, such as Argentina, Brazil India and Pakistan, construed the latest twist in

America's nuclear export policy as further evidence of US 'atomic imperialism'.

More troublesome, however, were the adverse reactions of America's senior allies for they greatly accentuated the already difficult problem of intra-alliance management confronting US diplomacy. It is worth noting that even the moderate proposals advanced by the Ford Administration had initially been given a cool reception by France, West Germany, Britain and Japan. Whereas the Americans were pressing for a concerted approach by supplier states, the Europeans and Japanese were insisting that any new controls should be subject to the approval of all countries concerned. Indeed, the West German government had strongly resisted the establishment of stricter safeguards which were not fully in accord with international agreements, notably Article IV of the NPT, and did not take account of the specific circumstances of countries depending on technology transfers for the development of their nuclear power programmes. Despite these objections the Europeans had moved some way towards the American position by accepting the principle of self-restraint enunciated first by the Zangger Committee and subsequently by the Nuclear Suppliers' Group. The shift in attitudes was confirmed by the announcement of the French government in December 1976 that it would no longer agree to the export of reprocessing technology, a stance also adopted by the West German government although not formally announced until June 1977.[84]

There were clear limits, however, to the concessions America's allies were willing to make. They were certainly not prepared to curtail their domestic enrichment or breeder reactor programmes. President Carter's call for a moratorium on plutonium recycling was unacceptable in that it threatened these programmes under the guise of effective arms control. Moreover, both the Europeans and Japanese were suspicious of the Carter package of stricter safeguards and assurances of fuel supply for they were seen as helping to maintain American dominance in fuel procurement and waste management policy. The British government, which had adopted a lower profile on the issue than either the French or German governments, was nevertheless sceptical of the implications of the US Administration's proposals. The British Foreign Secretary, David Owen, questioned, for example, whether President Carter's preference for the 'throw-away' cycle fully resolved the problem of plutonium accessibility. Would not the storage of spent fuel mean that large quantities of plutonium could be separated at any time and therefore require the same degree of international controls as would apply to reprocessing? And would the indefinite storage of unprocessed spent fuel elements be acceptable environmentally?[85]

The restriction in US nuclear export policy which caused greatest concern was the requirement that the importing country obtain US approval before reprocessing domestically or making available the technology to a third country. Equally objectionable in the eyes of America's allies was the process by which the new policy would be implemented, in particular the requirement that all existing nuclear co-operation agreements be renegotiated so as to align them with the new criteria set out in the Nuclear Non-Proliferation Act. Serious misgivings had also arisen because of the unknown conditions which might in future be attached to US approval for enrichment and reprocessing of American-supplied nuclear fuel, the unpredictable use of presidential powers, the prospect of a congressional veto against a presidential decision, and the possibility that new export criteria might be devised, which had the necessary support in both houses of Congress.[86]

But even before the Carter Administration had time to formulate the details of its policy, the President's vigorous opposition to the German–Brazilian deal had created serious strains in US–German relations. Chancellor Schmidt, far from yielding to American pressure, expedited the necessary authorisation for the transfer of enrichment and reprocessing know-how to Brazil. Clearly, the differences between the two countries involved more than a disagreement about the best way of preventing the further spread of nuclear weapons. Central to the dispute was the boldness of the German move in capturing an important slice of the international nuclear market, and this in a corner of the world the United States had traditionally regarded as its own domain.[87] The sales agreement with Brazil had to be secured not only because of its intrinsic economic value but in order to demonstrate Germany's reliability as a nuclear supplier. Economic competition between highly-developed capitalist countries had thus combined with different perspectives about military and energy security to destabilise the delicate balance underpinning the Atlantic alliance.

Western Europe and Japan, which had for many years been content to operate under the protection of the American economic and security umbrella, were now far more conscious of their separate interests and of their independent capacity to protect them.[88] Japan's determination to acquire an independent reprocessing capability and the possible interruption in the supply of US enriched fuel to Europe pending the renegotiation of the US–Euratom agreement represented two major areas of potential conflict. Soon after assuming office President Carter had made it known that, in keeping with his Administration's nuclear policy, he was opposed to, and would if necessary block, the commissioning of Japan's Tokai Mura demonstration reprocessing plant. Faced with Japanese intransigence and the need not to impair relations with Japan at a time when commercial and strategic issues were also under discussion, the United States modified its position and requested the Japanese to convert Tokai-Mura to a co-processing facility which would not separate the plutonium from the spent fuel.

The new American proposal proved no less unacceptable to the Japanese who considered that retrofitting the plant would be expensive but also in conflict with their stated aim to develop reprocessing on a commercial scale. America's implicit threat to cut off fuel supplies if it did not approve of Japan's nuclear plans merely strengthened Japanese resolve to strive towards greater nuclear independence.[89] A compromise was eventually reached in September 1977 by way of an interim agreement in which Japan undertook to carry out experimental co-processing work at its Tokai-Mura plant and to defer, at least for the duration of the International Nuclear Fuel Cycle Evaluation (INFCE), the use of plutonium in light water reactors and the construction of its planned plutonium conversion facility and 1000 tonnes/yr commercial reprocessing plant.[90] These Japanese gestures, however, represented little more than a face-saving formula for the United States, since Japan would now be able to proceed with reprocessing without fear of US retaliation. At best the United States had postponed resolution of the conflict for another two years.

In the European context, nuclear tensions which had been dormant since June 1977 surfaced once again following President Carter's signing into law of the Nuclear Non-Proliferation Act in 1978. The United States announced that it would not issue further licences for the export of nuclear fuels to members countries of the EEC until they agreed to renegotiate the current agreement covering the terms of such exports. As might be expected Euratom showed little inclination to follow this course. France, in particular, argued that European governments had no legal obligation to accept this unilateral demand and that no action should be taken before the conclusion of INFCE which was not expected before the end of 1979.

The US embargo formally came into effect in April 1978, although all licence applications whose paperwork had been completed by that date were approved by the NRC. Several other applications, however, were left pending.[91] In July 1978, Euratom agreed to negotiate, but on condition that the issues being studied at INFCE would not be considered and that the results of INFCE would be taken into account in the final negotiations. The Carter Administration was under strong pressure to take a firm stand from influential members of Congress who viewed the expansion of reprocessing at Windscale and La Hague as 'dangerously premature and obviously inconsistent with the INFCE initiative'. On the other hand, the President, anxious not to exacerbate tensions, accepted the Euratom face-saving formula, lifted the embargo, and despite inconclusive discussions authorised in February 1980 a dispensation of one year in the hope that substantive negotiations would take place after INFCE.[92] It had now become apparent that nuclear export policy would not be an effective instrument in America's bid to stop the reprocessing and breeder programmes of its major allies. Such difficulties as they encountered in this direction were almost entirely the result of domestic factors, whether technical, economic or political.

Even before the 1978 Act had come into force, the Carter Administration had considerably moderated the vigour of its non-proliferation diplomacy. The first signs of this trend appeared as early as May 1977 when at America's suggestion the major western powers agreed at their London summit to sponsor the INFCE Conference. Chancellor Schmidt, for his part, had given an assurance that no further contracts would be negotiated involving the sale of complete fuel cycle technology. Increasingly the emphasis in US non-proliferation policy was shifting to initiatives that could be taken in a domestic context. As for the international arena, America's diminishing options were reflected in new rhetoric stressing the need for greater understanding of energy security requirements and the value of bilateral and multilateral fuel assurance schemes.[93] By October 1978, US policy-makers were openly conceding that they 'could not unilaterally impose their will on others concerning how the nuclear fuel cycle should be structured.'[94] Diplomatic dialogue rather than the use of coercive instruments now formed the basis of the Carter strategy.[95]

The principal forum for such dialogue was to be the INFCE

Conference which held in first organising meeting in October 1977. From the American point of view, the overriding objective of the Conference was to establish an international consensus in favour of technical and institutional changes which would strengthen international safeguards, restrict the spread of sensitive technologies, and encourage the use of diversion-resistant processes.[96] Eight study groups were created for a two-year programme covering different aspects of the fuel cycle: fuel and heavy water availability; enrichment availability; assurances of long-term supply of technology and fuel services; reprocessing; waste management and disposal; advanced fuel cycle and reactor concepts. Each aspect was to be considered with particular regard to its proliferation implications. It soon emerged, however, that INFCE would not be able to achieve a technical consensus, much less a political agreement, which cut across national policy positions. Significantly, six of the eight study groups were chaired and run by countries whose views on the plutonium question were in conflict with those of the United States.

During the two-year evaluation, US representatives put forward several proposals for the restructuring of the fuel cycle. They suggested the establishment of an International Nuclear Fuel Authority (INFA) which would provide fuel services, including the storage of nuclear material and spent fuel; proposed the creation of a stockpile of enriched uranium accessible to nations willing to forgo enrichment and reprocessing facilities; declared America's willingness to provide other countries with reliable access to US enrichment services; and moderated the Carter Administration's previous emphasis on deferring the commercial introduction of reprocessing and breeder technologies. To buttress these proposals and initiatives the United States stressed the adequacy of natural uranium resources, the potential for more efficient utilisation of low-enriched uranium, and the positive contribution that unilateral and multilateral fuel guarantees could make to greater energy security.[97] The diminishing prospects for nuclear power and the consequent fall in the demand for natural and enriched uranium seemed to give added weight to American arguments, and by implication weakened the rationale for thermal recycle and breeder commercialisation.

Despite these favourable new elements in the negotiating process, Carter's policies in the end proved unacceptable to most allied and Third World governments. INFCE may have helped to avert a major diplomatic crisis between the United States and its allies in 1977–9 but it could not reconcile sharply diverging perceptions of the appropriate balance between economic self-interest and collective military security. The American attempt to defuse the controversy by seeking technical fixes to the non-proliferation problem was doomed to failure since the problem was itself the manifestation of a more profound conflict of state interests. Not only was the proliferation-proof nuclear fuel cycle an illusory objective, but the preference for any particular cycle, whatever its technical justification, was bound to advantage some and disadvantage others in the fiercely competitive structure of the international market-place.

The ambiguity inherent in the INFCE project was reflected in its conclusions. Neither the diplomatic language nor the highly technical calculations and forecasts contained in the final report could conceal the underlying disagreements.[98] Indeed, the only clear conclusion to emerge was that no conceivable fuel cycle could significantly reduce the proliferation hazard and that no single pattern of nuclear power development was likely to gain international acceptance. Both of these conclusions were at odds with the assumptions and expectations of US policy. INFCE had failed to achieve the international consensus desired by the Carter Administration.

The failure of America's non-proliferation strategy was in part the result of its internal contradictions which found expression in the uneasy tension between unilateral and multilateral initiatives. On the one hand, President Carter's early diplomacy and the restrictive provisions contained in the Nuclear Non-Proliferation Act suggested a willingness to go it alone and impose a new international safeguards regime on the rest of the world even at the risk of confrontation. On the other hand, the more conciliatory approach evidenced by the policy of incentives and the decision to initiate INFCE indicated a recognition of America's declining political and industrial leverage. To this extent the denial of access to US technology was no longer considered a sufficient instrument of policy. Export licensing arrangements could not by themselves ensure the ascendancy of American views given that the United States had lost its lead in reactor technology, that licensing arrangements governing the export of American technology were coming at an end, and that the supply of enrichment services had been substantially diversifield.[99]

Quite apart from the declining efficacy of American diplomatic and military influence, the unilateralist approach also suffered from an underlying incoherence in the formulation and execution of policy. In the first place, neither the Executive nor the Congress specified the relative importance of the non-proliferation objective within the overall framework of foreign and domestic policy. The competing claims of alliance management, commercial advantage (associated with the maximisation of US nuclear sales), and stabilisation of the international nuclear order were never fully reconciled. Even within the narrower confines of nuclear policy several critical issues were not resolved.

President Carter and his advisers were no doubt right in stressing the dangers entailed in the plutonium fuel cycle, but once-through fuel cycles could also be used to acquire a nuclear weapons capability. In addition to the plutonium route several existing and newly emerging enrichment technologies could be applied to the same end. According to one assessment, confirmed by INFCE's own conclusions, 'every form of every fissionable material in every nuclear fuel cycle can be used to make military bombs, either on its own or in combination with other ingredients made widely available by nuclear power.'[100] Whether it is technically or institutionally possible to organise the nuclear fuel cycle in ways which provide energy without providing weaponry was a question which US policy-makers largely ignored, perhaps because the answer would have raised fundamental and unpalatable questions about America's own commitment to nuclear fission as a source of energy. On the other hand, by sidestepping the issue, the Carter Administration handed its foreign critics powerful ammunition with which to challenge the intellectual foundations of its own policy.

Equally striking was the US failure to offer any principled grounds for accentuating the already discriminatory global structure implicit in the NPT system. For US export policy was ultimately reduced to promoting a new international division between states that could be relied upon not to divert reprocessing and plutonium recycle facilities for military purposes (i.e. major allies) and those that could not (i.e. minor allies and non-aligned nations). It was never made entirely clear why in the long run reprocessing facilities would be any safer in West German or Japanese hands than in Indian, South Korean or Taiwanese hands. The impression was thus created that US policy was governed more by national interest and the calculus of power than by an objective assessment of the dangers of nuclear proliferation. Finally, the unilateralist approach could not be pursued with any effectiveness so long as the state was unable to speak with one voice. As we have seen, disagreements between the White House and the Congress coloured every aspect of nuclear policy, and were especially visible in the provisions of the NNPA which allocated a substantial decision-making role to the Executive, the Legislature and the Nuclear Regulatory Commission. This division of powers reflected not only the traditional checks and balances operating within the American system of government but the political stalemate created by the major protagonists in the nuclear controversy.

Many of the same limiting factors hampered the conduct of multilateral diplomacy. The various multinational arrangements under discussion, not only the fuel assurances but the spent fuel and plutonium storage schemes, all required a much higher level of regulation and coordination than currently prevailed in international nuclear relations. The establishment of new institutions presupposed international agreement on the scope of their authority, voting arrangements, the criteria that would apply in setting contract conditions, and provisions for the enforcement of contracts. Even more problematic was the proposal advanced by Senator Ribicoff for the division of the world market for nuclear reactors into precisely defined shares among the major exporting nations.[101] Such an agreement was unlikely to eventuate against a background of competing economic and military interests.[102] The competitive pressures generated by the world market economy and the system of sovereign states thus made it unlikely that multinational blueprints would be any more efficacious than unilateral restrictions in overcoming the dangers of a proliferating world.

COMPROMISE AND COMPETITION

Well before the end of Carter's term of office, meagre results and adverse international reaction had combined to produce a clearly discernible shift in US non-proliferation policy. The underlying principles may not have been abandoned but the vigour with which they were pursued had largely subsided. Reagan's election to the presidency greatly accelerated this trend. The incoming Administration made no secret of the fact that it regarded denial of nuclear supply and other sanctions as weak instruments for preventing the dissemination of sensitive nuclear technologies. More to the point, the White House was now intent on restoring America's place in world nuclear trade. The renewed emphasis on commercial considerations was in response to the pressures exerted by the US nuclear industry which claimed to have lost during the Carter years some $9000 million in foreign orders to aggressive, government-backed European and Canadian suppliers.[103] In keeping with this new direction, the Reagan Administration's non-proliferation guidelines issued in July 1981[104] stressed the need for the United States to become a reliable supplier of nuclear materials and technology, urged 'expeditious action on export requests and approval requests', and instructed executive agencies and the NRC to act accordingly.

The need for pragmatism soon emerged as a dominant theme in official pronouncements. In an address to the Uranium Institute in London in September 1981, James Malone, Assistant Secretary for Oceans and International Environmental and Scientific Affairs, made clear the Administration's intention to re-establish the United States as a competitive participant in international nuclear commerce. In a later speech he explained that the aim was to 'enhance the international competitiveness of US nuclear exports by all appropriate means' in order to increase leverage with clients and ensure the economic viability of the US nuclear industry.[105] Nuclear export policy would now be based on the art of the possible rather than on preconceived notions of world order. The July 1981 guidelines were therefore designed to permit the 'natural development' of breeder and reprocessing capabilities among nations with advanced nuclear power programmes.

By June 1982 the President had agreed to sanction long-term programmatic arrangements for reprocessing and plutonium use in Japan, the EEC and perhaps other Western European countries. In response to congressional criticism that such blanket approval for the reprocessing of US-supplied nuclear fuel was inconsistent with the provisions of the NNPA, the Administration claimed that these agreements would involve 'only countries with effective commitments to non-proliferation . . . and where such activities do not constitute a proliferation risk and are under effective safeguards and controls.'[106] The inclination implicit in the Carter policy to divide customers into 'risk' and 'non-risk' categories, depending on their potential for military diversion of nuclear materials, was thus taken to its practical and logical conclusion.[107] Preventing the spread of nuclear explosive capability to additional countries was still described as a fundamental security and foreign policy objective, but to achieve it the United States would rely on diplomatic persuasion and non-nuclear inducements, notably more extensive sharing of intelligence and more liberal supply of conventional arms.

The policy of inducements, like the decision to expedite export licensing procedures, was intended to enhance America's commercial prospects, in this case by exploiting lucrative opportunities for arms sales in Third World countries. There was, however, another dimension to the policy, namely the wish to buttress the intricate network of security arrangements linking the United States with many parts of Asia, Africa and Latin America. Argentina, South Korea, Taiwan, Pakistan, Egypt, Israel and South Africa were seen as crucial to the success of this strategy. Finally, the enthusiastic advocacy of reprocessing and breeder technologies and the more flexible interpretation of the requirements of the NNPA not only accorded well with the preferences of the American nuclear lobby but helped to remove one of the elements of friction in intra-alliance relations.

In formulating his approach to non-proliferation President Reagan was much less preoccupied than his predecessor with establishing a sharp dividing line between the peaceful and military uses of the atom. The distinction was not seen as having much practical relevance for countries that had already acquired a nuclear weapons capability. The US programme for a vastly expanded nuclear arsenal, including thousands of new warheads for the MX, Trident and Cruise missiles, may well have contributed to the subtle shift in emphasis. The new requirements of US defence policy placed considerable pressure on available supplies of plutonium, which in turn resulted in proposals for government reprocessing of light water commercial spent fuel and the development of a laser isotope separation (LIS) process to produce special nuclear materials for nuclear weapons. This option, favoured by important elements within the nuclear and military establishment, was seen as breaking the reprocessing impasse in the United States and as having a profoundly beneficial impact on the American nuclear industry.[108] This option was openly canvassed by Energy Secretary James Edwards in September 1981 who argued that it would provide the plutonium needed for the US weapons programme and for fast breeders, and at the same time solve the industry's waste problem. Official statements subsequently attempted to playdown the significance of the remarks, claiming that military use of plutonium from commercial spent fuel was not currently contemplated and would occur only if deemed essential for national security reasons. Significantly, the weapons option was not completely ruled out. In any case, the very substantial funding – estimated at $560 million – for the development of the LIS process made little economic sense unless the underlying purpose was the future enrichment of plutonium from commercial spent fuel.[109]

The Reagan Administration had unambiguously subordinated the non-proliferation objective to considerations of national security and commercial competitiveness. In so doing it introduced into policy formulation a greater degree of internal consistency, without nevertheless fully resolving the problem of conflicting priorities. The more favourable attitude to reprocessing and plutonium recycle – despite or because of their military potential – raised difficult questions about the international dissemination of these technologies. As for the relaxation of nuclear export policy, though it might temporarily strengthen the hand of American suppliers in the world nuclear market, it was bound in the long run to invite a similar response from governments in Western Europe and Japan. A few examples may suffice to illustrate the dilemmas faced by US diplomacy as it sought to maximise the American position in what was now a new phase of savage competition in international nuclear commerce.

In a bid to protect US interests in the development of Taiwan's nuclear programme, the NRC agreed to expedite the licensing process by granting export approval to General Electric, Westinghouse and Combustion Engineering for the sale of two reactors to the Taiwan Power Company even before any of them had secured a firm contract.[110] The decision was in accord with the Reagan Administration's desire to maintain close military and economic ties with Taiwan. On the other hand, it was likely to complicate the already delicate relationship with China. The prospect of greater nuclear co-operation with the Chinese held great attraction for the United States. Westinghouse and its British licensee, National Nuclear Corporation, were eager to secure export authorisation for the supply of two 900 MWe reactors to Guandong province even before the Chinese had made a final decision to go ahead with the project. To pave the way for nuclear exports the Reagan Administration established a highl-level inter-agency group in the hope of finding a mutually acceptable safeguards formula. Several obstacles, however, stood in the way. China was neither a party to the NPT nor a member of the IAEA. It had steadfastly refused to allow international inspection of its nuclear facilities. Moreover, senior US officials had expressed misgivings about China's own role as a supplier of nuclear materials and equipment to such countries as

Argentina, South Africa, India and Pakistan,[111] all of which appeared in the American list of risk-category nations.

Nuclear relations with India proved equally intractable. At issue was the supply of US nuclear fuel for use in the Tarapur light water reactors. Although the two countries had reached agreement in 1963 on the conditions that would govern the supply of fuel, a new situation was created when the NNPA came into force in March 1978. Accordingly the NRC found that India no longer satisfied US export requirements. President Carter subsequently intervened by using the grace period allowed for in the Act and authorised the shipment of fuel. A resolution to override the President's decision gained the necessary majority in the House of Representatives but was narrowly defeated in the Senate. The breathing space, however, proved to no avail as the Indian government totally rejected the American demand for full-scope safeguards, thereby denying the Reagan Administration the option of a compromise formula. In November 1982 France agreed to supply the enriched fuel but without imposing the additional safeguards sought by the United States, or indeed the so-called pursuit and perpetuity clauses required by the London Suppliers Group.[112] The agreement did not provide the IAEA with the right to monitor any facility to which material from the Tarapur reactor might be transferred nor did it ensure that monitoring would continue after 1993. The more permissive attitude of the French government had thus enabled it to secure a foothold in what was previously American territory.

The American predicament proved still more difficult in the case of Pakistan for here the non-proliferation objective appeared to be in direct conflict with regional security interests. Once it became evident that Pakistan was building a centrifuge enrichment plant to produce weapons-grade uranium,[113] the Carter Administration responded by interrupting all economic and military aid. Subsequent reports suggested that Pakistan was using Libya as an intermediary to gain access to a source of unsafeguarded uranium, that it was manufacturing its own nuclear fuel for the KANUPP reactor, an unsafeguarded fuel fabrication plant, and that an unsafeguarded pilot reprocessing plant was in the final stages of construction.[114] Pakistan's purchase of components for its uranium centrifuge plant from members of the London Suppliers Group, notably Switzerland, had already exposed the serious loopholes in the London guidelines which precluded the export of items 'explicitly designed or prepared for' enrichment plants, but apparently not of equipment which could be described as having 'dual use'.[115] Despite the undeniable proliferation implications of Pakistan's nuclear activities, American attitudes underwent drastic change following the Soviet military intervention in Afghanistan. Formal assurances by the Zia government that it did not intend to develop nuclear weapons were now considered sufficient to justify the resumption of US military aid.

The desire to maintain close military and diplomatic links with a strategically situated client state may also help to explain Reagan's willingness to enter into negotiations with South Africa regarding US shipments of enriched fuel for the Koeberg reactors despite Pretoria's long-standing refusal to sign the NPT or accept full-scope safeguards.[116] Although no agreement was reached, the American initiative provided an opening for a French–Swiss–West German consortium to step in and make available the required fuel. In turning a blind eye to these arrangements, the United States may also have given the French government added encouragement to persist with its negotiations for the sale of a second nuclear power station to South Africa. The Reagan Administration's country-by-country approach, originally intended to endow US diplomacy with greater flexibility, had in the process created considerable confusion as to America's intentions, and provided its European competitors with a pretext for relaxing their own safeguards.

With European suppliers taking advantage of the ambiguities in the London guidelines and the US administration circumventing some of the more restrictive provisions of the NNPA, the painstaking efforts of previous years to establish an international consensus in favour of full-scope safeguards as a substitute for NPT membership appeared to have achieved little. The claim of the German and French governments that agreements they had secured involved the *de facto* if not *de jure* application of full-scope safeguards overlooked the fact that these arrangements did not preclude the future development of unsafeguarded but sensitive nuclear facilities. Having consented to European and Japanese plans for reprocessing and plutonium recycle, the question arose whether the United States would be able to resist similar pressures from Taiwan, South Korea, and perhaps other countries with ambitious nuclear power programmes. To compound the problem, countries like Brazil,

Argentina, India, Pakistan and South Africa had already developed or were on the verge of developing independent fuel cycle technology. With some of these countries likely to become suppliers of nuclear technology in their own right, the prospects of a stable international nuclear order were rapidly diminishing.

Both the failure of Carter's internationalist design and Reagan's subsequent retreat into pragmatism reflected in different ways America's declining capacity to shape the conditions of international nuclear commerce. That decline, itself part of a larger phenomenon, was a direct consequence of the reconstruction of the European and Japanese economies. The re-organisation of industry in these countries coupled with the gradual accumulation of capital and the growing sophistication of technological know-how had sharply reduced the American economic advantage. But in addition to the re-emergence of these major centres of power, semi-peripheral states and markets (e.g. Brazil, South Korea, Taiwan) were beginning to influence the international division of labour and to form industrial and technological alliances either amongst themselves or with one or other of the core states. The result was a progressively more heterogeneous and competitive international system which no single state, regardless of the military or economic resources at its disposal, could hope to control.

Nuclear trade could not but be affected by these profound changes in the structure of the world economy. If anything the trend towards multipolarity and competition was even more pronounced here. The peculiar features of nuclear technology which accounted for its far-reaching economic, political and military significance had necessitated a very high level of government intervention and extensive use of state capital even in countries which prided themselves on their commitment to free enterprise ideology. The built-in subsidies, export financing and other incentives enjoyed by nuclear corporations then gave rise to government-backed international competition. Such regulation of nuclear activities as states had been able to introduce within their national boundaries could not be readily transposed to the international arena, where no single state, group of states or multinational authority exercised effective control. The combined impact of world market forces and inter-state rivalries had driven controls over nuclear exports to the lowest common denominator. Increasing competition in nuclear commerce had gone hand-in-hand with declining institutional capacity to regulate the dissemination of nuclear technology and contain its military application.[117] In the highly fragmented and increasingly polarised system of international relations prevailing in the 1980s, the continuing dissemination of nuclear fuels, equipment and technology could not but increase the risk of nuclear proliferation.

8 Nuclear Power and the Crisis of Capitalism

In the preceding chapters we have attempted to analyse the intricate but often elusive interconnection between the nuclear industry and the state apparatus as it has developed in several capitalist countries. The purpose of the exercise has not been to argue that the linkage is peculiar to nuclear technology, that it assumes an identical form in all capitalist countries, or that it faithfully serves the interests of that section of industrial and financial capital most heavily committed to nuclear power development. Rather the aim has been to determine the nature and extent of state intervention, the degree to which it is influenced by the prevailing national and international environment, and its consequences for the state's economic, administrative and legitimating functions.

What makes the nuclear industry a fascinating and highly instructive case study of late capitalist development is its multifaceted yet highly integrated character which requires the state to intervene at several points and perform diverse and often conflicting functions. However strong the commitment to market principles, the nuclear fuel cycle presupposes, by the very fact of its organisational and technological complexity, a degree of centralised coordination which only the state is able to offer. For its part, the advanced capitalist state is naturally attracted to the nuclear option either because of its military potential, that is, its perceived contribution to external security, or because of its compatibility with policies of economic growth that rely on scientific and technological innovation, centralised energy systems and economies of scale. The resulting nexus between the political institutions of capitalist society and the nuclear project has meant that the vicissitudes experienced by this capital-intensive, financially and technically sensitive industry have spilled over into the larger political arena and affected the performance of the state's economic functions both nationally and internationally.

Before analysing more closely the evolving relationship between state and industry, it may be useful to situate that relationship in its widest historical context. Throughout the evolution of modern capitalism, the state has played a decisive role in the process of capital accumulation and provided the structural underpinning for the expansion of world trade and the growing interpenetration of national economies.[1] In the most recent phase, associated with the growth of transnational production, the state has again helped to create the legal, administrative and economic conditions conducive to capital expansion and the progressive integration of the world market economy. In the post-1945 period, national economic policy throughout much of the western world was premised on the Keynesian theory of state intervention which sought to offset low levels of private investment with higher rates of public spending. The growth of the public sector was considered an integral part of the strategy of demand management and a useful instrument for the regulation of the business cycle. More importantly, the American super-state, acting in concert with other advanced capitalist states, used it vast resources at the end of the war to re-organise the structure of national economies and loosen the national barriers which had hitherto restricted the development of the world economy. Taking advantage of this favourable domestic and international environment, transnational firms were able to initiate a programme of far-reaching industrial and geographical diversification.

The state's endogenous structural role in economic management thus became fully apparent in late capitalist society. Increasing reliance on advanced science and technology was now central to the re-organisation and accelerated circulation of capital, to increased labour productivity, to continued metropolitan dominance over the peripheral and semi-perpheral regions of the world. The function of the welfare state was to ensure sufficient effective demand, stabilise wages preferably at full employment, underwrite the research and development expenditures needed for continual technological innovation, and support national educational establishments capable of creating the levels of training and technical expertise required by corporate planners. An important aspect of this new reality was the militarisation of the growth economy through the allocation of public funds for costly, technologically innovative weapon systems – a process greatly facilitated and legitimised by the bipolar division of the world and the ensuing establishment of military alliances. Rapid technological change, its systematic application to the means of production, and the increasing integration of the means of production with the political apparatus of society had produced a new economic and political phenomenon variously described as the socio-industrial order,[2] the new industrial state,[3] the contract state,[4] or even the military-industrial complex.[5]

The unifying power of state planning, however, which equilibrates, adjusts and coordinates the diverse elements of a national economy, does not operate simply within a national context. It has to contend with world market forces and the international division of labour which they imply. To this extent the state is both a national and an international actor. Analytically, then, we are concerned not so much with the relationship between the state and the individual firm as between the state and transnational production, between the state system and the world economy, between a multiplicity of states and a single division of labour.

THE STATE AND NUCLEAR INDUSTRY

If it is true that the capitalist state has been central to the process of capital accumulation, and that such accumulation has been marked by increasing industrial and financial concentration, technological innovation, and centralisation of production and distribution systems, then it is not hard to understand why close institutional and ideological links should have developed between the state apparatus and the nuclear industry. Indeed, in each of the six countries we have examined, the commercialisation of nuclear energy came to depend largely on the state's administrative and financial resources. State intervention, whether through the intermediary of public electricity utilities or through direct government planning and expenditure aimed at maximising electricity consumption, was largely instrumental in generating the demand for nuclear electricity. The creation of market conditions capable of generating a higher rate of nuclear ordering was, in many instances, dictated by the financial requirements and productive capacity of the nuclear industry. Where the domestic market could not, as in the case of most European countries, sustain competing reactor designs or more than one manufacturer of nuclear steam supply systems, governments took the initiative in re-organising the industry, partly with view to achieving economies of scàle, reducing capital costs and ensuring long-term viability.

In addition to establishing the necessary technical and institutional framework for nuclear expansion, governments provided private capital with a wide range of incentives, including substantial subsidies, funding for research and development, training of operators, waiving of fuel use and fuel fabrication charges, and indemnity legislation providing for government liability in the even of accident. This support was critical in the initial period when nuclear power was not yet considered economic and industry and financial institutions were still reluctant to commit the necessary amount of risk capital. Governments, particularly in the United States, played an equally important role in the development of export markets through the transfer of technical skills and equipment and the supply of credit facilities and loan guarantees. Complementing these functions was the domestic and international regulatory framework devised by the state in order to facilitate and legitimise the operation of nuclear facilities and the dissemination of nuclear know-how, materials and equipment.

In harnessing the scientific, technological, organisational and financial resources of society in support of the nuclear project, the state did not necessarily or automatically represent the interests of particular segments of capital involved in the industry. Rather its task was to oversee a complex technical and administrative operation within the context of the international division of labour. Terms such as the nucleocracy or the nuclear-strategic-industrial complex have been devised in order to convey something of the multidimensional yet unified character of the nuclear decision-making process. The incorporation of the scientific and technological community into nuclear planning, dictated by the very nature of the project, was intended to take advantage of the prestige and respectability enjoyed by these professional groups in advanced industrial society. Attempts by the state to bring the nuclear fuel cycle under international or civilian control were influenced by the need to eliminate or at least obscure the more overt connection between nuclear energy and nuclear weaponry, thereby enhancing the legitimacy of the nuclear project.

The development of nuclear power required the capitalist state to extend its organisational authority and, at times, to act independently of the interests and objectives of private firms, although its actions were inevitably interlocked with those of transnational capital. By using the financial, administrative and coercive lever at its disposal, the state not only created the infrastructural conditions for nuclear production but placed research and development processes largely under its direct or indirect control. This trend was evident in the United States and Germany despite the firm ideological commitment to market principles and the strong financial and industrial base of private capital in both countries. It was even more conspicuous in the case of Britain, France and Sweden where the required level of scientific and technical development exceeded the capability of domestic capital. Where the resources of the national state were not sufficient to permit the full mastery of the fuel cycle, governments were attracted to various forms of international collaboration, hence the establishment of Euratom, CERN, Urenco, Eurodif, United Reprocessors and NERSA. Through these and other institutions new legal forms were brought into being reflecting the uneasy tension between the national and supranational organisation of state power, as well as the progressive fusion of state and private capital.

The function of the state, then, has been not merely to defend the interests of particular corporations, however large or powerful, but to regulate a complex socioeconomic system in which the development of the nuclear option was assigned an increasingly high priority. Indeed, the momentum achieved by the nuclear project was in large measure attributable to the initiatives of the state, which in many cases had to overcome the scepticism of private industry, particularly in the early stages of commercialisation. Although subsidies and other forms of state intervention were specifically aimed at maximising the profitability of nuclear investments, this was not necessarily the state's overriding objective but rather part of a larger technocratic design.

The degree and form of state intervention in each country depended to a considerable extent on the relative strength and competitive position of domestic capital within the world market economy. Where local manufacturers had an inadequate industrial base, or where several firms were competing for a limited domestic market, as was the case in Britain, France, Sweden and Brazil, the state intervened either to encourage the process of amalgamation or to ensure direct government participation in the reactor industry. This was often done with the support, but on occasions despite the resistance, of local manufacturing capital. The French government was instrumental in establishing Framatome as the sole reactor manufacturer with CEA as a substantial shareholder. In Britain a painful process of consolidation led to the creation of the National Nuclear Corporation with the UKAEA holding 35 per cent equity. In Sweden, the state joined ASEA to form a new company (ASEA–ATOM) specialising in reactor manufacturing with the state holding 50 per cent ownership. In the case of Brazil, nuclear power plant engineering and construction was placed entirely in the hands of the state-owned company NUCLEBRAS. This form of state intervention did not preclude foreign licensing arrangements although these were normally justified by reference to a transitional strategy leading to the long-term indigenisation of the nuclear industry.

In addition, then, to the need for coordination – the state's planning and forecasting agencies appeared well fitted to the task of regulating a capital-intensive and intricately interconnected technological system – the nuclear project also required the direct involvement of the state in industrial re-organisation. This was achieved either by the intrusion of the public sector into the productive process or by the state assuming a mediatory or even guiding role in the resolution of conflicts associated with the establishment of a manufacturing base. The state had, for example, to contend with the antagonism between foreign and indigenous capital. Its intervention, even when favouring the short-term penetration of transnational capital, was normally premised on the expectation that domestic firms would develop the necessary financial or technological maturity and eventually assert their autonomy. This claim was central to the rationale underlying the intervention of the French state and featured prominently in the Brazilian government's public defence of its nuclear policy. As events subsequently demonstrated, the capacity of the state to fulfil its promise of industrial independence varied widely from country to country.

But even in the national context, the private interests with a stake in the development of nuclear power were not necessarily homogeneous. In the initial stages at least, several firms were locked in fierce competition for a share of the domestic market. The elimination of less efficient firms inherent in the process of concentration and the rapid increase in the unit size of nuclear power plants gave rise to a series of political and economic convulsions which only the state could control or moderate. This is not to say that the state could automatically and effectively impose its will, or easily create out of the collision of opposing corporate interests the large diversified company capable of meeting high development costs and weathering cyclical variations in demand. In this respect the French state was much more successful than its British counterpart. Not only was it able to secure through Edf a sufficiently high nuclear ordering rate but it was instrumental in establishing an industrial structure that would have at least some prospect of successfully competing on the international market. The adroit use of economic and political leverage enabled the French state to offset the competitive edge which American and German firms would have normally enjoyed either because of their early development of light water reactor technology or because of their more robust industrial and financial base. State support for French industry had included extensive allocation of public funds to nuclear investment, a highly centralised system of site selection and plant licensing, the early commercialisation of the fast breeder, and development of the totality of services in the nuclear fuel cycle, in particular enrichment and reprocessing.

Although it achieved its clearest expression in the French nuclear programme, the twin notions of national interest and national independence were a recurring theme in the formulation and implementation of state objectives. In the first place, it was a useful instrument for promoting a unified national technological and economic strategy, especially in the face of powerful opposition from corporate interests likely to be disadvantaged by such a strategy. Closely related to this consideration was the desire, clearly visible in the West European context though much less evident in the Brazilian case, to strengthen the hand of domestic capital generally in what was rapidly becoming a highly competitive international environment. Finally, the stress on nationalism was intended to foster a public consensus which would legitimise the state's nuclear policies and the ideological premises on which they rested.

LEGITIMATION FUNCTION

The preoccupation with legitimacy assumed particular significance during the 1970s when nuclear energy became the subject of intense and widespread controversy. At issue was nuclear policy but also the wider economic project from which it stemmed. To this extend the critique of nuclear power represented a direct challenge to state authority. The anti-nuclear movement focused not merely on the safety and environmental implications of nuclear technology but on the policy of economic growth and the consequent stress on expanding and centralised energy systems. Philosophically and sociologically, therefore, the dispute about nuclear power has to be situated within a larger conflict of values, an ideological confrontation between the centre, which controls the productive process and uses the welfare state as the basis of capital accumulation, and the periphery sensitive to the destructive impact of the profit motivated post-industrial system.

Opposition to nuclear power thus became an integral part, perhaps the focal point, of a larger movement committed to resisting what was deemed to be the 'colonisation of the life-world'. The possibility of reactor accidents, the problem of radioactive wastes, the potential for military diversion, had generated within the body politic not only fear and a sense of powerlessness but also a readiness to resist these processes and their life-eroding consequences.[6] What gave added impetus to the critique of nuclearisation was its ability to integrate the local, national and international dimensions of protest as well as immediate and long-range concerns. At issue was the prevailing mode of production and consumption and the international competition for power and wealth which it expressed and reinforced. To the extent that the advanced capitalist state was seen as one of the main institutional props for this international division of labour, it inevitably became the target of anti-nuclear agitation and the arena for social and political upheaval.

The nuclear controversy generated both new and old forms of conflict, each superimposed on, and interacting with, the other. Although opposition to nuclear power did intrude in varying degrees into the conventional political process and received at least token attention from political parties and national parliaments, it would seem that, with the possible exception of the Swedish case, these institutions were more inclined to tackle traditional tasks of economic management and the administrative allocation of resources than the less tangible and more ethically oriented quality of life issues and concepts of risk-taking. The critique of nuclear power with its emphasis on endangered life-styles could not be easily contained within the established forms of institutional conflict, hence the recourse to sub-institutional or extra-parliamentary modes of dissent.

Given their relatively limited access to the formal decision-making process, the opponents of nuclear power were inevitably drawn to the politics of the public sphere, in a sense to communicative politics. Compared to trade unions and organisations with highly bureaucratised leadership structures and a preoccupation with 'economistic' issues, anti-nuclear groups were less vulnerable to incorporation, to social divisions based on ethnicity, race and sex, more favourably placed to create local, national and regional communication networks. Study circles, educational forums, local community campaigns, demonstrations, acts of civil disobedience were all intended to communicate the pervasive sense of insecurity, the revolt against anonymous or remote authority structures, the reassertion of individual initiative and responsibility. To this extent they represented a conscious break from the bureaucratic rationality and privatised universe characteristic of a mass production society.

The increasing incursion of the state – made necessary by nuclear expansion – into formerly private realms had thus provoked generalised hostility not only against the technology itself but also against the socio-cultural order which had given birth to it.[7] Following in the footsteps of other counter-culture movements, the opponents of nuclear power pointed to a new level of consciousness based on a universalist (communicative) ethic.[8] The motivational norms implicit in this ethic represented a critique of existing social reality and a direct challenge to the system's legitimising mechanisms. This is not to say that anti-nuclear ferment had succeeded in disrupting the technical apparatus of the state, much less in undermining the normative integration of the social system. A more accurate reading of the evidence would suggest that while dissent from nuclear othodoxy had produced delegitimising effects, these had not yet reached crisis proportions.

Even where opponents of nuclear power had succeeded in politicising the issue to the point of generating a public debate within and between established institutions, for example in Germany, Sweden and the United States, the mobilisation of the anti-nuclear case was still not sufficiently generalised or coordinated to compel more than a series of tactical retreats by the nucleocracy. The very decentralisation characteristic of the anti-nuclear movement in every country under review severely curtailed its ability to pursue a unified strategy which alone could have propelled it to the centre stage of the political arena.[9] On the other hand, it is also true that the articulation and dissemination of divergent political and technological perspectives and alternative enrgy options did considerably weaken the self-confidence of the nuclear establishment, sowed the seeds of division within its own ranks, and curbed its capacity to administer ambitious nuclear programmes, particularly in the adverse conditions associated with technical uncertainty and economic recession.

Enough will have been said to indicate that, despite their organisational limitations, anti-nuclear groups were an important component of a loosely structured but widespread movement calling into question the technocratic legitimation of late capitalism. As time went on, official claims regarding reactor safety, waste disposal, the capital costs of nuclear power or energy accounting were challenged by a growing number of scientists, technicians, economists, lawyers and others who fractured the façade of professional expertise and objectivity which had been so painstakingly erected around the nuclear project. The ensuing scientific-technical debate pointed to the absence of a professional consensus on the issue and confirmed the pivotal role of ethical norms. The net effect was to move the locus of decision-making from the inner confines of the bureaucratic apparatus to the wider political arena.

CONFLICT OF FUNCTIONS

The state for its part, intent on defusing a potentially destabilising conflict and reinforcing the legitimacy of the nuclear project, intervened through political parties, commissions and inquiries to depoliticise the controversy. To this end a two-pronged strategy was pursued which consisted on the one hand in reasserting the primacy of technical considerations and on the other in generating a measure of public consensus in support of state policies. Politics was redefined as the sphere for the technical elimination of dysfunctions and the avoidance of risks, with dysfunctions and risks viewed primarily from the vantage point of systemic stability and only indirectly in relation to human health, industrial safety or environmental protection. The reduction of the conflict to a series of technical arguments facilitated the performance of the state's administrative functions in that it excluded from public purview the normative questions likely to challenge the underlying premise of nuclear policy. The emphasis on technical expertise tended to disenfranchise the overwhelming majority of citizens and further limited their participation in the decision-making process.

The success of the strategy depended in no small measure on the ability of the state to co-opt the support of organised labour. Hence, the importance of the negotiated political wage in the capital- and growth-intensive sectors of the economy, and particularly in the nuclear industry. Formal or tacit agreements between governments, corporations and unions regarding employment and income helped to neutralise an important source of potential dissent. Similarly, the promise of material rewards, notably job and energy security, was instrumental in securing the acquiescence of the wider public and in persuading political parties, including those of the Left, of the electoral dangers of questioning too sharply the direction and underlying philosophy of the nuclear project. Another relevant factor was the degree to which the state was able to shape the contours of the political debate by harnessing the educational and media resources of society, which may help to explain the comparative advantage of centralised political systems in countering the impact of public intervention and, therefore, in implementing their respective nuclear programmes.

The technical complexity of the nuclear fuel cycle, the elaborate industrial and institutional infrastructure it required meant that the state was called upon to perform several distinct yet closely interconnected economic, administrative and legitimating functions. Despite the very considerable resources at the state's command, the very magnitude of these tasks placed severe constraints on its freedom of action. We have argued that in the economic arena state intervention was initially designed to reduce the costs of nuclear power generation and establish a stable market for nuclear electricity. This function, however, was greatly complicated by increasing public anxiety about the safety of nuclear installations, which in turn prompted both manufacturers and regulatory agencies to impose stricter safety standards and licensing procedures. The attempt to allay public fears and safeguard the legitimacy of nuclear power had thus resulted in escalating construction costs which adversely affected the economic attractiveness of the nuclear option.

It is not surprising, then, that against a background of economic recession, high inflation and high interest rates, not to mention the emerging oil glut on the world market, the electricity supply industry, particularly in the United States but also in Western Europe and Brazil, should have scaled down its projected reliance on nuclear power. Even in France, where the decline in nuclear expansion was much less pronounced, the 1980s pointed to a far more cautious attitude to nuclear planning than had prevailed in the preceding decade. The resulting slump in nuclear ordering had obvious implications for the reactor industry, even to the point of threatening the long-term viability of several manufacturing firms. These difficulties and uncertainties inevitably spread to other stages of the nuclear fuel cycle, significantly affected the economics of uranium mining, enrichment and reprocessing, and slowed down appreciably the commercialisation of the fast breeder reactor.

The unfavourable economic outlook of the late 1970s and early 1980s had greatly circumscribed the range of options available to the state. In conditions of rising costs and declining demand the twin tasks of energy forecasting and nuclear planning became increasingly problematic. To this extent nuclear policy had fallen victim to the more general crisis of economic management confronting the advanced capitalist state. To alleviate the plight of the industry governments and state instrumentalities experimented with a variety of legislative and administrative proposals aimed at lowering the temperature of political debate, streamlining licensing procedures, resolving technical problems, expediting waste management decisions, enhancing export prospects. The capacity of the state, however, to achieve these objectives varied widely from country to country. But even in France, where the centralised system of power and EdF's monopoly of the electricity supply industry could be used with considerable effect to coordinate the financial and organisational requirements of the industry, there were clear limits to state intervention. No amount of administrative efficiency, no public investment programme could offset the downturn in energy demand and economic activity or markedly increase the size of the domestic and international markets. As for the informational or public relations campaigns designed to contain the public debate and depoliticise the underlying issues, their success depended not only on the cohesiveness of the state apparatus but also on the susceptibility of the prevailing political culture to the messages or themes enunciated by the main protagonists in the controversy. Even where the policy-making process did not suffer from the fractional tendencies characteristic of the West German or American federal systems, the state could not always impose its will on the body politic without provoking sharp and debilitating political divisions. As we have already observed, the technical rationalisation of nuclear power, itself the subject of intense disagreement, was a strategy of diminishing efficacy. The Swedish case is perhaps the clearest example of a country with a highly sophisticated and technical apparatus, which though favourably disposed to nuclear energy, was unable to neutralise let alone suppress the countervailing political influence of the emerging ecological movement. In almost every country the attempted closure of the fuel cycle proved vulnerable to the vagaries of the political process which the state could influence but not fully control.

To secure compliance with its policies the state could proceed by way of intimidation and manipulation, but a coercive strategy of this kind would contradict the principles of equality and freedom on which the legitimacy of the system ultimately rested. Support for the nuclear industry could not be taken to the point of threatening the cohesion of the social system. On the other hand, state intervention, made necessary by the very sensitivity of the technology and the attendant risks to safety and security, could not but draw attention to the issues of choice, planning and control. The hand of the state as the regulator of the industry became increasingly visible, thereby contributing to the politicisation of the issue. This development, in turn, stimulated ever greater demands on the state whether in relation to disclosure of information, participation in decision-making, or the right of legal intervention. To reject these demands outright would have been to risk prolonged social and political instability. On the other hand to accede to these demands would have been to jettison the nuclear programme. The state was engaged in a delicate balancing act, in which administrative and financial support for the nuclear project could not be allowed to create a legitimation deficit. An incipient crisis of legitimacy had combined with the constraints implicit in the fiscal crisis to produce a very narrow margin of manoeuvrability in the state's performance of its administrative functions.

INTERNATIONAL DIVISION OF LABOUR

While the function of governments has been to formulate and implement a nuclear policy that is national in scope and consistent with national economic priorities, the nuclear industry has had to operate also in the context of an international division of labour characterised by stratification, competition and uneven development. Relations between metropolitan, semi-peripheral and peripheral states have mirrored and reinforced that divisions of labour. The development of national nuclear programmes has necessitated various forms of international technical and scientific collaboration, but has at the same time given rise to intense international economic and diplomatic competition. International nuclear relations have been subject to two contradictory processes: fragmentation a integration. It has been the function of the state to internalise and some sense reconcile these opposing tendencies.

In the aftermath of the second world war several countries, including the UK and Canada, proceeded to develop the commercial application of nuclear energy, but by virtue of its superior economic, technological and military capability, the United States was able to establish a more extensive and diversified nuclear programme. As a consequence of American ascendancy in light water technology and its commercial monopoly on enrichment, US firms had by 1974 built 70 per cent of the world's reactors and captured two-thirds of the export market. During 1968–73 US revenue from the export of reactor equipment had exceeded the combined revenues of all other nuclear exporters. Even as late as 1976 more than 80 per cent of all reactors on order were of the American type. America's commanding position in world nuclear trade, reflected in its dominance of the international regulatory framework, was eventually challenged in the wake of the reconstruction of European and Japanese capital. The launching of the Urenco and Eurodif projects in the early 1970s provided evidence that European industry was no longer willing to accept continued US control of the enrichment industry. The quest for fuel independence was strongly tied to the desire to enhance European competitiveness in reactor sales. By 1975, non-American firms were poised to capture an increasing proportion of America's nuclear export earnings.

Counter-measures taken by the Nixon, Ford and Carter Administrations to protect the American stake in international nuclear commerce, including proposals for multinational enrichment plants, changes in contractual arrangements governing US enrichment services, and attempts to institute much stricter international safeguards, did little to dissuade the Europeans or the Japanese from pursuing the course on which they had embarked. Given the limited opportunities afforded by domestic markets, European and to a lesser extent Canadian and Japanese firms became increasingly dependent on the export market to achieve the anticipated economies of scale. Quite apart from their balance of payments and employment implications, the sale of nuclear reactors, and enrichment and reprocessing services was seen as essential to future recoupment of public investments in the research, development and demonstration of nuclear technology. Domestic difficulties, which we have expressed as a deficit in the state's performance of its economic, administrative and

…, had greatly magnified the importance of the … accentuated the incidence of conflict and … international market economy.

… rivalries were directly related to the rise of new …s of power. It would be misleading, however, to suggest …iance nuclear relationships were now exclusively …a character. The International Atomic Energy Agency and …ystem, the recently formed Nuclear Suppliers' Group and …TO were important instruments in accommodating, or at least …ating, the plurality of opposing interests and objectives. …arly, Euratom and especially the OECD and its Nuclear Energy …ency, coupled with the western economic summit meetings, pro…ided opportunities for resolving conflicts or for attenuating their more disruptive consequences. The uneasy and fluctuating balance between the major nuclear suppliers did not in any case signify the complete decline of American power. The primacy of US influence, though much less conspicuous than before, was nevertheless still evident in the operation of the western security system and in international economic and financial transactions–a situation from which US nuclear export policy sought to derive maximum advantage.

Whereas American power could still be used to promote specific national objectives, it was much less able to perform a stabilising or coordinating role for the international system as a whole. President Carter's failure to gain widespread acceptance of his non-proliferation policy was indicative of this general trend. The increasing diversification of enrichment services, the fierce competition for reactor sales, the race for technological leadership in the development of fast breeder reactors, the sharply diverging approaches to international safeguards, in short the competition for nuclear spheres of influence, provided ample evidence of the polycentric tendencies emerging within the world capitalist system.

Several new alliances, much less formal than those which had arisen in the context of the Cold War, and economic and technological rather than military in character, were now in the process of formation. European assertiveness had given rise to a tacit Franco–German understanding based partly on French technology and German industrial muscle. It represented an economic equivalent to the Gaullist dream of a French-dominated strategic nuclear partnership. The agreement between the two countries in July 1977 for co-operation on fast breeder development barely three months after the announcement of the Carter policy and Germany's decision to conclude reprocessing contracts with Cogéma pointed to an emerging Franco–German axis. Attempts by the two countries to strengthen their overall economic position were complemented by a network of interlocking arrangements involving several other countries in the development of European enrichment, reprocessing and fast breeder industries. Minor alliances involving metropolitan and semi-peripheral countries were also developing. The special nuclear relationship between Germany on the one hand and Brazil and Argentina on the other, between France and South Africa, not to mention European forays into the Middle East, East and North-east Asia were an indication of rapidly changing economic and political alignments. They reflected the relative decline of the American state and as a consequence the destablishing transition from the politics of *hegemony* to the politics of *imperial rivalry*.[10] This instability was partially contained by a measure of co-operation amongst the metropolitan states and the residual influence of the United States both within the system as a whole and in each of its constituent units.

The deepest and most prolonged recession in the history of the nuclear industry had combined with a more evenly dispersed international balance of power to produce intense competition and precarious profit margins. The nuclear industry, with its high capital costs and increasing reliance on exports, was likely to experience severe structural pressure during the rest of the 1980s.[11] Even with a partial economic recovery, the continued viability of the industry in each country would depend on active state intervention. The state would still be expected to create the conditions for a stable domestic market and enhance the industry's competitive advantage on the international market. The disruptive impact of conflicting economic interests, which threatened to outweigh the regulatory potential of existing institutions, would pose a particularly painful dilemma for the state. It could either transfer some of its authority in the interests of more effective international regulation, or it could intervene more aggressively in defence of national interests. Either course of action carried with it considerable risk. Any attempt, for example to rationalise a country's nuclear industry so as to integrate into a new international order, would tend to advantage some domestic interests and disadvantage others, thereby creating new tensions within the nuclear establishment. On the other hand, a nationalist approach might simply serve to intensify international rivalry and expose the national industry to a fierce and debilitating struggle.

THE STATE AS THE ARENA OF CONFLICT

The political, economic and environmental constraints which had seriously prejudiced the prospects for nuclear expansion, particularly in the US and West Germany and to a lesser extent in Britain, Sweden and Brazil, prompted the state to pursue a more vigorous external policy in support of its domestic nuclear industry. Such a close alignment, however, between the state and domestic or even foreign capital tended to sharpen the clash of competing state interests. The world nuclear system gradually became the arena of intense strategic and economic divisions. The predicament facing the nuclear industry thus assumed an international dimension which further complicated the domestic functions the state was required to perform.

International competition compelled a reallocation of financial resources and a reassessment of the administrative arrangements governing the organisation of the nuclear fuel cycle. The state was the only entity capable of coordinated action aimed at lessening the impact of the recession, but such intervention was bound to upset the delicate balance of sectional interests. The nature and extent of state intervention were, in reality, dependent on the prevailing ideological climate and on the concrete power positions of contending interest groups within and outside the nuclear establishment. Any attempt on the part of the state to modify the mix of energy fuels, to restructure the reactor industry, to rationalise competition in the supply of fuel and equipment, to expedite licensing procedures, to simplify or relax safety and environmental requirements was bound to favour some interest groups at the expense of others. Such initiatives, even if they achieved their particular objective, might serve to heighten the intensity of the nuclear controversy.

Very often sharp differences existed about the optimal contribution of nuclear power to total energy consumption, about the most appropriate reactor technology, about the preferred mix of local and foreign capital when fostering an indigenous industry, about the necessary radiation and other safety standards, about the political and technical merits of alternative waste disposal schemes. All these were deeply divisive issues in which the state could intervene but at the risk of raising the temperature of political debate and diminishing the efficacy of its action. A highly centralised system of political authority might partially offset the constraints on state intervention, but even then the conditions created by the twin factors of stagflation and over-capacity would not be easily overcome.

These very factors made it unlikely that the US nuclear industry would see its fortunes restored in the 1980s. There was little prospect that nuclear energy would gain a substantial share of the power plant market. Despite the best endeavours of the Reagan Administration to reduce the regulatory burden and resolve the problems besetting the back end of the fuel cycle, little progress had been made. Whatever advantages industry might derive from these initiatives, they seemed likely to be offset by tight monetary policies, high interest rates and inadequate financial relief for the electricity utilities. The magnitude of the fiscal crisis, the fragmentation of the decision-making process and the intensity of localised protest were such as to severely limit the scope of government action notwithstanding the Administration's strong ideological sympathy for the speedy nuclearisation of the electricity supply industry.

The limits of state intervention were equally apparent in Europe, although their economic and institutional roots differed markedly from country to country. In West Germany, where nuclear power had become a deeply emotive issue, a concerted policy by the state to revive the industry seemed outside the reach of the nation's constitutional and legal processes and likely to accentuate political divisions with adverse effects on the state's legitimating function. In Britain, a sustained economic recession, falling demand for electricity, coal surpluses and rising capital costs provided little opportunity for effective state intervention. The vacillation of the state and the indecisiveness in the selection of the most appropriate reactor design expressed and reinforced the unresolved organisational structure of the industry.

In France a highly centralised technocratic system had successfully imposed an ambitious nuclear programme against resistance from the periphery. Even the ideological and pragmatic reservations of the Mitterand government were not sufficient to deflect nuclear policy from its previous course. But the administrative efficiency of the state could not fully compensate the continuing impact of the recession. It remained to be seen whether the politically-orchestrated export drive could offset the expected lower rate of nuclear ordering. In Sweden the state was instrumental in devising a political compromise designed to balance the need for legitimacy and the demands of the corporate sector and the technostructure. It had yet to be demonstrated whether that compromise would withstand the buffetting to which it would be subjected as a result of prolonged recession and an uncertain transitional period in the formulation and implementation of a sustainable energy policy. Adjustment pressures were likely to be particularly acute in Brazil where the cost of nuclear-generated electricity was rising steeply against the background of a much larger and more cheaply harnessed hydroelectric potential. Equally relevant was the increasing public hostility to the terms of the German–Brazilian deal which were widely perceived as inadequately preparing the ground for the full indigenisation of the industry.

Regardless of regional or local variations, the state throughout the advanced industrial world was drawn, as a direct result of the decline in the worldwide demand for nuclear power and the growth of manufacturing over-capacity, into competition for markets. To this end it offered financial incentives, arranged trade packages and made use of political and military leverage. As a corollary of this function the state was seeking to erect a highly protective shield around its domestic industry. Collaboration in research, development and marketing and even alliances with foreign companies were much less a sign of transnational coordination than devices aimed at improving national competitiveness. European, Japanese and American firms were increasingly locked into a fierce rivalry, each seeking to maintain its share of the market, each pressing for the structural rationalisation of the industry as a way of preserving its long-term capacity to design and manufacture pressure vessels, steam generators and other components.

In what is now a widely observable phenomenon, state intervention has become increasingly necessary but also less efficacious. The scope for government action by way of subsidy was limited by fiscal considerations, the inflationary spiral, and the political conflict inherent in any redistributive strategy likely to advantage the lower and middle strata of society. Opportunities for greater cost efficiency were also constrained by the technical and organisational intricacy of the fuel cycle, by deficiencies in the state's forecasting and planning agencies, and above all by the ever-present possibility of cultural and political dissent.

Efforts to neutralise the administrative deficit could well result in a legitimation deficit which would be equally prejudicial for the maintenance and expansion of the nuclear industry. Even the use of force, whether in the national or international arena, appeared to be of limited value. It was at best a contradictory instrument of policy in that recourse to it domestically might provoke a widespread and hostile reaction not only against nuclear technology but against the authority of the state. Externally, a show of force was likely to invite diplomatic, economic and military retaliation which no single state could effectively combat. By the late 1970s the crisis of capitalism had become national and international in character, each level feeding on, and interacting with, the other.

The increasing interpenetration of national economies coupled with the precarious balance underlying the domestic political process had greatly narrowed the range of national policy options while at the same time accentuating the need for state intervention. Nowhere was the dilemma of the advanced capitalist state more acutely experienced than in the field of nuclear policy, where competing claims on the state's limited resources and sharply divergent ideological perspectives had compounded the latent conflict between the state's productive and legitimising functions. In each of the case studies we have examined the state's response to the crisis entailed a complex but unsystematic bargaining strategy aimed at reconciling conflicting interests and priorities. Simultaneously, the trend towards international multipolarity, by exacerbating the competitive and anarchical tendencies within the world system, necessitated increased state planning and therefore a strengthening of the national capitalist state. To this extent the nuclear controversy was much more than a dispute about the appropriateness of a particular technology or a casualty of the world recession. It was the symptom of a deeper crisis, which itself reflected the contradiction between a capitalist system integrated by a single division of labour and a capitalist system divided between rival corporations and nation-states. The unfolding of that contradiction would in large measure shape the future of the nuclear industry.

Notes

CHAPTER 1

1. Although a great many accounts have been given of the origins of nuclear fission, the most revealing and reliable account remains that of Robert Jungk, *Brighter than a Thousand Suns* (trans. James Clengh), Harmondsworth, Penguin, 1960. For an interesting explanation of the progress made in nuclear weapons research in the Anglo-Saxon countries, as opposed to Germany, many of whose nationals played a leading role in the British and American weapons programme, see Bruce Page, 'The Creative Mind, Scientists, the Bomb and the Future', *New Statesman*, 19–26 December 1980, pp. 19–29.
2. For a personal but illuminating description of these events, see 'Leo Szilard: His Version of the Facts', Part Three, *The Bulletin of the Atomic Scientists* (hereafter referred to as *BAS*), vol. 35, no. 4, April 1979, pp. 28–32.
3. For a first-hand account, see Otto R. Frisch, 'Someone Turned on the Sun with a Switch', *Science and Public Affairs*, vol. 30, no. 4, April 1974, pp. 12–18.
4. See Elizabeth Young, *A Farewell to Arms Control*, Harmondsworth, Penguin, 1972, pp. 24–33.
5. This argument is developed at some length by Sheldon Novick, *The Electric War: The Fight Over Nuclear Power*, San Francisco, Sierra Club Books, 1976, pp. 26–8.
6. Richard G. Hewlett and Francis Duncan, *Atomic Shield 1947–52*, University Park, Penn., Pennsylvania State Press, 1969, p. 47.
7. For the release of this information we are indebted to the persistent efforts of David Alan Rosenberg who finally succeeded in breaking through the barrier of secrecy erected by the Atomic Energy Commission and maintained by government departments for nearly thirty-five years. See D.A. Rosenberg, 'U.S. Nuclear Stockpile, 1945 to 1950', *BAS*, May 1982, pp. 25–30.
8. I examine the composition of the military–industrial complex and its relationship to the security crisis in Joseph A. Camilleri, *Civilization in Crisis: Human Prospects in a Changing World*, Cambridge, Cambridge University Press, 1976, pp. 154–7. See also Fred J. Cook, *The Warfare*

State, New York, Macmillan, 1962; J.K. Galbraith, *The New Industrial State*, Harmondsworth, Penguin, 1974; Seymour Melman, *Pentagon Capitalism*, New York, McGraw-Hill, 1970; Herbert I. Schiller and Joseph D. Phillips (eds), *Superstate: Readings in Military–Industrial Complex*, Urbana, University of Illinois Press, 1970.

9. *House of Commons Debate* (*HCD*), 12 May 1948, vol. 450, col. 2117.
10. For the most exhaustive and carefully documented account of the early phase of Britain's atomic energy programme (and its overriding military objective), see Margaret Gowing assisted by Lorna Arnold, *Independence and Deterrence: Britain and Atomic Energy 1945–52*, 2 vols., London, Macmillan, 1974.
11. See J. Guéron, 'Atomic Energy in Continental Western Europe', *BAS* vol. 26, no. 6, June 1970, p. 63.
12. Alain Peyrefitte (*Le Mal Français*, Paris, Plon, 1976, p. 289) argues strongly that as far as the decision to build a French bomb is concerned, 'the Rubicon was crossed' on 26 December 1954. Lawrence Schienman (*Atomic Energy Policy in France under the Fourth Republic*, Princeton, Princeton University Press, 1965, pp. 116–22) on the other hand, believes the decision was much less positive, and that Mendès France simply tried not to foreclose France's military options.
13. The inexorable logic of the system pushing towards the acquisition of nuclear weapons is incisively examined by P. Simonnot, *Les Nucléocrates*, Presses Universitaires de Grenoble, 1978, pp. 225–35.
14. Eugene M. Zuckert, 'Policy Problems in the Development of Civilian Nuclear Power', *BAS*, vol. 8, no. 8, November 1952, p. 278.
15. See Sir Rudolf E. Peierls, 'Britain in the Atomic Age', *BAS*, vol. 26, no. 6, June 1970, p. 41.
16. The 1946 Atomic Energy Act was amended in 1951 to permit the US to share some nuclear information with its NATO allies, but the underlying intention at this stage was to strengthen military alliances rather than to promote commercial use of nuclear energy in Europe. See US House of Representatives Committee on International Relations, *Science, Technology and American Diplomacy*, Washington, US Government Printing Office, 1977, p. 142.
17. See C.I. Bernard *et al.*, *A Report on the International Control of Atomic Energy*, US Department of State, 2498, Washington DC, US Government Printing Office, 16 March 1946.
18. David E. Lilienthal, *Change, Hope and the Bomb*, Princeton, NJ, Princeton University Press, 1963, pp. 115–6.
19. See Philip Sporn, 'How Can Private Industry Best Participate in the Development of Atomic Energy', *BAS*, vol. 7, no. 2, February 1951, p. 49.
20. William L. Lawrence, *Men and Atoms*, New York, Simon & Schuster, 1959, p. 242.
21. Atomic Energy Act 1954, ch. 1, in *United States Statutes at Large*, vol. 68, Part I, Washington, US Government Printing Office, 1955, p. 921.

22. Sir John Cockcroft, 'The Development and Future of Nuclear Energy', *BAS*, vol. 6, no. 11, November 1950, p. 330.
23. *Science, Technology and American Diplomacy*, pp. 142–3.
24. Walker Iscard and Vincent Whitney, 'Atomic Power and Economic Development', *BAS*, vol. 5, no. 3, March 1949, p. 78.
25. Philip Sporn, 'Prospects in Industrial Application of Atomic Energy', *BAS*, vol. 6, nos. 8–9, Aug.–Sept. 1950, p. 320.
26. Philip Sporn, 'Prospects for Nuclear Power', *BAS*, vol. 9, no. 4, May 1953, p. 129.
27. William L. Lawrence, *Men and Atoms*, p. 240.
28. See J. Guéron, 'Atomic Energy in Continental Western Europe', *BAS*, vol. 26, no. 6, June 1970, p. 64; Sigvard Eklund, 'The International Atom', *BAS*, vol. 26, no. 6, June 1970, p. 58.
29. R.R. Wilson, 'The Conscience of a Physicist', *BAS*, vol. 26, no. 6, June 1970, p. 33.
30. Alice Kimbal Smith, 'Los Alamos: Focus of an Age', *BAS*, vol. 26, no. 6, June 1970, p. 17.
31. See Robert Gilpin, *France in the Age of the Scientific State*, Princeton, NJ, Princeton University Press, 1968, pp. 188–217.
32. For a much fuller examination of the 'scientific' contribution to the French nuclear programme, see Lawrence Scheinman, *Atomic Energy Policy in France Under the Fourth Republic*, esp. pp. 34–5, 49–57.
33. Much of this argument is drawn from the illuminating analysis by Daniel DuBarte, O.P. in 'Observations in the Relations between Science and the State', *BAS*, vol. 11, no. 4, April 1955, pp. 141–4.
34. This point is clearly brought out in one of the interviews conducted by Philippe Simonnot with the various representatives of the nuclear industry. The consensus among experts is described here as 'la vérité de groupe' (in-group perception of reality) and compared to an impenetrable fortress. See *Les Nucléocrates*, pp. 50–1.
35. This argument featured prominently in the official statement accompanying the proposal for the atomic energy programme (1952–7).
36. The call for a greater financial commitment found expression in the atomic energy decree of 20 May 1955.
37. See Gerhard Stoltenberg, *Staat und Wissenschaft*, Stuttgart, Seewald, 1969, pp. 25–62.
38. Speech delivered to the French National Assembly, 5 July 1956.
39. See Roger Williams, *The Nuclear Power Decisions: British Policies, 1953–78*, London, Croom Helm, 1980, pp. 23–6.
40. 'Le Développement nucléaire français depuis 1945', *Notes et Etudes Documentaires*, no. 3246, Paris, La Documentation Française, 1965, p. 6.
41. Simonnot, *Les Nucléocrates*, pp. 193–5.
42. See Henry R. Nau, *National Politics and International Technology: Nuclear Reactor Development in Western Europe*, Baltimore, Johns Hopkins University Press, 1974, pp. 72–6; also Bertrand Goldschmidt, *Le Complexe atomique*, Paris, Fayard, 1980, pp. 144–7.
43. Thomas E. Dewey, 'The Challenge of the Atomic Age' (speech given at

Phoenix, Arizona on 23 September 1948), *BAS*, vol. 4, no. 10, 1948, p. 297.

44. 'Report of the AEC Industrial Advisory Group', *BAS*, vol. 5, no. 2, February 1949, pp. 51–5.
45. 'The Electric Power Industry and the AEC', *BAS*, vol. 7, no. 11, November 1951, pp. 332–6.
46. Gordon Dean, 'Nuclear Power Development: AEC Policy Statement', reproduced in *BAS*, vol. 9, no. 8, October 1953, p. 314.
47. 'Atomic Energy and Private Enterprise: Joint Committee Hearings', reproduced in *BAS*, vol. 9, no. 8, October 1953, p. 310.
48. Edwin J. Putzell, Jr, 'The Prospects for Industry', *BAS*, vol. 8, no. 8, November 1952, pp. 275–7.
49. Eugene M. Zuckert, 'Policy Problems in the Development of Civilian Nuclear Power', *BAS*, vol. 8, no. 8, November 1972, pp. 277–9.
50. James R. Newman, 'The Atomic Energy Industry: An Experiment in Hybridisation', *Yale Law Journal*, vol. 60, no. 8, December 1951, pp. 1263–394.
51. For a useful discussion of the various phases in nuclear policy-making, particularly in the United States, see B. Goldschmidt, 'International Co-operation to Date', in *Proceedings of the OECD/NEA Symposium and International Co-operation in the Nuclear Field: Perspectives and Prospects*, Paris, 1978, pp. 22–34.
52. The export incentive as a factor in US nuclear power development is clearly outlined in Alvin M. Weinberg, 'How Shall We Establish a Nuclear Power Industry in the United States?', *BAS*, vol. 9, no. 4, May 1953, pp. 120–4. A similar analysis with respect to the British situation was offered by Franz Simon, 'Nuclear Power: A British View', *BAS*, vol. 9, no. 4, pp. 125–8.
53. See the evidence presented by AEC Commissioners to the US Congress, Joint Committee on Atomic Energy in, *Atomic Power and Private Enterprise*, 82nd Congress, 2nd session, December 1952.
54. US Congress, Joint Committee on Atomic Energy, *Report of the Panel on the Peaceful Uses of Atomic Energy*, 84th Congress, 2nd session, January 1956, p. 95.
55. US House of Representatives, Committee on International Relations, *Science, Technology and American Diplomacy*, 1977, p. 163.
56. Ibid., p. 164.
57. Ibid., pp. 169–70.
58. See C. Deubner, 'The Expansion of West German Capital and the Founding of Euratom', *International Organisation*, vol. 33, no. 2, Spring 1979, p. 216.
59. Ibid., pp. 222–3.
60. *A Target for Euratom*, reprinted in US Congress, Joint Committee on Atomic Energy, Hearings, *Proposed Euratom Agreements*, 85th Congress, 2nd session, 1958, pp. 38–64.
61. Ibid., p. 50.
62. G. Goldschmidt, *Les Rivalités Atomiques 1939–66*, Paris, Fayard, 1967.
63. *Science, Technology and American Diplomacy*, p. 210.

CHAPTER TWO

1. See Louis H. Roddis, 'AEC Power Demonstration Reactor Program', in *Commercial and International Developments in Atomic Energy*, New York, Atomic Industrial Forum, 1955, pp. 217–19.
2. Senator Clinton P. Anderson, 'The Outlook for the US Atomic Energy Program', *Nucleonics*, vol. 17, no. 3, March 1959, pp. 77–8.
3. *A Programme of Nuclear Power*, cmnd 9389, London, HMSO, February 1955.
4. *Capital Investment in the Coal, Gas and Electricity Industries*, Cmnd 132, London, HMSO, April 1957.
5. See 'British Government Speeds Nuclear Programme', *Nucleonics*, vol. 14, no. 12, December 1956, pp. S3–9.
6. Sir George Thomson, 'Britain's Drive for Atomic Power', *Foreign Affairs*, vol. 35, no. 1, October 1956, p. 98.
7. *The Nuclear Power Programme*, Cmnd 1083, London, HMSO, June 1960.
8. The rapidly changing fortunes of British nuclear industry during this period are carefully analysed in Williams, *The Nuclear Power Decisions*, pp. 60–79.
9. *The Second Nuclear Power Programme*, Cmnd 2335, London, HMSO, April 1964.
10. The decisive role of the nuclear establishment in determining British energy policy, particularly the decisions of the CEGB, is examined in Walter C. Patterson, *The Fissile Society: Energy, Electricity and the Nuclear Option*, London, Earth Resources Research Ltd, 1977, esp. pp. 24–8.
11. See B. Goldschmidt, *The Atomic Adventure*, (trans. Peter Beer), New York, Pergamon Press, pp. 97–101.
12. See 'France: Long View Taken in Fully-Fledged Nuclear Program', *Nuclear News*, September 1968, p. 36.
13. PEON, *Rapport sur les perspectives de développement des centrales nucléaires en France*, Paris, 1964.
14. 'Germany: Making Up for Lost Time is the Name of the Game', *Nuclear News*, September 1968, p. 39.
15. 'Financing Atomic Energy', *Nuclear Power*, March 1961, p. 79.
16. Germany, Federal Minister for Scientific Research, 3 *Atomprogramm der Bundesrepublik Deutschland 1968–72*, Bonn, Federal Ministry for Scientific Research, 1967.
17. See E.G. Malmlöw, 'Atomic Power in Sweden', *BAS*, February 1963, pp. 44–6; also 'Sweden's Nuclear Programme', *Nuclear Engineering*, vol. 5, May 1960, pp. 199–202.
18. Sten Sandstrom 'Sweden Looks to Own Needs with Eye also on Export Market', *Nuclear News*, September 1968, p. 46.
19. *Hearings on AEC Authorizing Legislation for Fiscal Year 1971, before the Joint Committee on Atomic Energy*, 91st Congress, 2nd Session, 1970, p. 1438.
20. This argument is developed at some length in Jaroslav G. Polach,

'Nuclear Power in Europe at the Crossroads', *BAS*, vol. 25, no. 8, October 1969, pp. 15–20.

21 *Report from the Select Committee on Science and Technology Section 1966–67, United Kingdom Nuclear Reactor Programme*, London, HMSO, 1967, p. xxviii.

22. Select Committee on Science and Technology, *Nuclear Power Policy Second Report*, HC–350 1972–3, Evidence and Appendices, p. 37.

23. The restructuring of French nuclear policy is examined by Nau, *National Politics and International Technology*, pp. 81–5.

24. For an incisive analysis of the 1968 PEON report, see Simonnot, *Les Nucléocrates*, pp. 246–51.

25. The meeting was held on 13 November 1969 and attended by the Prime Minister and the Ministers for Defence, Foreign Affairs, Economic and Financial Affairs, and Industrial and Scientific Development. Also present were the General Secretary of the Energy Department, the CEA's General Administrator and High Commissioner, and EdF's President and General Director. For a discussion of the changing direction of French nuclear policy at this time see Michel Vilain, 'Politique de l'énergie: les grandes orientations', *Revue Politique et Parlementaire*, vol. 72, no. 815, November 1970, pp. 47–51.

26. *UN Statistical Yearbook 1968*, New York, United Nations, 1969, pp. 353–60.

27. *Annual Report of the Board of Governors to the General Conference, 1 July 1969–30 June 1970* (IAEA Doc. GC(XIV)/430, 1970), p. 24.

28. For a critical examination of this line of argument, see Herman E. Daly, 'Electric Power, Employment, and Economic Growth: A Case Study of Growthmania', in H.E. Daly (ed.), *Toward a Steady-State Economy*, San Fancisco, W.H. Freeman & Co., 1973, pp. 252–77.

29. The factors contributing to overestimation in the British experience are discussed in *A Critique of the Electricity Industry* by the Energy Research Group, Open University, Milton Keynes, 1976, pp. 37–40.

30. Walker L. Cisler, 'Looking Ahead to the Last Quarter of the First Century of Electric Power in the United States', Edison Electric Institute, 22nd Annual Convention, June 1954. See also Theodore Baumeister, 'Steam and Electric Power – Its Past and Future', *Combustion*, December 1952.

31. The profligate use of energy by electricity utilities is described in Wilson Clark, *Energy for Survival: The Alternative to Extinction*, Garden City, NY, Anchor Books, 1975, pp. 125–65.

32. See 'Nuclear Plant Builders See a $1 Billion Market', *Business Review*, 5 March 1966, pp. 145–50.

33. Examined by Patterson, *The Fissile Society*, pp. 42–57.

34. See Appendix 39, by the Electricity Council, *Select Committee on Nationalised Industries: The Electricity Supply Industry* (HC 236 I–III), 1963.

35. Select Committee on Science and Technology, *Nuclear Power Policy*, Second Report, p. 33.

36. see evidence given by Mr F.J. Doggett, Deputy Chairman, Atomic

Energy Authority, in Select Committee on Science and Technology, *Nuclear Power Policy*, Second Report, Evidence and Appendices, p. 55.

37. See Nau, *National Politics and International Technology*, p. 86.
38. Sidney Hollands, 'Financing Atomic Energy', *Nuclear Power*, March 1961, p. 79.
39. See *The Development of Brazil: Report of Joint Brazil–United States Economic Development Commission*, Washington, DC, Institute of Inter-American Affairs, 1953, p. 154; also ECLA, *The Economic Development of Brazil*, United Nations, E/CN12/364, July 1955, p. 19.
40. *The Development of Brazil*, p. 158.
41. S.H. Robock, *Productive Uses of Nuclear Energy: Nuclear Power and Economic Development in Brazil.* National Planning Association, April 1957, p. 5.
42. J. Guéron *et al.* (eds), *The Economics of Nuclear Power*, vol. 1, London, Pergamon Press, 1956, p. 368.
43. The need for substantial government funding was clearly spelt out in the final report of the 12th American Assembly in October 1957, which brought together many of the leading scientists and executives associated with atomic energy. See 'Atomic for Power: US Policy in Atomic Energy Development', *Nucleonics*, vol. 15, no. 11, November 1957.
44. Senator Clinton P. Anderson, 'The Outlook for the US Atomic Energy Program', *Nucleonics*, vol. 17, no. 3, March 1959, p. 78.
45. See Frank K. Pittman (Director, Division of Reactor Development US AEC), 'The US Civilian Power Reactor Program', *Nuclear Engineering*, October 1960, p. 430.
46. The demand from business interests for increased government subsidy of nuclear power development became increasingly evident during 1958, particularly at the annual hearings conducted by the Joint Committee. See 'Battle over Reactor Subsidy', *Business Week*, 15 February 1958, p. 4; also US Congress, JCAE, *Comments of Reactor Designers and Industrial Representatives on the Proposal Expanded Civilian Nuclear Power Program*, Report, 85th Congress, 2nd session, December 1958, p. 60.
47. This approach was clearly spelt out by Dr Chauncey Starr, President of Atomics International Division of North American Aviation, Inc., in 'Industrial Viewpoint' *Nuclear Engineering*, October 1960, p. 431.
48. See F.G. Dawson, *Nuclear Power: Development and Management of a Technology*, Seattle, University of Washington Press, 1976, pp. 93–101.
49. W.S. Caldwell *et al.*, 'The 'Extraordinary Nuclear Occurrence' Threshold and Uncompensated Injury Under the Price–Anderson Act', *Rutgers–Camden Law Journal*, vol. 6, no. 2, Fall 1974, p. 379.
50. Ibid., p. 364.
51. See *Theoretical Possibilities and Consequences of Major Accidents in Large Nuclear Power Plants*, US AEC Report WASH–740, Government Printing Office, Washington, DC, 1957; and for a subsequent assessment, R.J. Mulvihill *et al.*, *Analysis of United States*

Power Reactor Accident Probability, PRC R-695, Los Angeles, Planning Research Corporation, 1965.

52. *Report from the Select Committee on Science and Technology*, 1972–3; *Nuclear Power Policy*, p. 102.
53. For a more detailed discussion of this point, see Patterson, *The Fissile Society*, pp. 70–1.
54. W.P. Warren, 'Reactor Exports and the UK AEA', *Nuclear Engineering*, vol. 3, no. 30, September 1958, pp. 367–8.
55. See W. Boulanger, 'The Development of Nuclear Law', in *Nuclear Law in a Developing World*, Vienna, International Atomic Energy Agency, 1969, p. 55.
56. See Syndicat CFDT de l'énergie atomique, *Le Dossier électro-nucléaire*, Paris, Editions du Seuil, 1980, pp. 377–89.
57. For a general review of nuclear legislation in European countries, refer to OECD, Nuclear Energy Agency, *Nuclear Legislation*, Paris, OECD, 1972; see also R.M. Stein, 'The European Nuclear Energy Agency', and H.J. Claesner, 'The European Atomic Energy Community' both in *Nuclear Law in a Developing World*, pp. 21–32, 39–46.
58. *Compilation of National and International Standards*, Oak Ridge, Tenn., Oak Ridge National Laboratory, Nuclear Safety Information Centre, Report no. ORNL–NSIC–78, October 1970, p. 44.
59. *Assessment of US and International Controls over the Peaceful Uses of Nuclear Energy*, Report to Congress of the Comptroller-General of the US, September 1976 (ID–76–60), p. 21.
60. *Science, Technology and American Diplomacy*, pp. 183–4.
61. US Congress, Senate Committee on Foreign Relations and Senate Members of the Joint Committee on Atomic Energy, *Hearings, Statute of the International Atomic Energy Agency*, 85th Congress, 1st Session, 1957, p. 175.

CHAPTER THREE

1. Many of the arguments in this chapter were first developed in my article, 'Ecological Politics: The Birth of a New Movement', *World Review*, vol. 17, no. 1, April 1978, pp. 45–59.
2. See 'Public Opposition to Nuclear Energy: Retrospect and Prospect', in *Sociopolitical Effects of Energy Use and Policy*, ed. C.T. Unseld *et al.*, Washington, DC, National Academy of Sciences, 1979, p. 263.
3. For a history and analysis of this controversy, see Dorothy Nelkin, *Nuclear Power and Its Critics: The Cayuga Lake Controversy*, Ithaca, NY, Cornell University Press, 1971.
4. *New York Times*, 31 January 1970.
5. The second phase of this conflict is again examined in detail by Dorothy Nelkin, in 'The Role of Experts in a Nuclear Siting Controversy', *BAS*, vol. 30, no. 9, November 1974, pp. 29–36.
6. For a further discussion of the Wyhl controversy, see Solange Fernex, 'Non-Violence Triumphant', *The Ecologist*, vol. 5, no. 10, 1975, pp. 372–85; and Peter Taylor, 'The Struggle Against Nuclear Power in Central Europe', *The Ecologist*, vol. 7, no. 6, 1977, pp. 217–22.
7. The centre–periphery relationship in the development of nuclear power

is graphically illustrated by Jim Falk, *Global Fission: The Battle Over Nuclear Power*, Melbourne, Oxford University Press Australia, 1982, pp. 172–99.

8. This process is well described by John Surrey and Charlotte Huggett, 'Opposition to Nuclear Power: A Review of International Experience', *Energy Policy*, vol. 4, no. 4, December 1976, pp. 286–307.
9. Uno Svedin, 'Sweden's Energy Debate: The Nuclear Controversy', *Energy Policy*, vol. 3, no. 3, September 1975, pp. 258–61.
10. See memorandum submitted by Amory Lovins and Walter Patterson to the Select Committee on Science and Technology, in *The Choice of a Reactor System*, First Report, Evidence HC 73 (1973–4); also the article by Lovins in *The Sunday Times*, 15 November 1973; and *Nuclear Power: Technical Bases for Ethical Concern*, London, FOE, 1974.
11. Royal Commission on Environmental Pollution, 6th Report, *Nuclear Power and the Environment*, Cmnd 6618, London, HMSO, 1976.
12. See Richard S. Lewis, *The Nuclear Power Rebellion: Citizen vs. the Atomic Industrial Establishment*, New York, Viking Press, 1972; also review of the book by Dean E. Abrahamson, in *BAS*, vol. 29, no. 5, May 1973, pp. 43–5.
13. See Arthur R. Tamplin and John W. Gofman, 'The Radiation Effects Controversy', *BAS*, vol. 26, no. 7, September 1970, pp. 2, 5–8.
14. For a graphic description of this debate as it emerged in several licensing hearings, see Lewis, *The Nuclear Power Rebellion*, pp. 109–47.
15. The UCS position is outlined in Daniel F. Ford and Henry W. Kendall, 'Nuclear Safety', *Environment*, vol. 14, no. 7, September 1972, pp. 2–9, 48.
16. US Nuclear Regulatory Commission, *Reactor Safety Study – An Assessment of Accident Risks in US Commercial Nuclear Power Plants*, Report no. (NUREG–75/104) WASH–1400, Washington, Government Printing Office, 1975.
17. See H.W. Kendall *et al.*, *Preliminary Review of the AEC Reactor Safety Study*, Cambridge, Mass., Union of Concerned Scientists, 1974; also H.W. Lewis *et al.*, 'Report to the American Physical Society by the Study Group on Light Water Reactor Safety' *Reviews of Modern Physics*, vol. 47, no. 1, Summer 1975, S1–S124; Frank von Hippel, 'Looking Back on the Rasmussen Report', *BAS*, vol. 33, no. 2, February 1977, pp. 42–7.
18. *The Sierra Club and Nuclear Power*, San Francisco, Sierra Club, 1975.
19. Committee of Inquiry: The Plutonium Economy, *The Plutonium Economy*, New York, National Council of the Churches of Christ, 1975.
20. See Lewis, *The Nuclear Power Rebellion*, pp. 232–58.
21. Dorothy Zinberg, 'The Public and Nuclear Waste Management', *BAS*, vol. 35, no. 1, January 1979, pp. 34–5.
22. Robert Gillette, 'Nuclear Safety (IV): Barriers to Communication', *Science*, vol. 177, 22 September 1972, p. 1080.
23. D. Ford and H. Kendall, 'Nuclear Misinformation', *Environment*, vol. 17, July–Aug. 1975, pp. 17–27.

24. 'Le Débat nucléaire', *Le Monde*, 6 March 1975, p. 12.
25. See J. Leite Lopes, 'Atoms in the Developing Countries', *BAS*, vol. 34, no. 4, April 1978, p. 34. The failure of adequate consultation with scientists, particularly with respect to energy alternatives, is also discussed by David Dickson, 'Brazil's Scientists Fan Doubts over Energy Priorities', *Nature*, vol. 275, 19 October 1978, pp. 578–80.
26. A summary of these arguments is given in Christoph Hohenemser, Roger Kasperson and Robert Kates, 'The Distrust of Nuclear Power', *Science*, vol. 196, 1 April 1977, pp. 25–34. See also Fred H. Schmidt and David Bodansky, *The Energy Controversy: The Fight over Nuclear Power*, San Francisco, Albion Publishing Co., 1976, pp. 56–64, 73–92.
27. Of the numerous ecological writings the following were particularly influential: Barry Commoner, *The Poverty of Power: Energy and the Economic Crisis*, New York, Alfred A. Knopf, 1976; Paul R. Ehrlich and Anne H. Ehrlich, *Population, Resources, Environment: Issues in Human Ecology*, San Francisco, W.H. Freeman & Co., 1970; Donella Meadows *et al.*, *The Limits to Growth*, New York, Universe Books, 1972.
28. Several studies of nuclear risk-perception have emphasised the role of pre-existing images of nuclear holocaust and of unconscious fears of the effects of radiation on genetic processes. See, for example, R. Lifton, 'Nuclear Energy and the Wisdom of the Body', *BAS*, vol. 32, no. 7, September 1976, pp. 16–20.
29. Some of the distinguishing characteristics of the European movement are indicated in William Sweet, 'The Opposition to Nuclear Power in Europe', *BAS*, vol. 33, no. 10, December 1977, pp. 40–7.
30. The emerging uneasiness about science and technology is well characterised by E. Shils, in *Civilization and Science: In Conflict or Collaboration*? CIBA Foundation Symposium, Amsterdam, Elsevier, 1972, p. 42. See also V. Ferkiss, *Technological Man, the Myth and the Reality*, New York, Braziller, 1969; L. Mumford, *The Myth of the Machine, vol. 1, Techniques and Human Development*, New York, Harcourt Brace Joranovich, 1967; J. Ellul, *The Technological Society* (trans. J. Wilkinson), New York, Alfred A. Knopf, 1956; and Ivan Illich, *Energy and Equity*, London, Calder & Boyars, 1974.
31. Todd R. La Porte and Daniel Metlay, 'Technology Observed: Attitudes of a Wary Public', *Science* vol. 188, no. 4184, April 1975, pp. 123.
32. See P. Lebreton, *L'Ex-croissance, Les Chemins de l'écologisme*, Paris, Denoël, 1978, Also J. Attali and M. Guillaume, *l'Antiéconomique*, Paris, Presses Universitaires de France, 1974.
33. This argument is well developed by Alan Roberts, 'The Politics of Nuclear Power', *Arena*, no. 41, 1976, pp. 22–47.
34. Claude G. Poncelet, 'A Taste of Things to Come', a paper presented at a conference of the Atomic Industrial Forum, reproduced in *Groundswell*, vol. 3, no. 3, April 1980, p. 4.
35. See Gérard Klein 'Politique nucléaire et stabilité sociale', *Revue Politique et Parlementaire*, vol. 77, no. 858, Oct.–Nov. 1975, pp. 28–37;

and Robert Jungk, *The Nuclear State* (trans. Eric Mosbacher), London, John Calder, 1979).

36. See position outlined by Brice Lalonde, in *Pourquoi les écologistes font-ils de la Politique*? (interview between J.-P. Ribes and B. Lalonde, S. Mascovici and R. Dumont), Paris, Seuil, 1978.
37. I examine the implications of the technocratic state in greater detail in *Civilisation in Crisis: Human Prospects in a Changing World*, pp. 12–46. For a fuller analysis of the ecological dimensions of the problem, see André Gorz, *Ecologie et Politique*, Paris, Seuil, 1978.
38. For an incisive account of the intellectual roots of the ecological movement, see Dorothy Nelkin and Michael Pollak, *The Atom Besieged: Extraparliamentary Dissent in France and Germany*, Cambridge, Mass., MIT Press, 1981, pp. 143–52.
39. The concept of an ecologically-oriented society has been canvassed in numerous writings, notably in Murray Bookchin, *Post-Scarcity Anarchism*, Berkeley, Cal., Ramparts, 1971; Ivan D. Illich, *Tools for Conviviality*, London, Calder & Boyar, 1973; H.E. Daly (ed.), *Toward a Steady-State Economy*, San Francisco, W.H. Freeman & Co., 1973; Warren A. Johnson and John Hardesty (eds), *Economic Growth vs. the Environment*, Belmont, Cali., Wadsworth Publishing Company, 1971.
40. *Energy and Nuclear Power*, statement approved by Friends of the Earth at their annual meeting, Washington, DC, 25 January 1976.
41. The ideological thrust of the French ecological movement is examined in some detail by Claude Journès, 'Les Idées politiques du mouvement écologique', *Revue Française de Science Politique*, vol. 29, no. 2, April 1979, pp. 230–54.
42. See Jean-Luc Parodi, 'Essai de problématique du mouvement écologiste: les écologistes et la tentation politique', *Revue Politique et Parlementaire*, vol. 81, no. 878, Jan.–Feb. 1979, pp. 25–43.
43. *Congressional Record*, Senate, vol. 121, 12 May 1975, pp. 13872–5. See also Environmental Action of Colorado, *The Direction of Nuclear Activists*, 1975, Denver, Col.
44. See Falk, *Global Fission*, pp. 184–5.
45. Surrey and Huggett, 'Opposition to Nuclear Power', p. 299.
46. *Der Spiegel*, 21 March 1977.
47. See *Wyhl Urteil*, compiled by the Badish-Elsässichen Citizen Action Groups, Dreisan Verlag, 1977.
48. Among the more widely read one would include: McKinley C. Olson, *Unacceptable Risk: The Nuclear Power Controversy*, New York, Bantam Books, 1976; John Berger, *The Unviable Option*, Palo Alto, Cal., Ramparts Press, 1976; Ralph Nader and John Abbots, *The Menace of Atomic Energy*, New York, W.W. Norton & Co., 1977.
49. See Amory Lovins, *Soft Energy Paths: Towards a Durable Peace*, Harmondsworth, Penguin, 1977. Although written primarily with the American context in mind, the book struck a responsive chord throughout much of the British environmental movement. Patterson's *The Fissile Society* was a much more direct attack on the planning and management of Britain's electricity supply industry but had a more limited audience.

50. Pierre Papon, 'Why France has had no Public Nuclear Debate', *Nature*, vol. 281, 13 September 1979, pp. 94–5.
51. Walter C. Patterson, 'The French Won't Let You', *Environment*, vol. 17, no. 5, July–Aug. 1975, pp. 2–3.
52. See GSIEN, *Electro-nucléaire: danger*, Paris, Seuil, 1977, pp. 7–12; also Philippe Garraud, 'Politique électro-nucléaire et mobilisation: la tentative de constitution d'un enjeu', *Revue Française de Science Politique*, vol. 29, no. 3, June 1979, pp. 457–60.
53. For an informative account of the proceedings and political significance of the inquiry, see Williams, *The Nuclear Power Decisions*, pp. 261–311.
54. For an assessment of the inquiry from an environmentalist perspective, see Czech Conroy, *What Choice Windscale?*, London, FOE, 1978.
55. See Daniel Boy, 'Le Vote écologiste en 1978', *Revue Française de Science Politique*, vol. 31, no. 2, April 1981, pp. 394–416.
56. Jean Luc Parodi, 'Eassi de problématique du mouvement écologiste: les écologistes et la tentation politique', p. 30.
57. Dean Abrahamson, 'Governments Fall as Consensus Gives Way to Debate', *BAS*, vol. 35, no. 9, November 1979, pp. 30–7.
58. 'Impossible to Vote a Clear "Yes" for Nuclear in Sweden', *NEI*, March 1980, pp. 24–6.
59. These dilemmas are graphically described in Nelkin and Pollak, *The Atom Besieged*, pp. 79–83.
60. *The Times*, 21 March 1977; also *Grohnde 19/3/1977. Dokumentation* compiled by various citizen action groups in the Hanover area, published by SOAK.
61. Falk, *Global Fission*, pp. 221–4.
62. *International Herald Tribune*, 1 August 1977. See also 'Le Désordre nucléaire', *L'Express*, 8–14 August 1977, pp. 23–8.
63. Falk, *Global Fission*, p. 188.
64. For a more detailed account, see Dave Elliott, *The Politics of Nuclear Power*, London, Pluto Press, 1978, pp. 122–3.
65. 'The International Connection: A View of the European Anti-Nuclear Movement', *Groundswell*, vol. 2, no. 8, Aug.–Sep. 1979, p. 15; also *The Guardian*, 7 May 1979, and Michael Flood, *Torness: Keep it Green*, London, FOE, 1979, pp. 39–43.
66. Harvey Wasserman, 'Confrontation at Seabrook', *The Progressive*, July 1977, pp. 11–12.
67. H. Kohn, 'Anti-Nuclear Spring Offensive', *Rolling Stone*, no. 268, 29 June 1978, pp. 13, 33–5.
68. *New York Times*, 8 May 1979.
69. *New York Times*, 25 September 1979.
70. Falk, *Global Fission*, pp. 218–19; and *Nucleonics Week*, 19 June 1980, pp. 1–2.
71. Fernex, 'Non-Violence Triumphant', p. 381.
72. *Declaration of the Salzburg Conference for a Non-Nuclear Future*, 29 April–1 May 1977, pp. 3–4.
73. The political consequences of the different German and French legal traditions are analysed in Dorothy Nelkin and Michael Pollak, 'French

and German Courts on Nuclear Power', *BAS*, May 1980, vol. 36, no. 5, pp. 36–42.

74. S. Ebbin and R. Caspar, *Citizen Groups and Nuclear Power Controversy: Uses of Scientific and Technological Information*, Cambridge, Mass., MIT Press, 1974, p. 4.
75. See Elliott, *The Politics of Nuclear Power*, pp. 45–52; also Les Dalton, *Trade Unions and Nuclear Power: An International Survey*, Nottingham, Spokesman, 1979.
76. *Le Monde*, 18 April 1975.
77. CFDT, *L'Electro-nucléaire en France*, Paris, Seuil, 1975.
78. See 'La CFDT conteste le choix tout nucléaire – tout électrique tout Américain', *Le Monde*, 15 May 1975; 'La CFDT demande la suspension du programme nucléaire pendant trois ans', *Le Monde*, 18 March 1976; 'La CFDT demande à Giscard d'Estaing la suspension pour trois ans du programme de développement nucléaire', *Le Monde*, 13 April 1976.
79. See Richard Grossman, 'Being Right is not Enough', *Environmental Action*, vol. 8, no. 16, 1976.
80. O. Renn, *Man, Technology and Risk: A Study on Intuitive Risk Assessment and Attitudes towards Nuclear Energy*, Kernforschungsanlage Jülich GmbH, Programmgruppe Kernenergie und Umwelt, June 1981, pp. 222–4.
81. *L'Express*, no. 1361, 8–14 August 1977, p. 26; see also 'Ce que pensent les Français', *Le Nouvel Observateur*, 8 August 1977, pp. 22–4.
82. Surrey and Huggett, 'Opposition to Nuclear Power', p. 302.
83. 'Public Opposition to Nuclear Energy: Retrospect and Prospect', pp. 273–4.
84. *New Society*, 31 March 1977.
85. G. Gallup, *Most See Need for Nuclear Power But Many Concerned About Safety*, Chicago, Field Newspaper Syndicate, 22 July 1976, p. 5.

CHAPTER FOUR

1. In *Civilization in Crisis: Human Prospects in a Changing World*, I have attempted to analyse the incipient crisis of legitimacy confronting the advanced industrial order in terms of the interacting and mutually reinforcing imbalances which permeate the fabric of national and international institutions. I have argued elsewhere that 'while required to provide the technocratic framework for capital accumulation, the capitalist state also needs to maintain the legitimacy of this process' ('The Advanced Capitalist State and the Contemporary World Crisis', *Science and Society*, vol. XLV, Summer 1981, p. 154). The state's need for legitimation is also clearly outlined in Ralph Miliband, *The State in Capitalist Society*, London, Quartet Books, 1973, pp. 161–236.
2. The constraints imposed on nuclear development by public opposition are incisively examined by Måns Lönnroth and William Walker, *The Viability of the Civil Nuclear Industry*, published by the Consultative Group on Nuclear Energy (jointly sponsored by the Rockefeller

Foundation and the Royal Institute of International Affairs), New York, 1973, pp. 46–7.

3. The principle of equal protection in relation to reactor emissions is examined by K.S. Schrader-Frechette, *Nuclear Power and Public Policy*, pp. 25–43.
4. Pierre Strohl, 'Nuclear Energy: Safety and Public Information', *OECD Observer*, no. 85, March 1977, p. 19.
5. W.O. Doub, 'Meeting the Challenge to Nuclear Energy Head-On', *Atomic Energy Law Journal*, vol. 15, no. 4, Winter 1974, p. 261.
6. W. Marshall, 'Nuclear Power and the Proliferation Issue', *Atom*, April 1978, pp. 78–102; also 'Proliferation and the Recycling of Plutonium', *Atom*, September 1978, pp. 234–41.
7. Dean Abrahamson, 'Governments Fall as Consensus Gives Way to Debate', *BAS*, vol. 35, no. 9, November 1979, pp. 30–7.
8. Thomas Cochran, 'Secrecy and Nuclear Power', *BAS*, Aug.–Sept. 1981, pp. 37–41; Mary M. Cheh, 'Secrecy: Why is it Still with Us?', *BAS*, December 1982, pp. 66–70.
9. See W.T. Keating, 'Politics, Energy and the Environment: The Role of Technology Assessment', *American Behavioural Scientist*, vol. 19, no. 1, Sept.–Oct. 1975, pp. 57–8.
10. See, for example, R. Gillette, 'At the AEC the Way of the Dissenter is Hard', *Science*, 5 May 1972, pp. 492–4; and Ford and Kendall, 'Nuclear Misinformation', pp. 19–20.
11. Particularly revealing in this regard are claims of several NRC employees who resigned to give free expression to their concerns. See Ronald Fluegge's letter of resignation reproduced in full in Jungk, *The Nuclear State*, pp. 78–9.
12. *Science* 19 May 1978, p. 753.
13. See Harold L. Nieburg, *Nuclear Secrecy and Foreign Policy*, Washington, Public Affairs Press, 1964; L. Douglas DeNike, 'Radioactive Malevolence', *BAS*, February 1974; Mason Wilrich and Theodore B. Taylor, *Nuclear Theft: Risks and Safeguards*, Cambridge, Mass., Ballinger Publishing Co., 1973; Peter Pringle and James Speiglman, *The Nuclear Barons*, London, Michael Joseph, 1983. For a graphic account of the illicit diversion of 200 tonnes of uranium, the concealment of the fact by the relevant authorities, and their failure to conduct a full-scale investigation, see Elaine Darenporh, Paul Eddy and Peter Gillman, *The Plumbat Affair*, London, Futura Publications, 1978.
14. Michael Flood and Robin Grove-White, *Nuclear Prospects: A Comment on the Individual the State and Nuclear Policy*, London, FOE UK, 1976.
15. See the debate on nuclear safety which took place in the House of Commons on 23 February 1976, in particular the intervention by Peter Viggers, *HCD*, vol. 906, cols. 127–31.
16. This conclusion emerges in two official reports: C. Coulais, 'Rapport fait au nom de la commission d'enquête parlementaire sur la situation de l'énergie en France', *Assemblée Nationale*, no. 1275, annexe au

procès verbal de la séance du 5.11.1974; M. Becam, 'Rapport au nom de la commission d'enquête parlementaire sur la pollution du littoral méditerranéen', *Assemblée Nationale*, no. 1273, annexe au procès verbal de la séance du 31.10.1974.

17. M. d'Ornano, contribution to debate on energy policy in the National Assembly, 1st session, 14 May 1975, *Journal Officiel* (Débats parlementaires), 15 May 1975, p. 2654.
18. See Hervé Kempf and Marie-France Toinet, 'Le débat nucléaire français', *Etudes*, no. 344, June 1976, pp. 53–7.
19. For an official perspective on the government's information campaign, see K. Lang, 'Information on Nuclear Energy in the Federal Republic of Germany', IAEA-CN-36/81, vol. 7, 1977, pp. 125–36.
20. Tovsten Kälvemark, 'Swedish Public Discussion on Nuclear Power', *Current Sweden*, no. 245, February 1980.
21. *HCD* 23 February 1976, vol. 906, col. 82.
22. Many of these arguments are rehearsed in 'Table ronde: quelle réponse aux problèmes énergétiques et financiers', *Revue Politique et Parlementaire*, May–June 1977, pp. 48–64 (esp. comments by Lucien Thiriet).
23. John Lenihan, 'Public Attitudes to Nuclear Energy', *Atom*, no. 253, November 1977, p. 323.
24. A short English summary of the Battelle study is given by V. Hartje and M. Dierkes, 'Impact Assessment and Participation: Case Studies in Nuclear Power Siting in West Germany', in D. Burkhardt and W. Ittelson (eds), *Environmental Assessment of Socioeconomic Systems* (Nato Conference Series Systems Science, vol. 3), New York, Plenum Press, 1978, pp. 561–67. See also Wolfgang Rüdig, 'Public Participation and Nuclear Politics', *Politics* (UK), vol. 1, no. 2, November 1981, pp. 35–7.
25. For a review of this literature see the study (carried out under the auspices of the Jülich Nuclear Research Centre) by Renn, *Man, Technology and Risk*, pp. 1–60.
26. During the first two years of President Reagan's term of office, the NRC acted to expedite specific plant hearings by reducing the scope for citizen intervention, and by significantly pruning the administrative and legal requirements of the licensing process. See 'The NRC Cracks Down on Interveners', *Groundswell*, vol. 5, no. 6, Nov.–Dec. 1982, pp. 1–5.
27. Cf. M. Georges and J. Molenat, 'Centrales françaises, tout le monde sera consulté', *L'Express*, 12–22 December 1974; 'M. d'Ornano réfléchit sur le courier de *l'Express*', L'Express, 21–7 April 1975.
28. See Walter C. Patterson, 'The Windscale Report: A Nuclear Apologia', *BAS*, vol. 34, no. 6, June 1978, pp. 44–9.
29. *The Windscale Inquiry*, report by the Hon. Mr Justice Parker, vol. 1 (report and annexes), London, HMSO, 1978. See also 'The Windscale Report: A Review', *Atom*, no. 259, May 1978, pp. 131–5.
30. *The Parker Inquiry*, Report by FOE presented to the Secretary of State for the Environment, 28 April 1978.

31. See J. Bugler, 'The Windscale Verdict', *New Statesman*, 10 March 1978, pp. 309–10.
32. The political context of the inquiry's decision is examined in Williams, *The Nuclear Power Decisions*, pp. 315–17.
33. This analysis is drawn largely from the account given by Nelkin and Pollack, 'French and German Courts on Nuclear Power', pp. 36–42.
34. Kerstin Niblaeus, 'National Referendum on Nuclear Power in Sweden', *Current Sweden*, no. 246, February 1980.
35. The nuclear implications of 'party impotence' are examined in some detail in Dorothy Nelkin and Michael Pollak, 'Political Parties and the Nuclear Energy Debate in France and Germany', *Comparative Politics*, vol. 12, no. 2, January 1980, pp. 127–41.
36. Jonathan Fox, 'Has Brazil Moved Toward State Capitalism?', *Latin American Perspectives*, vol. VI, no. 4, Fall 1979, pp. 64–86.
37. Philippe Faucher, 'Industrial Policy in a Dependent State: The Case of Brazil', *Latin American Perspectives*, vol. 7, no. 1, Winter 1980, pp. 3–22.
38. Details are cited in Falk, *Global Fission*, p. 127.
39. See J. Bugler, 'The Nuclear Politics of France', *New Statesman*, 26 August 1977, p. 266.
40. *The Atomic State and the People Who Have to Live in it*, published by the Campaign Against the Model West Germany, 1979, pp. 12–13.
41. Vera Rich, 'Berufsverbote Continues in spite of Resolutions', *Nature*, vol. 282, 6 December 1979, p. 549.
42. Marc Thivolle, 'Berufsverbote: Interdictions professionelles', *La Gueule Ouverte*, no. 185, 24 November 1977, pp. 11–12.
43. J. Habermas, *Legitimation Crisis* (trans. Thomas McCarthy), Boston, Beacon Press, 1975, p. 73.
44. For a fuller theoretical exposition of this argument, see Tony Woodiwiss, 'Critical Theory and the Capitalist State', *Economy and Society*, vol. 7, no. 2, May 1978, pp. 175–91; also David A. Gold, Clarence Y.H. Lo and Erik Olin Wright, 'Recent Developments in Marxist Theories of the Capitalist State', Part 1, *Monthly Review*, vol. 27, no. 5, October 1975, pp. 29–43; Part 2, *Monthly Review*, vol. 27, no. 6, November 1975, pp. 36–51.
45. The role of the state in giving shape to the politics of alienation is examined in Alan Wolfe, 'New Directions in the Marxist Theory of Politics', *Politics and Society*, vol. 4, no. 2, 1974, pp. 131–60.

CHAPTER FIVE

1. For a more detailed outline of the economic difficulties confronting the reactor industry in conditions of recession, See Måns Lönnroth and William Walker, *The Viability of the Civil Nuclear Industry*, published by the International Consultative Group on Nuclear Energy, London, 1979, pp. 71–7.
2. 'Communication on Energy: The Energy Future of West Germany', *Energy Policy*, December 1977, p. 341.

3. Casper Schuuring, 'West German Model Predicts Low Growth in Energy Demand', *Nature*, vol. 272, 30 March 1978, p. 393.
4. *ATW News* (published by Atomwirschaft–Atomtechnik), February 1982, p. 2.
5. M. Kempken, "L'Énergie nucléaire et l'opinion publique en République Fédérale d'Allemagne', *Energie Nucléaire*, vol. 14, no. 2, March–April 1972, p. 136.
6. See the outline of the 'standard scenario' given by Hartmut Bossel and Richard Denton, 'Energy Futures for the Federal Republic of Germany', *Energy Policy*, March 1977, p. 36.
7. Karl J. Sanerwalk, 'L'Industrie nucléaire allemande', *Energie Nucléaire*, vol. 14, no. 2, March–April 1972, p. 97.
8. Ulricht Däunert, 'Understanding the Structure of the Nuclear Industry", *Nuclear Engineering International* (hereafter referred to as *NEI*), May 1981, p. 31.
9. Andrew Buckoke, 'Nuclear Hiatus Hits West Germany Energy Markets', *New Scientist*, vol. 79, 7 September 1978, p. 670.
10. Otto Graf Lambsdorf, 'Why the Government Strongly Supports Nuclear Power', *NEI*, December 1978, p. 48.
11. For a detailed list of nuclear power stations in operation, under construction or at the planning stage as of 1980 see table in Wolf-J. Schmidt-Küster, 'The Role of Nuclear Power in Securing Future Energy Supplies', *NEI*, May 1981, p. 34.
12. Many of these problems are discussed by Thomas Roser, 'Where is the Market for the Nuclear Industry?', *NEI*, December 1978, pp. 54–6.
13. See Heinrich Mandel, 'Construction Costs of Nuclear Power Stations', *Energy Policy*, vol. 4, no. 1, March 1976, pp. 12–24.
14. Heinrich Mandel, 'Are Additions to Nuclear Capacity in Jeopardy?', *NEI*, December 1978, p. 50.
15. *Energièwirtzschaftliche Entwicklung in der Bundesrepublic Deutschland 1980/85*, Dresdner Bank AG, Frankfurt-am-Main, 1974. The estimates are also cited in Thomas Roser, 'Financing Nuclear Power for Germany', *NEI*, March 1975, pp. 177–8.
16. D. Schmidt and W. Mönig, 'The Electric Power Industry: Investment Requirements and their Financing', *Energy Policy*, March 1975, pp. 67–72.
17. See Gunther Radtke, 'Delays Help German Utilities Maintain Self-Financing Ratios', NEI, May 1979, pp. 64–5.
18. *NEI*, April 1981, p. 6; *NEI*, May 1982, p. 11; *NEI*, April 1983, p. 7.
19. Lambsdorf, 'Why the Government Strongly Supports Nuclear Power', p. 47.
20. *NEI*, June 1980, p. 10.
21. *Nucleonics Week*, 29 January 1981, p. 7.
22. *ATW News*, November 1981, p. 1.
23. *Nucleonics Week*, 19 June 1980, p. 7; 26 June 1980, p. 2.
24. See Otto Neck, *Policy-making in a Nuclear Programme: The Case of the West German Fast Breeder Reactor*, Lexington, Mass., Lexington Books, 1981, pp. 223–9.

25. A. Brandstetter, 'The Tripartite Fast Breeder Programme: A Utility/Industry View', *NEI*, July 1976, p. 41.
26. H.H. Hennies *et al.*, 'Status and Perspectives of German Breeder Development', *Atomwirtschaft*, March 1981, p. 156.
27. *Der Spiegel*, no. 17, 1981, p. 37; *NEI*, January 1983, p. 5.
28. Däunert, 'Understanding the Nature of the Nuclear Industry', p. 30.
29. *ATW News*, October 1981, p. 1.
30. *NEI*, April 1982, pp. 4–5.
31. Commissariat à l'Energie Atomique, 1979 Energy Summary.
32. *Annuaire Statistique de la France 1976*, Paris, Ministère de l'Economie et des Finances, p. 214.
33. Ibid., p. 219.
34. *Annuaire Statistique de la France 1980*, p. 249.
35. Ibid., p. 257.
36. These projections are cited in *Rapport de la Commission de l'Energie*, Paris, la Documentation Française, 1976, p. 18.
37. Commissiariat à l'Energie Atomique, 1979 Energy Summary; also M. Pecqueur, 'Energy in the 80s: Shouldn't We Bid 'No Trump'?', *Atomwirtschaft*, Aug.–Sept. 1980, p. 427.
38. Richard Masters, 'Political Will, a Key Factor in Large Nuclear Programme', *NEI*, March 1979, p. 47.
39. See *France and the Nuclear Option*, interview with President Giscard d'Estaing, 18 January 1980, Paris, Département des Relations Publiques, CEA, p. 2; and Pecqueur, 'Energy in the 80s', p. 424.
40. See Peter Bunyard and Edward Goldsmith, 'France – Country of the Atom', *The Ecologist*, vol. 11, no. 6, December 1981, pp. 293–6.
41. Masters, 'Political Will, a Key Factor in Large Nuclear Programme', p. 50.
42. Syndicat CFDT de l'Énergie Atomique, *Le Dossier Électronucléaire*, p. 420.
43. See Simon Rippon, 'Sorting Out the Industry', *NEI*, January 1977, p. 77.
44. *Le Monde*, 15 June 1976, p. 40.
45. Ibid., 10 November 1976, p. 34.
46. Ibid., 24 January 1981.
47. Michel Hug, 'How the French Programme is Benefiting from Standardisation, *NEI*, July 1981, pp. 29–32.
48. *NEI*, July 1981, p. 6.
49. Ibid., September 1981, p. 6.
50. Ibid., February 1982, p. 3.
51. *Le Monde* 9 October 1981.
52. Ibid., 7 November 1981.
53. 'French Nuclear Industry Running out of Steam', *The Christian Science Monitor*, 30 December 1982, pp. 1, 6. See also *NEI*, May 1983, p. 4.
54. The evolution of the French breeder programme is described in George A. Vendryes, 'Super Phénix: A Full-Scale Breeder Reactor', *Scientific American*, vol. 236, no. 3, March 1977, pp. 26–35.
55. See Bernard Guillemard, 'Start Up of Phénix', *NEI*, May 1974,

pp. 411–14; and M. Aubert and C. Boulinier, 'The Phénix 4 Fast Breeder Power Plant', *NEI*, July 1974, pp. 563–6.

56. 'Phénix Down Again', *NEI*, November 1977, p. 8.
57. William D. Metz, 'European Breeders (1): France Leads the Way', *Science* 25 December 1975, pp. 1279–81.
58. See 'Creys-Malville (Super-Phénix)', reprinted from June 1978 issue of *Nuclear Engineering International.*
59. Framatone subsequently acquired full ownership of Novatome. CEA was nevertheless able to exert influence as a result of the restructuring of Framatome which conferred on CEA a virtual power of veto. See 'Super Phénix Keeps to Schedule', *NEI*, May 1982, p. 5.
60. M. Rapin, 'Five Countries Work Together on the 1200 MWe Fast Breeder', *NEI*, April 1981, pp. 39–41.
61. 'FBR Agreement Signed', *NEI*, August 1977, p. 93.
62. A critical analysis of the economic of the French breeder is offered in 'L'Utopie SurgénéRatrice', *La Gazette Nucléaire*, (GSIEN publication), no. 25, March–April 1979.
63. *Britain's Energy Resources*, London, Central Office of Information, 1980, p. 4.
64. *Financial Times European Energy Report*, 8 September 1980, p. 2.
65. R. Papadopoulos, 'Growth and Overcapacity in the UK Electricity Industry', *Energy Policy*, vol. 9, no. 2, June 1981, p. 153.
66. *Nuclear Power*, The Government's Response to the Select Committee on Energy's Report on the Nuclear Power Programme Session 1980–81, HC 114–1, London, HMSO, 1981, p. 8.
67. 'CEGB's Nuclear Generation Falls', *NEI*, September 1981, p. 5.
68. R.L.R. Nicholson, 'The Nuclear Power Paradox in the UK', Energy Policy, vol. 1, no. 1, June 1973, p. 42. See also 'Future Prospects for Energy Supply and Demand', *Atom*, no. 196, February 1973; L.G. Brookes, 'Towards an All-Electric Economy', *Atom*, no. 202, August 1973. A UKAEA forecast for 2030 of 426 GWe is given in Royal Commission on Environment Pollution, Sixth Report, *Nuclear Power and the Environment*, pp. 182–3.
69. *Energy Policy*, A Consultative Document, presented to Parliament by the Secretary of State for Energy in February 1978, Cmnd 7101, London, HMSO, 1978, p. 55.
70. Mr Varley's statement to the House of Commons (2 May 1974) is reproduced in *Atom*, no. 212, June 1974, pp. 121–2.
71. *Nuclear Energy in Britain*, London, Central Office of Information, 1980, pp. 8–10.
72. As late as 1978, the CEGB was projecting the commissioning of 8000 MWe of nuclear power by 1990 and a possible installation rate of 5000–10,000 MWe a year by the late 1990s (*NEI*, March 1979, p. 16).
73. Papadopoulos, 'Growth and Overcapacity in the UK Nuclear Industry', p. 154.
74. Committee for the Study of the Economics of Nuclear Electricity (CSENE), *Nuclear Energy: The Real Costs*, CSENE, Worthyvale Manor, Camelford, Cornwall, 1982, p. 6.

75. Monopolies and Mergers Commission, *Report on the Central Electricity Generating Board*, HC 315, London, HMSO, 1981, p. 285.
76. These calculations are outlined in some detail in 'How the CEGB calculates its Nuclear Costs', *NEI*, September 1980, pp. 23–6.
77. Monopolies and Mergers Commission, *Report on the CEGB*, pp. 290–2.
78. Reference here is to the CSENE study (fn 72). See also Colin Sweet, 'Nuclear Power Costs in the UK', *Energy Policy*, June 1978, pp. 107–18.
79. CSENE, *Nuclear Energy: The Real Costs*, p. 4.
80. House of Commons Select Committee on Science and Technology, Session 1968–9, p. 125, Q. 659.
81. House of Commons Select Committee on Energy 1980–1, *The Government's Statement on the New Nuclear Power Programme*, vol. 1, HC 114–1, London, HMSO, 1981, p. 18.
82. These arguments are outlined in the first report of the Select Committee on Energy 1980–1, pp. 49–55.
83. *Atom*, no. 280, February 1980, pp. 34–5.
84. Ibid., no. 282, April 1980, p. 111.
85. Select Committee on Energy 1980–1, *The Government's Statement on the New Nuclear Power Programme*, vol. 1, pp. 82–4.
86. *Nucleonics Week*, 13 March 1980, p. 2.
87. *Nuclear Power*, The Government's Response to the Select Committee on Energy's Report, pp. 4, 10, 12–13.
88. See the UKAEA submission to the public hearings on the projected CDFR, convened by the British Council of Churches in December 1976, in D. Cosling and H. Montefiore (eds), *Nuclear Crisis: A Question of Breeding*, Dorchester, Prism Press, 1977, pp. 104–5.
89. "Major Split Over Big British Breeder Programme', *Nucleonics Week*, 30 November 1978, p. 1.
90. *Nucleonics Week*, 10 January 1980, p. 2.
91. Ibid., 18 September 1980, p. 2.
92. *Guidelines for Energy Policy*, Stokholm, Ministry of Industry, 1981, p. 6.
93. See R.U. Gradin, 'The Energy Situation and Nuclear Power', *NEI*, January 1976, p. 35.
94. *Guidelines for Energy Policy*, pp. 28–9.
95. See Olle Gimstedt, 'Sweden's Road to a Firm Nuclear Programme', *Nuclear Europe*, vol. 2, no. 1, January 1982, pp. 9–12; and 'Nuclear Power in Sweden', *Atom*, no. 274, August 1979, p. 217.
96. *Swedish Nuclear News*, no. 1, May 1980, p. 7.
97. See M. Lönnroth, T.B. Johansson and P. Steer, 'Sweden Beyond Oil: Nuclear Commitments and Solar Options', *Science*, vol. 208, no. 4444, 9 May 1980, pp. 562–3.
98. See Erik Jeffs, 'Decision Time Draws Near for Sweden's Nuclear Projects', *Energy International*, vol. 14, no. 12, December 1977, pp. 19–22; also Emar Eskilsson, 'Swedish Nuclear Prospects Brighten

but Government Decision Awaited', *Energy International*, vol. 15, no. 10, October 1978, pp. 33–4.

99. 'Nuclear Power in Sweden', *Atom*, no. 274, August 1979, pp. 217–18.
100. 'After the Referendum', *Atom*, no. 285, July 1980, pp. 179–80.
101. *Guidelines for Energy Policy*, pp. 4, 6–8, 42–6.
102. US Department of the Interior, Bureau of Mines, *Minerals Yearbook, 1976, vol. 1: Metals, Minerals and Fuels*, Washington, GPO, 1978, pp. 44–7.
103. *Statistical Abstract of the United States 1979*, p. 608.
104. See *Development, Growth and State of the Nuclear Industry*, Hearings before the Joint Committee on Atomic Energy Congress of the United States, 93rd Congress, 2nd session, Washington, GPO, 1974, appendix 1, p. 501.
105. ERDA, *United States Uranium Requirements*, Office of Planning, Analysis and Evaluation presented by Edward J. Hanrahan at the Uranium Industry Seminar, Grand Junction Col., October 1976.
106. These estimates were given in *World Nuclear Power and its Fuel Cycle after Three Mile Island: A Guide for Marketing and Strategic Planning*, and reproduced in *NEI*, April 1982, p. 9.
107. *Development, Growth and State of the Nuclear Industry*, pp. 497–503.
108. C.D. Goodwin (ed.), *Energy Policy in Perspective*, Washington, Brookings Institution, 1981, p. 702.
109. *Groundswell*, vol. 4, no. 1, February 1981, pp. 6–7.
110. Ibid., vol. 5, no. 2, March–April 1982, pp. 8–9.
111. Charles Komanoff, 'Nuclear Power Costs: Past, Present, Future', *Groundwell*, vol. 2, no. 8, Aug.–Sept. 1979, pp. 4–6; also by the same author, *Power Plant Cost Escalation*, New York, Komanoff Energy Associates, 1981; and 'Nuclear Energy Costs: The US Experience', *The Ecologist*, vol. 11, no. 6, 1981, pp. 298–301.
112. Results of the study of Ebasco Services of New York City are cited in E. Faltermayer, 'Nuclear Power after Three Mile Island', *Fortune*, 7 May 1979, p. 118.
113. 'Safety Drowns in Sea of Regulations', *NEI*, April 1980, pp. 10–11.
114. R.G. Lester, *Nuclear Power Plant Leads Times*, New York, ICGNE, 1978, p. 24.
115. J.S. Katzin, 'Effects of Inflation and Recession on Nuclear Project Financing in the USA', *NEI*, March 1975, pp. 184–6.
116. See Geoffrey Greenhaugh, 'Nuclear Lead Times: Are They Too Long?', *Energy International*, vol. 17, no. 4, 1980, pp. 22–4.
117. R. Masters, 'Combustion Engineering Adjusts to Slump in Nuclear Market', *NEI*, November 1980, pp. 25–9.
118. G.C. Masche and R. Daub, 'Services and the Nuclear After-Market', *NEI*, May 1980, pp. 42–5; see also *Business Week*, 31 August 1981, pp. 81–2.
119. See President Nixon's message to Congress, 18 April 1973, in Weekly Compilation of Presidential Documents, vol. 9, no. 16, 23 April 1973, p. 397.
120. *Development, Growth and State of the Nuclear Industry*, p. 117.

121. See speech by Robert Fri, Deputy Administrator ERDA, to World Nuclear Fuel Market, Washington, DC, 23 September 1975.
122. Joseph M. Hendric, 'How NRC is Working for a More Up-to-Date Licensing Process', *NEI*, November 1977, pp. 51–2.
123. P. Feinmark, 'Reagan's Energy Plan: Leave it to The Marketplace', *Ambio*, vol. 11, no. 2, 1982, pp. 20–3.
124. AEC, *LMFBR, Proposed Final Environmental Statement*, WASH-1535, Washington, DC, US Government Printing Office, 1974.
125. See E. Abel, 'In the U.S.A.: Atomic Energy on Trial', *Nuclear Law Bulletin*, no. 13, April 1974, pp. 56–65.
126. A. Robert Smith, 'The Breeder Reactor: Another SST', *BAS*, October 1974, pp. 12–13.
127. See *Can the US Breeder Reactor Development Program be Accelerated by Using Foreign Technology*?, Report to the Joint Economic Committee, US Congress, by the Comptroller General of the United States, May 1976, pp. ii, 3-8.
128. *Considerations for Commercialising the Liquid Metal Fast Breeder Reactor*, Report to the Congress by the Comptroller General of the United States, November 1976, p. 35
129. Thomas B. Cochran, *The Liquid Metal Fast Breeder Reactor: An Environmental and Economic Critique*, Baltimore, Resources for the Future, Inc., 1974.
130. For President Carter's full statement, see *Department of State Bulletin*, 2 May 1977, pp. 429–50.
131. E.S. Beckjord, 'Maintaining an Effective Breeder Reactor Programme', *NEI*, November 1977, pp. 55–6.
132. K. Johnston, 'US Industry Remains Unconvinced by Carter', *NEI*, May 1978, pp. 36–8; 'GAO Backs Breeder and not Reprocessing', *Nuclear News*, September 1977, p. 33.
133. Republica Federativa do Brasil, Ministerio das Minas é Energia, *Relatorio de Actividudes 1977*, p. 114.
134. Federative Republic of Brazil, Ministry of Mines and Energy, *National Energy Balance 1978*, p. 10.
135. Federative Republic of Brazil, Ministry of Mines and Energy, *National Energy Balance 1976*, p. 20.
136. *National Energy Balance 1978*, p. 12; *National Energy Balance 1980*, p. 20.
137. *National Energy Balance 1978*, p. 10.
138. C.S.M. Pinto *et al.*, *Organization and Development of the Brazilian Nuclear Programme*, paper presented to IAEA International Conference on Nuclear Power and Its Fuel Cycle, Salzburg, Austria, 2–13 May 1977, p. 4.
139. *NEI*, June 1979, p. 11.
140. 'Brazil Cuts Programme', *NEI*, April 1982, p. 11.
141. See Robert Wesson, *The United States and Brazil: Limits of Influence*, New York, Praeger, 1981, pp. 76–8; and Edward F. Wonder, *Nuclear Fuel and American Foreign Policy*, Boulder, Col., Wastview Press, 1977, p. 287.

142. Federative Republic of Brazil, *The Brazilian Nuclear Program*, Brasilia, March 1977.
143. 'Brazil's Megawatt Megalomonia', *The Economist*, 7 October 1978.
144. *NEI*, April 1981, pp. 5–6.
145. 'Brazil Cuts Programme', p. 11.
146. See M. Bazin, 'The Politics of Power in Brazil', *Nature*, vol. 284, 24 April 1980, p. 656.
147. *Nucleonics Week*, 31 May 1979.
148. *NEI*, June 1979, p. 11.
149. D. Smith, 'Brazil Throws down Gauntlet to Carter as Work Starts on Angra 2 & 3', *NEI*, May 1977, p. 37.
150. Pinto *et al.*, *Organization and Development of the Brazilian Nuclear Programme*, pp. 8–11; also David Fishlock, 'Brazil's Nuclear Industry Is Now in Business', *NEI*, November 1976, p. 38.
151. See William Perry and Sheila Kern, 'The Brazilian Nuclear Programme in a Foreign Policy Context', *Comparative Strategy*, vol. 1, nos. 1–2, 1978, pp. 53–70.
152. See Norman Gall, 'Atoms for Brazil, Dangers for All', *Foreign Policy*, no. 23, Summer 1976, pp. 163–4. For an outline of the official view on autarky, see The Brazilian Nuclear Programme', *Brazil Trade and Industry*, no. 42, 1977 (published by the Ministry of Trade and External Relations), p. 15.
153. See Marcos Arruda, 'A Study of Capitalism in Brazil', *Latin American Perspectives*, vol. 6, no. 4, Fall 1979, pp. 32–44.
154. Bazin, 'The Politics of Power in Brazil', pp. 656–7.

CHAPTER SIX

1. See Joint OECD/NEA Report, *World Uranium and Thorium Resources*, Paris, 1965; Joint OECD/NEA-IAEA Report, *Uranium: Resources, Production and Demand*, Paris, 1970; Joint OECD/NEA-IAEA Report, *Uranium: Resources, Production and Demand*, Paris, 1975.
2. Joint OECD/NEA-IAEA Report, *Uranium: Resources, Production and Demand*, Paris, 1977.
3. See *US Commercial Nuclear Power: A Status Report*, Washington, Federal Energy Administration, September 1977, p. 5.
4. Joint OECD/NEA-IAEA Report, *Uranium: Resources, Production and Demand*, Paris, 1982.
5. See *Nuclear Fuels Policy*, Report of the Atlantic Council's Nuclear Fuels Policy Working Group, Boulder, Col., Westview Press, 1976, pp. 36–57.
6. *Nuexco Monthly Report on the Uranium Market*, no. 159, November 1981; 'Uranium Supply and Demand Examined', *NEI*, June 1982, p. 15. The IAEA had previously predicted a production capability of 92,000 tonnes per year by 1985 ('Uranium Supply and Demand', *IAEA Bulletin*, vol. 20, no. 1, 1978, p. 21).
7. See 'Uncertainty Hovers over the Uranium Market', *NEI*, October

1980, p. 28; 'An Industry View of the Outlook for Uranium', *NEI*, September 1981, p. 26.

8. Joint OECD/NEA-IAEA Report, 1977, pp. 20–1.
9. Ibid., pp. 23–4.
10. W.A. Baldwin and Z. Cowman, *Heavier than Lead: Does the US Uranium Mining and Milling Industry Face a Financial Catastrophe?*, paper prepared for Friends of the Earth, San Francisco, Cal., May 1980.
11. Joint OECD-NEA-IAEA Report, 1977, pp. 20–1.
12. 'Péchiney Ugine Kuhlmann: From Uranium Prospecting to Fuel Fabrication', *NEI*, January 1975, pp. 31–7.
13. See J.-P. Silve, 'Fuel Cycle Industry Combines Private and Public Enterprise', *NEI*, December 1976, pp. 55–7.
14. The Monopolies and Mergers Commission, *Central Electricity Generating Board*, pp. 172–3.
15. 'Quellen der Natururanversorgung für die Bundesrepublik', *Atomwirtschaft*, December 1977, p. 649.
16. Ministry of Mines and Energy, Federative Republic of Brazil, *National Energy Balance 1978*, pp. 17–18.
17. 'An Industry View of the Outlook for Uranium' *NEI*, September 1981, p. 25.
18. The drastic fall in projections of uranium demand had occurred despite the fact that the proposed recycling of uranium was now unlikely to prove economical in comparison with the price of newly-mined uranium. See Terence Price, 'The Uranium Market – Economic and Political Factors', *Atom*, no. 265, November 1978, pp. 290–4.
19. See Thomas L. Neff and Henry D. Jacoby, *Nuclear Fuel Assurance: Origins, Trends and Policy Issues*, MIT Energy Laboratory Report No. MIT-EL 79–103, MIT, Cambridge, Mass., February 1979.
20. See *International Uranium Supply and Demand*, Hearing before the Subcommittee on Oversight and Investigation of the Committee on Interstate and Foreign Commerce, House of Representatives, 94th Congress, 2nd session, November 1976, Washington, US Government Printing Office, 1977, pp. 364–73; and *Survey of United States Uranium Marketing Activity*, Washington, DC, US Department of Energy, May 1978, p. 24.
21. The impact of US enrichment contracting policies on uranium requirements is analysed in some detail in Vince Taylor, *The Myth of Uranium Scarcity*, Los Angeles, Cal., Pan Heuristics, 1977, pp. 8–14.
22. For the most comprehensive examination of the uranium cartel, see June H. Taylor and Michael D. Yokell, *Yellowcake: The International Uranium Cartel*, New York, Pergamon Press, 1979.
23. See P.J. Shirrington, 'The Marketing of Uranium', *Australian Foreign Affairs Record*, vol. 53, no. 4, April 1982, p. 160.
24. *Allocation of Uranium Enrichment Services to Fuel Foreign and Domestic Nuclear Reactors*, Report to the Committee on Foreign Affairs House of Representatives by the Comptroller General of the United States, March 1975, p. 3.
25. 'The President's Message to the Congress Outlining Administrative

Actions and Legislative Proposals to create a Competitive Private Uranium Enrichment Industry – June 26 1975'.

26. These arguments are considered more fully in *Uranium Enrichment: Alternatives for Meeting the Nation's Needs and their Implications for the Federal Budget*, Congressional Budget Office, Background Paper no. 7, 18 Mary 1976; and *Nuclear Power: Issues and Choices*, Report of the Nuclear Energy Policy Study Group, Cambridge, Mass., Ballinger Publishing Co., 1977, pp. 374–6.
27. The rationale, function and consequences of these multilateral initiatives are examined at some length in Edward F. Wonder, *Nuclear Fuel and American Foreign Policy: Multilateralization for Uranium Enrichment*, Boulder Col., Westview Press, 1977.
28. See Vince Taylor, *How the US Government Created the Uranium Crisis (and the Coming Uranium Bust)*, Los Angeles, Cal., Pan Heuristics, 1977, pp. 25–6.
29. *Allocation of Uranium Enrichment Services to Fuel Foreign and Domestic Nuclear Reactors*, pp. 5–6.
30. See Allen L. Hammond, 'Uranium: Will There Be a Shortage or an Embarrassment of Enrichment?', *Science*, vol. 192, 28 May 1976, p. 866.
31. This analysis is developed in much greater detail in Taylor, *How the US Government Created the Uranium Crisis*, pp. 38–58.
32. The President's decision was supported by the General Accounting Office. See *Centrifuge Enrichment: Benefits and Risks*, Report by the Comptroller General of the United States, 7 March 1978.
33. See statement by William R. Voigt, Jr, Director Division of Uranium Resources and Enrichment, US Department of Energy, in *Hearings Before the Sub-Committee on Energy Research, Development and Demonstration, US Senate*, 9 February 1978, p. 9.
34. *Uranium Enrichment Policies and Operations: Status and Future Needs*, Report to the Congress by the Comptroller General of the United States, 18 November 1977, pp. 15–20.
35. Proven centrifuge technology could not be transferred to Brazil because of objections from Britain and the Netherlands, West Germany's Urenco partners. For a fuller discussion of this question, see Hartmut Krugmann, 'The German-Brazilian Nuclear Deal', *BAS*, February 1981, pp. 32–6.
36. For a full analysis of worldwide enrichment capacity as of this date, see *Enrichment Availability*, Report of INFCE Working Group 2, Vienna, International Atomic Energy Agency, 1980, pp. 12–13.
37. For a survey of major new enrichment projects, see *NEI*, November 1976, pp. 49–62.
38. Dick Kovan, 'Urenco Opens its Centrifuged Doors', *NEI*, December 1977, pp. 25–7; Sir John Hill, 'Benefits from Joint Activities in Nuclear Fuel Services', *NEI*, April 1981, pp. 30–2.
39. *The Economist*, 11 March 1978, p. 61; *NEI*, August 1978, p. 3.
40. See Simon Rippon, 'Enrichment Prospects for the 1980s', *Energy International*, vol. 14, no. 5, May 1977, pp. 43; and Tom Wilkie,

'Tricastin Points the Road to Energy Independence', *NEI*, October 1980, pp. 41–5.

41. See P. Bander et al., 'Competing for the Non-USA Enrichment Markets', *NEI*, October 1980, pp. 37–41.
42. Wilkie, 'Tricastin Points the Road to Energy Independence', pp. 41–5.
43. 'World Enrichment Over-Capacity', *Nature*, 28 October 1982, p. 773.
44. C. Joyce, 'Row Breaks Out about Uranium Enrichment', *New Scientist*, vol. 88, no. 1229, 17 November 1980, p. 555; 'The Changing Face of Enrichment', *NEI*, February 1981, p. 13–14.
45. For a survey of progress made in the development of commercial reprocessing in the United States and Western Europe, see Simon Rippon, 'Reprocessing – What Went Wrong?', *NEI*, February 1976, pp. 17–27.
46. G. Rossney, 'Reprocessing in Europe', *NEI*, April–May 1976, p. 20.
47. 'La Hague: French Face Bright Prospects for Commercial Oxide Fuel Reprocessing', *Nuclear News*, November 1978, p. 58.
48. The OECD/NEA was established in 1972 to replace the OECD's European Nuclear Energy Agency on the adhesion of Japan as a full member. In a report issued in 1977 the Agency argued that 'present commitments to establish reprocessing capacity are insufficient to meet the projected demand for such services if the reprocessing option is pursued' (*Reprocessing of Spent Nuclear Fuels in OECD Countries*, Paris, OECD, 1977, p. 9).
49. For a summary of the OECD/NEA's principal findings, see Richard Masters, 'The Economic and Environmental Benefits of Reprocessing and Recycle', *NEI*, May 1977, p. 31.
50. This was one of the major premises on which Justice Parker had based his recommendations and which the British Government used in support of its decision to proceed with the expansion of Windscale's reprocessing capacity. See 'The Windscale Debate', *Atom*, no. 259, May 1978, p. 143.
51. Many of these arguments are canvassed in A.J. O'Donnell, R.O. Sanderg and R.E. Brookbank Sr, 'Restoring Commercial Reprocessing in the United States', *NEI*, August 1982, pp. 30–3.
52. Rippon, 'La Hague: French Face Bright Prospects for Commercial Oxide Fuel Reprocessing', p. 62; and 'Le Retraitement', *La Gazette Nucléaire*, no. 24, February 1979, p. 14.
53. 'Japan/UK Reprocessing Contract Signed', *NEI*, June 1978, p. 8.
54. See Frank Barnaby, 'Nuclear Power and Proliferation', *New Scientist*, 21 July 1977, pp. 168–9; and, by the same author, 'An Unclear Division for Germany', *New Scientist*, 26 April 1979, p. 267.
55. *HCD*, 14 May 1981, p. 338.
56. '... But Do Reprocessing Plants Work Reliably?' *NEI*, September 1982, p. 13.
57. See Richard Severo, 'Nuclear Recycling: Key Issues Raised', *New York Times*, 17 April 1977; and 'Reprocessing: How Necessary is it for the Near Term?', *Science*, vol. 196, 1 April 1977, pp. 43–5; W.

Bebbington, 'The Reprocessing of Nuclear Fuels', *Scientific American*, vol. 235, no. 6, December 1976, pp. 30–41.

58. *NEI*, November 1973, p. 483.
59. The concerns of the trade union are outlined in *L'Usine de La Hague*, Saclay, SNPEA–CFDT, 1976.
60. 'Close to the Brink', *Nature*, vol. 290, 16 April 1981, p. 538.
61. *Final Generic Environmental Statement on the Use of Recycle Plutonium in Mixed Oxide Fuel in Light Water Cooled Reactors (GESMO)*, Report of Nuclear Regulatory Commission, August 1976. For a discussion of the economic difficulties of reprocessing, see Marvin Resnikoff, 'Expensive Enrichment', *Environment*, vol. 17, no. 5, July–Aug. 1975, pp. 28–35.
62. *Nuclear Power: Issues and Choices*, p. 325.
63. These arguments are canvassed in 'Reprocessing: Right to Pause and Think', *Nature*, vol. 264, 23–30 December 1976.
64. 'Ford–Mitre Study: Nuclear Power Yes, Plutonium No', *Science*, vol. 196, 1 April 1977, p. 41.
65. The redefinition of aims is described in Klaus Hopfrer, 'Planners Backtrack after German Nuclear Inquiry', *Nature*, vol. 278, 26 April 1979, pp. 774–5.
66. Williams, *The Nuclear Power Decisions*, pp. 304–7.
67. Jonathan Holtorp, 'The Reasons behind BNFL's Corporate Plan', *NEI*, August 1981, pp. 15–21.
68. 'West Germany: Eyeball to Eyeball over Nuclear Fuel Reprocessing', *Nature*, vol. 278, 22 March 1979, pp. 296–7.
69. *NEI*, April 1980, p. 5.
70. *NEI*, July 1981, p. 4.
71. 'Still Searching for Reprocessing Site', *NEI*, January 1982, p. 11; 'DWK's Search for Site Moves Forward', *NEI*, September 1982, p. 3.
72. 'German Utilities Sign Reprocessing Contracts with Cogéma', *NEI*, May 1978, p. 6.
73. *Spent Nuclear Fuel and Radioactive Waste*, A summary of a report by the Swedish Government Committee on Radioactive Waste, Stockholm, 1976, pp. 10–11.
74. Thomas B. Johansson and Peter Steen, 'What To Do with Radioactive Waste?', *BAS*, vol. 35, no. 9, November 1979, p. 38.
75. Erik Svenke, *Swedish Policy for the Back End of the Nuclear Fuel Cycle*, address delivered at the Uranium Institute Sixth Annual Symposium, 2–4 September 1981, p. 4.
76. 'Mounting Waste', *NEI*, November 1979, p. 15.
77. *Royal Commission on Environmental Pollution, 6th Report, Nuclear Power and the Environment*, London, HMSO, 1976.
78. *Ranger Uranium Environmental Inquiry, First Report*, Canberra, Australian Government Publishing Service, 1976, p. 110.
79. *Objectives, Concepts and Strategies for the Management of Radioactive Waste Arising from Nuclear Power*, Paris, OECD, 1979.
80. *Spent Fuel Management*, Report of INFCE Working Group 6, Vienna, IAEA, 1980, p. 9.

81. Ibid., pp. 13–14.
82. CEA, *Vitrification of High Level Waste Solutions at Marcoule, France*, paper presented at European Nuclear Conference, Hamburg, May 1979.
83. 'Vitrification Inches Towards a Solution', *NEI*, November 1980, p. 13.
84. *Nucleonics Week*, 15 November 1979 and 19 June 1980.
85. Ingvar Vivstad, 'Swedish Utilities Design Completely Safe Disposal Route', *NEI*, January 1978, pp. 45–8.
86. See B. Gustafsson, 'Sweden Goes for Control Temporary Storage Facility', *NEI*, October 1980, pp. 51–2; and *CLAB, Central Storage Facility for Spent Fuel*, Stockholm, SKBF, 1982.
87. *Report on the Current Situation with respect to Nuclear Fuel and the Operations of SKBF During the Period November 1981–October 1982*, Report to the Swedish Ministry of Industry, Stockholm, 1982, p. 21.
88. Svenke, *Swedish Policy for the Back End of the Nuclear Fuel Cycle*, pp. 2–4.
89. *Atom*, no. 299, September 1981, p. 251.
90. *A Review of Cmnd 884 'The Control of Radioactive Wastes'*, report by an expert group made to the Radioactive Waste Management Committee (available from the Department of the Environment, London).
91. See 'Need to Evaluate Waste Disposal Options', *NEI*, November 1979, pp. 25–6.
92. John Lewis, 'Davy Jones's Nuclear Locker', *New Scientist*, vol. 91, no. 1263, pp. 227–9.
93. D.W. Clelland and A.D.W. Corbet, 'Vitrifying Britain's Waste', *NEI*, August 1982, p. 335.
94. 'Radioactive Waste Management', *Atom*, no. 279, January 1980, pp. 15–17.
95. 'Engineered Storage "Should be Considered" for HLW', *Atom*, no. 298, August 1981, p. 204.
96. 'The Disposal of High Level Nuclear Wastes', *Atom*, no. 300, October 1981.
97. 'Vitrification Inches Towards a Solution', *NEI*, November 1980, pp. 13–14.
98. K. Kopfner, 'Germany to Decentralise Nuclear Waste Treatment', *Nature*, vol 281, 11 October 1979, p. 419.
99. 'New Spent Fuel Policy Unveiled', *Science* vol. 198, 11 November 1977, p. 591.
100. See US Department of Energy, *Report to the President by the Interagency Review Group on Nuclear Waste Management*, March 1979, TID-29442; US Nuclear Regulatory Commission, Office of Nuclear Materials Safety and Standards, *Regulation of Federal Radioactive Waste Materials*, September 1979, NUREG-0527.
101. The White House, Office of the Press Secretary, *Fact Sheet: The President's Program on Radioactive Waste Management*, 12 February 1980.
102. 'Congress and Carter Clash on Waste', *NEI*, June 1980, p. 11; 'US

Senate Stalls', *Nature*, vol. 289, 1 January 1981, p. 7; 'US Confusion on Waste Management', *NEI*, June 1981, pp. 13–4.

103. M.H. Raudenbush and Lawrence J. Smith, 'New Directions in US Waste Management', *NEI*, May 1982, pp. 21–2.
104. *Groundswell*, vol. 6, no. 1, Jan.–Feb. 1983, pp. 1–4, 9.
105. E.L. Draper and R.E.L. Stanford, 'US Utilities Concerned about Waste Storage', *NEI*, August 1982, pp. 15–16.
106. 'No Time to Waste for Congress', *NEI*, June 1982, pp. 6–7.

CHAPTER SEVEN

1. See Jean Klein, 'Ventes d'armes et d'équipements nucléaires: les politiques des Etats-Unis et des pays d'Europe Occidentale depuis la guerre d'octobre 1973', *Politique Etrangère*, 40° année, no. 1, 1974, pp. 603–20.
2. Cited in Sverre Lodgaard, 'International Nuclear Commerce, Structures, Trends, and Proliferation Potentials', *Bulletin of Peace Proposals*, vol. 18, no. 1, 1977, p. 15.
3. *Energy Prospects to 1985*, vols. 1 and 11, Paris, OECD, 1975.
4. *Market Survey for Nuclear Power in Developing Countries*, Vienna, IAEA, 1974.
5. Atomic Industrial Forum estimate, reported in *Nucleonics Week*, 10 June 1976, p. 8.
6. See S. Jaishankar and C. Raja Motian, 'Nuclear Cartelisation: Theory and Practice', *Economic and Political Weekly*, 14 May 1977, p. 799; also Carl Walske, 'Nuclear Electric Power and the Proliferation of Nuclear Weapon States', *International Security*, Winter 1977.
7. An early indication of the trend is given in 'The Prospects for the World Nuclear Energy Market', *NEI*, April–May 1976, pp. 91–109.
8. BNFL, *Tenth Annual Report Accounts 1980–81*, p. 39.
9. 'Brazil Intends to Export Nuclear Technology, Says Minister Cals', *Nucleonics Week*, 21 May 1977, pp. 6–7.
10. For a complete tabulation of international trade in power reactors as of 31 December 1978, see 'Nuclear Power and Nuclear Proliferation: Export Policies and Proliferation Resistance', in *World Armaments and Disarmament: SIPRI Yearbook 1979*, London, Taylor & Francis, 1979, pp. 308–11.
11. For an overview of the main competitors in the international reactor market, see Paul L. Joskow, 'The International Nuclear Industry Today', *Foreign Affairs*, vol. 54, no. 4, July 1976, pp. 789–803.
12. 'How Westinghouse Is Consolidating its International Lead', *NEI*, December 1975, pp. 999–1007.
13. The impact of domestic standardisation on the company's export performance is examined in Richard Masters, 'Standardisation and Quality are Priorities at Kraftwerk Union', *NEI*, August 1976, pp. 39–47.
14. *Overview of Nuclear Export Policies of Major Foreign Supplier Nations*, Study by the Staff of the US General Accounting Office, 21 October 1977, p. 21.

15. 'Framatome's Licence with Westinghouse will be Ended Permanently', *Nucleonics Week*, 24 April 1980, pp. 9–10.
16. Per Ragnarson, 'What Role for Sweden's Industry?' *NEI*, February 1979, pp. 15–16.
17. See *ASEA Journal*, vol. 47, no. 1, 1974, p. 21; vol. 48, no. 1, 1975, p. 22.
18. 'Asea–Atom Looks at the USA', *NEI*, February 1982, pp. 9–10.
19. 'Vendors Jockey for Position as Korea Prepares for New NSSS Bids', *Nucleonics Week*, 24 April 1980; and 'Korea: An Expanding Economy Trying to Gain Energy Independence', *NEI*, February 1980, pp. 13–14. The technical deficiencies and safety dangers arising from the rapid expansion of South Korea's nuclear programme are examined in *Far Eastern Economic Review*, 3 March 1983, pp. 68–9, and 10 March 1983, pp. 59–60.
20. 'France Succeeds in South Korea', *NEI*, December 1980, p. 3.
21. See Namiki Nozomi, 'South Korea: The Nuclear Industry's Last Hurrah', *Ampo*, vol. 13, no. 1, 1981, p. 45.
22. R. Masters, 'Is China a Market for Nuclear Power?', *NEI*, May 1979, p. 13–14.
23. *Nucleonics Week*, 11 February 1982, p. 1; *Far Eastern Economic Review*, 19 May 1983, pp. 80–1.
24. Ibid., 20 May 1976.
25. Ibid., 28 January 1982, p. 1.
26. 'Debris Clouds Iraq's plan to Go Nuclear', *Business Week*, 22 June 1981, pp. 37–8; see also *BAS*, Aug.–Sept. 1981, pp. 8–13.
27. 'Iran Plans World's Fourth Biggest Nuclear Programme', *NEI*, March 1977, pp. 31–3; see also 'Iran-Half of Generating Capacity Nuclear by 1992', *NEI*, March 1978, pp. 13–14.
28. *NEI*, December 1977, p. 62; *Nucleonics Week*, 11 May 1978; *NEI*, June 1978, p. 7.
29. *The Times*, 21 May 1976; see also D.J. Ramos, 'Following Koeberg's Progress', *NEI*, July 1981, pp. 39–40.
30. A closely documented account of the nuclear relationship between South Africa and the major western exporters, in particular West Germany, will be found in Zdenek Cervenka and Barbara Rogers, *The Nuclear Axis*, New York, Times Book, 1978.
31. 'Planning for Nuclear Self-Sufficiency', *NEI*, September 1982, pp. 30–2.
32. 'Kraftwerk Union to Build Atucha II', *NEI*, November 1979.
33. *Nucleonics Week*, 24 January 1980, pp. 4–5; Ibid, 28 January 1982, p. 2.
34. See 'The increase in International Nuclear Transactions', *World Armaments and Disarmament SIPRI Yearbook 1977*, Cambridge, Mass., MIT Press, 1977, pp. 29–51.
35. *US Financial Assistance in the Development of Foreign Nuclear Energy Programs*, Report to the Committee on International Relations, House of Representatives, by the Comptroller General of the United States, 28 May 1975, pp. 3–4.
36. See Peter Hayes and Tim Shorrock, 'Dumping Reactors in Asia: The

US Export–Import Bank and Nuclear Power in South Korea', *Ampo*, vol. 14, no. 1, 1982, pp. 30–5.

37. *The Economics of Export Promotion*, unpublished paper prepared by the US Arms Control and Disarmament Agency, February 1976, p. 2.
38. 'Brazil Is Getting Large and Long-Term Financing', *Nucleonics Week*, 22 July 1976, p. 13.
39. *Overview of Nuclear Export Policies of Major Foreign Supplier Nations*, p. 19; see also 'The US Nuclear Power Industry Cries for Help', *Business Week*, 31 August 1981, pp. 70–1.
40. For a brief history of these initiatives, see B. Sanders and R. Rometsch, 'Safeguards Against the Use of Nuclear Material for Weapons', *NEI*, September 1975, pp. 682–4. For an official French perspective see Bertrand Goldschmidt, 'Le Contrôle de l'énergie atomique et la non-prolifération', *Politique Etrangère*, 42 année, Nos. 3–, 1977, pp. 413–30.
41. 'World List of Nuclear Powers', *Nuclear News*, February 1976.
42. Frank Barnaby, 'Diversion of Plutonium and Proliferation of Nuclear Weapons', in J. Rotblat (ed.), *Nuclear Reactors: To Breed or not to Breed*?, London, Taylor & Francis, 1977, p. 89.
43. *World Armaments and Disarmament SIPRI Yearbook 1978*, p. 33.
44. See Lewis A. Dunn, 'Nuclear "Gray Marketeering"', *International Security*, vol. 1, no. 3, Winter 1977, pp. 107–18.
45. See *Assessment of US and International Controls over the Peaceful Use of Nuclear Energy*, Report to the Congress by the Comptroller General of the US, September 1976, pp. 26–7.
46. Many of these weaknesses were reported in the confidential *Special Safeguards Implementation Report*, prepared for the IAEA Board of Governors, June 1977.
47. I discuss the military potential of reactor-grade plutonium in 'The Myth of the Peaceful Atom', *Millemum: Journal of International Affairs*, vol. 6, no. 2, Autumn 1977, pp. 111–27.
48. *Plutonium, Proliferation and Policy*, remarks of Victor Gilinsky to MIT, 1 November 1976, pp. 9–10; see also the masterful analysis by Albert Wohlstetter *et al.*, 'The Military Potential of Civilian Nuclear Energy: Moving Towards Life in a Nuclear Armed Crowd', *Minerva*, no. 15, Autumn/Winter 1977, pp. 387–538.
49. Robert Wesson, *United States and Brazil: Limits of Influence*, pp. 79–80.
50. See William W. Lowrance, 'Nuclear Futures for Sale: To Brazil from West Germany, 1975', *International Security*, vol. 1, no. 2, Fall 1976, pp. 147–66.
51. *New York Times*, 13 June 1975, p. 36.
52. A useful account of India's nuclear test and its proliferation implications will be found in John Maddox, *Prospects for Nuclear Proliferation*, Adelphi Papers, no. 113, London, International Institute for Strategic Studies, 1975, pp. 14–22.
53. Shirin Takhir-Kheli 'Pakistan's Nuclear Option and US Policy', *Orbis*, vol. 22, no. 2, Summer 1978, p. 367.

54. *Regional Rivalries and Nuclear Responses*, vol. 1, Los Angeles, Pan Heuristics, 1978, pp. 71–6; see also Richard K. Betts, 'Nuclear Proliferation and Regional Rivalry: Speculations on South Asia', *Orbis*, vol. 23, no. 1, Spring 1979, pp. 167–84.
55. 'Bonn's Atom Offer to Iran Stirs a Debate on Sharing', *New York Times*, 18 April 1976, pp. 1, 20.
56. See Lincoln P. Bloomfield, 'Nuclear Spread and World Order', *Foreign Affairs*, vol. 53, no. 4, July 1976, pp. 743–55.
57. The deliberations and conclusions of the conference are examined in Keith D. Suter, 'The 1975 Review Conference of the Nuclear Non-Proliferation Treaty', *Australian Outlook*, vol. 30, no. 2, August 1976, pp. 322–40.
58. These and other inconsistencies in American export policies are acknowledged by Senator Abraham Ribicoff in 'A Market Sharing Approach to the World Nuclear Sales Problem', pp. 764–6; see also General Accounting Office Report, *US International Nuclear Safeguards – Are They Being Effectively Exercised*?, ID76–21, 9 February 1976.
59. See remarks by Victor Gilinsky, NRC Commissioner, at the Conference on Nuclear Safeguards, Atomic Industrial Forum, 4 December 976.
60. Hearings before the Sub-committee on Arms Control, International Organisations and Security Agreements of the Committee on Foreign Relations, 94th Congress, 1st and 2nd sessions on non-proliferation issues, 24 October 1975, Washington, US Government Printing Office, 1977, p. 239.
61. Hearings before Senate Committee on Government Operations, 9 March 1976, Washington, US Government Printing Office, 1976, p. 786.
62. ACDA, *Arms Control Report*, 15th Annual Report to the Congress, July 1976, pp. 50–6.
63. Gilinsky, *Plutonium, Proliferation and Policy*, p. 5.
64. See the statement by Henry Kissinger before the Senate Committee on Government Operations, in *Department of State Bulletin DSB*, 29 March 1976, p. 407. These guidelines were formalised in a public statement dated 21 September 1977 and released by the Nuclear Suppliers' Group in early 1978. The text is reproduced in *Survival*, vol. 20, no. 2, March/April 1978, pp. 85–7.
65. For an analysis of these limitations, see Steven J. Baker, 'Monopoly or Cartel?', *Foreign Policy*, no. 23, Summer 1976, p. 217.
66. These opposing approaches are incisively outlined in Bertrand Goldschmidt, 'A Historical Survey of Non-Proliferation Policies', *International Security*, vol. 2, no. 1, Summer 1977, pp. 69–87.
67. See Zalmay Khalilzad, 'Pakistan and the Bomb', *BAS*, January 1980, p. 12.
68. The evolution of French non-proliferation policy, particularly under Giscard d'Estaing, is analysed in Pierre Lellouche, 'France in the International Nuclear Energy Controversy: A New Policy under

Giscard d'Estaing', *Orbis*, vol. 22, no. 4, Winter 1979, pp. 951–65. The author stresses the break with the Gaullist approach, the willingness to move some distance towards the American position, but the refusal to develop a coherent non-proliferation policy which would constrain the growth of France's nuclear industry or its diplomatic freedom of action.

69. Conseil Supérieur de Politique Nucléaire Extérieure, *Foreign Nuclear Policy*, Paris, French Press and Information Service Release, 1976.
70. The negative impact of US diplomacy is described in Charles K. Ebinger, *International Politics of Nuclear Energy*, pp. 63–6; see also Wesson, *The United States and Brazil: Limits of Influence*, pp. 80–2.
71. See the statement by Joseph S. Nye, Jr to the sub-committee on Arms Control, Oceans and International Environment of the Committee on Foreign Relations, US Senate, 95th Congress, 1st session, Washington, US Government Printing Office, 1977, p. 27. Joseph Nye as Deputy Under-Secretary of State for Security Assistance and Technology and Chairman of the National Security Council Group on Non-Proliferation was the principal architect of Carter's non-proliferation policy. His most comprehensive outline of its underlying rationale will be found in 'Non-Proliferation: A Long-Term Strategy', *Foreign Affairs*, vol. 56, no. 3, April 1978, pp. 601–23. Of particular interest is the emphasis on the elements of continuity with policy under previous Administrations.
72. These measures were part of Carter's seven-point plan announced in April 1977; see *Remarks of the President on Nuclear Energy Policy*, Office of the White House Press Secretary, 7 April 1977.
73. For a fuller analysis of these aspects of Carter's policy, see William R. Prendergast, 'US Foreign Policy and Nuclear Proliferation', *Naval War College Review*, Summer 1978, pp. 49–65.
74. See *Message from the President of the United States*, referred to in the Committees on International Relations and Science and Technology, 95th Congress, 1st session, 28 April 1977.
75. Statement by Joseph S. Nye made before the Sub-committee on Energy Nuclear Proliferation and Federal Services of the Senate Committee on Government Affairs, 6 May 1977, in DSB, 30 May 1977, p. 560.
76. 'Spent Nuclear Fuels Policy', DSB, 14 November 1977, p. 665.
77. See the statement by President Carter, made on signing HR 8638 into law on 10 March 1978, in DSB, April 1978, pp. 50–1.
78. For a detailed analysis of the Act, see Frederick Williams, 'The US Congress and Non-Proliferation', *International Security*, vol. 3, no. 2, Fall 1978, pp. 45–50.
79. Chauncery Starr, 'Nuclear Power and Weapons Proliferation – The Thin Link', *Nuclear News*, June 1977, p. 55.
80. 'Plea for Free Transfer of Nuclear Technology', *Nuclear News*, June 1977, pp. 86–96.
81. See his address to the British Nuclear Energy Society, 8 December 1977, *Atom*, no. 258, April 1978, pp. 107–8.

82. T.T. Poulouse, 'Atomic Colonialism', BAS, vol. 34, no. 8, October, 1978, p. 59. An official presentation of the same argument is offered by Munir Ahmad Khan, Chairman of the Pakistan Atomic Energy Commission, in *Nuclear Energy and International Co-operation: A Third World Perspective of the Erosion of Confidence*, London, International Consultative Group on Nuclear Energy, 1979.
83. T.T. Poulouse, 'Nuclear Proliferation: A Third World Perspective', *Round Table*, no. 274, April 1979, pp. 154–68.
84. 'Paris and Bonn Alter Nuclear Stand', *Science*, vol. 195, 7 January 1977, p. 32.
85. Speech by the Foreign and Commonwealth Secretary, the Rt. Hon. Dr David Owen to the Royal Institute of International Affairs, 19 May 1977, *Atom*, no. 249, July 1977, pp. 132–5.
86. For a detailed outline of these objections, see Gunter Hildenbrand, 'A German Reaction to US Non-Proliferation Policy', *International Security*, vol. 3, no. 2, Fall 1978, pp. 51–6.
87. The impact of nuclear issues on the German–American relationship is discussed in Manfred Knapp, 'Bonn–Washington: Co-operation and Competition', *Aussen Politik*, vol. 29, no. 4, 1978, pp. 387–400. See also Roger Morgan, *West Germany's Foreign Policy Agenda*, Beverley Hills, Cal., published for the Center for Strategic and International Studies, Georgetown University, Washington DC by Sage Publications, 1978, pp. 32–44; and Marion Dönhoff, 'Bonn and Washington: The Strained Relationship', *Foreign Affairs*, vol. 57, no. 5, Summer 1979, pp. 1052–64.
88. See Lawrence G. Franks, 'The Carter Administration's Clash with European Economic Interests', *The Atlantic Community Quarterly*, vol. 16, no. 4, Winter 1978–9. pp. 440–51.
89. Charles K. Ebinger, *International Politics of Nuclear Energy*, pp. 66–8.
90. 'US, Japan Sign Determination for Nuclear Facility', DSB, 10 October 1977, pp. 460–2; see also Joseph S. Nye, Jr, 'US Policy on Supply of US-Origin Nuclear Material', DSB, January 1979, pp. 44–5.
91. D. Dickson, 'US Embargoes Nuclear Fuel Exports to Europe', *Nature*, vol. 272, 27 April 1978, p. 746.
92. See also DSB, May 1980, 'Split Over Nuclear Export Licensing', *Nature*, vol. 284, 20 March 1980, p. 201.
93. For an indication of the shift to the language of low-key diplomacy, see address by Joseph S. Nye before the Uranium Institute, 12 July 1978, in DSB, October 1978, pp. 38–42.
94. Address by Joseph S. Nye, Jr before the Atomic Industrial Forum, 23 October 1978, in DSB, January 1979, p. 41.
95. The factors making for a less assertive non-proliferation strategy are examined in Michael Brenner, 'Carter's Non-Proliferation Strategy: Fuel Assurances and Energy Security', *Orbis*, vol. 22, no. 2, Summer 1978, pp. 333–56.
96. Nye, 'Non-Proliferation: A Long-Term Strategy', p. 615.

97. Steven J. Warneke, 'Non-Proliferation and INFCE: An Interim Assessment, *Survival*, vol. 21, no. 3, May–June 1979, pp. 116–24.
98. The ambiguity and limitations of the INFCE study are stressed in Lellouche, 'International Nuclear Politics', *Foreign Affairs*, vol. 58, no. 2, Winter 1979–80, pp. 336–52; see also Ian Smart, 'INFCE Brings International Agreement on Nuclear Fuel Cycle No Nearer', *Nature*, vol. 283, 28 February 1980, pp. 808–9.
99. Gerard Smith and George Rathjens, 'Reassessing Nuclear Non-Proliferation Policy', *Foreign Affairs*, vol. 59, no. 4, Spring 1981, pp. 886–7.
100. Amory B. Lovins, L. Hunter Lovins and Leonard Ross, 'Nuclear Power and Nuclear Bombs', *Foreign Affairs*, vol. 58, no. 5, Summer 1980, p. 1144.
101. See no. 58 above; and Michael Mandelbaum, 'A Nuclear Exporters' Cartel', BAS, June 1977, pp. 42–50.
102. Jaishankar and Raja Motian, 'Nuclear Cartelisation: Theory and Practice', pp. 798–802.
103. 'Reactivating the US as a Nuclear Exporter', *Business Week*, 18 May 1981, p. 54D.
104. DSB, September 1981, pp. 60–1.
105. Cited in William J. Lanouette, 'Reagan's Non-Policy', BAS, Aug.–Sept. 1982, p. 33.
106. See the official statement by the Department of State, 9 June 1982, in DSB, September 1982, p. 52; and *Nucleonics Week*, 7 June 1982, pp. 2–3.
107. 'US Aims To Be a More Reliable Supplier', NEI, August 1981, p. 3.
108. See the paper by A.T. Peaslee, Jr, 'Some Political Issues Related to Future Special Nuclear Materials Production', Los Alamos National Laboratory, New Mexico, August 1981.
109. See the statement by Thomas Cochran and Barbara Finamore on behalf of NRDC before the sub-committee on Oversight and Investigation of the House Committee on Interior and Insular Affairs, 1 October 1981.
110. NEI, April 1981, p. 4.
111. See the reports by Robert Manning, in *Far Eastern Economic Review*, 8 January 1982, p. 28, 26 November 1982, pp. 19–20.
112. Mohan Ram, 'French Finesse', *Far Eastern Economic Review*, 3 December 1982, pp. 39–40.
113. In 1978 these reports were confirmed by the CIA which claimed to have photographic evidence of the heavily-guarded plant at Kahuta. See Thomas F. Dorian and Leonard S. Spector, 'Covert Nuclear Trade and the International Non-Proliferation Regime', *Journal of International Affairs*, vol. 35, no. 1, Spring–Summer 1981, p. 58.
114. Ibid., pp. 61–2.
115. Attempts by the Zangger Committee to establish a tighter system of export controls on centrifuge enrichment technology, even if successful would be too late to forestall Pakistan's uranium enrichment programme (see *NEI*, January 1983, p. 9).

116. 'US Nuclear Exports Generate Confusion', *Business Week*, 9 November 1981, pp. 26–7.
117. For a succinct outline of current trends, see John Holdren, 'Nuclear Power and Nuclear Weapons: The Connection is Dangerous', BAS, January 1983, pp. 40–5.

CHAPTER EIGHT

1. The endogenous structural role of the state in the management of the national economy is examined in Joachim Hirsch, 'Elements of a Materialist Theory of the State', *International Journal of Politics*, vol. 7, no. 2, 1977, pp. 9–82.
2. Raymond Aron, *Progress and Disillusion: The Dialectics of Modern Society*, London, Pall Mall Press, 1968.
3. John Kenneth Galbraith, *The New Industrial State*, Harmondsworth, Penguin, 1974.
4. H.L. Nieburg, *In the Name of the Science*, Chicago, Quadrangle Books, 1966.
5. Sidney Lens, *The Military–Industrial Complex*, Philadelphia, Philadelphia University Press, 1970; see also Seymour Melman, *Pentagon Capitalism*, New York, McGraw Hill, 1970; and Steven Rosen (ed.), *Testing the Theory of the Military–Industrial Complex*, Lexington, Mass., D.C. Heath & Co., 1973.
6. Risk perception as a consequence of over-complexity is analysed by Jürgen Habermas, 'New Social Movements', *Telos*, Fall 1981, pp. 35–6.
7. See David Hill, 'Crisis Tendencies, Legitimation and the State', in J.A. Thompson and D. Held (eds), *Habermas, Critical Debates*, London, Macmillan, 1982.
8. For a discussion of the 'communicative' dimension of politics, see Tony Woodiwiss, 'Critical Theory and the Capitalist State', *Economy and Society*, vol. 7, no. 2, May 1978, pp. 175–91.
9. 'A Fresh Portrait of the Anti–Nuclear Movement', *Groundswell*, vol. 5, no. 4, July/Aug. 1982, pp. 1–7.
10. I have examined the changing framework for the internationalisation of economic activity, particularly in the period since 1945, in 'The Advanced Capitalist State and the Contemporary World Crisis', *Science and Society*, vol. XLV, no. 2, Summer 1981, pp. 130–58.
11. 'World Power Plant Industry in Recession', *NEI*, November 1981, pp. 15–16.

Select Bibliography

This bibliography refers only to some of the more useful secondary material readily available in books. For official sources and articles consult the notes for each chapter.

A Time to Choose: America's Energy Future, Final Report by the Energy Policy Project of the Ford Foundation. Cambridge, Mass., Ballinger Publishing Co., 1974.

Boyle, Godfrey, *Nuclear Power: The Windscale Controversy*, Milton Keynes, Open University Press, 1978.

Bunyard, Peter, *Nuclear Britain*, London, New English Library, 1981.

Bupp, I.C. and Derian, J.C, *Light Water: How the Nuclear Dream Dissolved*, New York, Basic Books, 1978.

Burn, D., *Nuclear Power and the Energy Crisis: Politics and the Atomic Industry*, London, Macmillan, 1978.

Chayes Abram and Lewis W. Bennett (eds), *International Arrangements for Nuclear Fuel Reprocessing*. Cambridge, Mass., Ballinger Publishing Co., 1977.

Colson, J.P., *Le Nucléaire sans les français*, Paris, Maspéro, 1977.

Commoner, Barry, *The Politics of Energy*, New York, Alfred A. Knopf, 1979.

Connolly, Thomas J., Hansen Ulf, Wolfgang, Jack and Beckurts Karl-Heinz, *World Nuclear Energy Paths*, New York, The Rockefeller Foundation, 1979.

Dawson, Frank G., *Nuclear Power: Development and Management of a Technology*, Seattle, University of Washington Press, 1976.

Duschesneau, Thomas, D., *Competition in the US Energy Industry*. Cambridge, Mass., Ballinger Publishing Co., 1975.

Duffy, G.C. and Adams, G., *Power Politics: The Nuclear Industry and Nuclear Exports*. New York, Council on Economic Priorities, 1978.

Ebinger, Charles K., *International Politics of Nuclear Energy*, The Washington Papers, vol. VI, Beverly Hills/London, Sage Publications, 1978.

Fagnani, F. and Nicolon A. (eds), *Nucléopolis: Matériaux pour l'Analyse d'ure Société Nucléaire*. Grenoble, Presses Universitates de Grenoble, 1979.

Falk, Jim, *Global Fission: The Battle over Nuclear Power*, Melbourne, Oxford University Press, 1982.

Goldschmidt, Bertrand, *Le Complexe atomique: Histoire politique de l'énergie nucléaire*, Paris, Fayard, 1980.

Gravelaine, F. de and O'Dy, S., *L'Etat EdF*, Paris, Alain Moreau, 1978.

Gray, John E. *et al., International Cooperation on Breeder Reactors*. New York, The Rockefeller Foundation, 1978.

Imai, Ryukichi, *Nuclear Energy and Nuclear Proliferation*, Boulder, Col., Westview Press, 1980.

Jungk, Robert, *Brighter than a Thousand Suns*, Harmondsworth, Penguin, 1958.

Jungk, Robert, *The Nuclear State* (trans. Eric Mosbacher), London, John Calder, 1979.

Lefever, Ernest W., *Nuclear Arms in the Third World: US Policy Dilemma*. Washington, DC, The Brookings Institution, 1979.

Lenoir, Y., *Technocractie Française*, Paris, Pauvert, 1977.

Lewis, R.S., *The Nuclear Power Rebellion: Citizens vs. the Atomic Industrial Establishment*, New York, Viking Press, 1972.

Lönroth, M. and Walker, W., *The Viability of the Civil Nuclear Industry*. New York/London, The Rockefeller Foundation/The Royal Institute of International Affairs, 1979.

Metzger, H.P., *The Atomic Establishment*, New York, Simon & Schuster, 1972.

Morgan, Roger, *West Germany's Foreign Policy Agenda*, Washington Papers, vol. VI, Beverly Hills/London, Sage Publications, 1978.

Mullenbach, Philip, *Civilian Nuclear Power: Economic Issues and Policy Formation*, Honolulu, East-West Center Press, 1966.

Myers, Desaix B., *The Nuclear Power Debate: Moral, Economic, Technical and Political Issues*, New York, Praeger, 1977.

Nau, Henry R., *National Politics and International Technology: Nuclear Reactor Development in Western Europe*, Baltimore, Johns Hopkins University Press, 1974.

Nelkin, Dorothy and Pollak, Michael, *The Atom Beseiged: Extraparliamentary Dissent in France and Germany*. Cambridge, Mass., The MIT Press, 1981.

Nuclear Power: Issues and Choices, Report of the Nuclear Energy Policy Study Group, Cambridge, Mass., Ballinger Publishing Co., 1977.

Pringle, Peter and Spiegelman James, *The Nuclear Barons*, London, Michael Joseph, 1982.

Rotblat, J. (ed.), *Nuclear Reactors: To Breed or not to Breed*?, Taylor & Francis, 1977.

Scheinman, L., *Atomic Energy Policy in France under the Fourth Republic*. Princeton, NJ, Princeton University Press, 1965.

Schrader-Frechette, K.S., *Nuclear Power and Public Policy: the Social and Ethical Problems of Fission Technology*. Dordrecht, Holland, D. Reidel Publishing Co., 1980.

Simonnot, Philippe, *Les Nucléocrates*, Grenoble, Presses Universitaires de Grenoble, 1978.

Stott, Martin and Taylor, Peter, *The Nuclear Controversy*, London, Town & Country Planning Association Political Research Group, 1980.

Syndicat CFDT de l'Energie Atomique, *Le Dossier Électronucléaire*, Paris, Editions du Seuil, 1980.

Taix, Gabriel, *Aux Portes de l'Enfer Atomique*, Paris, Agence Parisienne de Distribution, 1975.

Vernon, John Mitcham, *Public Investment Planning in Civilian Nuclear Power*, Durham, NC, Duke University Press, 1971.

Weart, Spencer R., *Scientists in Power*, Cambridge, Mass., Harvard University Press, 1979.

Williams, Roger, *The Nuclear Power Decisions: British Policies, 1953–78*, London, Croom Helm, 1980.

Willrich, Mason, *The Global Politics of Nuclear Energy*, New York, Praeger, 1971.

Willrich, Mason (ed.), *International Safeguards and Nuclear Industry*, Baltimore, Johns Hopkins University Press, 1975.

Willrich, Mason and Taylor, Ted, *Nuclear Theft; Risks and Safeguards*, Cambridge, Mass., Ballinger Publishing Co., 1974.

Yager, Joseph A., with the assistance of Ralph T. Mabry, Jr, *International Cooperation in Nuclear Energy*. Washington, DC, Brookings Institution, c. 1981.

Index